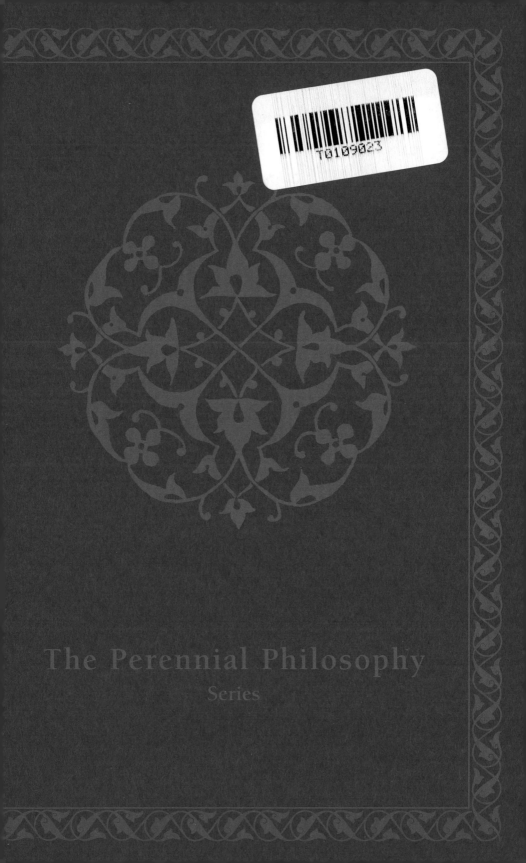

The Perennial Philosophy

Series

About this Book

"The essays in [*Living in Amida's Universal Vow*] provide us with a broad and in-depth perspective of Shin Buddhism. Contributors range from those who lived a century ago to those who are very active in the present time, from Buddhist scholars to Christian theologians, and from ardent believers to critics who speak from a more detached standpoint. The essays are relatively short and highly readable. Many of them were originally written in Japanese, but the English translations are of superb quality."

—**Toshikazu Arai**, Soai University, Osaka, Japan, author of *Lectures on Tannisho*

"*Living in Amida's Universal Vow* reveals some key aspects of the extraordinary breadth and profundity of Shin Buddhism, exemplified by a well chosen sampling of the thought of leading Shin Buddhist scholars and clergy over the past century. This book is both inspiring and thought-provoking. It presents penetrating essays, many of which have hitherto only been available in Japanese. This book provides a real contribution to the understanding of what in the West is still a relatively little-known branch of Buddhism, Jodo-Shinshu (or Shin Buddhism). Jodo-Shinshu is perhaps the most popular and widespread form of Buddhism in Japan, where it originated 800 years ago. This book presents Shin Buddhism from a truly modern and intellectually well-founded perspective. Shin Buddhism, ostensibly the 'easy path' of Buddha Dharma, constitutes in reality a challenge to experience life in a fundamentally compassionate and fully authentic way. This book presents readers with the profundity of the Nembutsu path of 'Deep Hearing,' or responding to the call of the boundless compassion and unsurpassed wisdom of Amida Buddha's universal vow to rescue us from our lives blinded by consuming passions. It will provide insight to the educated reading public as well as a wealth of information useful not only to Buddhist students but also to students of Eastern culture and comparative religion at the collegiate and graduate levels."

—**Richard St. Clair**, founder of the Boston Shinshu Buddhist Sangha

"Because the message of Shinran reflects his deep honesty concerning human existential realities, and because these are the very basis of true enlightenment, the intellectuals of our day should be attracted to his teachings."

—**Reverend Koju Fujieda**, formerly of Fukui Medical University

"This volume is an excellent collection of both classic and contemporary essays on the Shin Buddhist tradition by noted Japanese and Western scholars."

—**Duncan Ryuken Williams**, University of California, Irvine

"*Living in Amida's Universal Vow* provides readers a good opportunity to learn about Pure Land Buddhism as taught by a lay tradition that claims the largest following of any Japanese sect. These essays indicate some new directions to Western Buddhism as it continues to develop as a lay practice."

—**Norman Waddell**, Otani University, Kyoto, Japan, author of *Essential Teachings of Zen Master Hakuin* and *Zen Words for the Heart: Hakuin's Commentary on the Heart Sutra*

"Shin, the Buddhism of the heart, is the most popular form of Buddhism in Japan but it is still the least known in the West. This valuable collection of previously published articles, of interest to specialists and non-specialists alike, will help to establish Shin in the English speaking world."

—**Roger Corless**, Duke University, author of *The Vision of Buddhism*

World Wisdom
The Library of Perennial Philosophy

The Library of Perennial Philosophy is dedicated to the exposition of the timeless Truth underlying the diverse religions. This Truth, often referred to as the *Sophia Perennis*—or Perennial Wisdom—finds its expression in the revealed Scriptures as well as the writings of the great sages and the artistic creations of the traditional worlds.

The Perennial Philosophy provides the intellectual principles capable of explaining both the formal contradictions and the transcendent unity of the great religions.

Ranging from the writings of the great sages of the past, to the perennialist authors of our time, each series of our Library has a different focus. As a whole, they express the inner unanimity, transforming radiance, and irreplaceable values of the great spiritual traditions.

Living in Amida's Universal Vow: Essays in Shin Buddhism appears as one of our selections in the Perennial Philosophy series.

The Perennial Philosophy Series

In the beginning of the Twentieth Century, a school of thought arose which has focused on the enunciation and explanation of the Perennial Philosophy. Deeply rooted in the sense of the sacred, the writings of its leading exponents establish an indispensable foundation for understanding the timeless Truth and spiritual practices which live in the heart of all religions. Some of these titles are companion volumes to the Treasures of the World's Religions series, which allows a comparison of the writings of the great sages of the past with the perennialist authors of our time.

LIVING IN AMIDA'S UNIVERSAL VOW

ESSAYS IN SHIN BUDDHISM

EDITED BY

ALFRED BLOOM

FOREWORD BY

TAITETSU UNNO

World Wisdom

Living in Amida's Universal Vow: Essays in Shin Buddhism
© 2004 World Wisdom, Inc.

Library of Congress Cataloging-in-Publication Data

Living in Amida's universal vow : essays in Shin Buddhism / edited by Alfred Bloom ;
foreword by Taitetsu Unno.
p. cm. -- (The Perennial philosophy series) Includes bibliographical references.
ISBN 0-941532-54-2 (pbk. : alk. paper)
1. Shin (Sect)--Doctrines. I. Bloom, Alfred. II. Series.
BQ8718.3.L58 2004
294.3'926--dc22

2004006768

Printed on acid-free paper in Canada

For information address World Wisdom, Inc.
P.O. Box 2682, Bloomington, Indiana 47402-2682

TABLE OF CONTENTS

III. Modern Issues in Shin Thought

IV. Historical and Comparative Perspectives

FOREWORD

In the Spring of 2003 my wife and I traveled throughout Southeast Asia where we visited various places designated as World Historical Sites: Angkor Wat, Halong Bay, Luang Prabang, Plain of Jars, and so forth. During the trip, we heard a saying that nicely sums up the peoples and cultures of three Buddhist countries: "In Vietnam people grow rice, in Cambodia people watch rice growing, and in Laos people listen to rice growing." This aphorism reminds me of a story from the life of Buddha. Once when Shakyamuni Buddha, together with his disciples, was making the rounds for alms, a prominent landowner and farmer criticized him, saying:

> I, O ascetic, plough and sow; and having ploughed and sown, I eat. You also, O ascetic, should plough and sow; and having plowed and sown, you should eat.

He was criticizing the Buddha for depending on alms and not engaging in productive work, whereupon the Buddha replied:

> I, too, O Brahmin, plough and sow; and having plowed and sown, I eat.

Both the farmer and the Buddha are engaged in cultivation, but of a different sort. One cultivates the field and obtains a harvest, while the other cultivates the hearts and minds of people to develop true, real, and sincere human beings. This story suggests that religious life requires cultivation or practice, requiring the commitment of the total person, physical, psychological, and spiritual.

The aphorism also brought to mind three kinds of practices that parallel different attitudes to rice growing: practice as a means to an end (growing rice), practice as focusing on the process rather than on the end (watching), and practice in which the end expresses itself (listening). This requires some explanation.

First, practice as a means to an end. We all enter the path of Buddha Dharma with some clear objective: to attain peace of mind, resolve personal issues, grapple with questions of life and death, and ultimately, to realize the goal of Buddhahood. Second, however, practice soon becomes centered on the process itself and not on the end, whereby we are made to see hidden dimensions of self not evident to ordinary reflection or discursive reason. Third, our practice becomes expressive of the end itself; that is, it manifests the working of the Buddha. What does this mean? In Pure Land Buddhism, whenever we call on the Name of the Buddha, *namu-amida-butsu*, we become attuned to the power of the compassionate Buddha, and in doing so we ultimately hear the calling from the Buddha to which we respond by saying "*namu-amida-butsu*." This is called "deep hearing."

The act of invocation originates from the side of the Buddha; hence, it is called Great Practice. The adjective "great" contains the wisdom and compassion of the Buddha whose "practice" or activity is directed solely to karma-bound beings for their liberation and freedom. True religious life is ultimately not dependent on human agency but on the working of the Buddha to which we entrust our total self. This was a radical idea in medieval Japan, and it required the maturing of time and history for it to become recognized as a legitimate path to enlightenment. That time arrived in the year 1052, according to Japanese reckoning, the first year of *mappo*, an age of unprecedented turbulence and chaos when life was precarious and the world began to disintegrate.

Shinran, the founder of Shin Buddhism, lived in such an age, regarded by everyone as the end-time of history, confirmed by crumbling social and political orders, civil wars rampant among the contending warrior clans, natural disasters that swept the country several times—droughts, famines, pestilences, and earthquakes, and above all great monastic centers that were marked by decadence, nepotism, and political intrigues with monk-soldiers threatening imperial rule. This idea of *mappo* had already existed in China since the sixth century, but the acute sense of historical crises was confined there to the Buddhist world, whereas in Japan the sense of doom and destruction was all-pervasive, affecting all quarters of society.

Mappo for Shinran, however, was not only a matter of external chaos in society but a matter of internal unease, a keen sense of infinite finitude and the burden of cyclic life. Following the lead of his teacher Hōnen, he plumbed the depth of Buddhist scriptures and the writings of earlier Pure Land teachers to discover the salvific path particularly suited for the age of religious and spiritual bankruptcy: the Great Practice of the Buddha manifested in each saying of the *nembutsu* by anyone so inclined.

As a practice, nothing could be simpler, for it can be undertaken by anyone, anywhere, and at any time; and nothing could be more effective, being the active manifestation of the Buddha in the midst of everyday life, and not a self-generated human act with no guarantees for success. This, of course, was a great boon for Shinran, who saw himself as a failed monk in Tendai monastic practices, and who identified with all those hitherto excluded from entering the gates of Buddhism: hunters, fishermen, and butchers called "evil" for taking life; peasants and merchants regarded as "bad" in the eyes of the cultured elites; women of all classes considered "defiled" and monks and nuns who had violated the precepts. Those considered evil, bad, defiled, and fallen were now the primary concern of the compassionate Buddha, who selected the saying of *nembutsu* as the religious practice most suited to meet their needs.

Great Practice, the intoning of *nembutsu*, is a spontaneous and natural expression of *shinjin*, defined as "the true and real heart of Amida Buddha" brought to life within a person. According to Shinran, it is "the one thought-moment of time reaching its ultimate limits when the awakening of *shinjin* occurs." The horizontal, linear course of life is broken through by the vertical timeless reality. This intersection is *shinjin*—an awakening here and now that is the basis of creative living in the world and of becoming fully engaged with the challenges of history.

The goal of traditional Pure Land practice was to attain birth in the Pure Land after death. Shinran, however, taught that it is to be realized here and now when the mind and heart of the Buddha enters and takes over a person's life. When this occurs, a person attains the stage of nonretrogression, a major goal in all Buddhist paths whereby there is only forward progression to enlightenment and no fear of backsliding into delusions.

Shin Buddhism is slowly becoming known in the world as an alternative to the monastic paths to liberation and freedom. Since it is rooted deeply in the everyday life of the lay populace, it is available to anyone: young or old, woman or man, good or evil. The articles contained in this anthology, covering a wide range of subject matters, will help the reader gain a broader knowledge and deeper appreciation for this unique lay-oriented path to Buddhahood. The editor, Alfred Bloom, has once again rendered a great service towards the introduction of Shin Buddhism and its relevance for the world today. It is another stellar achievement of a lifetime devoted to the study of Shinran and the practice of Jodo Shinshu.

TAITETSU UNNO
Professor Emeritus of Religion
Smith College

INTRODUCTION

Though it has been in the West for over one hundred years, Pure Land and Shin Buddhism has been little known or understood among Western peoples. The reasons for this are varied, but with the growing availability of important scholarly studies and easily understood popular interpretations, seekers now have the opportunity to encounter the richness and depth of the tradition. It is the intention of this anthology to contribute to a greater understanding of Pure Land teaching in particular and Buddhism in general.

Since World War II a broad increase of interest in Japanese culture resulted from the occupation of Japan and the development of intimate economic relations between Japan and America. Buddhism especially gained greater respect notably with the introduction of Zen Buddhism through the efforts of Dr. D. T. Suzuki and a host of other teachers who settled in the West. In addition, the dispersion of Tibetan Buddhism and the visibility of the Dalai Lama throughout Western countries has also been a very significant factor in the growth of interest in Buddhism. The Vietnam War brought a focus on Buddhist monks who resisted the war, sacrificing themselves by self immolation. Thich Nhat Hanh, a noted Zen monk, carried the message of peace to the West. Programs in Buddhism and Asian cultures were established in many universities and colleges.

Widespread religious ferment in Western society has been expressed in movements designated as New Age Spirituality. These newly arisen religious groups attract individuals who have become increasingly dissatisfied or disillusioned with their traditional faiths. Seeking alternative paths for dealing with their personal problems and understanding life, they often turn to one of the many forms of Buddhism.

Despite the renewed interest in religion, the significance of Pure Land teaching and appreciation of its spiritual character as an important approach to understanding human existence have lagged behind other traditions such as Zen, Tibetan, and Theravadan forms of Buddhist teaching and meditation. Pure Land faith appears as a popular, other-worldly path, mainly concerned with death and afterlife and lacking in such features as meditation and social awareness.

Closely identified with the Japanese-American or Canadian communities, Pure Land Buddhism appears to some people as an exclusively Japanese religion without realizing that it is a universal faith open to all peoples. However, there has been an increase in the number of clergy whose knowledge of western culture and language enables them to build bridges of understanding between religions and cultures in their communities. In addition the Institute of Buddhist Studies in Berkeley, California, which is sponsored by the Shin Buddhist Churches of America, has been created to train clergy in America and to integrate Buddhism into the life of the nation through its participation in the complex of Christian seminaries, the Graduate Theological Union. The Honpa Hongwanji Mission of Hawaii has established the Pacific Buddhist Academy high school and college preparatory school based on Buddhist philosophy and peace studies.

Over the years a wide variety of literature has developed with the translation of sacred texts such as *The Three Pure Land Sūtras* by Dr. Hisao Inagaki, and the *Collected Works of Shinran*, as well as more popular texts such as Dr. Taitetsu Unno's *River of Fire and River of Water* and *Shin Buddhism: Bits of Rubble Turn into Gold*, both designed to explain and interpret Pure Land and Shin Buddhist teaching in ways western people can comprehend through touchpoints in western experience and thought.

This anthology provides a sampling of the resources available for the study Shin Pure Land Buddhism through a variety of essays from important and influential journals. It is common for people to look for a book to study a subject. However, there is a rich resource hidden in journals, which often sit untouched on library shelves in our universities. The journals publish papers presented at scholarly meetings or are the results of scholars' creative research. Lay people are not generally familiar with these resources, because they do not have easy access to university libraries or hold membership in the scholarly societies that publish them.

This volume proposes to remedy the situation by offering essays by noted scholars. The anthology reveals the serious intellectual and spiritual character of the teaching, while also enabling the reader to gain a perspective on its significance for modern society. Some scholars are adherents of the teaching, while others regard it as an important object of study. Whatever their motivation, they bring to bear skills and insights which can assist us in evaluating the meaning of the teaching for ourselves personally. We can also observe various styles of presentation and theoretical perspectives, demonstrating that diversity rather than uniformity is a mark of vital religious reflection. The essays will show that Pure Land teaching has many dimensions as a living tradition, and is capable of giving meaning to everyday life, while inspiring commitment to the service of humanity.

The title *Living in Amida's Universal Vow* indicates that Buddhism is for living, not merely for dying or the afterlife. Afterlife, of course, is an important concern for everyone. One of the first questions to arise in religious discussion is what happens to me when I die? However, the answer to that question brings us immediately back to this life where the quality of our spiritual life *now* holds implications for any life to follow. Since religious reality, however one conceives it, must be the same here and hereafter, encountering that reality *now* in the context of our living is an important indicator of what any future life would be.

*

* *

The Pure Land and Shin tradition evolved from a large body of literature mainly originating in India from which three texts became central: the *Larger Sūtra of Eternal Life*, *The Sūtra of Contemplation on Eternal Life*, and the *Shorter Pure Land Sūtra*. While the normative, monastic tradition focused on meditation, a popular tradition emerged in China which promised salvation for ordinary people through the merit of reciting the name of the Buddha. Their recitations accorded with their respective mother tongues (in Sanskrit, *Namo Amitabhaya Buddhaya*; Chinese, *Namo O mi to fu*; Korean, *Namo Amit'a Bul*, or Japanese, *Namu Amida Butsu*).

Amitabha/Amitayus Amida Buddha is the Buddha of the Western Paradise. In Sanskrit the term *Amita* means Infinite, thus Infinite Light or Life respectively. According to the foundational myth, Amida became Buddha as a result of perfecting a series of forty-eight Vows by which he promised to establish an ideal world where it would be easy and natural to attain enlightenment and eternal release from the bondage to the cycles of births and deaths. The story sets forth a model of compassion that provides direction for the way we should approach life here and now.

The Universal Vow represents the aspiration or desire of the Buddha that all beings be included in his unconditional compassion. The Vow is a potent symbol signifying that the Buddha ceaselessly works in and through the reality of our lives and world to realize his promise of our ultimate fulfillment. The essays in this volume in their various ways constitute reflections on the Vow and the many ways it can be understood to be active in our lives.

Initially Amitabha/Amitayus was one among many Buddhas in Buddhist Mahayana cosmology, but eventually he became widely revered and worshiped throughout East Asia. The myth of his becoming Buddha offered a comprehensive and inclusive path of birth into the Pure Land based on his unconditional compassion and wisdom. Other Buddhas and Bodhisattvas came to be viewed as his manifestations.

The phrase chanted to secure birth in the Pure Land is "I take refuge in Amida Buddha" (in Japanese *Namu Amida Butsu*, the most widely known form). It is termed the *Nembutsu* in Japanese, which means thinking on the Buddha, and can mean either meditation or chanting. While chanting of the name was a part of various rituals and meditative practices by monks, some Sūtras advocated it for ordinary people as a method for accumulating merit for birth into Amida's Pure Land and eventual perfect enlightenment. There would be no more fear or prospect of birth in the world of suffering and ignorance. The Pure Land teaching thereby became a stratum in all Buddhist traditions in China, Vietnam, Korea, and Japan as a subsidiary means available to the common person.

In Japan in the 13th century, there was a flourishing of the human spirit stimulated by violence and disruption as a new social and political order arose, dominated by a warrior ethos, with the city of Kamakura in Eastern Japan as its center. In this turbulent age there were several prominent teachers representing the spectrum of Buddhism in Japan at the time.

Among them, Hōnen (1133-1212) is known as the founder of the independent Pure Land School. He dedicated himself to propagating the recitation of the name of Amida Buddha as the only effective means of salvation for all people, including monks, living in the last age of the decline and disappearance of the Buddhist teaching (*mappo*).

Mappo is a theory of the decline of Buddhism: people through many centuries forgot the true aims of Buddhism, replacing its discipline of enlightenment with self-seeking advancement or benefits. Hōnen believed that the traditional practices of Buddhism were inadequate because they were not required by Amida's Vow or the masses of people were incapable of achieving the ideal of enlightenment. He noted that the Vow of Amida did not require wealth, education, moral or religious ability, which were esteemed by the religious establishment. These conditions were possessed only by a few, and, therefore, could not be the criteria for attaining birth or enlightenment. Amida's compassion must be open to all regardless of their social or religious status. Therefore, based on Hōnen's view of the Pure Land Sūtras, the account of Amida's Vows, and the character of the times, Pure Land teaching was considered the only path to enlightenment for the people of this age.

Hōnen had several disciples. Shinran (1173-1262) became the best known and most influential in later times. He claimed that he carried on the mission of Hōnen to interpret the spirit of the Vow in the broadest way. The tradition which emerged from Shinran's teaching is known as the Jodo Shinshu, or True Teaching of the Pure Land in contrast to sects developed by other disciples as the successors of Hōnen, which came to be known as Jodo-shu, the Pure Land Sect. The Pure Land sects together became the leading religious movement of popular Buddhism in Japan. Among the majority of immigrants from Japan to the West, Jodo Shinshu, or Shin Buddhist adherents, was the largest group.

Shinran's teaching is distinguished by his stress on the gift of faith-true entrusting by Amida and the understanding that the recitation of the name is to express gratitude and not to seek merit. Shinran removed any basis for egocentrism and ego-advancement through religious adherence. We are simply passion-ridden, foolish beings with no virtue to claim any superiority. Further, the assurance of birth-enlightenment is given in this life.

In its basic teaching Pure Land spirituality appears simple, inspiring the criticism that it is merely a superficial path for the masses. However, study of the interpretations and implications of the teaching reveals that it is more sophisticated and complex, and embodies a deep spiritual ideal of hope and compassion which embraces all beings without discrimination. It is this spirit that we are attempting to illuminate through this volume.

Introduction

*
* *

The volume is divided into four sections. The first presents "Modern Shin Buddhist Thinkers" who were pivotal figures in establishing Shin Buddhism as a modern system of thought at a time when Japan opened its doors to the West. During this period Japanese Buddhists were confronted by issues arising from the emergence of a modern secular state and from Christianity. In meeting the challenges of the time it was important to highlight the aspect of personal religious experience as the basis of adherence rather than any traditional institutional connection.

Kiyozawa Manshi's (1863-1903) brief essays, "The Great Path of Absolute Other Power" and "My Faith" are his famous statements concerning the personal meaning of Other Power in his life, as he faced the ravages of tuberculosis. They are deeply personal statements, written a few days before his death at the end of his short life of forty-one years. Here he stresses the importance of faith and the limitations of human endeavor. The essay reveals Kiyozawa's deep religious subjectivity and awareness, which contrasted with formal, traditional adherence to the teaching encouraged by the institution and assumed by the ordinary follower. His teaching is marked by a concern for the inner commitment of the person whose life is illuminated by it, and provides eloquent insight into the depth of his personal awareness of this central aspect of Pure Land teaching.

Kiyozawa is known as a religious reformer, spending a good part of his young life trying to revitalize the Shin tradition which had simply accommodated itself to the Meiji political order. He attempted to focus attention on the necessity of a personal, inner awareness as the basis for commitment and living, in contrast to formal, external adherence to an institution.

He initiated the Spirituality movement (*Seishinshugi*), which was criticized because it appeared subjective and individualistic, neglecting society. While not considered a social reformer as such, his teachings are not without social implications, since activity in society requires a foundation in the human spirit to struggle against exploitative social forces. Given more time, he might have revealed his approach to society more clearly.

Soga Ryojin, author of "The Significance of Dharmakara Bodhisattva as Earthly Savior," was a leading disciple of Kiyozawa. Though Soga's thought is complex and requires considerable reflection, it is an important resource for studying the deeper aspects of Shin thought. He reinterpreted traditional Shin teaching to establish its character as a modern system of thought. Particularly, he focused on the dynamic spiritual reality of Dharmakara Bodhisattva—the protagonist of the Amida myth—within one's psyche in the process of salvation. Dharmakara symbolizes Vow Power who is "born directly in the hearts and minds of human beings." He is the voice rising from the depths of our own heart that seeks salvation, while at the same time he is the savior who answers that call. From this identification in which the "Tathāgata becomes me," he saves us from within our "darkness of suffering and despair" as we become aware within ourselves of the unity of the seeker and the Savior. This dynamic relation is the basis for deep religious subjectivity expressed as true entrusting (*shinjin*) and reflects an interest in the inner religious experience of the individual as against adherence to abstract doctrines and external membership in an institution.

Kaneko Daiei's "The Meaning of Salvation in the Doctrine of Pure Land Buddhism" offers a concise presentation of the fundamentals of Shin Buddhism by one of the major Shin scholars of the last century. He also was a disciple of Kiyozawa Manshi, pursuing interest in religious subjectivity or awareness on a broad scale.

Kaneko defines salvation in Buddhism as liberation from the bondage of ignorance and suffering within the context of our existential human condition. More than self-concern, he emphasizes the Mahayana Buddhist principle of the interrelation and interdependence of all beings. Liberation is indivisible and there can be no liberation without liberating others. The Pure Land approach is significant as the only way out of the existential situation without leaving home or society. Rejecting the popular notion of Pure Land teaching as seeking happiness in another world, Kaneko sees it as an expression of the deeper Mahayana spirit of seeking enlightenment together with others in this world.

While highlighting the work of Hōnen, Kaneko finds that Shinran was the first to realize the significance of the awakening of faith. Here the *Nembutsu* is more than just the recitation of a formula; it is the expression of our human desire for salvation. However, as faith becomes mature it transforms to the call of Amida to awaken and take refuge in him.

This understanding makes it possible to endure sufferings in life and to be transformed in our awareness, becoming more compassionate and tolerant of others. We know that we are not essentially different from those we might deem evil, and the Vow has been given for all. Based on this thought there are implications for religious awareness and ethical relations. We do not act out of moral obligation or duty but through humility based on our awareness of "foolish being" (*bombu*). We relate positively to others, setting aside blame and self-righteousness, thereby creating the conditions for peace.

Dr. Daisetz T. Suzuki's series of three essays, "Shin Buddhism"(Parts I, II, III), explain the meaning and significance of various topics in traditional Shin Buddhist thought such as Amida Buddha, the Primal Vow, Shin Buddhism and Mahayana Buddhism, The Name and *Nembutsu*, Self Power and Other Power. While Dr. Suzuki is noted primarily for his advocacy of Zen, we have included his article here because in his later life he focused on Shin Buddhism through various essays, notably his study of Asahara Saichi, an ardent Shin Buddhist devotee, and his translation of Shinran's major work *Teaching Practice Faith*

Realization (*Kyogyoshinsho*), which he was unable to complete before he passed away.

The second section, "Interpretations of Shin Buddhism," brings together a variety of contemporary discussions which display the range of concerns taken up by scholars and indicate the breadth and depth of Shin thought.

Takeuchi Yoshinori's "Centering and the World Beyond" discusses eschatology in Buddhism in relation to Shinran's description of his passing through three stages to true entrusting. In this series of stages Shinran declares that his spiritual development passed through the stage of the Nineteenth Vow, which promises birth in the Pure Land through the self-power practices of morality and meditation. He then turned to the Twentieth Vow which promises birth through the recitation of the *Nembutsu*, finally reaching the stage of true entrusting in Other Power of the Eighteenth Vow. This personal process expresses the temporality of human existence and the expanding development of religious consciousness.

Taitetsu Unno, in his "The Practice of Jodo-shinshu," provides a digest of the basic teaching and character of Shin Buddhism. He summarizes the development of the *Nembutsu* from forms of meditation and recitation to its understanding as a call of Amida and expression of trust whereby the *Nembutsu* "wakens us to the liberating power that sanctifies life." He explains the religious implications of this perspective.

Omine Akira's "*Shinjin* is the Eternal Now" interprets the nature of birth in the Pure Land and true entrusting, emphasizing its reality here and now. This means that when faith arises, one encounters the eternal within time. Omine points out that Shinran reinterpreted the Buddhist teaching of "entering the ranks of the truly settled," which was traditionally considered an attainment in the afterlife. According to Shinran, one attains this status in this life through the encounter with eternity *now*, in true entrusting. This is the basis for a meaningful life even within a "vain and futile world." He maintains that "any Buddha that cannot come to the world of ordinary beings is powerless." Likewise the Pure Land cannot be a far-off world, but must be actively working in this world. There is a reciprocity, a dialogue, between the Pure Land and this world. Through *shinjin*, true entrusting, we take part in the life of this world, relying on the Buddha's Vow power.

Alfred Bloom, "Shinran's Vision of Absolute Compassion," discusses the meaning of compassion in Pure Land Buddhism in the context of the history of religion, focusing on Shinran and his concept of Amida as the Eternal Buddha. Shinran's understanding of Amida's absolute compassion, he argues, released the believer from the fear and oppressions of folk beliefs and transcended the accidental, adventitious conditions of life such as class, social position, spiritual capacity, education or moral character. Amida's compassion is the motivating force of reality and history, symbolized in the figures of Dharmakara Bodhisattva and Amida Buddha, thereby providing a basis for a meaningful and hopeful life within a suffering world.

Dennis Hirota's, "Religious Transformation and Language in Shinran" takes up the role of language in the process of the arising of true entrusting and its consequent transformation of self-understanding and the understanding of the world in Shin Buddhism. Shinran's approach, through its dependence on language, contrasts with such traditions as Zen which aims to break through our ordinary thinking and conceptualization. Hirota observes two phases in this process, designated as "hearing the Name" and the aspect of performance of practice in "saying the Name." By encountering the Dharma in the first phase the objectified, absolutized self is dissolved. All calculative, moralistic thinking becomes meaningless. In the second phase a new self-understanding emerges in which inconceivable reality, experienced as the Name, *Namu Amida Butsu*, is apprehended as the non-dual, underlying, contemporaneous reality of one's life. While one recognizes one's historical, samsaric conditionedness, there is the simultaneous recognition that the Name as reality pervades one's whole existence, past, present, and future and is not limited to one moment. While the passions and ignorance remain as our existential condition, they no longer dominate one's life. Moreover, through the reality of the Name present in one's life, rather than being passive, one may participate in the world with a more acute sense of the pain our existence may bring to the world, and gratitude that we may become a locus for the activity of wisdom-compassion.

Ueda Yoshifumi, "Freedom and Necessity in Shinran's Concept of Karma," presents a detailed treatment of the concept of karma in Shinran's thought. Professor Ueda deals with the question created by Shinran's statement that for the person on the unobstructed path of *Nembutsu* there is no karmic retribution for evils committed after the reception of *shinjin*. His thesis is that Shinran's concept of karma is not a matter of individual, personal will, but the condition of temporality running from past through the present to the future. The believer experiences his present as the bearer of the infinite karma from the past, which is released through the experience of *shinjin*. We can see this illustrated in the postscript of the *Tannisho* where Shinran expressed his gratitude for the Primal Vow by which Amida saved him despite his heavy burden of karma. In effect it points to personal religious experience through which the ego is transformed by being made aware of its karmic bondage. Such an awareness marks one's embrace by the compassion of Amida Buddha and a decisive turning toward non-egoic compassion. Thus, as Shinran states, the evil is transformed to good. From this arises the possibility of authentic existence where our awareness of our karmic heritage is given deeper meaning through complementary awareness of the Buddha's compassion and wisdom embracing that heritage. It inspires within us the "mind of great compassion" which motivates positive living and action in the world.

Murakami Sokusui's, "Joy of Shinran: Rethinking the Traditional Shinshu Views on the Concept of the Stage of Truly Settled" is also a study of the concept of the stage of the truly settled in Shinran's thought and its resultant joy in present religious life. This concept is an important feature of Mahayana and Pure Land Buddhism. According to scripture, it is attained on birth into the Pure Land. For Shinran, however, it is a stage received at the moment of true entrusting and decisively marks a shift in attitude and religious consciousness.

Shinran reinterpreted the traditional teaching that our present joy in faith is in anticipation of our birth in the Pure Land after death. In contrast he declares that he does not rejoice in future birth in the Pure Land as a result of the tenacity of his passions.[1] For Shinran our joy in the teaching arises from the fact that we have *now* been embraced by Amida's Vow. This orientation exhibits the this-worldly focus of his teaching. The discussion of the presentness of salvation and the orientation to the future has its root in the *Sangowakuran* controversy in the Nishi Hongwanji branch of Shin Buddhism in the late 18th and early 19th centuries. The term *Sangowakuran* means the confusion concerning the relation of salvation and the three acts of body, mouth, and mind which are involved with faith.

The subtlety of Shinran's view is perhaps lost on the greater number of followers who believe that faith is in anticipation of future life in the Pure Land rather than an experience of the assurance that Amida has *already* saved us *now* through *shinjin*. In Shinran's thought the moment of true entrusting is the moment of birth and in the realization that our minds are spiritually already in the Pure Land we are freed from the fears that attend the afterlife for the ordinary traditional person. This is why Shinran rejected the deathbed practices of Pure Land tradition which focus on future afterlife.

Reflection on Shinran's perspective concerning the entry in this life, at the moment of entrusting, into the truly settled stage (*shojoju*) enables Shin Buddhism to offer a more dynamic stance in participating in the affairs of this world, as we become more sensitive to Amida's working *now* and the reality of the Pure Land behind the looming contradictions and sufferings that pervade our modern world.

The third section is "Modern Issues in Shin Thought." The focus of these essays is on the contribution of Shin Buddhism to society. Galen Amstutz, "Shinran and Authority in Buddhism," discusses how Shinran's reinterpretation of Pure Land Buddhism transformed the traditional understanding of monasticism and institutional Buddhism. He focuses on the conceptual triangle of *eko*, transfer (or directing) of merit, the Buddhist awareness of *akunin shoki* (the awareness that the evil person is the true object of Amida's Vows), and institutional

---

[1] *Collected Works of Shinran* (Kyoto: Jodo Shinshu Hongwanji-ha, 1997), p. 125, #113.

transcendence implied in the concept of *hiso-hizoku*, being neither priest nor lay person, by which Shinran described his own position in Buddhism. His analysis leads him to the conclusion that far from being a weak or failed individual, Shinran was a shrewd and profoundly rebellious individual, offering a challenge to traditional, conventional religious institutions.

Gerhard Schepers, "Shinran and Modern Individualism," discusses the discovery of the self in Hōnen and Shinran and their influence in modern Japan. While noting the emergence of the modern individual in the West, he observes that in Japan the focus on the independence of the individual arose with Hōnen and Shinran, in association with the salvation promised in Pure Land teaching. It becomes particularly clear in Shinran, with his declaration that Amida made his Vow for Shinran alone. Schepers asserts that "Shinran's thought could prove to be one of the few traditional beliefs in Japan, if not the only one, that, while preserving the continuity of tradition, can provide a basis for the individual in order to face the challenge of modern society." This is reflected in the strong interest in Shinran and his charismatic personality in Japan with his potential for criticism and reform. Despite differences of interpretation of the meaning of Shinran's teaching among scholars, Schepers notes that the critical spirit of Shinran has remarkably survived in Shin tradition and has inspired reform movements such as Kiyozawa's in the major branches, Otani and Honpa Hongwanji.

Futaba Kenko, "Shinran and Human Dignity: Opening an Historic Horizon," counters the view that Pure Land teaching only offers bliss in the afterlife. The author takes note of efforts to recover the true understanding of Shin from the traditional view. He explores the implications of the teaching which supports human dignity and human rights. Futaba himself represents one of the efforts striving for reinterpretation and reform in Shin Buddhism, stressing that Shinran opened the way to a new society in Japan.

Ama Toshimaro, "Towards a Shin Buddhist Social Ethics," deals with the wartime use of Buddhism by the government, the problem of the two truth theory, and the social approach of Kiyozawa Manshi and Takagi Kenmyo. Japan's defeat in World War II raised the question of social ethics as citizens became more participatory in the many political, economic, educational, and environmental problems of modern society. Because Shin Buddhism, in particular, supported the modern imperial nation, Shin Buddhists are challenged to take up the question of social ethics. The Vietnamese Buddhists' opposition to war provides a good example of Buddhists working to end war and to eradicate suffering in society. The origin of the idea of "engaged Buddhism" may be traced to these efforts.

Ama observes that Shin Buddhist doctrine has sometimes inhibited the development of social ethics by the belief that Other Power refers to the attainment of salvation and not the resolution of issues in worldly society. Things are left to others and followers only accept reality as it is. He maintains that this is a misunderstanding of the teaching. A major contributor to the misunderstanding has been the teaching of the two truths, mundane and supramundane. The concept is not a core doctrinal issue for Shin Buddhism but arose out of the social history of the movement. The thrust toward developing a social ethic, however, appeared with Kiyozawa Manshi and Takagi Kenmyo.

Kiyozawa in effect rejected the prevailing distinction of the two truths which placed religion in the service of the state. It was his view that greater awareness of the Infinite would lead to greater concern for one's fellow human being. However, it was particularly the effort of Takagi Kenmyo that represented Amida's compassion in society. Though he died in prison in 1914, his work was reevaluated in the 1960s and he was reinstated by the Otani denomination in 1996. He had been defrocked and imprisoned because of his implication in an attempt to assassinate the Emperor in 1911. Despite the complexities of modern society, Ama concludes that Shin Buddhist faith cannot be indifferent to events in the actual world.

As an example of an early engaged Buddhist, we have included the essay of Takagi Kenmyo, entitled "My Socialism," which gives his personal interpretation of this doctrine based on Buddhist ideals, particularly the Pure Land as the ideal society. It illustrates the potentiality of Shin Buddhism to inspire compassionate action in society.

Kenneth K. Tanaka's "Ethics in American Jodo Shinshu: Trans-Ethical Responsibility," though pastoral in intent, takes up an important issue for Shin Buddhism in the West, and particularly in America. This is the role of ethics. The concern for ethics arises from the social context of Shin Buddhism where questions of ethical relations are constantly discussed. The author, preliminary to dealing with modern ethics in Shin Buddhism, outlines the meaning of ethics, Buddhist ethics, Shinran's thought on soteriology and ethics, and post-Shinran ethical thought till Rennyo, the eighth Abbot in the 15th century. With this background, he states that for Shin Buddhism to grow in the West it will be necessary to integrate ethical concerns into its teachings.

While throughout its history Shin Buddhism has taken up ethical issues, it has generally turned to non-Buddhist resources such as Confucianism for its basic values. He further notes that Shin Buddhism in America has created liturgical literature which reflects ethical concerns due to the emphasis on secular life and the here and now in American culture. Turning to the basis or motivation for ethics, the author presents a concept called "trans-ethical responsibility."

The trans-ethical dimension goes beyond secular, goal-oriented, or religious obligatory ethics to stress responsibility. This sense of responsibility derives from self reflection in the context of a higher soteriological life. That is, it is grounded in religious awareness and brings about a transformation resulting from becoming aware of the gap between the source of salvation and one's own ego propensities. It comes about when the individual becomes deeply aware of the inadequacy of his self-motivated, self-willed efforts to fulfill ethical principles or norms. Awareness of the gap between himself and the ideal may lead the person to an understanding of his true self illuminated by higher spiritual ideals and bring about a transformation in approach to ethical life.

In the conclusion of the essay, the author sets forth a variety of guidelines for specific issues with touchpoints in Shin teaching that can assist an individual in making decisions. These involve such questions as abortion, capital punishment, social welfare, and the environment.

The fourth section takes up "Historical and Comparative Perspectives." Here the authors call attention to the historical roots of Shinran's thought, or intercultural and interreligious considerations which indicate the broader religious significance of Pure Land and Shin in our modern world.

Bando Shojun's, "Shinran's Indebtedness to T'an-luan" discusses the influence of T'an-luan (476-542), an early Chinese proponent of Pure Land teaching. T'an-luan contributed to Shinran's interpretation in significant areas of Buddhist thought, such as philosophy, the principle of Self Power and Other Power, and transfer of merit. The importance of T'an-luan for Shinran may be observed in the fact that the name Shinran is taken in part from the Japanese pronunciation of the Chinese Don*ran*. The *shin* is from Ten*shin* or Vasubandhu (5th century) a major Indian Buddhist teacher. T'an-luan, along with Vasubandhu is one of the seven major teachers making up Shinran's Pure Land lineage.

Allan A. Andrews, "Pure Land Buddhist Hermeneutics: Hōnen's Interpretation of *Nembutsu*," discusses Hōnen's approaches in determining the truth or value of Pure Land teaching for attaining enlightenment. These approaches are through reason, through scripture, and through appeal to a revered teacher. It is a comprehensive treatment of Hōnen's justification of the sole practice of *Nembutsu* as the only means for all people in the last age to be born in the Pure Land.

Frithjof Schuon's, "David, Shankara, Hōnen" establishes three comparative spiritual types, illustrated by David, the alleged author of the Psalms in the Bible, Shankara, the founder of the Indian Vedanta school of philosophy, and Hōnen, the founder of the Pure Land sect in Japan. Each represents a basic mode of spirituality, denoted as the way of prayer, the way of intellect or metaphysical discernment, and the way of grace and saving trust.

Our concluding essay constitutes a challenge to Shin Buddhism, as well as all faiths. Professor Takeda's "Mutual Transformation of Pure Land Buddhism and Christianity" summarizes various approaches to Buddhist-Christian dialogue presented by major scholars such as the late Nishitani Keiji, a Buddhist philosopher, and John Cobb, Takizawa Katsumi, Gordon Kaufman, and John Hick, all Christian theologians. He indicates their basic theses, while explaining where he differs with each.

Taking note of the challenge which the modern pluralistic situation poses for Buddhism and other traditions, he affirms that the issue whether the view of salvation through Amida Buddha is true or not can only be resolved by dialogue and comparison.

He concludes that he accepts the truth theory of pluralism whereby the criterion of truth of one's own faith means also to recognize the criterion of truth of other faiths, otherwise there can be no meaningful dialogue. From this position he suggests an even more radical pluralist position which is based on a postmodern world view where everything is interconnected in organic, non-substantial relationship, open to the future with potentially new creativity and without resistance to self-transformation resulting from dialogue. Rather than dialogue seen as imposed by external conditions, it should arise from within one's own faith standpoint.

We trust that this limited selection of essays will attest to the depth and potential meaning of the Pure Land teaching in the context of contemporary religious studies. We also hope that the broadening understanding of the teaching will strengthen its participation and effectiveness in contemporary religious dialogue, and that as it evolves through the dialogue process it will join with other faiths in increasing spiritual awareness and commitment in our complex and fragmented world.

The editor is very grateful to World Wisdom Inc., particularly its commissioning editor Barry McDonald, for recognizing the significance of Pure Land and Shin thought and affording this opportunity to explore the diverse resources available in the journals. The editor also wishes to thank the various contributors or their translators for their generous permission to reprint their essays. Further, the editor recognizes that the selection of essays is a matter of personal judgment and accepts responsibility for whatever is lacking in the choices made in this volume.

ALFRED BLOOM
Professor Emeritus
University of Hawaii

I. MODERN SHIN BUDDHIST THINKERS

CHAPTER 1

"THE GREAT PATH OF ABSOLUTE OTHER POWER" AND "MY FAITH"

—KIYOZAWA MANSHI

(TRANSLATED WITH AN INTRODUCTION BY BANDŌ SHŌJUN)

Introduction

Modern Japanese Buddhism produced at its very start a great but truly tragic figure. Kiyozawa Manshi[1] was born in 1863, and died in 1903. Though it was only for forty years that he lived on this earth, his original thought commanded a special prominence even in the Meiji Period (1868-1912) when numerous new schools of thought flourished. His short life as an exemplary Buddhist, moreover, had vital significance as signaling a turning point in the history of modern Buddhism. In 1888, after graduating from Tokyo Imperial University where he studied religious philosophy, the twenty-six year old Kiyozawa was requested by authorities of the Higashi Honganji Order of the Pure Land Shin Sect to which he belonged to return to Kyoto to take up the task of educating young priests. To ready himself, he embarked on a life of asceticism, which he called "Minimum Possible," for a period of four years. This "experiment," carried to the utmost of his human capacity, caused him to fall victim to consumption. But it also enabled him to gain a profound understanding of the finite limits of human ability, and brought his spirituality to full maturity. He felt that Shin teaching could achieve a far-reaching mission. At the dawn of the Meiji Period, Shinran's teachings were scarcely noticed by philosophical circles, being simply regarded as a belief of ignorant country people. It was, nevertheless, this religious teaching on which Kiyozawa based his hopes, not merely for the Japanese people, but for all mankind. Commanding an overall view of the faltering fortunes of his own Otani Order, loaded down as it was with the heavy burdens of a rigidly organized feudal society, Kiyozawa's inner aspirations for revitalizing Buddhism could not help but burst out in the form of an attempt to reform the order.

His attempt in this direction, however, proved an utter failure. The vigorous reformation movement lasted for two years but failed to realize any noticeable

3

results. During this time he suffered repeated hemorrhages of the lungs, caused by an aggravation of his chronic disease. He was finally excommunicated by the Order, and rejected by those around him. Family complications then occurred which vexed him even further. Returning to his home temple, he was led to thoughts of suicide. He remained at home in complete silence for two years, hoping to recuperate from his illness. It was during this time that he experienced an epoch-making conversion.

Ever since the failure of his reformation movement, he had devoted himself to repeated readings of the Agama Sūtras. One day he felt he had for the first time encountered the true spirit of the Buddha. He happened to read the Greek Stoic philosopher Epictetus,[2] and his mind underwent a further transformation. The teaching of *nil admirari* ("Do not be affected by anything") advocated by Epictetus provided the struggling Kiyozawa with a profound peace of mind. He describes this as being not a fragmentary happiness, or a mere sense of satisfaction, but something absolute, a state in which living itself means unconditional happiness.

In 1899, aged thirty-seven, he had become so highly regarded by the Shin authorities (who had by then reinstated him) that he was entrusted with the project of setting up a new college in Tokyo. This college, named *Shinshū Daigaku,*[3] was the forerunner of the present Otani University in Kyoto. Ailing as he was, he went to Tokyo and began his work. At the same time there formed around him a small gathering of youths who admired and respected his noble character, known as the Kōkōdō[4] group. The activities of this group attracted more world attention than any of the other Buddhist groups in the Meiji Period. They published a monthly organ, *Seishinkai* [5] ("Spiritual World") which became one of the most well-read and influential Buddhist magazines throughout the Meiji and Taishō Periods. Through this magazine, Kiyozawa kept expressing his faith, and his movement became known as *Seishin shugi* [6] ("Spiritualism"), in keeping with the journal's name.

Zettai Tariki no Taidō [7] ("The Great Path of Absolute Other Power") was written first in Kiyozawa's diary, Rōsenki,[8] and initially published in the *Seishinkai* in a slightly edited form by Tada Kanae, one of his disciples. The original Japanese text, which is known by heart by many Shin followers even today, is marked by the nobleness of its sentiment and elegance of its expression. It may be said to be a concise expression of the author's sincere religious faith, the record of the outpouring of his religious inspiration as he arrived at final resolution of his religious quest.

In autumn, 1902, he resigned all his posts and in ill health returned to his temple in Aichi Prefecture. Half a year later, on 6th July, 1903, he passed away at the youthful age of forty-one. A week before death, he wrote an article entitled *"Ware wa kaku no gotoku Nyorai o shinzu"*[9] ("I Believe in Tathāgata in this Way"), summing up his lifelong search for the Way. The editor of the *Seishinkai*, in which the work first appeared in June of 1903, changed the title to *"Waga*

Shinnen"[10] ("My Faith"), which had been the subtitle, and that is the title by which it has become known. In it he expresses in full detail the process of the development of his unadulterated faith in Tathāgata. This article has earned the reputation of being one of the most outstanding confessions of religious faith of modern Japan. Kiyozawa acknowledges repentantly his utter ignorance and incompetence in the presence of Tathāgata, and records his deep sense of gratitude and heart-felt praise of Tathāgata for the wondrous fact that he, by virtue of the faith granted him, should be enabled to live in a peaceful and calm state of mind amidst this turbulent world so full of suffering.

I have used the text found in Professor Terakawa Shunshō's edition of Kiyozawa's selected writings, entitled *Waga Shinnen*[11] (Bunmeidō: Kyoto, 1971, pp. 41-50). I am also indebted to Professor Terakawa's remarks accompanying the text as well as to his unpublished article, "Kiyozawa Manshi," for the information in this Introduction.

"The Great Path of Absolute Other Power"

I

This my self is none other than that which, following the way of suchness and entrusting itself to the wondrous working that is absolute and infinite, has settled down of itself in the present situation.

By entrusting myself to the absolute and infinite, I am beyond fears of the problem of life-and-death. And with the problem of life-and-death beyond our fears, how much more so problems of lesser importance! Banishment is welcome. Imprisonment is bearable. How should we be concerned with censures, rejections, or humiliations? Rather let us enjoy above all else what has been accorded to us by the absolute and infinite.

II

The infinite variety of the myriad phenomena of the universe belongs to the wondrous workings of the one great mystery. And yet we simply take it for granted, regarding it all as a natural phenomenon, paying no respect or regard to it. Were we not endowed with any knowledge or sensibility, there would be no problem. But we are in fact endowed with them, and we remain insensitive to them. How then can we avoid being termed perverted?

The reflection of a single color, the fragrance of a single scent, can never appear of themselves. The appearance of all these phenomena is without exception caused by the power of that one great mystery. Not only color and scent, what

5

of the arising of our "selves"? No matter where the self's original source or final destination may lie, nothing lies within the domain of our own will. Not only are our previous lives and our after-lives not subject to our own will, the appearance and disappearance of our thoughts at this very moment is not a matter at our own dispensation. We are absolutely within the hands of the Other Power.

III

We are bound to die. But even if we die we shall never be reduced to extinction. We are not made up of life alone; death belongs to us as well. Our existence is composed of both life and death. We are not to be dependent upon life and death; we are spiritual beings existing beyond life and death.

Nevertheless, life and death cannot be decided by our own free will. They are solely dependent for their being upon the wondrous working of the Other Power that transcends our thought. We should, therefore, never be swayed by joy or grief in the face of life and death. And not only then; we should conduct ourselves likewise in the face of all the other occurrences. We should rather admire the wondrous workings of the infinite Other Power as manifested in the infinite variety of occurrences in the universe.

IV

Do not supplicate. Do not demand. What is lacking in you? If you feel any lack, does it not testify to your unbelief? Has the Tathāgata not given you all that is necessary for you? Even if what has been given is not sufficient, is it not true that there could be nothing else truly satisfying to you? If you suffer in the thought that something is lacking in you, then you should cultivate yourself all the more and learn to find peace in the Tathāgata's great command. It would be mean and low to expect something of others, an insult to the Tathāgata's great command. Although the Tathāgata is untouched by any insult, what about your own suffering?

V

Where is the infinite Other Power? It is visible in all your receiving, which is a manifestation of the infinite Other Power. Revere and cherish it, and thus be thankful to the Tathāgata's enormous blessing. Yet in order to satisfy yourself you are running after external things, following others, without seeking satisfaction within yourself. Are you not mistaken?

Chasing after external things is the source of greed. Following others is the source of anger.

VI

What is the way to cultivate oneself? You should better reflect and examine yourself. See into the great Way. If you see into the great Way, you will never feel any lack no matter what is given to you. And then you will never seek anything in others. When this happens, you will never quarrel with others. Being content in oneself, not demanding anything, not quarrelling—can there be anything in the world more powerful? Can there be anything on earth more comprehensive? Thus, not until we attain this can we manifest a great cause of independence and freedom. Such an individual self is never hurt by external things or by other people. One who harbors apprehensions of being hurt is utterly deluded. One should rid himself completely of illusion and delusion.

VII

An independent man must always stand atop the rock of life-and-death. He must as a matter of course be prepared for annihilation or for death by starvation. He should accept food and clothing, if at all, only when he is thus prepared. If all is exhausted, he should calmly go to death. A man with wife and children, however, should give priority to their food and clothing, give all he has to them. He should take himself only what is left. He should not worry how they will be fed and clad if he should die. A firm faith in the great path of the absolute Other Power is more than enough against such apprehensions. The great path will never disregard them. Someway or other they will be able to find a way of subsistence. If by chance they cannot find it, it means the great path is commanding them to die. They are simply to accept their lot. Socrates said: "When I was in Thessaly, away from home, Heaven was gracious enough to sustain my family through the magnanimity of others. Even if I were to go to a far-away land now, how could Heaven fail to look after them?"

"My Faith"

I should like now to dwell a bit on the ideas of "faith" and "Tathāgata," to which I often refer, in order to clarify what they actually mean.

I should hardly have to mention that my faith refers to the mode of my belief in Tathāgata, which is made up of two factors: belief and Tathāgata. Outwardly these two appear to be two different things, but for me these two are one. What is my faith? It is to believe in Tathāgata. What is the Tathāgata to which I refer? It is Reality, upon which my faith is based. In dualistic terms, it has two aspects; the believer and what he believes in. It might be said that in me the former is my faith, and the latter is Tathāgata. In other words, it is a matter of distinction between the believing *ki*[12] and the *hō*[13] which is believed in. I shall

7

not be concerned any longer with technical terms such as *nō-jo*[14] (subjective aspect-objective aspect) and *ki-hō*, since they are liable to obscure what should be made clear.

There are a number of problems to be clarified: what is meant by "I believe"; why I attempt such a thing as belief; what benefit it has; and so forth. First, as for the benefit, my agony and suffering are eliminated by the act of believing. This I might call the salvational benefit. Be that as it may, when this faith arises in my mind as I agonize and suffer from various influences and circumstances, I immediately acquire peace and tranquility. In other words, when my faith makes an appearance, it permeates my mind, taking the place of all other illusory thoughts. When this faith is there, though I suffer incursions of any influence or circumstance, I can never be provoked into agony or suffering. Such a susceptible, over-sensitive fellow as I have become on account of my illness could never be free from acute agony and suffering were it not for this faith. I am convinced this kind of faith is essential even for those who, though healthy, are beset by suffering. Should I express the joy and gratitude of my religious feeling, it would be none other than to call it the joy in the actual experience of having all my agony and suffering swept away by virtue of my faith.

Second, as to why I attempt to believe in this Tathāgata, I would answer: because it involves the benefit mentioned above. But there are other reasons. The benefit comes only after the act of believing. Before, no one can know if benefit will follow. Of course, there is no reason one could not believe in the testimony of others, but a belief based on hearsay remains uncertain. A conviction in the presence or absence of real benefit appears solely in one's own experience. My faith in the Tathāgata, however, is not necessarily based on its benefits but upon certain other grounds of great import.

You may ask what they are. My faith in the Tathāgata may be traced until the ultimate limits of my knowledge. Without speaking of the time I lacked serious resolve concerning the question of human life, once I came to tackle the problem more soberly, I felt compelled to inquire into the meaning of life at all costs. This quest finally reached a stage where I found life's meaning to be inscrutable. This experience brought about my belief in the Tathāgata. There may be room for suspecting that my following this course was not accidental, for the need for such an inquiry is not necessary in order to have faith. For me, however, such a course of events was necessary. It is an integral part of my faith to believe that my self-power is useless. In order for me to believe that my self-power is of no avail, it was necessary to exhaust the entire resources of my knowledge and devices, to the extent I could no longer hold up my head. This was a process most trying for me. Even before this final apex was reached, a number of temporary conclusions were drawn from time to time as to the nature of religious faith. But one after another they would invariably be undermined. One can never escape this calamity so long as one is hopeful of establishing religious faith by way of logic or learning.

What good is, what evil is, what truth is, what untruth is, what happiness is, what unhappiness is—none of these are finally within our grasp. The most vital point in my faith is that I came to give myself up entirely to the Tathāgata upon realizing that everything is after all beyond my grasp.

Third, what then is the nature of my faith? It consists in believing in the Tathāgata. It is Reality, in which I am capable of believing and in which I cannot help but believe. The Tathāgata in which I am capable of believing is the fundamental potential, which quickens this helpless self, whose ability is nil and who is incapable of becoming independent, to realize its true individuality. That is to say, the Tathāgata in which I believe is the basic potentiality that enables me who am utterly incapable of discriminating between good and evil, truth and untruth, happiness and unhappiness, and therefore unable to make even a single move in any direction, left or right, forward or backward in this world fraught with discriminations of good and evil, truth and untruth, happiness and unhappiness—to live and die in this world dispassionately and calmly. Without putting faith in this Tathāgata, I can neither live nor die. I cannot help but believe in this Tathāgata. This is the Tathāgata in which I feel compelled to believe.

The above is a general outline as to the nature of my faith. From the first point of view, the Tathāgata is for me infinite compassion. From the second, the Tathāgata is for me infinite wisdom. From the third, the Tathāgata is for me infinite potentiality. Thus my faith consists in believing in the reality of infinite compassion, wisdom, and potentiality.

First, because the Tathāgata is infinite compassion, the Tathāgata deigns to give me calm and peace as soon as my faith is established. The Tathāgata of my belief renders me great happiness while in this world, even before the advent of an after-life. I am not incapable, however, of attaining some measure of happiness from certain other things. But no happiness is superior to the happiness accorded by faith. Therefore, the happiness deriving from faith is the greatest happiness of my life. It is the happiness I acutely experience day and night. I shall not speak of happiness in the next life here, since I have not yet experienced it myself.

Second, because the Tathāgata is infinite wisdom, the Tathāgata always deigns to illuminate and protect me and to deliver me from bondage to the illusions of evil knowledge and views. One is apt, owing to his common custom, to fall unawares into vain reasoning in supporting his study and inquiries. At times, we even go so far as to attempt to prove the infinite, compassionate Reality by way of finite and crude speculations. With the establishment of faith, however, even if we fall into such deluded states for a while, we are finally induced to renouncing all such reasoning, and to reflecting upon our unreasonable attitude. The awareness expressed in the maxim, "Knowledge consists in knowing that one does not know what is beyond his knowledge," is indeed the pinnacle of man's knowledge. Nevertheless, we cannot easily rest assured in it. I myself have held most presumptuous opinions. But, thanks to faith, I can now respectfully acknowledge and appreciate the confessions of "Hōnen, an ignoramus," and the "foolish, bald-headed Shinran," and I can truly rest assured with this ignorant self. Personally speaking, I formerly found it most difficult to escape from the delusion of attempting to inquire into the perfect standard or the infinite reality by way of finite, imperfect, human knowledge, while declaring myself to be finite and imperfect. Formerly, I also used to feel the whole universe crumble and all society reduced to chaos when I lost sight of the standards of truth and morality. But now I am convinced that the standards of truth and morality could not possibly be raised by human knowledge.

Third, because the Tathāgata is infinite potentiality, the Tathāgata deigns to accord me a great potentiality through faith. Ordinarily, it is customary for us to decide our action or attitude through our own deliberation and discrimination. But once confronted with an event more complicated in nature, we find it less easy to maneuver our deliberations and discriminations. It is for this reason, as we gradually proceed to attempt studies and inquiries with a view to finding the standard and the reality, it becomes increasingly difficult for us to make decisions as to our actions, and we are finally cornered, at a loss what to do. To be prudent in speech and actions, not to break the law, not to violate the moral codes, not to lose one's decorum, not to be unmannerly; obligations, to oneself and to others, at home, in society, to parents, to the lord, to husbands, to wives, to brothers, to friends, to the good, to the wicked, to the superior, to infants, and so forth, even obligations deriving from mundane ethical teachings—these are never very easy. If we attempt to observe them faithfully, we are bound for the grief of "impossibility." I have experienced a great deal of suffering, confronted with this impossibility. If I had had to suffer endlessly on its account, I might have committed suicide long ago. Thanks to religion, however, I was able to escape this suffering, and now I no longer feel the need to commit suicide. That is, by placing faith in the Tathāgata of infinite compassion I remain today in peace and tranquility.

How then does the Tathāgata of infinite compassion accord to me such peace? He delivers me by assuming all responsibilities for my Śākyamuni. No sinful act can cause any hindrance before the Tathāgata. There is no need for me to discriminate between good and evil, just and unjust. No matter what they are, I can simply follow my own will, my own aspiration to do anything. Whether they are errors or crimes, I do not worry at all over my actions. The Tathāgata deigns to assume entire responsibility for all my acts. I am able to rest in continual peace by simply putting my faith in this Tathāgata. The Tathāgata's potentiality is infinite. The Tathāgata's potentiality is supreme. The Tathāgata's potentiality is at all times omnipresent. The Tathāgata's potentiality comprehends the ten directions and acts freely and unrestrictedly. I take refuge in the wondrous power of the Tathāgata and receive great peace and calm. Surrendering the great matter of life and death to the Tathāgata, I never feel any unrest or dissatisfaction.

A proverb has it: "Death and life are the decree of Heaven; wealth and rank depend upon the will of Heaven." The Tathāgata in which I believe is the basic ground for the decree and will of Heaven.

NOTES

1 清沢満之.

2 60?-120? C.E.

3 真宗大学.

4 浩々堂.

5 精神界.

6 精神主義.

7 絶対他力の大道.

8 臘扇記; *Rōsen* ("a fan in winter") was a pen-name of Kiyozawa's.

9 我は此の如く如来を信ず.

10 我が信念.

11 わが信念.

12 機.

13 法.

14 能-所.

CHAPTER 2

THE SIGNIFICANCE OF DHARMAKARA BODHISATTVA AS EARTHLY SAVIOR

—SOGA RYOJIN

(TRANSLATED BY WAYNE S. YOKOYAMA AND HIROSHI SUZUKI)[1]

I

It was through discussions we had in early June last year [1912] at Kaneko Daiei's place in Takata that I had an insight which I articulated as "The Tathāgata becomes me," and further discussions in late August at Akegarasu Haya's place inspired me to expand it to, "The Tathāgata becoming me is the Tathāgata's way of saving me." Then around October it finally dawned on me: "The unity of Tathāgata and self is the birth of Dharmakara Bodhisattva." Thus, I came to realize that the unity of Tathāgata and self is sewn up part and parcel with the event of Dharmakara Bodhisattva's birth. While such matters may not have concerned others in the least, they have been a constant source of annoyance to me these past twenty years. At times I got so worked up about it I thought I would go stark raving mad. Day after day I would thumb through the sacred writings, but could garner no clue as to the significance of these passages. My situation was aggravated by the fact I was beset by all the trivial problems that have colored these dark and troubled times of contemporary Japan. And so attaining this level of clarity was like a ray of light shining at the end of a long and dark tunnel. I am at a loss for words when it comes to expressing just how I feel. But there was a part of me that was not content to remain silent, and so from October of last year I began to publish portions of my confessions in the "Storming Winds, Pelting Rain" column I have been contributing to *The World of Spirituality* journal. I also published an essay called "Dharmakara Bhikṣu in the Present World as the One Awakened to the Eternal Buddha-mind" in the January [1913] issue of *The Inexhaustible Light* journal. After these pieces came out I received words of encouragement from friends far and wide, but this only made me question my own position further, forcing me to confront some of my deepest fears. Looking back on this time I am surprised by the boldness and sheer arrogance of the enterprise, and I cannot help but lament the paucity of the intellectual resources at my command as I engaged the task. Now as I reflect the matter, I see that, as in the Zen phrase, "Originally there is not a single thing" (Hui-neng), I was a person who had nothing, but through the help of numerous friends along the way, even those whom I had made light of or were contemptuous of, I was made to benefit greatly from the inspiring thoughts they turned over to me, a fact that impresses me greatly even now.

II

Though I knew of the name of Dharmakara Bodhisattva from long before and regarded it as a major concept, truth is, I must confess, there was a long stretch of time when I could make neither heads nor tails of it. Of course neither could I understand the concept of the Land of Bliss, that realm which lay tens of thousands of millions of buddha lands to the west. But as I cannot imagine this world of reality to be the Land of Bliss, then like it or not I had to capitulate to that western Land of Bliss. But when it came to Dharmakara Bodhisattva and his awakening to the Original Vow after five kalpas contemplation and his aeons of practice to fulfill that Vow, I simply could not bring myself to believe that account, nor did I feel myself under any obligation to do so. As a child I was taught Shinran's *Hymn of True Faith*, and although I couldn t understand it, I remember being moved by the passage, "In the causal stage as Bodhisattva Dharmakara … he undertook five kalpas contemplation and vowed that his Name would resound throughout the universe." The simple-hearted believers who heard the part about the five kalpas contemplation would be moved to tears. But once I started to think for myself, whatever attraction I had to this Practice of the Vow in the causal state soon faded, and instead I found myself interested exclusively in the name "Tathāgata of Light radiating unhindered in all directions." For the time being I rationalized the matter by saying that the so-called great law of cause and effect fell into the category of things inscrutable. Yet since it was unlikely that humankind could extract itself from beneath the weight of such a universal principle, I would explain it away by saying that in order for the Tathāgata to inform humankind of the Original Vow, the Tathāgata had to transmit its message by manipulating the great law of cause and effect that governs the human thought processes. But truth is, I was so enamored by the imagery of Tathāgata's radiant Light that it exclusively guided my thoughts to the point of virtually destroying any budding interest I might have had in the Vow practice in causal state of Dharmakara Bhikṣu.

In short, though I would go around talking up the theme of holding to the central belief in the Original Vow, truth was I regarded the Original Vow to be nothing more than simply the great spiritual energy of the Tathāgata's true awakening. Dharmakara Bhikṣu was nothing more than the name of a bit character who transiently appeared for a brief five kalpas contemplation in the greater scenario of the Tathāgata's eternal drama. Moreover, it was a drama that did not require our appearance on stage. For all extents and purposes, my savior was still the emanating out of eternity Tathāgata of Light radiating unhindered in every direction.

III

But when the eternal Tathāgata of Light radiating unhindered in every direction becomes the object of our veneration, as a projection of our ideals it ceases to function as our world savior. This kind of self-serving and intellectualized belief is enmeshed in the *satori* of the so-called Holy Path of self-power. Salvation is a matter of reality. The great problem is what we must do as the protagonists in the real life drama of human life. There is no salvation in store for us when we count on empty ideals to pull us through. All the gods, buddhas, and bodhisattvas in every direction in time and space manifest human ideals. As the Name of the Tathāgata of Light radiating unhindered in every direction contains the sum merit of every god, buddha, and bodhisattva there is, it symbolizes the concrete unification of all human ideals, and it is only natural that we should direct our deepest aspirations to that quarter. But if we are so enamored with the Light merely as an ideal, we must ask ourselves: Is the light of wisdom that issues from the truth of that ideal world sufficient to rend this long dark night of ignorance? Is it sufficient to serve as the proverbial raft that works to dispel the real suffering we have to endure on the great sea of life and death? When we step aboard the great Vow ship of compassion, our ideals at last match with our realities for the first time, and the sea of human life with its real suffering as such becomes harmoniously integrated into the vast sea of Light radiating in all its fullness and glory. Distance ourselves from that great Vow ship of compassion and the sea reverts to the watery vale of suffering it was before. But it is futile to talk about a Light unhindered shining its rays on the sea of suffering if it holds no benefit for those drowning in its depths. The realities we face here and now demand not some empty notion of light, but the ship of the Universal Vow sailing forth dynamically on the seas of human life. An eternal Tathāgata of timeless truth can never be our savior as we stand face to face with life's realities. To mediate the gap between the human and Buddha world, a real world savior has to be one who too merges with this world of reality.

In the Christian concept of Trinity, Jesus Christ serves as mediator between God and man, and it is this very role as mediator that makes it impossible for Jesus to truly fulfill his role as world savior directly. If we conceive of God the Father as eternal light, this points to the impossibility of God being able to make intimate contact with the world of human reality. Even if God were the creator of this world, once this world of reality came into being, there would be an absolute demarcation between God and this world, such that each exists completely independent of the other. God of course may be said to be in possession of an original dimension through which God holds dominion over the world of man; but God as such is unable to either better the human condition or to work out man's deliverance. God's utter isolation is especially evident in God's act of sending God's beloved son Jesus into this real world, and it is through Jesus'role as world savior and as medium to the spiritual world that we learn of the design of this God isolated in eternity to become one with humankind.

Thus, between the Parent of eternal light and we humans who have fallen into the sea of life and death, there is a gap as great as that between heaven and earth. Indeed, his influence would seem not to reach where we are. That is why he appears in this world in the form of the human-buddha savior Dharmakara Bodhisattva, his light mingling with the dust of this world.

IV

The question now engages us: Who is this Dharmakara Bodhisattva? Where did he make his appearance in this world, where did he make the Original Vow, where did he practice, where did he attain supreme enlightenment? We could say he attained supreme enlightenment in the Pure Land in the west, a realm transcending our real world. But the question remains as to the birth of our hu-man-buddha mediator. In the case of Christ, however enshrouded he may be as an apotheosis of Light, it is clear he is an historical figure. The claim that Christ is well qualified to be the savior in this real world is in part grounded in his tak-ing this real world as the foundation of his ministry; but at the same time his inability to achieve that goal of savior may be attributed to the fact he occurs as an historical figure. For however great he may be, in final analysis is he not just another human being? And as far as being a soul in need of deliverance he would have to be a person no different from us. In so being, then, our man-God mediator loses his credentials as savior of those caught up in the real world. For how can such an individual be my savior when he is, as always, who he is and I am always who I am? Even if Christ were a manifestation issuing from the heavenly world, it would be impossible for him as an individual to act as savior to me, another individual. If in this capacity he is unable to become the new sav-ior, his role would then be reduced simply to being nothing more than the first discoverer of a new truth: that God is father to humankind. Christianity in its outward form may thus seem to resemble our religion of so-called other-power salvation, but strip away the mask and it turns out to be just another teaching based on the ideals of self-power, the idea that man can save himself by his own efforts. From his ideal world all God can do is shed his light on the ever-deepen-ing quandary of human karma, and while we may look to this god in adoration all we can do is cry in vain at our efforts to save ourselves.

By contrast, Dharmakara Bodhisattva is never presented as an historical figure. Instead he is born directly in the hearts and minds of human beings. That voice beckoning to living beings everywhere does not come to us from on high, from the lofty reaches of the world of pure light, nor are we being beckoned to by some one objectively distinct personality who exists as an individual separate from us. The voice of Dharmakara Bodhisattva issues forth from within the breast of each person trapped in the darkness of suffering and despair. When the Original Vow of Dharmakara Bodhisattva is described as the proverbial raft on the great sea of life and death, it points to the issuing forth of that voice from the depths of our hearts, from the very bowels of the earth on which we stand. In contrast to all of the idealistic religions of the world that I call "religions of Heaven," only our religion of salvation in Dharmakara Bodhisattva stands apart as the sole "religion of Earth." Many are the "religions of Light," but only our Shin Buddhism is a "religion of the Vow ship." Only our Shin Buddhism is a religion addressing the real world each of us is experiencing, and as such it is a religion offering true salvation. Phrases such as "ordinary life is where the karma for awakening matures" and "the two truth theory of ultimate truth and worldly truth" may well express the salvation Reality offers, but in truth they pay no more than lip service to it. Why is it, one wonders, that there are so many who, whilst singing paeans of praise to the Light as it might turn out in some future time, pass their lives in vain in this sea of life and death, only to vanish forever into its depths? The truth is that our Shin Buddhism, like the many Light-praising religions throughout the world, also sings praises to the Light the Tathāgata disperses in every direction. But as we sing these paeans of praise to the Light we are not suspended in midair. Our feet are planted firmly on the deck of the Vow ship crossing the great sea of life and death. We are no longer isolated individuals who at death vanish forever. Though we continue to remain in the midst of the great sea of life, as long as we are passengers aboard the great ship of the Vow we are forever separated from the cycle of life and death. When we are not mindful of that ship, though we may live out our days pleasantly we are not truly living up to our name as those who praise the Light. And when our reality follows the timeless trajectory that has guided its course, we at last reach that place where we are destined. For we are not people suspended in midair.

All the buddhas, bodhisattvas, and gods of time and space beckon to us from the heavens above, and while each of them has their own special light, it is the Lord of Blazing Light, Amida Tathāgata, that consolidates all these lights into one. But the adoration of such a buddha and salvation by such a buddha are not the same thing. Although it is said that the gods and buddhas never abandon us and call to us and shine their light on us constantly, when we utterly helpless beings stand face to face with the problem of saving ourselves and address the question of what options we have, we must abandon those gods and buddhas and leave them behind. Their beckoning may be said to exist on some ideal plane, but they have made no original vow to rescue us in the real world. Strictly speaking, the Original Vow is limited to Dharmakara Bodhisattva's Forty-eight Vows. Although there is a tendency to take other-power salvation lightly, our founder Shinran Shonin ascribed true other power solely to the power of

Tathāgata's Original Vow. But here we must ask ourselves: What is the power of Tathāgata's Original Vow? It has to be the ability to save this self of ours trapped in the web of the real world. It cannot be like a picture of a tasty treat that does nothing for us. Ultimately, though, the power of the great compassionate Avalokiteśvara is like this kind of picture; it has no footing in our real world, and as such is nothing more than another pretty story. Dharmakara Bodhisattva's Original Vow is of a completely different order. On the one hand, as human-buddha mediator he is Amida Tathāgata who attained timeless Buddhahood; at the same time, he is the person who truly seeks salvation. I have expressed this truth and reality in words of confession as, "The Tathāgata is perfectly identical to myself," and also in my intuitive statement, "The Tathāgata becomes me." The main principle operative in this process of salvation is the Unity of Seeker (religious conviction) and Dharma (Tathāgata); for one undergoing this process it could also be expressed as the Unity of Buddha-mind (religious conviction) and Ordinary mind (evil karma). In this single unit called Dharmakara Bodhisattva, we pay reverence to the majestic power of the Tathāgata who embodies timeless truth; at the same time, awakening to the harsh truth of the karmic evil of our life we see ourselves single-mindedly taking refuge in that Tathāgata. Thus, in Dharmakara Bodhisattva, we find a Tathāgata as parent and ourselves as sentient beings without any third-party mediator; it is the Tathāgata as such sheerly identified with us sentient beings. In this configuration the first person "I" is perfectly identified with the second person "You," wherein the objective state of our religious conviction is at the same time the subjective state of the Tathāgata's religious conviction. The call for help of those seeking to be saved is at the very same moment the savior's answer to that call. It is the Tathāgata's urging us to "Trust in me" occurring at the very same moment as the seeker's act of entrusting in that Tathāgata. In this logic Dharmakara Bodhisattva is the passenger aboard ship and at the very same time he is the commander of the ship. This renowned author of the Original Vow is at the very same time the humble seeker for whom the Vow is intended. Thus when I reflect on the character of Dharmakara Bodhisattva and the circumstances and significance of his birth, I am both amazed and impressed by the mystery of what he embodies.

NOTES

[1] Readers may also take note that there is an alternative translation by Fr. Jan Van Bragt, "Savior on Earth: The Meaning of Dharmakara Bodhisattva's Advent," in *An Anthology of Modern Shin Buddhist Writings* (Kyoto: Otani University, 2001).—*Ed.*

CHAPTER 3

THE MEANING OF SALVATION IN THE DOCTRINE OF PURE LAND BUDDHISM

—KANEKO DAIEI

(TRANSLATED AND ADAPTED BY SAKAMOTO HIROSHI)

It goes without saying that, for all its profound philosophical systems, Buddhism is essentially a doctrine of liberation. In Buddhism, no salvation is conceivable except the liberation through Enlightenment from the bondage of ignorance and suffering. But does this apply equally to the doctrine of Pure Land Buddhism (the Shin and other Pure Land schools of Buddhism) in which faith in Amida (Amitabha Buddha) has prime importance, or is Pure Land Buddhism virtually a soteriological religion, despite its Buddhist background?

In this article, I, as a Buddhist thinker, shall attempt to make clear the meaning of salvation in the doctrine of Pure Land Buddhism.

I Suffering

Semantically, the term "salvation" means the liberation or emancipation of one from the predicament into which he is fallen. This is equally true of the Japanese term *sukui* or *kyūsai*.[1] In other words, "salvation" semantically presupposes some predicament, whatever it may be. What, then, is the human situation which Buddhism envisages as the predicament from which man should be liberated? The Buddhist answer to this question is widely known: "The suffering of life." But the term "suffering of life" is vague and indefinite in meaning. It needs further definition and clarification. What does it specifically mean? To make its meaning clear, we should turn our eyes to human life as an ever flowing duration or continuum.

One thing to be noted of our life is that it flows on, ever alternating between "doing" and "undergoing." This alternation between doing and undergoing, however, is by no means a lawless, orderless movement. It is ruled by a kind of law, so to speak, a law of inter-causation or mutual conditioning. We do, and our "doing" inevitably makes its influence felt on our way of feeling, sensing, and thinking, directly as well as indirectly (—through its effects on our environment). Our way of feeling, sensing, and thinking thus influenced then inevitably conditions the further steps of our doing.

It is true that an awareness of this law has been expressed very early in mythology and folklore, and later in religion, philosophy, and psychology. It is, indeed, one aspect of wisdom that underlies the process of human civilization. Broadly speaking, however, the bearers of this wisdom have been those who have naïvely affirmed life with its impulses, cravings, and desires, and have sought to gratify life's wants ever better; that is, they applied their awareness of this law for the better enjoyment of life. Life itself was never radically questioned. They remained strangers to the tragic sense of life and to the negation of life. Their wisdom had something analogous to the "wisdom of instinct," as Fabre called it.

Buddhism started with a keen sense of the painfulness of life and sought in all seriousness to penetrate to the nature and origination of the suffering of life. It declared that no human experience could be free from suffering. In other words, the life as we actually live it is, after all, suffering. This declaration may sound bold and too pessimistic. However, it should be remembered that the declaration is made from the viewpoint of Enlightenment, from a penetrating insight into the origination of suffering.

Buddhism teaches that all sufferings of life originate in delusion (*kleśa*). Intellectually, delusion is ignorance (*avidyā*), that is, the ignorance of the emptiness (*śūnyatā*) or suchness (*tathātā*) of things and events. Emotionally, delusion is primarily a thirsty craving (*tṛṣṇā*). Possessed by delusion, we are irresistibly involved in matters of love and hate, gain and loss, honor and dishonor, aggression and defense, in short, in things and events of the world. The result is that we suffer.

The process of our life alternating between doing and undergoing referred to above is thus seen by Buddhism as a vicious circle under the spell of delusion between doing (*karma*) and suffering. Delusion causes us to do deluded things in our actual life; the deluded things done cause us to suffer; and the suffering tends to cause us to become more and more deluded, and so on endlessly. The law that rules over this process is the law of karmic causation.

The origination of suffering as stated above makes the nature of suffering clear. In Buddhism, suffering primarily means the painful uneasiness or anxiety of being deluded. As such, suffering is pregnant with an urge, even if subconscious or semi-conscious, to break through delusion. It is precisely in this sense that suffering is declared to be universal in human life. Some one might be conscious of such suffering, but very feebly and only in the exceptional moments of affliction or depression. Another might have no experience of it. Nevertheless, no one is exempt from such suffering, as long as he is human. In other words, everyone is potentially a sufferer.

II Our Inner Togetherness

One thing should be remembered in connection with the problem of suffering: every one of us human beings is deeply interrelated with fellow beings in an *inner togetherness*. It can hardly be doubted that we are so born as to be sensitive of our inner togetherness. Do we not implicitly mean this when we use the term "we"? In this sense, our inner togetherness may be called "we-ness." As long as our fellow beings are unhappy, none of us can remain aloof from them. We can not but share the unhappiness with them. Because of the inner togetherness of man, sympathy can be awakened within us.

The consciousness of the inner togetherness of man finds its fullest and sublimest expressions in the sphere of religion. Mahayana Buddhism is especially emphatic about the principle of "seeking for emancipation from suffering together with fellow beings." In the *Vimalakīrtinirdeśa* we read, "I (*Vimalakīrti*) suffer, because my fellow beings suffer." This is precisely what the term compassion (*karuṇā*) means. The Mahayana principle of "together with fellow beings" may naturally lead to the vision of the Dharma: The Dharma through which I am truly saved from suffering must be the same Dharma through which all my fellow beings are equally saved, that is, the Dharma that is *adequate* to all the human beings. But what, then, is meant by the term "adequate"?

We actually live in a world in which we find ourselves bound to others by family, neighborhood, occupational, religious, political and other countless ties. Our life situation is largely conditioned by these ties. Above all the family tie has a fundamental importance in conditioning our life situation. Most men and women are actually living a home life. No one doubts that home life is the normal way of living. The life of the homeless one, secluded from family and society, however sublime its purpose may be, is exceptional. Most people make much of their home and family, and are ready to accept all the cares accompanying their home life. They believe that man is so born as to live and love home life for all its cares and troubles. It is true that home life is exposed to the danger of disintegration in the highly industrialized society of today. Nevertheless, the home does not seem to have lost its primary importance in human life.

However, it is definitely in the home as well as in social life that we experience the full strength of delusion over us. The foliage of delusion is exuberant on the soil of home and social life. The delusive passions such as attachment, hatred, anger, fear, jealousy, enmity, perverseness, and aggressiveness become intensified in the tensions of human relationships. It is undoubtedly such delusive passions and their results that afflict us. Suffering is thus inevitable for us beings in the world. To suffer because of being submerged in the world—this is precisely our existential situation.

The Chinese Buddhist master, Shan-tao,[2] undoubtedly had this existential situation in mind when he wrote as follows:

I am actually an ordinary, sinful being who has been, from time immemorial, sunken in and carried down by the current of birth-and-death. Any hope to be helped out of this current has been wholly denied to me.[3]

Some commentary may be needed on those words. By the term "I". Shan-tao definitely means the we-ness or inner togetherness referred to above. He represents here all the human beings in the world. Otherwise, this sentence is not meaningful. The "sinfulness" mentioned here does not refer to any personal sin, but to the sinfulness of the delusion of human existence itself. The phrase "from time immemorial" may be taken to express how long the delusive circle between karma and suffering has been repeated up to the present. In short, this passage expresses a penetrating insight into the existential situation in which man is inevitably bound to suffering, and as such still has a vital meaning for the present day world.

The doctrine of Pure Land Buddhism has appeared as the Dharma that is truly adequate to such an existential situation of man, the Dharma through which alone we can be saved as we are in the world, that is, without deserting home or social life.

III   The Dharma Adequate to all Ordinary Beings

The doctrine of Pure Land Buddhism has a long history of transmission throughout India, China, and Japan. Among the masters who transmitted the doctrine, Tan-luan[4] and the above-cited Shan-tao were exceedingly influential over their own times and over posterity. But the fundamental significance of the Pure Land doctrine as the Dharma truly adequate to all ordinary beings was for the first time positively established by the Japanese master, Hōnen,[5] who resolutely declared the independence of the Pure Land doctrine from all other Buddhist schools. The depth of Hōnen's faith which remained as yet unexpressed by himself was subsequently fully grasped and given a profound and most thoroughgoing expression by Shinran.[6] The mark that distinguishes both these masters is their decided preference of "our" salvation to "my" emancipation. They firmly stood on the ground of the inner togetherness of man.

In his childhood, Hōnen was exhorted by his dying father, who was murdered by his jealous competitor, to become a Buddhist monk and quest for the Dharma through which is emptied every discrimination between friend and foe, love and hate, and through which true peace is attained. He followed his father's dying will and became a monk of the Tendai sect of Buddhism. His elaborate study of the sūtras and śāstras as well as his rigorous disciplinary practices for many years in the monastery on Mt. Hiei were exclusively devoted to the purpose of attaining that Dharma. But all his efforts brought him no light. This is no wonder, considering that the Buddhist quest which had been traditionally undertaken in the monastery was fundamentally directed to the personal emancipation of each monk, while Hōnen's quest was exclusively for the salvation of all human beings in the world. Had his chief concern been personal emancipation, he would have believed that he was steadily marching on the right path to the goal.

The sinfulness of man was continually a problem that confronted Hōnen. The popular belief of the day that sinfulness can be expiated by the virtue of leaving home and becoming a Buddhist monk was unacceptable to him. Sinfulness was nothing other than the deludedness because of which man endlessly alternates between evil karma and suffering, thus afflicting others as well as himself. As such it was definitely a problem of man, not a mere personal problem. The personal solution of this problem might be conceivable, of course, and in fact a great number of Buddhist monks have sought a solution of this sort. The sense of our inner togetherness, however, makes this sort of solution less meaningful. Unless "we" can be saved, what is the meaning of "my" emancipation? Hōnen thus exclusively sought the Dharma through which all the human beings can be equally saved, and at last he discovered this Dharma in the Pure Land doctrine.

In this connection, a reference may be given to the critical view that faith in the Pure Land is dominantly motivated by the desire for happiness or enjoyment after death. As regards the deteriorated and secularized form of the Pure Land cult which is observable among the masses, this criticism is irrefutable. Regarding the genuine form of faith in the Pure Land, however, it is completely wrong. As stated above, in Pure Land Buddhism and, accordingly, in the genuine faith in the Pure Land, the prime concern is the salvation of all of us human beings from the predicament of suffering. This concern is really furthest from the egocentric desire for happiness and enjoyment. The spirit of Mahayana Buddhism which emphasizes "seeking Enlightenment together with all fellow beings" is most vitally and thoroughly embodied in Pure Land Buddhism.

IV The Pure Land and the Original Vow

In the first section I made a reference to suchness, stating that suchness is emptiness, and vice versa. In other words, suchness is the reality of things and events. Beyond suchness no Ultimate Reality is conceivable. It is primarily because of ignorance that we remain blind to suchness and are attached to the illusory images and views of things and events.

It is, however, the common faith of all Buddhists that suchness is attainable for everyone. In this respect, the Pure Land Buddhists are no exception. But the Pure Land Buddhists have something unique in their view of suchness. For they believe that while suchness is attainable in principle for everyone, one would never be able to embody suchness in one's own personality as long as one remains in the world. To remain in the world means not to be liberated from the power of delusion. With this thought, they paid keen attention to the dynamic aspect of suchness. What, then, is the dynamic aspect of suchness?

In the first place, guided by the sūtras relating to the Pure Land, they learned to comprehend suchness in terms of land, namely, as the Pure Land. As the land of suchness which illumines, empties, and purifies our delusion, the Pure Land is the land of Wisdom (*jñāna*, as flowing out of *prajñā*). Shinran defined it as the land of infinite light (Wisdom). Suchness now appears as the land of infinite light. Illumined by light of the Pure Land, we come to know the delusiveness of this world. Such is the basic conception of the Pure Land. But the dynamic aspect of suchness can not be fully expressed by the idea of the Pure Land alone.

Secondly, the Pure Land masters further learned to comprehend the dynamic character of suchness in terms of personality, namely, as the Original Vow of Amida Tathāgata. The term "*tathāgata*" means "the one who emerges out of suchness." "*Amida*" (derived from *amitāyus-amitābha*) means "infinite." As such Amida Tathāgata symbolizes the dynamic operation of suchness which is expressed as infinite compassion and Wisdom, even though he appears as an individual Buddha in the sūtras relating to him. According to the *Larger Sūtra of Eternal Life*, out of the sincerest desire of delivering all beings from suffering Amida took an incomparably excellent vow when he was in the original, disciplinary stage as a Bodhisattva (*Dharmākara* by name), which he has already fulfilled. This vow is called the Original Vow. The Original Vow is thus Amida's fullest self-expression and, accordingly, the sublimest self-expression of suchness in terms of Tathāgatahood or bodhisattvahood.

The *Larger Sūtra* shows that the Original Vow is differentiated into forty eight items. They are interrelated with each other in a subtle way. They cannot be discussed fully in this paper, but for the present the following should be remembered as the essentials of the Original Vow:

1) It is vowed that Amida's Name should appear as embodying all the virtues or efficiencies that have any bearing whatever on the salvation or deliverance of all human beings, and, when the Name appears, it should sound throughout the lands in ten directions.[7]
2) It is vowed that anyone who, hearing Amida's Name praised, awakens faith in Amida's Sincerity and keeps Amida's Name with him, should be assuredly reborn in the Pure Land.
3) It is vowed that the Pure Land should be completed as the land in which all the reborn ones should attain nirvāṇa.

We notice from the descriptions above that two important things are vowed in the Original Vow regarding the problem of our salvation: One is the rebirth in the Pure Land; the other is the awakening of faith in Amida's Sincerity.

The rebirth in the Pure Land that is held to take place after death has been the central concern of most Pure Land masters as well as followers for a long time. It was really inconceivable for them to attain Enlightenment in this life. The

Buddhist monastic disciplines were so difficult to accomplish. They wished to attain Enlightenment after death in the Pure Land, relying on Amida's Original Vow. As a general tendency, faith in Amida's Original Vow was regarded merely as a requisite to the rebirth. They hardly realized the profound significance of the awakening of faith. It is, indeed, Shinran who for the first time realized this in its full significance. He was revolutionary in shifting the prime importance, hitherto attached to the problem of rebirth or Enlightenment, to the problem of the awakening of faith. Faith is essential; once true faith is awakened and established, the rebirth in the Pure Land will take place as a natural result. For Shinran, the awakening of faith in Amida's Sincerity really meant salvation.

V The Awakening of Faith in Amida's Sincerity

Shinran coped in all seriousness and tenacity with the problem of faith. He suffered long in his search for pure faith. Any form of faith, so long as it remains an expression of the will to believe, can never be pure. It is branded with a self-willed character. It is mixed and defiled with calculation, self-interest, suppressed doubt, etc. Pure faith must be something cleared of all these defilements and mixtures. As such genuine faith is most difficult to attain, because it could not take place without some otherness coming from beyond and working upon us. How, then, does pure faith in Amida become possible for us?

Influenced by Shan-tao's *Commentary on the Meditation Sūtra*, Shinran came to hit upon the "Sincerity" of Amida. He learned to see all that Amida did —and does—as the expression of Amida's Sincerity. The Original Vow itself is the loftiest, sublimest expression of his Sincerity. Suchness has now appeared as Sincerity in the Tathāgatahood of Amida. Ever disclosing himself in the sound of his Name, Amida the All-Sincere One untiringly works upon us. He turns himself over us. His Sincerity radiates itself as boundless illumination and compassion. Precisely as a genuine response called forth by his Sincerity, the awakening of faith in Amida's Original Vow takes place in us, when the time is fully ripe.

In the awakening of faith, we experience a breaking through at the root of the delusion. We realize how delusive, insincere and sinful we have been. Our self-complacency breaks down this moment. We are emptied through and through. At the same moment, however, we find ourselves decisively taken in by Amida's Sincerity. We for the first time attain true restfulness, because the deepest root of our existential anxiety or suffering, namely, ignorance, is cut through for ever. It is still true that the foliage of actual sufferings does not perish; so long as we remain in the world, there is no escaping them. We have to undergo them. But they no longer disturb the fundamental restfulness and serenity. Further, in this experience of awakening we find ourselves firmly standing on the way which leads straight to the Pure Land. It is the way of *nembutsu* or going with Amida's Name.

What, then, is the *nembutsu*? It is definitely *our* act, *our* practice, which has been chosen by Amida for *us* to do in the Original Vow. Regarding the nembutsu as our act, Hōnen declares as follows:

> By nembutsu I do not mean the practice of contemplating as engaged in by the sages of China and our country. Nor is it the recitation of the Buddha's name practiced as the result of understanding the meaning of the term "nen" (thinking). It is just to recite "Namu-Amida-Butsu" without doubting that this will issue in rebirth in the Pure Land.[8]

Both the contemplative form of nembutsu and the vocal form of nembutsu as resulting from some special understanding are rejected by Hōnen, because they are after all, distortions into special forms of nembutsu capable of being practiced only by the gifted ones. None of these practices can be *our* act as originally intended by Amida. The *nembutsu* intended by Amida himself as our act, Hōnen concludes, consists of reciting "Namu-Amida-Butsu," that is, calling Amida's Name, out of faith in his Original Vow. As such, the *nembutsu* originates in Amida's Sincerity itself. Its significance is clear: it is meant to be that which every one of us can easily practice. It is precisely that which enables us to go straight along the way of "no hindrance." Shinran, too, when he developed a profound comprehension of *nembutsu*, took the same position as Hōnen.

VI   The Maturing of the Time for the Awakening of Faith

Our next problem is: How do we come to be awakened to Amida's Sincerity and surrender ourselves to it? How does the time become mature and full for the awakening of faith? From the viewpoint of practice, I would like to emphasize that the time is matured for faith through—and only through—the *nembutsu*.

According to Manshi Kiyozawa, it is not that we believe in the Tathāgata because of his existence but the Tathāgata exists because of our faith in him.[9] This is basically true of the relationship between the Tathāgata's existence and the practice of *nembutsu*: It is not that we practice the *nembutsu* because of the Tathāgata's existence; the Tathāgata exists because of our practice of *nembutsu*.

In the last analysis, *nembutsu*, and nothing but *nembutsu*, makes us realize what the Tathāgata is in reality. It is true that we are attracted to the *nembutsu* by hearing of Amida Tathāgata, but it is even more true that Amida's Sincerity becomes really understandable and appreciable to us through the *nembutsu*. It is more than probable that it was from this insight that Amida himself specifically chose, in his Original Vow, the *nembutsu* as *our* practice. In this sense, I would prefer to say: "In the beginning, the *nembutsu* was."

In the process of the life of *nembutsu*, time is matured for the awakening of faith. At the outset, however, *nembutsu* expresses our urgent need for salvation from suffering. Under the pressure of existential suffering, we cry, so to speak, for salvation while calling the Name of Amida. But there is no hope of this need being satisfied from without by, say, some savior god. The need is not the kind of need which can be satisfied in such a way. What we can do in this situation is, in so far as we are existentially inclined to the teaching of *nembutsu*, patiently to seek to realize the deepest meaning of the teaching, while intently practicing the *nembutsu*.

A revolution takes place in our *nembutsu*-mindedness itself when the time is ripe. The *nembutsu* is no more a mere expression of our desire for salvation this moment; it now appears as the very vehicle through which Amida's Sincerity of awakening and receiving us becomes fully audible and understandable. We who have been calling Amida's Name for salvation now turn out to be the ones who, all the while, have been called by Amida to awake and take refuge in him. The well-known definition of religion by Schleiermacher as the "feeling (or consciousness) of absolute dependence" becomes acceptable to the Pure Land Buddhists, too, on the ground of this revolutionary experience. Shinran himself has written: "The Tathāgata has already taken his Vow and turned over the Act (that is, the nembutsu completed by himself) to us for our Act." [10]

As mentioned in the previous section, so long as we still live in the world, the actual sufferings of life do not cease to press upon us even after we are awakened to Amida's Sincerity. But we do not now desperately grope for the liberation from suffering. We are always with Amida's Name, that is, with *nembutsu*, wherever we may be or wherever we may go. We never call Amida's Name without returning at that same moment to the fundamental restfulness and serenity of being saved by Amida's Sincerity. This return to the original experience of the awakening of faith refreshes us and enables us to brace ourselves for natural but courageous living. We are thus, through *nembutsu*, enabled to pass the impassable current of sufferings in every moment. To be enabled to pass the impassable—this is precisely what salvation means in the Pure Land doctrine. This life of *nembutsu* is designated as the way that leads straight to the Pure Land.

VII The Fruits which Faith Bears in Actual Life

What fruits does faith in the Pure Land bear in actual life? Does it introduce something novel into life?

As already observed, Pure Land Buddhism has disclosed itself as the Dharma which is truly adequate to *our* existential situation. From this fact it naturally follows that the Pure Land doctrine makes its adherents all the more sensitive of the inner togetherness and interrelatedness of human beings. Once we are awakened to the Original Vow that has been vowed for all beings, we can no more look on others' follies or evil deeds with coldness; we can no more look on other's suffering with indifference. In a similar situation or under similar conditions, each of us might have done the same thing. We are all "ordinary beings," as Prince Shotoku has declared. With this thought we are emptied of all unreasonable contempt for evildoers and actors of folly. Arrogance now gives place to *humility*. What we can do is, first of all, to pray heartily that all our fellow beings, including the persons in question, might awaken to Amida's boundless Sincerity and boundless compassion, as expressed in the Original Vow; then we must do all that we can do to help bring about this awakening.

It is the experience of the awakening of faith which, emptying and purifying us of delusive thoughts and emotions, enables us to live in accordance with suchness, that is, to live naturally. This life of naturalness is lived in and through the practice of *nembutsu*. The humility just mentioned is one aspect of the life of naturalness. Another aspect of this life is *tenderness* or tender-heartedness. The boundless compassion of Amida, when we awaken to it and accept it, melts away to tenderness our deep-seated obstinacy and self-complacency. We are thus enabled to confront every problem open-mindedly, flexibly and unprejudicedly.

This reminds us that in Buddhism any wrath whatsoever is rejected as sin. Even if the wrath is an emphatic expression of the justice of God, that makes no difference to Buddhism. Wrath is a violent, destructive emotion. It must be melted and transformed into tenderness by the boundless compassion of Amida.

In its expression in human relationships, tenderness may bear something in common with tolerance. This something should not, however, be confused with the toleration which is based on the temporary, political suppression of the impulse to justify oneself and blame the other. The tolerance on the part of the *nembutsu* adherents is essentially rooted in repentance and humility for the fact that the same evil (which is "tolerated") is finally characteristic of us all. Further, the selflessness of repentance and humility exerts an immense influence upon others. It naturally calms others and induces them to reflect upon themselves. It thus helps to purify others. The repentance and humility spring from faith in Amida's boundless Sincerity and are renewed every moment through the *nembutsu*. It is in this sense that the *nembutsu* is called the "purifying act." The *nembutsu* purifies not only the *nembutsu*-adherents themselves but also those who come into contact with them.

In this connection, a reference may be made to Shinran's assertion that "the *nembutsu* is the way of no-hindrance."[11] A careless reading might suggest to the reader that Shinran is here emphasizing the overwhelming supernatural power of the *nembutsu* to clear away every hindrance and obstacle blocking the *nembutsu*-adherent's way to the Pure Land. But this is a sheer misunderstanding. The word "no-hindrance" should be interpreted never in terms of *power* but always in terms of *spirituality*. Shinran's statement should be interpreted as follows: The *nembutsu*-adherent naturally confronts with tenderness and humility every problem that comes about. The tenderness and humility themselves make for no-hindrance. Consequently, Shinran's idea of no-hindrance bears no color of license or antinomianism.

All of the above has a vital bearing on the problem of morality. What, then, is the basic attitude of the *nembutsu*-adherent to the problem of morality? They all pay due respect to the importance of morality. It is a pity, however, that we can never do good in the complete sense of the term, considering the fact that our impulse to justify ourselves and to blame others is finally characteristic of us all. This fact shows how deep we have been submerged in the current of birth-and-death, as deplored by Shan-tao. Therefore, we need by every means to listen to, to awaken to, and thus to be purified by the Original Vow.

Not out of the consciousness of moral obligation or duty, but immediately out of the humility which arises from being awakened to Amida's Sincerity, the *nembutsu*-adherent seeks to attain a warm reconciliation and communion with others. It has often been the case with excellent *nembutsu*-adherents that the humility, tenderness, and gratefulness to Amida which shine out of their personality, quite naturally influence others around them and thus bring about genuine peace in their local community. Is not such virtue surely what morality envisages as its ideal? Bearing this in mind, Shinran says, "There is no good that surpasses the nembutsu."[12]

World peace is our urgent, serious problem. It goes without saying that it can never be brought about by any temporizing measures. Political toleration or appeasement will not avail much. The foundation of peace must be firmly laid in the depth of human nature.

In this situation, the doctrine of Pure Land Buddhism may well be rediscovered as a valuable source for bringing peace. I do not mean that the awakening to the Original Vow of Amida Tathāgata is a panacea for all the problems of man. However, it should never be overlooked that Pure Land Buddhism has long been, and continues to be in the present, the Dharma that is adequate to the existential situation of all ordinary beings, and, further, that it has borne to the *nembutsu*-adherents above described spiritual fruits, all of which have great importance for the problem of peace.

NOTES

[1] 救済 *Kyūsai* is a compound of the Chinese characters, 救 which means "to keep one from harm," and 済 which means "to ferry one across."

[2] 善導 J. Zendō (613-681), an eminent Chinese Buddhist master, especially important in the Pure Land traditions of Buddhism in China and Japan.

[3] Shan-tao, 観経疏 *A Commentary on the Meditation Sūtra*, Vol. 4: Exposition of the goods that are meant for the practically minded, (not the contemplatively disposed,), to practice.

[4] 曇鸞 (476-542), an eminent Chinese Buddhist master, especially important in the Pure Land traditions of Buddhism in China and Japan. His main work is 往生論註 *A Commentary on Vasubandhu's Treatise on the Pure Land.*

[4] 法然 (1133-1212), founder of the Pure Land (Jōdo) school of Buddhism in Japan and teacher to Shinran. His main work is the 選択集 *Senjakushū.*

[6] 親鸞 (1173-1262), founder of the Shin (Jōdo Shin) school of Buddhism. The most important of his numerous works is 教行信証 the *Kyō-gyō-shin-shō.*

[5] In the tradition of Pure Land Buddhism, the term "Name" as applied to Amida Tathāgata is something much more than name in the usual sense of the term. According to the tradition, Amida's Name stores all of his virtues or efficiencies and, when uttered, the virtues are actualized in the utterer himself. How to interpret the actualization of the virtues has been a problem for the *nembutsu*-adherents to tackle existentially.

[6] Hōnen, 一枚起請文 the *One Sheet Document.*

[7] Manshi Kiyozawa (1863-1903), an eminent Buddhist leader in Japan in Meiji Era. As for his thought, refer to S. Yamabe (ed.), *Selected Essays of Manshi Kiyozawa* (tr. by K. Tajima & F. Shacklock), 1936.

[8] Shinran, *Kyō-gyō-shin-shō* (The collection of passages relating the true and real teaching, practice, faith, and attainment of the Pure Land), Vol. 2: The collection of passages relating to the practice that is true and real.

[9] 歎異抄

Tannishō ("A tract deploring heresies of faith," compiled by Yuien, one of Shinran's direct disciples), Section 7.

[10] *Tannishō*, Section 1.

CHAPTER 4

SHIN BUDDHISM (PART ONE)[1]

—DAISETZ T. SUZUKI

Those of you who are accustomed to listening to the usual explanations of Pure Land Buddhism may find my lectures on this subject unusual and unorthodox, but I am willing to take that criticism. Ordinarily speaking, Pure Land doctrine is heavily laden with all kinds of what I call "accretions," which are not altogether necessary in order for modern people to get at the gist of the teaching.

For instance, Amida is the principal subject of Pure Land Buddhism. He is represented as being so many feet in height and endowed with the excellent physical features of a great man; he emits beams of light from his body, illuminating the world—not just one world, but many worlds, defying human calculation or measurement; and on every ray of light that comes out of his body, in fact, from every pore of his skin, there are so many Buddha-lands, decorated in a most extravagant manner. The descriptions almost exceed the imagination.

Of course this too is the product of man's mind, so I cannot really say it is beyond human imagination. But we can see how the Indian mind, more than any other, is richly endowed with the ability to create imagery. When you read the sūtras and listen to the old ways of explaining Pure Land doctrine, you will be surprised at how differently those people viewed such things, when compared with our modern way of thinking.

I am not going to touch upon these traditional aspects of the doctrine, so I am afraid my own explanations will be somewhat prosaic, devoid of the usual glamour and rich imagery. In a way, it will be Amida religion brought down to earth; but at the same time the doctrine is not to be treated from the intellectual point of view, on the relative plane of thought. It is after all altogether beyond human intellection.

The Pure Land and Amida are revealed on this earth, though not as is taught by orthodox preachers. The Pure Land is not many millions and millions of miles away to the west. According to my explanation, the Pure Land is right here. Those who have eyes to see it can see it right here, even in this very hall. Amida is not presiding over a Pure Land beyond our reach. His Pure Land is this dirty earth itself. When I explain things in this way I am going directly against the traditional or conventional Pure Land doctrine. However, I have my own explanations and interpretations, and perhaps after these lectures are over you will agree with them, though of that I cannot be quite sure!

A Japanese Shin Buddhist friend of mine in Brazil recently wrote to me, requesting that I write out the essential teachings of the Pure Land school in English for the Buddhists there, because they found it difficult to translate such things from Japanese into Portuguese. He wanted me to present it so as to make Amida and Pure Land doctrine appear somewhat similar to Christianity, at least superficially, and yet to retain characteristic features of the Pure Land doctrine. So I sent the following to him. Whether he agreed with my views or not, I do not know. You might say I wrote it for my own edification.[2]

First: We believe in Amida Butsu, Amitabha Buddha, as Savior of all beings. ("Savior" is not a word often used among Buddhists; it is a kind of condescension to the Christian way of thinking.) This Amida Buddha is eternal life and infinite light. And all beings are born in sin and laden with sin. (This idea of sin is to be specially interpreted to give it a Buddhist color, which I will do later on.)

Second: We believe in Amida Buddha as our Oya-sama. (Sometimes the more familiar "Oya-san" is used in place of "Oya-sama," but the latter is more generally used. Oya-sama, in this context, means love or compassion. Strictly speaking, there is no word corresponding to Oya-sama in English or any European languages. *Oya* means parent, and *-sama* is an honorific suffix. *Oya* can mean either father or mother, and can also mean both of them; not separately, but mother and father as one. Motherly qualities and fatherly qualities are united in Oya. In Christianity God is addressed as Father: "Our father which art in Heaven." But Oya-sama is not in heaven, nor is Oya-sama the Father. Oya-sama is neither a "he" nor a "she." I don't like to say "it," so I am at a loss what to say. Oya-sama is such a peculiar word, so endearing and at the same time so full of religious significance.)

Third: We believe that salvation ("salvation" is not a good word here, but I am trying to comply with my friend's request) consists in pronouncing the name of Amida in sincerity and with devotion. (This pronouncing the name of Amida may not be considered so important, but names have certain magical powers. When a name is uttered, the object bearing that name is conjured up.)

In *The Arabian Nights' Entertainments*, when the devil's name is pronounced, the devil appears. Among some primitive peoples, the name of the supreme being is kept a secret. It is revealed only to those who have gone through certain rituals. The initiate is led by one of the elders of the religion into a dense forest where there is no danger of being overheard by anybody. Then the elder reveals the name to him. By knowing the name, the initiate is now fully qualified as a leader himself. The name plays an important role in religious life.

Amida's name is pronounced in sincerity and with devotion. The formula is *Namu-amida-butsu*. *Butsu* is Buddha, *namu* means "I take refuge": I take refuge in Amida Buddha. Or we may take *namu* as meaning adoration to Amida Buddha. It is a simple formula. There is nothing especially mysterious about it, and you may wonder how this name or phrase could have such wonderful power.

Now I have to say something about *hongan*. *Hongan*, according to my interpretation, is the primal will. This primal will is at the foundation of all reality. *Hongan* as expressed in the *Sūtra of Eternal Life* consists of 48 different vows, but all 48 may be summarized in one basic vow, or *hongan*, which is: Amida wants to save all beings. Amida desires to have all beings brought over to his land, which is the land of purity and bliss. And those who earnestly, sincerely, and devotedly believe in Amida, will all be born in the Pure Land.

This birth does not take place after what is called death. To sincere followers of the Pure Land, instead of being born in the Pure Land, the Pure Land itself is created or comes into existence when we sincerely pronounce *Namu-amida-butsu*. Therefore, instead of going over to the Pure Land, the Pure Land comes to us. In a way, we are carrying the Pure Land within us all along, and when we pronounce that magic formula *Namu-amida-butsu*, we become conscious of the presence of the Pure Land around us, or rather, in us.

The *hon* of *hongan* means original or primal, and *gan* is generally translated "vow." But I have misgivings about using vow as an equivalent for *gan*. Sometimes it is translated "prayer." *Gan* means literally "wish" or "desire." Philosophically speaking, it may be better to say "will," so that *hongan* would be rendered "primal will." Why *gan* cannot properly be translated as "vow," "prayer," "wish," or "desire" will become clearer later. I am just trying to give you an idea now of how I interpret some of these terms.

I

I wrote a little book called *A Miscellany on the Shin Teaching of Buddhism* which was published in Japan in 1949. It contains rather fragmentary explanations of the Shin teaching, but parts of it may be helpful in gaining a general view of Shin Pure Land Buddhism.

The Pure Land teaching originated in China, but it reached its full development in the Japanese Shin school of Pure Land Buddhism. The Shin school is the culmination of Pure Land thought, and that culmination took place in Japan. The Japanese may not have very many original ideas to contribute to world thought or world culture, but in Shin we find one major contribution Japanese can make to the outside world. There is one other major Buddhist school that developed in Japan, the Nichiren sect. But all the other schools more or less trace their origin as well as their form either to China or to India. Nichiren is more or less related to the nationalistic spirit of Japan and is often confused with nationalism. But Shin is absolutely free of such connections; in that respect, Shin is remarkable.

Shinran, the founder of the Shin sect, was born in Kyoto about eight hundred years ago. He is generally made out to be of noble lineage, but that I suspect is fiction. His family was probably relatively cultured and may well have belonged to the higher levels of society, but their connection, if any, to the aristocracy was I think remote. In any case, his real religious development took place when he was exiled to the country, far from the capital, the center of culture in those days. He was a follower of Hōnen, founder of the Pure Land (Jōdo) school in Japan. Hōnen's influence was very great at the time, and priests belonging to the older established schools did not like that. Somehow they contrived to have Hōnen banished to Tosa, then a remote area of the country. Shinran was also exiled, to the northern part of Japan. His decisive religious experience really took place during this exile, while he was living among the common people. He understood well their spiritual needs. In those days Buddhism was somewhat aristocratic, and the study of Buddhism was mainly confined to the learned few, who were rather addicted to learning. But Shinran knew that mere learning was not the way to religious experience. There had to be a more direct way that did not require the medium of learning or ritual. In fact, to experience a full awakening of the religious consciousness, all such things must first be cast aside. Such mediums would only interfere with our attempts to directly attain this full awakening, which is the consummation of the religious life. Shinran came to realize this himself, and he finally found the most direct way to the attainment of this awakening.

Let me read a bit now from *A Miscellany on the Shin Teaching*:

Of all the developments Mahayana Buddhism has achieved in the Far East, the most remarkable one is the Shin teaching of the Pure Land school. It is remarkable, according to my judgment, chiefly for the reason that geographically its birthplace is Japan and historically it is the latest and highest evolution the Pure Land teaching could have reached. The Pure Land idea originated in India (because the sūtras used by this sect were originally compiled in India, the ideas must have developed first in India) and the sūtras devoted to its exposition were compiled probably about three hundred years after Buddha (that is, about one or two centuries before the Christian era). The school bearing its name, however, started in China towards the end of the fifth century when the White Lotus Society was organized by Hui-yüan (334-416) and his friends in 403. The idea of a Buddha-land which is presided over by a Buddha is probably as old as Buddhism, but a school based upon the desire to be born in such a land in order to attain the final end of the Buddhist life, did not fully materialize until Buddhism began to flourish in China as a practical religion. It took the Japanese genius of the thirteenth century to mature it further into the teaching of the Shin school. Some may wonder how the Mahayana could have expanded into the doctrine of Pure Land faith, which apparently stands in direct contradiction to the Buddha's supposedly original teaching of self-reliance and enlightenment by means of *prajñā*.[3]

II

[Dr. Suzuki explains the following Shin terms at the blackboard]

Amida is standing on one side, and on the other side is *bombu* (or *bompu*), the ordinary people, just as we all are. We sometimes see this term rendered as "all beings" in English. Amida Buddha is the *hō* (Dharma), and we *bombu* are *ki*.

Hō and *ki* are difficult terms to translate. *Hō* is on the other side and *ki* is on this side. Religious teachings start from the relationship between them. *Hō* might be considered as corresponding to God or Christ, and *ki* is this sinful person. *Hō* is the other-power, and *ki* is self-power. Other-power and self-power stand in contrast; and in order to be born in the Pure Land, self-power is to be altogether abandoned and other-power embraced. In fact, when self-power is embraced by other-power, self-power turns into other-power; or, other-power "takes up" self-power altogether.

Or again, on one side we have the Pure Land, and on the other side this world. "This world" is more commonly called *shaba* in Japanese and Chinese—it is a Sanskrit term originally. The other world is called Jōdo. (*Jō* means pure, *do* is land, or "Pure Land.") *Shaba* is, we might say, the land of defilement. So there is Jōdo, the land of purity, or the Pure Land, and *shaba*, the defiled land. The Pure Land is the realm of the absolute, and *shaba* the realm of relativity.

When we pronounce *Namu-amida-butsu*, Amida is on one side and *namu* is on the other. *Namu* represents self-power or *ki*; Amida is *hō*, the other-power. *Namu-amida-butsu* symbolizes the unification of *ki* and *hō*, Amida and *bompu*, self-power and other-power, *shaba* and Pure Land—they are unified, identified. So when *Namu-amida-butsu* is pronounced, it represents or symbolizes the unification of the two. "Unification" is not an adequate term, but its meaning will hopefully become clearer.

Now Amida is on the other side, the *bompu* is on this side, and *shaba* is where we are. The Pure Land reveals itself when we realize what we are, or, what Amida is. Other-power is very much emphasized in Shin teaching. When Amida and other-power are understood, the Pure Land will be understood too. When Amida's essential quality is understood, *hongan* and compassion, or love, also become known. It is just like holding a cloth at the central part; if you pull the middle up, all the rest comes with it.

SHIN BUDDHISM (PART TWO)[4]

In giving names to objects we commonly fall into the error of thinking that the names stand for the actual objects themselves. This is a danger that is always present in name-giving, but we cannot on that account disregard the importance of names. Names represent a form of discrimination; they help us distinguish one thing from another, and this enables us to know their nature to some extent. Without a name, an object could not be distinguished from other objects. Distinguishing or discriminating helps us in this way to understand the objects around us. But names are not everything.

Man is also distinguished from other beings in that he is a toolmaker. Names are also a sort of tool; we can put them to use to better deal with the objects around us. But there is also a tyranny of tools. We make and surround ourselves with tools of all kinds, whereupon the tools begin to tyrannize us. Instead of us using them, they turn against their inventor. We become the tools of the tools we make.

This situation is especially noticeable in modern life. We invent machines, and they in turn control human affairs. Machines, especially in recent years, have inextricably entered our lives. We now must try to adjust ourselves to machines, for once they are out of our hands they refuse to obey our will.

In our intellectual endeavors, our ideas can be despotic too. We cannot always be in control of ideas. We invent or construct ideas and concepts to make life more convenient. Then these very ideas which we intended to be so convenient become unmanageable and control the inventors themselves. Scholars invent ideas and then forget that they invented them in order to deal with certain realities. For instance, each of the branches of science, whether it is called biology, psychology, or astronomy, has its own premises, its own hypotheses. Each branch organizes the fields it has chosen—stars, animals, fish, and so on—and deals with those realities according to the special concepts its scientists have invented to enable them to handle the subjects of their research. Whatever situation comes along in the pursuit of their research or exercise of their ideas that does not happen to be amenable to those ideas, they drop. Instead of dropping the ideas and trying to create new ones in order to overcome the unexpected difficulties that arise, they stick to the old ideas they invented and try to make the new realities fit the old concepts. Or else they simply exclude those things which cannot easily be worked into the network of ideas they have invented.

I have heard that some scientists have themselves compared their methods to catching fish in a net with standardized meshes; those fish which fail to be scooped up in the net will be dropped and unaccounted for. They just take up those that can be caught in their net and try to explain their catch by means of their ready-made ideas. The fish that remain uncaught are treated as if they did not even exist. "These exist," say the scientists of those that have been caught in the net. All the other fish are nonexistent.

The same can be said of astronomy. Those stars which do not come within the scope of the telescope are usually neglected. Yet more powerful telescopes are developed to enable the astronomers to make more extensive and deeper surveys of the heavens. But when asked about the parts of space that lie beyond the scope of their present telescopes, they tend to disregard the question. Sometimes they go as far as to say that space is empty beyond a certain group of stars. Certain galaxies make up their astronomical maps, and beyond those, they say, there is a void.

But such conclusions are altogether unwarranted. If scientists would limit their conclusions to what they could survey or measure, and admitted that they did not know beyond that, and did not venture any theory or any hypothesis, that would be all right. But blinded by their success within these boundaries, they try to extend that success beyond them, as if they had already surveyed and measured those unknown parts. Most scientists make this mistake, and, unfortunately, people tend to rely on what the scientists say.

To be truly scientific, they must always qualify their statements, because they always start from certain established hypotheses. Formerly scientists couldn't explain light, so they invented what they called "wave theory." But wave theory did not account for all the phenomena connected with light, so they then came up with what they called "quantum theory," which made explanations of certain other phenomena possible. But later they came to discover that to explain all the phenomena, they had to use both theories. The trouble with that, I am told, is that the two hypotheses contradict each other. If the wave theory is adopted, the quantum theory must be thrown out; if the quantum theory is taken up, the wave theory must be discarded. Yet the phenomena themselves exist, and scientists cannot deny their reality. So however contradictory it is on a logical plane, they have to adopt both theories, and somehow make them compatible.

All our surveys of reality are accomplished by means of our five senses. If we possessed another sense, or two or three more senses, besides the five we already have, then we might perceive an altogether different universe.

To say that what we experience via our five senses exhausts reality is a totally unfounded presumption on our part. We can say that within the limits of our five senses and intellect the world is understood so, explained so, interpreted so. But there is no way to deny the existence of something (though it may not be proper to call it a "thing") higher, deeper, and more pervasive which may lie beyond the ken of our five senses and intellect. If we do have some such extra sense within us, even though it is largely undeveloped—and some people do claim to have that kind of sense or faculty—then we may have another way of coming in contact with reality that is deeper and more extensive than our ordinary sensory and intellectual experience. It would be arrogant for someone to deny the existence of a higher and deeper "intuition," and declare, "Nothing can exist outside my sensory or intellectual perceptions."

Now let me write the six Chinese characters "Na-mu-a-mi-da-butsu" on the blackboard. This is called the Nembutsu and is the cornerstone of the entire Pure Land teaching. Namu-amida-butsu is also known as the *Myōgō*, or Name of Amida Buddha, although it contains something more than the *Myōgō* itself. The efficacy of the *Myōgō* enables us to be born in Amida's Pure Land, to realize the highest reality, and fully grasp the ultimate truth. *Myōgō* does not work on the level of our senses and intellect, which are relative; it works on the part of our mind or being that lies beyond the senses and intellect. Those who are addicted to intellection would probably deny the efficacy of the *Myōgō* to explore those fields of human being which are beyond and cannot be surveyed by intellection, and deny as well the existence of such fields.

In religious life there is a phenomenon that we call "faith." Faith is a strange and wonderful thing. Ordinarily, we speak of "faith," or "belief," in a context of something beyond our ordinary comprehension that cannot be certified by our ordinary knowledge. Yet in religious faith there is something more to be considered. We have to venture into the life that is opened up by faith.

In the relative sense of faith, the one we use in ordinary life, we can say, "I cannot believe it unless I have seen it or heard it personally." We may nevertheless believe something not by means of direct personal experience but through the communication of our friends or books. And if we judge the basis of that belief to be strong and verifiable enough, we will accept it as true, even if the proof lies outside of our direct personal experience.

But in religious belief there is something more. Even if our intellect is unable to verify it objectively or scientifically, there is something in religious faith which somehow compels us to accept it as reality. Though we may not have experienced it, it still almost demands our acceptance, whether we will or not. Theologians talk about "accepting faith" as a kind of perilous decision we have to make. It is a venturesome deed or experience, a plunging into an unknown region and deciding to risk our faith and destiny.

I am afraid that people who accept such a theology are still on the plane of relativity. The fact is, we are compelled—there is no choice—to accept faith. All religions contain a similar element. Instead of Amida being taken into our life or being, we are carried away by Amida. This is how the *Myōgō* starts to live and become actual life within Shin devotees. Some people ask about the significance of the *Myōgō* and how it could possibly be so efficacious as to take us to Amida and make us be born in the Land of Purity. As long as a person has such doubt or suspicion or hesitancy in accepting the *Myōgō* in true faith, then he or she is not yet within its working.

The Indian sūtras tell of a mythical golden-winged bird of enormous size that eats dragons for its food. The dragons live deep in the ocean, but when the golden-winged bird soaring high above detects the dragons down at the bottom of the ocean, it sweeps down from the sky; the waves open up and it picks the dragons out of the deep and eats them. Of course the dragons are afraid of the approach of the bird and dread becoming its meal.

Someone once asked a Buddhist teacher, "What does the bird who has broken through the net eat?" The mythical bird who has broken through the net is perfectly free, absolute master of itself. We ourselves are caught up in various kinds of nets, mostly of our own making. They may not really exist, but we imagine ourselves caught in them. This bird—that is, one of us who has been spiritually enlightened—is one who has broken through all the nets and now enjoys perfect freedom. Now the question to the Buddhist teacher, "What food does such a bird eat?" is the same as asking, What kind of life does an enlightened man, one who is spiritually free, lead? Or, What kind of life would a person lead who believes totally in the *Myōgō* and is possessed by Amida. What kind of person would he be?

Most people ask questions of this kind as if the question had nothing to do with them at all. What is the use of trying to know about such matters, when we should instead be such a person ourselves. But that is how we are made; this curiosity is a frailty of human nature. At the same time, this is what makes our lives distinguishable from those of the other animals—they don't ask these questions.

The master then said: "Come through the net yourself. Then I will tell you." Once through the net, no telling is needed. He will know for himself. Instead of asking idle questions about the life of the spiritually free, why not free yourself and see for yourself what kind of life it is? The same can be said of questions about the life of a Shin devotee. Americans sometimes ask me what significance the message of Buddhism has for our modern life. We may explain the kinds of benefits, advantages, material or otherwise, which come, for example, from belief in the *Myōgō*. But instead of being informed by someone else about the advantages that might accrue from accepting the *Myōgō*, they should just accept the *Myōgō*; and try … no, not try, just live it. Then they will know what it means.

This is what distinguishes religious life from relative, worldly life. In the relative life we want to know beforehand all that may result from our doing this or that; then we proceed to take action expecting a certain outcome. But religious life consists in accepting and knowing, and at the same time living that which is beyond knowledge. So in knowing and living, living is knowledge, and knowing is living. This kind of difference sharply distinguishes the religious from the worldly life. In actual fact there is no such thing as spiritual life distinguished from worldly life. Worldly life is spiritual life, and vice versa. It is just that we become blinded and confused in our encounters with the world. Just as scientists are caught in the nets they weave for themselves, we too, in taking all our inventions for realities, are blinded by them. We have to fight these unrealities. Actually, to call them unrealities is not exactly correct, for they are, with reservations, real enough. That is something we frequently fail to recognize or acknowledge.

Now regarding the *Myōgō*, Shinran, the founder of the Shin sect, says, "One pronouncing of the *Myōgō* is enough to make you be born in the Pure Land." Birth in the Pure Land is not an event that happens after death, as is popularly assumed. It takes place as we are living this life.

I was reading a Christian book recently in which the author speaks about Christ being born in the soul. We generally think Christ was born on a certain date in history, at a certain place on earth. This occurred not in the usual biological way but through the miraculous power of God.

But this Christian author says that Christ is born in our soul. And when that birth is recognized, when we become conscious of Christ's birth in our soul, that is when we are saved. So Christ is born in the course of history, but that historical event takes place in our own spiritual life. Christ is born, and we must become conscious of his birth in us. He is not born just anywhere, but in us, every day, at every moment; not once in history, but repeatedly, everywhere, at every moment.

And according to this author, his birth is dependent on our dying to ourselves. We must die to what we call the ego. When the ego is altogether forsaken and the soul is no more disturbed, there will be no anxiety, annoyance, or worries whatever, for all worries come from being addicted to the idea of the self. Therefore, when the self is completely given up, all the disturbances are quieted, and absolute peace prevails in the soul, which, he says, is "silence."

It is remarkable to see this Christian writer speak of silence. When silence prevails in the soul, that is the moment Christ is born in our soul. So silence is needed. When everything is kept in silence, that is the time, the opportunity, for spiritual being to enter our soul. Silence is attained when the self is given up; when the self is given up, the consciousness of dualistic thoughts is altogether nullified; that is to say, no dualism exists.

When I say dualism does not exist I do not mean that duality itself is annihilated. While the duality remains, an identification takes place; the two are left as two, and yet there is a state of identity. That is the moment silence prevails. When there are two ("two" means more than two, that is, multiplicity), noise of various kinds usually results, a disturbance which needs to be quieted. But this silence is not achieved by the annihilation of multiplicity. Multiplicity is left as multiplicity, yet silence prevails, not underneath, not inside, not outside, but here. The realization of this silence is simultaneously the birth of Christ. They occur synchronously.

Similarly, the *Myōgō* enters our active life when there is no longer any *Myōgō* but Amida; Amida becomes the *Myōgō* and the *Myōgō* becomes Amida. The last time, I spoke about the relationship between *ki*, we ordinary beings, and *hō*, Amida Buddha, or the Dharma. When the *Myōgō* is pronounced and we are conscious of saying Namu to Amida, and when Amida is listening to us say Namu, there will be no identity, no silence. One is calling out to the other, and the other is looking down or looking up. There is dualism or disturbance, not silence.

But when Namu is Amida and Amida is Namu, when *ki* is *hō* and *hō* is *ki*, there is silence. That is, the *Myōgō* is absolutely identified with Amida. The *Myōgō* ceases to be the name of somebody who exists outside the one who pronounces the *Myōgō*. Then a perfect identity, or absolute identity, prevails, but this identity is not to be called "oneness." When we say "one," we are apt to interpret that one numerically, that is, as standing against two, three, four, and so on. But this oneness is absolute oneness, and absolute oneness goes beyond all measurement. In absolute oneness or identity, the *Myōgō* is Amida, Amida is the *Myōgō*. There is no separation between the two; there is a perfect or absolute identity of *ki* and *hō*.

This is when absolute faith is realized. This is the moment, as indicated by Shinran, that "Namu-amida-butsu (*Myōgō*), pronounced once, is enough to save you." That "once," an absolute once, is something utterly mysterious.

SHIN BUDDHISM (PART THREE)[5]

Now, *jiriki* is self-power, and *tariki* is other-power. The Pure Land school is known as the Other-power School because it teaches that the other-power is most important in attaining rebirth in the Pure Land. Rebirth in the Pure Land, or regeneration, or enlightenment, or salvation—whatever name we may give to the end of our religious efforts—comes from the other-power, not from the self-power. This is the contention of the Shin followers.

The other-power is opposed to what is known in theology as synergism. Synergism means that in the work of salvation man has to do his share just as much as God does his. This is Christian terminology. The Shin school may therefore be called monergism, in contradistinction to synergism. *Syn* means together, and *ergism* (*ergo*) means work—"working together." Monergism means working alone. Thus in *tariki*, *tariki* alone is working, without self-power entering. The Other-power School therefore is monergism, and not synergism. It is all in the working of Amida, and we ordinary people living relative existences are powerless to bring about our birth in the Pure Land, or, in another word, to bring about our enlightenment.

This distinction between synergism and monergism may be described in this way: The mother cat when she carries her kittens from one place to another takes hold of the neck of each of the kittens. That is monergism because the kittens just let the mother carry them. In the case of monkeys, however, baby monkeys are carried on their mother's back; the baby monkey must cling to the mother's body by means of their limbs or tails. So the mother is not doing the work alone; the baby monkeys too must do their part. The cat's way is monergism—the mother alone does the work; while the monkey's way is synergism—the two working together.

In Shin teaching, Amida is the only important power that is at work; we just let Amida do his work. We don't add anything of our own to Amida's working. This other-power doctrine, or monergism, is based on the idea that we humans are all relative-minded, and as long as we are so constituted there is nothing in us or no power which will enable us to cross the stream of birth-and-death. Amida must come from the other side to carry us on his boat of "all-efficient vows"—that is, by means of his *hongan*, his *praṇidhāna* ("vow-prayer").

There is a deep and impassable chasm between Amida and ourselves, who are so heavily burdened with karmic hindrance. And we can't shake off this hindrance by our own means. Amida must come and help us, extending his arms from the farther end. This is what is generally taught by the Shin school.

But, from another point of view, however ignorant, impotent, and helpless we may be, we will never be able to grasp Amida's arms unless we exhaust all our own efforts to reach that other end. It is all well and good to say the other-power does everything on our behalf and we just let it do its work. We must, however, become conscious of the other-power working in us. Unless we are conscious of Amida's doing, we will never be saved. We can never be certain of our birth in the Pure Land, or the fact that we have attained enlightenment. Consciousness is necessary. To acquire this consciousness we must strive, exhausting all our efforts to cross the stream by ourselves. Amida may be beckoning to us to come to the other shore where he is standing, but we cannot even see him until we have done our part to the limit of our power. Self-power may not ultimately carry us across the stream. But, at the same time, Amida cannot help us by extending his arms until we have realized that our self-power is worthless, is of no account, in achieving our salvation. Only when we have made use of our self-power will we recognize Amida's help and become conscious of it. Without this consciousness, there will be no regeneration whatever.

The other-power is all-important, but this all-importantness is known only to those who have striven by means of self-power to attempt the impossible.

This realization of the worthlessness of self-power may also be Amida's doing. And in fact it is. But until we come to the realization, this recognition—the fact that Amida has been doing all this for us and in us—would not be ours. Therefore, striving is a prerequisite for all realizations. Spiritually or metaphysically speaking, everything is ultimately from Amida. But after all we are relative beings, and so, we cannot be expected to arrive at this viewpoint without having first struggled on this plane of relativity. The crossing from the relative plane to the transcendental or absolute plane—or other-power plane—may be impossible, logically speaking, but it appears an impossibility only before we have tried everything on this side. So, the relativity of our existence, the striving or complete exhausting of ourselves, and self-power—these are all synonyms. In Japanese, this is known as *hakarai*. It is a technical term in Shin doctrine.

This may correspond to the Christian idea of pride. Christians are, in a way, not so philosophical as Buddhists and, except possibly the theologians, do not use such terms as self-power or other-power. Ordinarily, Christians use the word "pride," which exactly corresponds to the Shin idea of *jiriki*, self-power. This pride means self-assertion, pride in one's worthiness, pride in being able to accomplish something, and so on. To rely on self-power is pride, and this pride is difficult to uproot, as is self-power. In this relative world, we are constantly dependent on self-power. On the moral plane, especially, we are forever talking about individual responsibilities, making one's own choice, and coming to a decision—all products of self-power. As long as we live in a moral world, individual responsibility is essential. If we went on without any sense of responsibility, society would be in chaos and end in self-destruction. Self-power in this sense is a necessary part of living in this world of relativity. Self-power, or pride, is all right as long as things are going on smoothly, when we do not encounter any hindrance, or anything that frustrates our ambitions, imaginations, or ideals. But as soon as we encounter something which stands athwart the way we want to go, then we are forced to reflect upon ourselves.

Such obstructions may be enormous, not only individually but collectively. Our society is getting more and more complex, the hindrances or obstructions are becoming more collective in nature and single individuals feel less responsible for them. But as long as a society is a community of individuals, each individual, whether conscious of it or not, will have to be responsible to some degree for what his society does, for what society imposes upon its members. When we encounter such hindrances we reflect upon ourselves and find we are altogether impotent to overcome them. The very moment we encounter insurmountable difficulties, we reflect, and soon find our self-power altogether inadequate to cope with the problem. We are seized with feelings of frustration, breeding in our minds anxiety, uncertainty, fear, and worry—familiar features of modern life. This is where pride fails to provide an answer. Pride has to curb itself; it must give way to something higher or stronger. Then pride is humiliated. As long as we live in our relative world, on this plane of conditionality, we cannot avoid obstacles and hindrances. We are sure to encounter them.

Earlier Buddhists used to say, "Life is suffering, life is pain." And we are compelled to try to escape from it, or to transcend the necessity of being bound to birth-and-death. They used to use the term "emancipation," or "liberation," or "escape." Nowadays, instead of such terminology, we say, "to attain freedom," or "to transcend," or "to synthesize," and so on.

In opposition to the terms "relativity," "striving," "self-power," "*hakarai*," and "pride," we have "transcending," "making no efforts." This relative world of ours is characterized by all kinds of striving. Unless we strive we can't get anything—that is the very condition of relative existence. However, in religious life, effortlessness prevails—there is no striving. Self-power is replaced by other-power, pride by humility, *hakarai* by *jinen hōni*.

Here are a few more translations or paraphrases of what Shinran, the founder of the Shin school, says about *jinen hōni*, that is *anata-makase*, or "Let thy Will be done." It is somewhat scholastic, but it may interest you.

"*Ji* of *jinen* means 'of itself' or 'by itself.'" *Ji* literally means "things as they are," or "self," as it is not due to the designing of man but Amida's vow that man is born in the Pure Land. Man is led naturally or spontaneously—this is the meaning of *nen*—to the Pure Land. The devotee does not make any conscious self-designing efforts, for self-power is altogether ineffective to achieve the end of being born in the Pure Land. *Jinen* thus means that because one's rebirth in the Pure Land is wholly due to the working of Amida's vow-power, the devotee is simply to believe in Amida and let his vow work itself out.

When I say "birth in the Pure Land" I wish this to be understood in a more modern way. That is, going to the Pure Land is not an event that takes place after death, but while alive. We are carrying the Pure Land with us all the time. In fact, the Pure Land surrounds us everywhere. This lecture room itself is the Pure Land. We become conscious of it, we recognize that Amida has come to help us only because we have striven and come to the end of our strivings. It is then that *jinen hōni* comes along.

"*Hōni* means 'It is so because it is so.'" We cannot give any reason for our being here. Why do we live here? The answer will be, "We live because we live." Explanations for our existence will inevitably result in a contradiction. When we come face to face with such a contradiction we cannot live on even for a moment. Fortunately, however, contradiction does not get the better of us, we get the better of contradiction.

In this connection, with the *tariki* and *jiriki*, other-power and self-power, idea, it means this: It is in the nature of Amida's vow-power that we are born in the Pure Land. Therefore, the way in which other-power works may be defined as "meaning with no-meaning." This is a contradiction or a paradox. When we talk about "meaning" we wish the word to signify something, but in religious experience "meaning" is a meaning of no meaning. That is to say, its working is so natural, so spontaneous, so effortless, so absolutely free, that it works as if it were not working.

*
* *

"In order for the devotee to be saved by Amida and be welcomed to Amida's Pure Land, he must recite the *Myōgō, Namu-amida-butsu*, in all sincerity. As far as the devotee is concerned, he does not know what is good or bad for him. All is left to Amida. This is what I, Shinran, have learned."

This is what Shinran says. He does not know good from bad, for all is left to Amida. This may seem to go directly against our moral consciousness, or what we call conscience. But from the religious point of view, what we think is good is not necessarily good all the time, or absolutely good. For good may turn into bad at any time and vice versa. So we cannot be the absolute judge of moral good or moral evil. When by Amida's help we go beyond all this, and everything is left to Amida's working, when we realize or become conscious of Amida's working in everything we do, whether it be good or bad, then all is good. As long as we live on the relative plane, this will remain a paradox, inexplicable and incomprehensible.

"Amida's vow," Shinran continues, "is meant to make us all attain supreme Buddhahood." As I said before, when supreme enlightenment is attained, we realize the actual existence of the Pure Land, the fact that we are right in the midst of the Pure Land. Supreme Buddhahood, which is the same as supreme enlightenment, is realized when we find we are in the Pure Land itself.

Shinran goes on: "Buddha is formless, and because of his formlessness he is known as 'all by itself.'" All physical things have forms, and ideas have something to designate, but when Buddhists say "formlessness," they mean neither physical form nor intellectualization. We are in the world of "formlessness" when we go beyond the materiality of things and our habits of intellectualizing. The Buddhist term "formlessness" is also known as *jinen*, "all by itself," "to exist by itself."

"If Amida had a form he would not be called Supreme Tathāgata, *Nyorai*. He is called Amida in order to let us know his formlessness. This is what Shinran has learned. Once you have understood this you need not concern yourself with *jinen* any longer." This is important. When we realize that we are really in the world of "formlessness," we need not talk about *jinen*, "being by itself," any more.

Shinran goes on: "When you turn your attention to it, the meaningless meaning assumes a meaning, defeating its own purpose." When we talk about "being by itself," we no longer are "being by itself"; there is no more "meaningless meaning." Meaning has something to mean; it points to something else. When we are that meaning itself, we need not talk about meaning any more. When we are *jinen* itself, there is no more need to discuss it because we are *jinen*. As soon as we begin to think, all kinds of difficulties arise, but when we don't think, everything is all right. By "not thinking," I don't mean that we must be animal-like; we must remain human and yet be like "the lilies of the field," or "the fowls of the air." Shinran says, "All this comes from *butchi* (*Buddhajñā*; Buddha-intellect, or Buddha-wisdom)." *Butchi* is something that goes beyond our relative way of thinking; it is the "other-power." The term other-power is a more dynamic conception; while *butchi* is more dialectic or metaphysical.

From his commentary on *Jinen Hōni* ("Being by Itself"), we can see what understanding Shinran had of the working of Amida's vow-power, or of the other-power. "Meaningless meaning" may be thought of as something devoid of sense—literally, meaningless, without any definite content whereby we can concretely grasp its significance. But the idea is this: there was no teleology or eschatological conception on the part of Amida when he made those forty-eight vows. All the ideas expressed in them are the spontaneous outflow of his great infinite compassion, his great compassionate heart, embracing everything and extending to the farthest and endless ends of the world. And this infinite compassion is Amida himself. Amida has no ulterior motive. He simply feels sorry for us suffering beings, and wishes to save us from going through an endless cycle of birth-and-death. Amida's vows are the spontaneous expression of his love or compassion. This "going beyond teleology," or "purposelessness" may sound strange at first, for everything we do in this world usually has a purpose. But religious life consists in attaining this "purposelessness," "going beyond teleology," "meaningless meaning," and so on. This is what is called *anata-makase*, or "Let thy Will be done," "going beyond self-power and letting Amida do his work through us or in us." Thus there are no prayers in Buddhism in the strict sense of the term. For when you pray to gain something you will never get anything; when you pray for nothing you gain everything.

During the Tokugawa era, there was a man in Japan called Issa who was noted for his haiku. Issa expressed his idea of "Let thy Will be done," but in his case it has no religious implication. In fact, he was being pressed by worldly affairs, and it was out of his desperate situation that he uttered this haiku at the end of the year. I still remember when I was very young we paid everything we owed to the tradespeople at the end of the year. In my day it was twice a year, once in July and once at the year end. If we could not pay by mid-July, we left it to the end of the year, and if we could not pay then, we went broke. Issa was in a similar predicament. I will give his verse first in Japanese. Those who understand Japanese might appreciate it:

> *Tomokaku mo*
> *Anata-makase no*
> *Toshi no kure*

Issa was obviously in great distress: "I, being at the end of the year, having no money whatever to pay my accounts, have no choice but to let Amida do his Will." If indeed Amida could look after Issa's problem, all would be well, for Issa was really desperately poor. In fact, worldly poverty and spiritual "poverty" often have a great deal to do with each other, going hand in hand.

In reading Eckhart, I found a story you might like to hear. It is entitled "Meister Eckhart's daughter":

> A daughter came to the preaching cloister and asked for Meister Eckhart. The doorman asked, "Whom shall I announce?"
>
> "I don't know," she said.
>
> "Why don't you know?"
>
> "Because I am neither a girl, nor a woman, nor a husband, nor a wife, nor a widow, nor a virgin, nor a master, nor a maid, nor a servant."
>
> The doorman went to Meister Eckhart and said:
>
> "Come out here and see the strangest creature you ever heard of. Let me go with you, and you stick your head out and ask, 'Who wants me?'"

Meister Eckhart did so, and she gave him the same reply she had made to the doorman. Then Meister Eckhart said:

"My dear child, what you say is right and sensible, but explain to me what you mean." She said:

"If I were a girl, I should be still in my first innocence; if I were a woman, I should always be giving birth in my soul to the eternal word; if I were a husband, I should put up a stiff resistance to all evil; if I were a wife, I should keep faith with my dear one, whom I married; if I were a widow, I should be always longing for the one I love; if I were a virgin, I should be reverently devout; if I were a servant-maid, in humility I should count myself lower than God or any creature; if I were a man-servant, I should be hard at work, always serving my lord with my whole heart. But since of all these I am neither one, I am just a something among somethings, and so I go."

Then Meister Eckhart went in and said to his pupils:

"It seems to me that I have just listened to the purest person I have ever known." (Blakney translation, pp. 252-3).

This is quite an interesting story. But I have something to say here: This strange daughter said, "Of all these, I am neither one." That is, she is not any of all those enumerated above. She mixes the worldly sense with the spiritual sense; that is, for example, "if I were a husband, I should put up a stiff resistance to all evil." This may be taken in a worldly or in a spiritual sense, I believe. If one were engaged in spiritual life, or otherwise, there will be some end to perform. If you designate this or that, if you have some work to accomplish, some role to perform, you will have *something*. But she says, "Since of all these I am neither one, I am just a something among somethings … "

I wouldn't say this. I would say, "I am just a nothing among somethings, and so I go." "So I go" is *jinen hōni*. It is *sonomama*. It is "Let thy Will be done."

NOTES

[1] This is the first of a series of talks given by D.T Suzuki before the members of the New York Buddhist Academy in the spring of 1958. We wish to thank the Matsugaoka Library, Kamakura, for permission to publish it here.—*Ed.*

[2] The portions in parentheses in the following three paragraphs contain Dr. Suzuki's comments on the original written statement he sent to his friend.—*Ed.*

[3] The text given here has been revised to include several revisions written into the author's personal copy. The remarks set off by brackets are comments made during the lecture.—*Ed.*

[4] This is the second of a series of talks given by D. T. Suzuki at the New York Buddhist Academy in the spring of 1958. We wish to thank the Matsugaoka Library, Kamakura, for permission to publish it here.—*Ed.*

[5] This is the third and final installment of a series of talks given before members of the New York Buddhist Academy in the spring of 1958.—*Ed.*

II. INTERPRETATIONS OF SHIN BUDDHISM

CHAPTER 5

CENTERING AND THE WORLD BEYOND

—TAKEUCHI YOSHINORI

(EDITED AND TRANSLATED BY JAMES W. HEISIG)

I Eschatology and the Stages of History

To locate the origins of eschatological thought and belief in Buddhism we have to go back to the early period of Indian Buddhism. In the Pali canon there are already a few indications of the later developments this belief would undergo, a fact that comes out particularly clearly when we compare the Pali texts with the corresponding Chinese translations. The Chinese texts even show coincidences of terminology here and there with later teachings, though hardly with the same rigor of definition.

In general, Buddhist eschatology includes three periods. First is the era of *correct dharma*, which is to last for some five hundred—or, according to alternate traditions, for up to one thousand—years after the death of the Buddha. During this period the doctrine of the Buddha would be followed perfectly, and his disciples would be able to reap the fruits of saving wisdom in this world.

After this first era of five hundred or a thousand years such saintly discipleship would disappear. There would be many disciples of the Buddha who would in fact follow their master's path and perfectly carry out religious practice as had once been done, but they would no longer be able to reap the fruits of saving wisdom. This era of *falsified dharma* would last another five hundred (or one thousand) years.

Finally would begin the era of the *final dharma*, the time of the last things. This is to continue until the year 10,000, a period in which neither redemptive enlightenment nor genuine religious practice would be found. Deprived of their spiritual vitality, the sūtras would become mere corpses, until finally with the year 10,000 the whole world would go up in flames in the great kalpa-fire, and the sūtras would sink into the bowels of the earth or the depths of the sea.

Another method of reckoning eschatology proceeds more according to historical events. Here the duration of the various segments of time is about five times longer than actual historical reality itself. In the Mahāyāna text known as the *Ta-chi-yüeh-tsang-ching*, we also find predictions of the Buddha that speak of five basic eras to follow his death. According to that text, in the first phase, the disciples would be able to attain wisdom with steadfastness; in the second phase, they would be able to attain contemplation with steadfastness; in the third, to hear and see many things with steadfastness; in the fourth, to erect stūpas, virtue, and bliss and to arrive at penitence with stability; in the fifth phase, however, the pure dharma would become hidden and cease to function, which would be the cause of great strife and leave behind only a few good ones. This account goes on to tell of events that would wreak havoc on the period to follow.

These two methods of reckoning time, when combined, produce numerous predictions, as we see particularly in those times of persecution when schisms proclaimed the end of the "falsified era."

The sūtras in which these eschatological ideas were used were soon translated into Chinese and caused a great flare-up of anxiety in China, leading people to believe that the world had entered into its third era, the time of the last things. (All of this occurred around the middle of the sixth century of the Christian era.) Actually, Chinese Buddhism after a time experienced the same fate as had befallen Indian Buddhism. After the flowering of Buddhist philosophy in China, a period of persecution suddenly broke out, and it was then that the predictions of the horrible events to occur in the eschaton and their descriptions in the sūtras became a pressing problem for all Buddhists. A Chinese emperor, inspired by Confucianism, banned Buddhism from his realm, forbidding the people to believe in Buddhism and decreeing that all monks return to the lay state. But in spite of all the misery that this persecution brought, Chinese Buddhism did not die out. Quite the contrary, it became purified and took to reflecting once again and with firm spiritual intensity on its true aims.

Thus after the golden age of theoretical Buddhism, when cities had invariably been preferred as the center of teaching, a new orientation came about: the existential and practical religion of Buddhism. The two important representatives of this new orientation are Zen and Shin (or Pure Land) Buddhism.

From an eschatological standpoint, Shin Buddhism is the more important. It is instructive to note that in most cases its predecessors were those very scholars who had previously devoted themselves to writing commentaries on the sūtras. But under the influence of the words and deeds of their religious leaders, and profoundly gripped by the temporality of human being, people turned themselves to belief in the Pure Land.

The temporality of human existence here has to be seen in the sense of a general destiny that affects the human in each particular period of time. Precisely how this belief in the Pure Land developed its own existential problematic is something we shall not pursue in detail here. I would rather restrict myself to the final phase of this development, the religious efficacy of Shin Buddhism in Japan, and in particular the influence of Shinran (1173-1262).

II Shinran and the Phenomenology of Religious Consciousness

According to Shinran, the three periods of eschatological history—the rise and fall of the sūtras as spiritual forces—correspond to the transformations of the spirit that religious individuals must each pass through in their own inner experience. Furthermore, these three transformations of the spirit are intimately linked by Shinran to three vows that Amida Buddha, out of his great and merciful compassion (*karuṇā*), made on behalf of sinful humans in order to lead them into the Pure Land. The triad that this sets up of the threefold vow, the threefold movement of eschatology, and the threefold transformation of the religious individual represents a central relationship that we may, without exaggeration, liken to the Hegelian triad of the absolute spirit, the objective spirit, and the subjective spirit. There is such a dialectic method of a "phenomenology of the religious spirit" at work in the way Shinran develops the final part of his major work, the *Kyōgyōshinshō* (*The Teaching, Practice, Faith, and Enlightenment*).

The first stage of the religious spirit, according to Shinran, is aesthetic and ethical. The nineteenth vow of the Buddha is cited:

> After I have attained Buddahood, there will be sentient beings in the ten quarters who raise the Bodhi-Mind, practice various meritorious acts, and desire to be born in my land with sincere aspiration; if, on the eve of their death, I should not appear before them surrounded by a host of [sacred] beings, may I not attend the Perfect Bodhi.[1]

In Shinran's interpretation, this vow corresponds to the religious observance that the *Amitāyurdhyāna-sūtra* (The Meditation Sūtra) urges on neophytes. The Sūtra requires a particular form of contemplation of believers: the *kasiṇa* meditation on the setting sun, and river, and the lapis lazuli that culminates in a vision of the Pure Land in all its splendors and including the figure of Amida Buddha himself. Together with these thirteen stages of contemplation, which proceed from the easy to the difficult, the Meditation Sūtra urges the believer to perform meritorious deeds, but the list of virtues laid out here proceeds in the opposite direction, beginning with the highest good and proceeding to the lower forms of virtue. Even for those who throughout their entire lives have done nothing good, the promise of future redemption through the grace of Buddha is held for the one who, instructed by a good master, will confess his sinfulness on his deathbed and pronounce the name of the Buddha ten times.

A certain confusion appears at this point in the way the Meditation Sūtra has been constructed, and Chinese and Japanese Buddhists have tried to explain its meaning in numerous ways. Many argue that the Pure Land, into which all— saints, fools, and wicked alike—can be taken up, cannot be the real realm of the highest salvation, since the highest must always be the most difficult and therefore the most rarely attained. Moreover, they go on, the assertion that one can be saved by pronouncing the name of the Buddha ten times should be taken in an indefinite sense, as a way of animating neophytes to set out on the path to *nirvāṇa*.

Those who view the matter from an eschatological consciousness come to a different understanding. For them no person in the present—that is, in the eschaton—can become a saint or enlightened one by his or her own powers, since the power of time necessarily and unavoidably conditions the sins of all people. Only the grace of Amida Buddha can bring redemption in this time. The idealism of a theoretical Buddhism that abstracts from time cannot understand how the essence of Amida Buddha can be achieved powerfully in the midst of time, and how in this achievement of the essence of Amida Buddha the reality of the Buddha is accomplished through *karuṇā*. For Shinran, calling on the name of the Buddha is not only our deed, but much more the original essence or essential achievement of the Buddha himself. The pronouncing of the name *is* the Buddha; it is nothing other than the fulfillment of his vow. This is how the pronouncing of the name of Amida Buddha becomes the source of salvation. The achievement of the essence of the Buddha is thus at the same time our own achievement. It is our appropriation of the essence of the Buddha.

Hence we see in the Meditation Sūtra a duality of a "revealed" and a "concealed" sense. *Revealed* refers to what is clear and true for a *given consciousness*, while *concealed* refers to what is clear and true only for *genuine belief*. (In this regard, Hegel also uses the two notions of *für das Bewusstsein* and *für uns* —or *für den Philosophen*—in his phenomenology.) What consciousness first and directly believes to be true and good collapses with the experience of failure, and in its place what had first been at work in hidden fashion gives rise to an achievement of our innermost heart.

For Shinran, *kasiṇa* contemplation stands for contemplation in general. It is also the easiest form of contemplation because it is centered on a specific object. Furthermore, the virtues that are listed are in turn easier than contemplation, since the good of virtuous deeds is the good of an extraverted, *scattered* consciousness, while the good of contemplation is the good of an introverted and *centered* consciousness.

But one who lives in the latter days is no longer able to center the mind as the holy sages of old were able to do. The ardent longing for salvation means that one forever experiences an inner dividedness at the ground of one's being and that zeal for the highest good always sees radical evil as one's essence. But it is precisely at the point of this dividedness and doubt within consciousness that we are able, under the right circumstances, to encounter the name of Amida Buddha, who "comes like a great ship from the yonder shore over the sea of life and struggle to help humanity."[2]

According to Shinran, this encounter with the name of Amida Buddha represents the second stage in religious consciousness. He cites the twentieth vow of the Buddha:

> If, after I have attained Buddhahood, beings in the ten quarters who, having heard my Name, direct their thoughts towards my land, plant various roots of virtue, and

desire to be born in my land by sincerely turning their merits [towards it], should not ultimately attain Birth, may I not attain the Perfect Bodhi.[3]

In Shinran's explanation, this vow signifies the religious decision to direct oneself with one's whole being to the Pure Land. It is a decision that one arrives at only by trodding the path of despair, only through confessing one's own finiteness and sinfulness. It is here that for the first time one is able to experience the powerful grace from the beyond and to belong to that Pure Land. Shinran often speaks of his experience of religious decision, as we read in one of his conversations with his disciples:

> When we believe that we are to be born in the Pure Land being saved by Amida's inconceivable Vow, there rises up within us the desire to utter the Nembutsu [name of the Buddha]. At that moment we share in the benefit of "being embraced and not forsaken."
>
> We should know that Amida's Original Vow does not discriminate whether one is young or old, good or evil, and that Faith alone is of supreme importance, for it is the Vow that seeks to save the sentient beings burdened with grave sins and fiery passions.
>
> Therefore, if we have Faith in the Original Vow no other good is needed, because there is no good surpassing the Nembutsu. Nor should evil be feared, because there is no evil capable of obstructing Amida's Original Vow.[4]

Shinran here puts his religious decision in intimate relationship with the root of all virtues, namely, with the name of the Buddha. The contrast between virtues and their root is set up still sharper in another passage:

> Even a good person is born in the Pure Land, how much more so is an evil person! However, people in the world usually say, "Even an evil person is born in the Pure Land, how much more so is a good person." At first sight this view seems to be reasonable, but it is contrary to the purport of the Original Vow of the Other-Power. The reason is that, as those who practice good by their self-power lack the mind to rely wholly on the Other-Power, they are not in accordance with the Original Vow of Amida. However, if they convert their minds of self-power and trust the Other-Power, their Birth in the True Land of Recompense is assured.
>
> Amida made his Vow out of compassion for us who are full of evil passions and who are unable to set ourselves free from saṃsāra by any practice. Since the purpose of His Vow is to have evil persons attain Buddhahood, the evil person who trusts the Other-Power is especially the one who has the right cause for Birth in the Pure Land. Hence the words, "Even a good person is born in the Pure Land, how much more so is an evil person."[5]

In still another passage he says to his followers:

> The aim of your visit to me, after crossing over the boundaries of more than ten

provinces at the risk of your lives, is solely to ask me the way to Birth in the Land of Utmost Bliss.

However, if you find something unfathomable in me and suppose that I know a way to Birth other than the Nembutsu, and that I am well-versed in the Buddhist doctrines, it is a grave mistake on your part. If so, then there are many distinguished scholars in the Southern Capital and on the Northern Mountain, whom you had better call upon and ask, to your satisfaction, about the essentials of Birth.

As for me, Shinran, there is nothing left but to receive and believe the teaching of the Venerable Master—that we are saved by Amida merely through the utterance of the Nembutsu.

I am entirely ignorant as to whether the Nembutsu is really the cause of Birth in the Pure Land, or whether it is the karma which will cause me to fall into hell.

I will have no regrets even though I should have been deceived by Hōnen Shōnin,[6] and, thus, by uttering the Nembutsu, I should fall into hell. The reason is that, if I could become Buddha by performing some other practice and fell into hell by uttering the Nembutsu, then, I might feel regret at having been deceived. But since I am incapable of any practice whatsoever, hell would definitely be my dwelling anyway.

If the Original Vow of Amida is true, then Śākyamuni's sermons cannot be untrue. If the Buddha's words are true, then Zendō's[7] comments cannot be untrue. If Zendō's comments are true, how can Hōnen's sayings be false? If Hōnen's sayings are true, what I, Shinran, say cannot possibly be false, either. After all is said, such is the faith of this simpleton. Beyond this, it is entirely left up to each one of you whether you accept and believe in the Nembutsu or reject it.[8]

The passage has the ring of Pascal's *logique du pari*. In his own way, Shinran was seeking a relationship between evidence and risk in the decision to faith. In a poetical work he writes:

Be it that the great chiliocosm be aflame,
He who dares to pass through the fire
To hear the Sacred Name of the Buddha,
Will attain the Non-retrogressive Stage forever.[9]

The fire of the great chiliocosm is the fire of the end of the world. The eschatological confession of Shinran concerning our human existence arrives in the second stage of religious awakening at its highest seriousness. How one is able to awaken the root of virtue (the name of Buddha) he explains thoroughly and with dialectical clarity.

Just as the first stage corresponds to the Meditation Sūtra, so the second corresponds to the short *Sukhāvatī-vyūha-sūtra* (also called the Amida Sūtra), where we find the following description:

If a believer centers himself and calls on the name of Amida Buddha for one or two days or for as many as seven days, the Buddha will certainly appear to that believer on his deathbed and receive him into the Pure Land.[10]

To hear this and confirm it in oneself is for Shinran the repetition of decision. The utterance of the name of Buddha ten times is the same as the affirmation of the name for seven days. Indeed, to utter the name once on one's deathbed in all resoluteness to convert, and to utter it repeatedly throughout one's entire life, mean the same thing.

But in this very repetition of the name the step from the second stage to the third, which is always certain to reach the goal, since it means being escorted by Amida Buddha himself, is achieved. The way from the second to the third stage involves the contradiction within us between our pride on the one hand, and our will to surrender totally to dependence on the Buddha on the other. The first encounter, which seems to us already to be an absolute experience of the other—of the transcendent itself—is in fact at first only our own experience, our own egoistic reaction. What is concealed to consciousness becomes clear to it through the repetition of the religious decision, that is, through adherence to the name. One might also say that the proximity and the distance of the Pure Land to our world opens up for the first time dimensions in which our believing minds and hearts are able to experience in a real sense the event of transcendence. This means that the eschatological destiny of our human existence is for the first time able to be consciously appropriated through the achievement of the step from the second to the third stage. Only one who has walked this path can recognize the genuine reality of eschatology, just as only one who has awakened can gain insight into the dream.

Conversely, Shinran defines the second stage of religious consciousness, in which one considers oneself to have surrendered utterly and completely to the name of the Buddha, as the "misappropriation of the name" (the gift of the Buddha) on our part. The believer's intention to surrender to the name of the Buddha actually entails the acceptance of this name not as a pure gift from the yonder shore but rather as one's own merit for one's own profit. This perversity of consciousness, which lies hidden deep in the ground of our human existence in the form of the principle of ego, is the very thing that the classical school of Indian Buddhism known as the Vijñānavāda referred to as the *mano nāma vijñāna*. In Shinran, however, the problem of effecting a reversal of the perversion at the ground of our being (*āśraya-parāvṛtti*) is put in terms that connect it intimately with the utterance of the name of the Buddha and thus make it at once more concrete and phenomenologically more perceptive than the merely abstract and hence difficult-to-comprehend speculation of the Vijñānavādin.

Let us not forget, though, that awakening from the dream is not enlightenment and the achieving of saving wisdom. In eschatological terms the absolute knowledge we are speaking of is what the saint is able to accomplish as the fruit of individual effort during the first stage. It is also the ideal that religious individuals in our own day aim at when, viewed from the vantage point of the believer, they walk the path of "self-redemption." In contrast, for the believer the proximity and distance of the Pure Land maintains its significance permanently on the way to that Land. The realization of the name of Amida Buddha in the world (the vow of Amida Buddha) renders possible a faith-transcendence in a double sense: as a transcending that occurs by way of a transdescending, and a transcending that always occurs at once with a transdescending.

The correlatedness of transcendence and transdescendence is not only something essential for the believer but points to a double meaning of the Buddha himself: Tathāgata, the one who has trod the path from this world to the world beyond (*nirvāṇa*), and likewise the one who has come to the path of this world from the world beyond. The name of Amida Buddha is precisely the way on which the Buddha, as the coming-and-going one, can encounter the believer for the first time as a person. Hegel described this characteristic of the Absolute with the term *egressus est regressus*. But Shinran sought to characterize these two movements in closest correlatedness with the essence of the name of Buddha as the duplicity of the Buddha. Here we cannot enter into detail on his theological thought. Instead, some concluding remarks should be made on Buddhist eschatology in its transcending and transdescending characteristics in terms of two other aspects, the subjective and the objective, since this double meaning of the eschaton is always present for the believer.

The eschatological age is repeated again and again in its particulars. Of course, we do not possess in everyday life the fruit of saving wisdom, as do the saints, but, like them, we are free of anxiety and doubt in this sea of sin and death because we are blind. We become aware of the real bottomlessness of life only when we feel the pressure of their affects. Only then are we driven to the quest of the true self and of true being as something completely different from this impermanent world. In all earnestness we strive for the ideal of the theoretical and the ethical. But this idealistic rein on life turns out in fact to be in vain, and the truths that accompany it to be only imaginary truths. Thus our striving, with all its intensity and seriousness, eventually drives us to the point of shipwreck. Our existence loses that quiet and freedom from anxiety that seemed to correspond to a saving wisdom at the first stage. It comes to despair of its own activity and in so doing repeats the first and second eras of world history. At the very abyss of the essence of our existence we encounter the name of Buddha. Yet even on the path of encountering this name of the Buddha we must be led to a further despair, since we have yet to learn how deep the abyss of nihility of ego is, how absurd our own pride is in entering onto the path for the first time. Only in the repetition of the religious decision do we experience the difficulty (and at the same time the simplicity or, one might say, the simple difficulty) of preserving the essence of the name. It is like someone excavating a well who has to bore through the layers of earth one after another until reaching the real, richest underground watercourse, in order then to let the water gush forth from its inexhaustible source. In the same way, one must wander perseveringly through the many torments of the heart so that the genuine achievement of an encounter with the name of Buddha (the steadfast utterance of the name) can take place in one's innermost being. Just as in the well the whole pressure of the earth is concentrated at one point in the flow, so too in the genuine utterance of the name of Buddha is the entire power of the eschaton centered on the utterance of the name and the power of depression is transformed into the power of ascension, of freely gushing forth. The greater the depression, the greater the force of the spring upwards. This is what we described above as the correlatedness of transcending and transdescending. In this way the essence of the eschaton is recalled and repeated in us when we have experienced how to encounter the name of the Buddha authentically and confirm it in ourselves. In this experience we perceive the sense of what is contained in the eschatological myth:

> All the sūtras of the Buddha will sink into the bowels of the earth or the depths of the sea except for those that preach the Pure Land, which will remain for a hundred years after the time of the final kalpa-fire in order to save humans burdened with affliction.

The survival of the sūtras here means the workings of the name of the Buddha. These sūtras represent the total working of the Buddha, which, as an object of encounter, is qualitatively different from what is meant by the usual sūtras of "self-redemption." As a vow, it calls out to us entirely on its own, without our having any part in it insofar as we are capable of learning the correct correspondence and making a decision with regard to it. What Karl Barth had to say regarding revelation and religion, and what Paul Tillich was later to say in opposition to Barth's position, calls to mind the problem of religions of grace that Rudolf Otto has characterized as the difference between the way of the cat and the way of the monkey.[11] One ought not, however, confuse Tillich's position with a synenergism. The grace of God alone is active insofar as the believer has arrived ek-statically (transcending-transdescending) on the way of encounter, but not like a car bumping into a careless pedestrian on the street. Even reason can become ek-static of itself if it reaches its own ground through the contradiction of itself and, reassuming its activity from there, allows itself to enter into communication with the transcendent—in a word, insofar as it is authentically dialectical.

III The Return to Primitive Buddhism

As we have already stated above, from the very outset the appraisal of the first two eschatological eras is very ambiguous, since the first era of pure dharma is also at the same time the flowering of Hīnayāna, while the second era of falsified dharma must be seen as the flowering of Mahāyāna; and also because this way of reckoning time in general has come into India from Mahāyāna. As we read clearly in the Mahāmāyā Sūtra, Nāgārjuna and Vasubandhu themselves belonged to the second, false era.

For the Chinese and, in particular, for the Japanese Pure Land sects the problem is perfectly clear. The Chinese Pure Land sect first became conscious of the meaning of the third era, whose beginning was the setting for their own time of tribulation. On Shinran's reckoning, Japanese Buddhism entered into the third era with Prince Shōtoku's decision to lead a life according to the later principles of the Pure Land sect.[12] The extreme temporal and geographical distance of Japan from Primitive Buddhism stimulated the yearning for a return to authentic Buddhism precisely at the end of ancient times and the onset of the Middle Ages with its movement "back to the spirit of primitive Buddhism" and its profession of an eschatological point of view infused with a sense of the philosophy of history. One of the outcomes of this event was that Shinran became aware that the time of the greatest distance from primitive Buddhism could correspond in an authentic sense with the fulfillment of the vow of Amida Buddha, which is what Gotama the Buddha was really preaching.

Nishitani Keiji has expressed himself on this problem, and I rely on his views, at the same time complementing them with my own, for the remaining pages of this chapter.

The impact of the reformation that took place in Japanese Buddhism during the Middle Ages was so rich, so radical, and so forward that in the entire history of Japan only the Meiji Restoration can be likened to it in significance. The Meiji Restoration, however, lacked religious underpinnings and hence the medieval reformation remains for Japan the only substantial achievement of a cultural synthesis and a firmly grounded unity of life that is rooted deep in the religious consciousness of the Japanese.

Prior to this time Japanese Buddhism stood at the "aesthetic" stage. One can ignore here the philosophy and speculations of the monks of the time, since that was the work of only a few intellectuals functioning independently of the popular beliefs of the age. In contrast, the great masses of the people believed in a Buddha who would bestow on them the gift of happiness and who was supposed to aid them in avoiding danger. Through Buddhist teachings and through their own experience, they knew of the impermanence and untruth of everyday life, even though they continued to depend on it, hoping that the Buddha would provide them with benefits in their perils. They depended on the proof of miracles that, in their minds, would only occur rarely and under extraordinary circumstances. They believed in the charism contained in things and persons and did not take the significance of a true Buddhist life all that seriously. The splendid, romantic ceremonies of the Tendai sect and other sects of Japanese Buddhism of the time were enough to satisfy what the people needed. Their preference for the proof and witness of the rare miraculous event (which are nothing other than another form of the "fruit of saving wisdom" taught by the six heretical teachers) shows us that Buddhism in Japan had not at the time effected a complete unification of religious life with profane life.

This spiritual relation is intimately bound up with the fact that at the time Buddhism was believed in *aesthetically*. One would marvel at the beauty of the paintings and statues of the Buddha and stand in awe of the magnificence of the Pure Land. This attitude betrays a mixture of the sense of "denying world and life" and "affirming world and life," two poles charging each other through mutual mediation. We can refer to this attitude as "aesthetic" in that the pole of affirmation, while seasoned with the negative pole, was positive and strong, leaving people so much the more dependent on enjoying the things of life.

As the setting sun brings to the fore the colors of the foliage and sharpens the outline of things on earth, even as it projects a lustrous shining of colors in the sky as if in the Pure Land, only for the whole brilliance of the scene to disappear quickly back into darkness, so is life seen only in terms of the contradiction of this world and the world beyond, of the negative and the affirmative, only a fantasy-unity of beauty in which no more than a fleeting, apparent harmony of the two is achieved. It only covers over the contradiction without really sublating it into a higher order. Only with eschatological belief is this Buddhism made conscious, in unconditional clarity, of the radical incompatibility between the profane world and religious truth. Viewed in its authentic sense, the dharma of the Buddha is eternal and there should be no such thing as an eschatology in Buddhism. But this unity of "is" and "ought" is not really able to rule over the whole reach of the profane world. It only comes about rarely—pure and beautiful, but fading—quickly to melt away again like snow on a sunny day. In order to save oneself in this disunity, one has to preserve a "beautiful soul" untainted by the outer world. The aesthetic posture of this belief finds a strong expression in the painting and poetry of the period.

Eschatology first brought to the fore clearly and in its entirety the gap between the everyday and the religious that is perpetually with us. Yet through the sublation of this contradiction in life the religious truth contained in the concreteness of everyday life becomes realized and our life on earth is made holy and religious. The mutual interpenetration of the spiritual and the earthly was first established in Japan through the reforms of Zen and Shin Buddhism. Genuine eschatological belief is thus necessary for the purification and practice of a Buddhist way of life.[13]

NOTES

[1] *Kyōgyōshinshō* (教行信証), VI, 3. ET: *The Teaching, Practice, Faith, and Enlightenment*, Ryukoku Translation Series, vol. 5 (Kyoto, 1966), p. 165.

[2] 正像末和讃 (Shōzōmatsu-wasan, *The Praise of the Grace of Amida Buddha in the Last Things*), n. 53.

[3] *Kyōgyōshinshō*, VI, 39 (see n. 1 above), p.194.

[4] *Tannishō* (歎異抄), I. ET: *Notes Lamenting Differences*, Ryukoku Translation Series, vol. 2 (Kyoto, 1962), pp. 15-16.

[5] *Tannishō*, III, (see n. 4 above), pp. 22f.

[6] Hōnen Shōnin (1133-1212) was Shinran's teacher and founder of the Japanese Pure Land sect.

[7] Zendō (613-681), the Japanization of the Chinese name of Shan-tao, was the fifth of the Seven Patriarchs of Shin Buddhism, and was one of the prominent teachers of the T'ang Dynasty.

[8] *Tannishō*, II (see n. 4 above), pp. 20f.

[9] *Jōdo-wasan* (浄土和讃), n. 31. ET: *The Hymns on the Pure Land*, Ryukoku Translation Series, vol. 4 (Kyoto, 1965), p 59.

[10] The passage appears in v. 10 and has been somewhat abbreviated. The complete text of the sūtra appears in vol. 49/2 of the *Sacred Books of the East* (Oxford University Press, 1894), pp. 89-102.

[11] "When a mother ape falls into danger, her young immediately cling fast to her, and when she makes a leap to safety, they are saved, by the act of the mother it is true, but in such a way that the young *cooperates* a little, because it clings to the mother *by its own act*. It is therefore a synergist. But when danger threatens a cat with her young, the mother cat takes the young in her mouth. The young one does nothing for its salvation. It remains merely passive. All cooperation is excluded" (R. Otto, *India's Religion of Grace and Christianity Compared and Contrasted*, trans. F.H. Foster [London, SCM Press, 1930], p. 56).

[12] Shōtoku Taishi (574-622) was a Japanese prince and devoted advocate of Buddhism, and is commonly credited with having secured the introduction of Buddhism into Japan.

[13] See M. Kōsaka and K. Nishitani, 日本的なるもの―その系譜と構造 (*The Genealogy and Structure of Things Japanese*), *Jiyū*, December 1959, pp. 110-31, January 1960, pp. 104-22.

CHAPTER 6

THE PRACTICE OF JODO-SHINSHU

—TAITETSU UNNO

The question most frequently asked of a Shin Buddhist is, what is your practice? The obvious answer is the practice of compassion. As Buddhists, our task is to manifest compassion in everyday life, beginning with members of our own family and extending it to all of society. But when one really tries to practice compassion, expressing care, concern, empathy, and love, all the while respecting the autonomy and dignity of the other, one encounters a huge obstacle. And that obstacle is never the other, but rather one's own self-centered ego. This awareness is the starting point of the Shin Buddhist path.

Among the many branches of Buddhism, the better-known ones in North America are today represented by various forms of Zen, Tibetan Buddhism, and Vipassana practices, but there are many other branches that are found in the Asian landscape. One of them is the Pure Land branch of Mahayana Buddhism, whose deep roots go back to the South Asian world that produced many scriptures, including the Pure Land scriptures, in the first century B.C.E. A major offshoot of this branch that emerged in thirteenth-century Japan is Jodo-shinshu, or Shin Buddhism.

While Theravada Buddhism venerates a single buddha, the historical Shakyamuni, Mahayana Buddhism has many buddhas who play principal roles in the different scriptures. They include such figures as Akshobya Buddha, Maitreya Buddha, Vairochana Buddha, Bhaishajyaguru Buddha, and Amitabha or Amitayus Buddha, who is the Buddha in the Pure Land scriptures. In East Asia, however, the two titles—Amitabha, Immeasurable Light, and Amitayus, Immeasurable Life—are combined into the contracted form, Amita or Amida.

The two primary scriptures of Pure Land that originated in India are called the *Larger Sukhavati-vyuha Sūtra* and the *Smaller Sukhavati-vyuha Sūtra*. *Sukhavati-vyuha* means the "adornment of the realm of bliss." A third scripture of Central Asian or Chinese origin, dating from about the fourth century C.E., is the *Kuan wu-liang-shou ching*, or the *Sūtra on the Contemplation of the Buddha of Immeasurable Life* (abbreviated to *Contemplation Sūtra*). These three are called the *Triple Sūtra of Pure Land Buddhism*.

The *Larger Sūtra* describes the career of a bodhisattva by the name of Dharmakara, who makes forty-eight vows before a buddha known as Sovereign Monarch of the World. The vows promise to relieve the sufferings of people and replace them with peace and comfort. When Dharmakara fulfills and completes all the vows, he attains buddhahood and becomes known as Amida Buddha. The most important among them is the Eighteenth Vow, also called the Primal Vow, which manifests the nonjudgmental and all-embracing compassion of Amida.

The *Smaller Sūtra* is a highly imaginative portrayal of the realm of enlightenment in very concrete terms: bejeweled railings, nettings, trees; bathing pools lined with golden sands and with steps of gold, silver, lapis lazuli, and crystal; pavilions covered with exquisite jewels built on the earth made of gold. The atmosphere is filled with celestial music, rare and exquisite birds, and a subtle breeze blowing through jeweled trees which produces a harmonious chorus. This rich and gaudy description is said to be a manifestation of emptiness (*shunyata*) that expresses itself freely in any way it chooses. Since reality is empty of permanent being, and all things are in flux, it can take any form.

The *Contemplation Sūtra* begins with the tragedy of Rajagriha, which occurred during the time of the historical Buddha. Prince Ajatasatru, incited by Devadatta, a cousin and rival of Shakyamuni, imprisons his father, the king, and later his mother, the queen. In distress, Queen Vaidehi calls for Shakyamuni Buddha to counsel her. The Buddha shows countless Pure Lands, among which Vaidehi selects the Pure Land of Amida and aspires to be born in that land. The Buddha describes sixteen forms of meditative and non-meditative contemplations by which birth in the Pure Land is assured.

The Pure Land scriptures were popularized in China and various lineages of practice derived from them evolved. Important commentaries and studies began appearing beginning in the fourth century C.E. When these scriptures were introduced into Japan in the sixth century they did not attract much attention, but gradually they inspired monks and nuns among the six schools of the Nara Period (710-794) to pursue Pure Land practices.

It was in the Heian Period (794-1191), however, that Pure Land beliefs began to have a major impact on some of the monastic institutions and the general culture. It became an inspiration for art and architecture, as well as for poetry and literature, producing, for example, the first major narrative in world literature, *The Tale of Genji* by Lady Murasaki, in the eleventh century. The two Buddhist schools of Heian, known as Shingon and Tendai, also embraced aspects of Pure Land teachings, but it is the Tendai practice known as the Samadhi of Constant Practice that is significant for our purposes. This practice, originally conceived by Chih-i (538-597), the founder of the T'ien-t'ai school in China, was a ninety-day circumambulation of the image of Amida Buddha, while constantly reciting the Name of Amida with almost no rest or sleep.

In 1175 a charismatic figure by the name of Hōnen, a monk of the Tendai order, appeared and proclaimed the founding of a separate and independent Pure Land school called Jodo-shu (*Jodo* means "Pure Land" and *shu* is "school"). His basic tenet is summed up in the phrase, "In the path of Sages one perfects wisdom and achieves enlightenment; in the path of Pure Land one returns to the foolish self to be saved by Amida." The basic practice that Hōnen recommended was the single-hearted recitation of *nembutsu*, the Name of Amida: *Namu-Amida-Butsu*.

This practice of recitative *nembutsu* changed the course of Japanese Buddhism, for the monastic paths, patronized by the imperial court and the nobility, excluded the masses until Hōnen founded the independent Jodo School. Then the gates to liberation and freedom were wide open, welcoming those who had hitherto been excluded: women of all classes; hunters, butchers, and fishermen, who took life to make a living; peasants and merchants considered ignorant and "bad" in the eyes of the upper classes; and monks and nuns who had violated the precepts.

Among Hōnen's many followers, it was Shinran (1173-1263) who followed in his footsteps to penetrate the inner dynamics of intoning the *nembutsu*, rejecting mechanical repetition and clarifying its source as the boundless compassion that is Amida Buddha. Thus, the saying of *nembutsu* is received basically as a call from Amida, but simultaneously it is our response to that call. Being a devoted student of Hōnen, Shinran disclaimed any following, but his lineage kept alive his memory and teaching, which eventually became recognized as another Pure Land school, known as Jodo-shinshu (*shin* means "true and real" and *shu* here means "tenet"). Although Shinran used the term Jodo-shinshu to mean "the true and real tenet of Pure Land (as taught by Hōnen)," today it is used as the name of an independent school, widely referred to in the West as Shin Buddhism.

*

* *

Buddhism is a path of supreme optimism, for one of its basic tenets is that no human life or experience is to be wasted, abandoned or forgotten, but all should be transformed into a source of vibrant life, deep wisdom, and compassionate living. On the everyday level of experience, Shin Buddhists speak of this transformation as "bits of rubble turn into gold."

This metaphor comes from Tz'u-min, the Chinese Pure Land master of the eighth century, who proclaims the working of boundless compassion called Amida, the Buddha of Immeasurable Light and Life, as follows:

> The Buddha, in the causal stage, made the universal vow:
> When beings hear my Name and think on me, I will come to welcome each of them,
> Not discriminating at all between the poor and the rich and well born,
> Not discriminating between the inferior and highly gifted,
> Not choosing the learned and those upholding pure precepts,
> Nor rejecting those who break precepts and whose evil karma is profound.
> Solely making beings turn about and abundantly say the *nembutsu*,
> I can make bits of rubble change into gold.[1]

When we are made aware of the neglected aspect of ourselves, hidden in darkness, which hinders our practice of compassion on a consistent, thorough-going basis, we are already being touched by the light of boundless compassion that is Amida Buddha. This light not only illuminates our darkness, it transforms it, so that we try our best to be compassionate with a sense of humility and gratitude, mindful of our karmic limitations. Humility arises for having been shown our karma-bound self, yet grateful for the boundless compassion that inspires us to act with a new and vigorous appreciation for life.

All this is contained in the saying of *nembutsu*: *Namu-Amida-Butsu*. It consists of two parts integrated as one: the being of self-enclosure and deep egocentricity, symbolized by *namu*, illuminated and transformed by boundless compassion, *amida-butsu*.

The *nembutsu* is the flowing call of the Buddha of Immeasurable Light and Life, coming from the fathomless center of life itself, as well as our response to that call without any hesitation or calculation. Thus it is not a petitionary act, a mindless, mechanical repetition, or a mantra with magical powers.

This calling of *nembutsu* awakens us to a liberating power that sanctifies all life, because it comes from beyond the small-minded self that is always engaged in calculating life only in terms of gain or loss, winning or losing. Sooner or later we will respond to this call, if we are ever to know a sense of security and well-being. If I were to translate *nembutsu* into English, it would be the "Name-that-calls," for it calls us to awaken to our fullest potential to become true, real, and sincere human beings.

What is essential, then, is not the number of times voiced, nor even the purity of heart involved, but simply the deep hearing of the Name-that-calls to which we want to respond. The goal of deep hearing is to bring about a fundamental change in one's life, such that one realizes liberation and freedom in the midst of worldly entanglements, daily responsibilities, and constant agitations. This path is for everyone, especially lay people, in our contemporary world, because the *nembutsu* path has no requirements except the recognition of an indisputable fact: the problems in our daily life can be ultimately transmuted into sources of self-knowledge and received wisdom.

The process of deep hearing culminates with our birth in the Pure Land, but the Pure Land is not the ultimate goal. It is a mere way station from which we return to our world of saṃsāra. Now endowed with wisdom and compassion, the welfare and salvation of all beings become the ultimate concern. The return, however, is inseparable from the going, both made possible by the centrifugal force of boundless compassion. Such is the ultimate expansion and deepening of the bodhisattva ideal, which breaks through conventional notions of time and space.

According to Shinran, religious awakening is the realization of timeless time in each moment of temporal activity. The ultimate dimension breaks into the historical dimension, the timeless penetrates time. In his words, "One thought-moment is time at its ultimate limit, where the realization of *shinjin* takes place."

The "one thought-moment" underscores the irreplaceable, ultimate value of the here and now. It is the moment that vertical time breaks through into horizontal or linear time, the absolute penetrating the relative. In Buddhist discourse it is also the moment of formless reality, called dharmakaya, appearing as the Primal Vow of Amida in human consciousness.

Such an experience of time was the basis of Shinran's reinterpretation of "birth in the Pure Land," changing its original futuristic connotation into a radical affirmation of the here and now. He interprets the scripture that states, "Then they attain birth," to suggest an immediacy not apparent in the original. Thus, in his commentary, Shinran states: "'Then' means immediately; 'immediately' means without any passage of time, without any passage of days."

Historically, for over a thousand years, the Pure Land symbolized various ideals of the religious life. Foremost among them was the representation of the perfect realm to pursue the path of enlightenment, unobstructed by the din, commotion, and entanglements of our samsaric world. It was also the place to which the dying would be welcomed by Amida Buddha and his retinue of bodhisattvas coming down from the sky. In fact, a deathbed ritual was developed in medieval Japan to ensure successful birth into the Pure Land. A folding screen with a painting of Amida Buddha, looking down from among mountain peaks, was placed above the bed of the dying person. A string attached to the heart of Amida would be extended and firmly grasped by the dying, so that there would be no chance of getting lost on the way to the Pure Land.

Shinran rejected this popular deathbed ritual as causing greater anxiety about death and dying, as well as revealing a lack of trust in the Primal Vow. He states:

> The idea of Amida's coming at the moment of death is for those who seek to gain birth in the Pure Land by performing religious practices, for they are the practicers of self-power. The moment of death is of central concern for such people … The person of true *shinjin*, however, abides in the stage of the truly settled, for he has already been grasped, never to be abandoned. There is no need to wait in anticipation for the moment of death, no need to rely on Amida's coming. At the time *shinjin* becomes settled, birth too becomes settled; there is no need for deathbed rites that prepare one for Amida's coming.

There is no need for such a deathbed ritual, because birth in the Pure Land occurs in the awakening to *shinjin* here and now. *Shinjin* is a kind of trust where doubt is nonexistent and assertion of any kind is unnecessary. It is different from the popular notions of faith, which contain a vast range of meanings, mostly based on a dualistic view that focuses on an object outside of oneself. It is more appropriate to use words taken from ordinary life to translate *shinjin* into English, words such as trust, confidence, steadfastness, certainty, which do not involve any kind of duality. Since it also has nothing to do with the fickle mind of human beings, I translate *shinjin* as "true entrusting," an entrusting that is made possible by that which is true and real, namely, Amida Buddha.

In the initial engagement, both Amida and Pure Land are regarded as objects, dualistically conceived, but in mature engagement they become an integral part of a fundamental awakening, such that the practitioner and Amida/Pure Land are experienced as nondual reality.[2]

The primary goal of Shin Buddhism is life lived in mature engagement with the buddhadharma. The ultimate goal of deep hearing is not *satori* or enlightenment but true entrusting. In the words of Shinran,

> For the foolish and ignorant who are ever sinking in birth-and-death, the multitudes turning in transmigration, it is not attainment of the unexcelled, incomparable fruit of enlightenment that is difficult; the genuine difficulty is realizing true and real *shinjin*.

The "genuine difficulty" comes from our deep-rooted self-clinging that will not open up to "true and real *shinjin*" that is the unconditional gift of boundless compassion. Shinran describes true and real *shinjin* variously: as diamond-like, because it is not dependent on the ego-self and hence is indestructible; as the settled state, because it is not subject to our emotional upheavals; and as nonretrogression, because there is no backsliding into confusion and darkness. Toward the end of his life, Shinran called *shinjin* a state equal to the Tathāgata or Buddha; that is, it is not identical with buddhahood but equals it, since supreme enlightenment will be attained necessarily as its natural consequence.

In carefully interpreting the writings of past masters of the Pure Land tradition from his own experiential reading, Shinran concluded that the three basic attitudes stipulated in the Eighteenth Vow—sincere mind, joyful entrusting, and aspiration for the Pure Land—can be unified as the single heart-mind of Amida working in foolish beings to bring about true entrusting.

Shinran frequently uses the expression "returning to the ocean of Primal Vow" for *shinjin*. He likens it to the great ocean that does not discriminate between good and bad, young and old, men and women, noble and humble. Nor does it differentiate between practitioner and non-practitioner, sudden and gradual attainment, right and wrong contemplation, once-calling and many-calling. The working of *shinjin* is ultimately "inconceivable, inexplicable, and indescribable. It is like the medicine that eradicates all poisons. The medicine of the Tathāgata's Vow destroys the poison of our wisdom and foolishness."

When we think that we have attained some kind of wisdom, it is nothing but arrogance, and as such it poisons us and those around us. Only the medicine of *nembutsu* can eradicate such a toxic condition. But just as an ordinary person does not know the base chemicals in a prescription medicine, yet derives good from it, so likewise the practitioner of the Shin path cannot fathom the depth of *nembutsu* life, yet receives inconceivable benefits from it.

*
*   *

The Shin Buddhist path makes no undue demands on its followers, physical or otherwise, except one: *the giving up of the ego-self.* Consistent with the original teaching of Shakyamuni Buddha, Shin regards the ego-self as another human construct but with such deep roots in one's karmic past that it is impossible to give up. Hence sometimes it is called *karmic self,* but since it creates suffering for oneself and others, it is also the self of *karmic evil.* Because of its deep roots in countless lives past, becoming free of the ego-self so that true and real personhood might emerge is not an easy matter. This is where the working of boundless compassion in the form of the Primal Vow comes to nullify the ego-self and transform it into its opposite. Since all the work is done by the invisible Other Power, the path of Pure Land is deemed the Easy Path, but to experience this in all its depth and height is another matter. Hence the scriptures remind us that, "The path is easy but few are those who take it."

According to the Pure Land tradition, it was the philosopher Nagarjuna (second and third century C.E.) who first characterized the path of Pure Land as the "easy path," in contrast to the path of Sages labeled as the "difficult path." While it is burdensome to carry a heavy load on one's back and travel by foot to reach one's goal, it is much easier to be carried on a ferry and transported on the waterway to the same destination. Thus the Primal Vow of Amida, the Buddha of Immeasurable Light and Immeasurable Life, is likened to a huge vessel that carries all beings to the other shore of supreme enlightenment. In the words of Shinran,

> It is a great torch in the long night of ignorance;
> Do not lament that your wisdom-eye is dark.
> It is a ship on the vast ocean of birth-and-death;
> Do not grieve that your karmic obstructions are heavy.

The Pure Land path may be open to misunderstanding, if and when seen through the popular notions of faith-oriented religion. The problem is compounded by another set of well-known Pure Land terms—"self-power" and "Other Power"—first enunciated by T'an-luan in the early sixth century. While self-power is identified with the difficult path of Sages and Other Power with the easy path of Pure Land, our concern is with the existence of self-power within Other Power. That is, self-power is the natural inclination to assert the power of the ego-self to reach a goal, but it is necessary to realize that ultimately it is ineffectual and fruitless on the path of supreme enlightenment. Yet at the same time, it is a necessary stage on the path where self-power is also appreciated, in reflection, as the working of Other Power.

69

The proper relationship of these two terms may be illustrated by the example of sailing on the high seas. In order for the sailboat to catch the wind (Other Power), the sailor must first undertake a variety of tasks (self-power). The sails, of course, must be put up, but countless unseen preparations are necessary: studying the weather forecasts, judging the prevailing wind velocity and the movements of the ocean currents, mastering the use of various navigational tools. All this requires time, effort, and hard work, similar to the preliminary work required on the Pure Land path.

All this preparation, however, will not move the ship. When all preparations have been completed and the sails have been hoisted, one must now wait with patience and alertness for the wind to blow. Such a state of waiting is required, for the wind of Other Power is beyond human control. When the wind does blow, however, the sailboat is ready to cruise effortlessly on the high seas with lightness and alacrity.

Such must have been the feeling of Shinran, who, after twenty years of relentless quest and search as a Tendai monk, abandoned it for the path of *nembutsu*. His joy is expressed with exuberance:

> Now, as I ride on the ship of the great compassionate vow and sail on the expansive ocean of wondrous light, the breeze of highest virtue blows peacefully and calms the waves of pain and sorrow. Quickly shall I reach the land of immeasurable light and attain unexcelled peace and freedom.

When freed of egoistic designs and calculations, life unfolds freely, in spite of unavoidable difficulties. But a new kind of wisdom is bestowed on a person, so that he or she can negotiate through the labyrinth called life. This wisdom is not something acquired or gained, as in the Path of Sages; rather, it is bestowed or granted to the person of *nembutsu*, who is a foolish being.

Shinran never claimed to have a special message, nor did he cry out that he came to save the world. His focus was always on the working of the Buddha of Immeasurable Light and Life, the luminosity that enabled him to see through the falsities and shams he himself was subject to as an ordinary human being. In our age of spiritual masters, gurus, and charlatans, it is refreshing to hear the voice of Shinran writing at the age of eighty-six:

> Not really knowing right from wrong,
> Not really knowing false from true,
> I lack even small love and small compassion,
> And yet, for fame and name, enjoy teaching others.

But for that very reason he saw himself as the supreme candidate for transformation by boundless compassion. Thus, he could claim without being pretentious or pompous:

Although I am without shame or remorse
And totally lack truth or sincerity,

The Name of Amida directed to me
Makes virtues abound in the ten directions of the universe.

In the long and grand history of Buddhism, Shinran gives hope that the most foolish being, lost and confused, can be transformed into its opposite, for the power of boundless compassion can make "bits of rubble turn into gold."

The unhindered light filling the ten quarters
Shines on the beings in the darkness of ignorance
And unfailingly brings to attainment of nirvāṇa
The person who realizes the one thought-moment of joy.

Through the benefit of the unhindered light,
We realize *shinjin* of vast, majestic virtues,
And the ice of our blind passions necessarily melts,
Immediately becoming water of enlightenment.

Obstructions of karmic evil turn into virtues;
It is like the relation of ice and water:
The more the ice, the more the water;
The more the obstructions, the more the virtues.

The ocean of the inconceivable Name does not hold unchanged
The corpses of the five grave offenses and slander of the dharma;
The myriad rivers of evil acts, on entering it,
Become one in taste with the ocean water of virtues.

Rivers of blind passions, on entering the ocean
The great, compassionate Vow
Of unhindered light filling the ten quarters
Become one in taste with that sea of wisdom.[3]

NOTES

[1] Passage quoted in *The Collected Works of Shinran, Volume I* (Kyoto: Jodo Shinshu Hong-wanji-ha, 1997). This volume contains the complete works of Shinran in English translation and all quotations by Shinran in this article are from this work.

[2] The distinction between initial and mature engagement was first made by Dennis Hitota, ed., *Towards a Contemporary Understanding of Shin Buddhism* (Albany, New York: SUNY Press, 2000), pp. 33-72.

[3] Shinran, *Hymns of the Pure Land Masters*, from *The Collected Works of Shinran, Volume I*.

CHAPTER 7

SHINJIN IS THE ETERNAL NOW[1]

—OMINE AKIRA

(TRANSLATED BY DAVID MATSUMOTO)

In the *Jodo Shinshu* teachings, the notion of "birth in the Pure Land" (*Ojo Jodo*) has long been set forth. Rephrasing this with modern terminology, "birth in the Pure Land" refers to the path along which human beings can truly live. The meaning of "birth," therefore, is not that one goes to the Land of Ultimate Bliss after death and then lives over there. Some are prone to think that, by approaching the Chinese word for "birth" (*Ojo*) from the standpoint of the order of the characters, it must mean that one first "goes" (*O, yuku*) and after that "lives" (*Sho, iku*). However, how are we able to go to the Pure Land? That becomes a problem. The answer is that the person who truly lives in this world is able to go to the Pure Land. That person is "born." Therefore, it is not that one goes there and is able to live. If one does not truly live before that, that is, here and now, in this world, then that person will not realize enlightenment in the Pure Land. This is what Shinran Shonin teaches us.

The doctrinal expression for this is that, without *shinjin*, one can never go to the Pure Land. *Shinjin* means to truly live. In the first Letter of Shinran's *Collection of Letters* (*Mattosho*), there is this famous phrase: "At the moment that *shinjin* is settled, one's birth is settled." With these splendid words, Shinran Shonin expresses the foundation of *Jodo Shinshu*. When is one's birth settled? It is settled, not after death, but at the moment that one entrusts in the Buddha. In other words, when an ordinary being entrusts oneself to the great life of the Tathāgata in this world, her birth is already settled. One does not go to the Land of Ultimate Bliss and then live. The person who truly lives is able to go to Ultimate Bliss. Therefore, from the perspective of their meaning, the order of the characters (*Ojo*) is reversed. Instead of "to go and be born," the true meaning is "to be born and go." If we do not engage in "thinking," then *Jodo Shinshu* will be wrongly understood. Shinran Shonin says that "In the one thought-moment of *shinjin*, birth is settled." In the instant of true entrusting, the eternal becomes manifested. In the one thought-moment of *shinjin*, the experience of encountering the eternal is referred to as the "settlement of *shinjin*" (*shinjin ketsujo*). One encounters the eternal now in the very midst of time.

Faith in *Jodo Shinshu* is this experience of encountering the "eternal now." The "eternal now" is a famous expression of Kitaro Nishida. The eternal now is not a temporal now. Rather, it is the now in which time has been broken through. In other words, it refers to time in which the eternal enters into time. There is no now, other than the now into which the eternal has entered. The now which is not connected to the eternal through *shinjin* will soon flow away. Within human life, there is no now. We may try to specify the now to the hour, minute, or second, but that now soon flows away; it does not halt for even an instant. The *Larger Sūtra of Immeasurable Life* describes this situation with the words, "It passes in vain." Without *shinjin*, human life simply passes in vain.

If human life were only a matter of being within time, then it would be just like being without time. Up until today, I have lived a number of decades. But, while it seems to have been a long time, it also does not seem to have been long at all. Time always seems to be moving faster and faster. When I was a child, it felt as though the days passed slowly until the New Year. But, these days, it comes around before I know it. When it comes to time then, no matter how long of a time period it may be, in the end it flows completely away, leaving nothing. Within time, we cannot catch hold of any now. The now that I speak of now is now in the past.

However, in *shinjin*, the now which one could not previously catch hold of can be attained. The person who entrusts in the Tathāgata comes into contact with that which does not flow away and therefore the now can be secured. A person who does not rely upon the Tathāgata is one who seeks to protect himself through his own self-power. Such a person can never attain the now. Shinran Shonin was the first one to interpret "the ranks of the truly settled in the present life" as "at the moment shinjin is settled, one's birth is settled." He emphasizes that one is able to come into contact with eternal life, not in another world, but at this time and in this world in which one is living.

This was Shinran's magnificent discovery. Up until then, people had thought that one would probably encounter eternity after going to that world. In this world, they believed, there is nothing eternal; everything is futile. However, this kind of Pure Land teaching was a woeful, unhappy one. There are people who still believe that the world of ordinary beings contains nothing eternal, and that, upon going to the Land of Ultimate Bliss, one may meet the great assembly of Buddhas there. But theirs is a very miserable *Jodo Shinshu*. It is not the *Jodo Shinshu*, which is the true essence of the Pure Land way as set forth by Shinran Shonin. Their kind of *Jodo Shinshu* is based on a wrong understanding.

The world of ordinary beings may be vain and futile, but the true essence of the Pure Land Way exists where beings who live in the midst of that futile world can hear the Word of Amida Buddha. That is to say, Shinran Shonin's teaching is that any Buddha that cannot come to the world of ordinary beings is powerless. Any Tathāgata that simply remains in the Pure Land waiting for us is powerless. An Amida Buddha or Pure Land of Ultimate Bliss that does not exercise any power in this present life is not the real Buddha or Land. This was Shinran Shonin's magnificent discovery. His teaching that "at the moment that *shinjin* is settled, one's birth is settled," refers to the moment that the first ray of Light from the Pure Land reaches this world.

This point was not clear in the Pure Land teachings prior to Shinran Shonin. It seems that it took a long time before this truth of Buddhism could be truly unearthed and could be recognized as true. The *Larger Sūtra of Immeasurable Life* was produced at around the beginning of the Common Era, but it took until the Kamakura Period in the thirteenth century before its essence could be made clear. Perhaps that is how it had to be. Because it involves religious truth, it could not have been clearly understood from the very outset. When it comes to revealing religious truth to human beings, it seems as though history is necessary. We do not know why this truth was revealed during the Kamakura Period and not during the preceding Heian Period. Perhaps that was the result of some kind of chance occurrence or perhaps some kind of fate of the historical world. The primary essence of the truth set forth in the *Larger Sūtra of Immeasurable Life* was discovered by Shinran, a religious genius in thirteenth century Japan. We must give some thought to this auspicious event. It is our great joy that the genius known as Shinran was able to discover the very core of Śākyamuni Buddha's teaching.

According to Shinran Shonin the eternal world is not a separate world of the after-life which is different from our temporal world. True, eternal power exists where the eternal enters into time. Therefore, a Pure Land that is not actively working in this world is not the true Pure Land. The Pure Land that comes into this world is the true Pure Land. I agree completely with Shinran. If the Pure Land does not come into this world, it makes no difference whether it exists or not. Shinran Shonin expressed this idea simply by saying that there is a constant coming and going between the *saha* world and the Pure Land. If the *saha* world and the Pure Land were to stand in mutual opposition without any interchange, it would not be the true Pure Land. A Pure Land that cannot come and go is no good. Without any interchange, it is the same as hell. When two human beings remain silent toward each other, it is just like hell. In contrast, when there is dialogue between people, even though they may be far removed from each other, the world is alive and harmonious. No matter how close people may be to each other, if they do not converse with each other, it is as if they were separated by 1,000 miles.

In the Pure Land traditions prior to Shinran Shonin, it was believed that beings had to go from here over to a realm called the Pure Land of Ultimate Bliss. "Birth" in that Land meant that a person would go there once and for all, and never return. It was believed, for example, that one would go there and be able to meet one's deceased father or child. Since, in this world, there are only ordinary beings in this world and no Buddhas at all, it was thought that, by just going over there, something would work out. This is how people used to think.

Shinran Shonin did not think in that way. His idea, in contrast, was that "directing of virtue" (*eko*) possesses two aspects: the aspect of going (*oso eko*) and the aspect of returning (*genso eko*). Stated simply, *Jodo Shinshu*, as the true essence of the Pure Land way, signifies a mutual interchange of life between the saha world and the Pure Land. It is the great "circulating current" (*kanryu*) of the life of the Tathāgata, which goes and returns. The true aspect of our human life is revealed, floating atop the great life of the Buddha which flows from this world to the Pure Land and from the Pure Land back to this world. Shinran Shonin said that our human life rides atop the current of great life as it flows and circulates. The flow of life goes around and around; it goes and returns, returns and goes. The reason for this is that life never remains still. Anything that remains still remains in a dead world. If life does not move, then it is not life. There is a constant coming and going between this world and that world. This is the natural state of the world of life. That being the case, simply living for a long time in this world is not true living. That is the same as coming to a standstill. Therefore, we must quickly go to the Pure Land of Ultimate Bliss. Then, upon going there, we do not remain there, but must return to this world once again in order to save people who continue to wander in delusion.

Human life is not a straight line, in which a person is born at one time, does a variety of things for a while and then ends up buried in a graveyard. That human life would be dead. Human life in a straight line would be a dead and fragmentary human life. In contrast, life fundamentally takes the form of a great, moving circle. To entrust in the Tathāgata is to ride atop the flow of this "circulating current" of life. We tend to be under the impression that entrusting in the Buddha requires us to focus on something within our minds. However, Shinran Shonin said that *shinjin* is to ride on and rely upon the Tathāgata's Vow power. *Shinjin* of Other Power means that we take part in this great current of life. In order to participate in it, we need to discard our egos. In *shinjin* it is not our delusions and blind passions that are discarded. Instead, as we are carried upon the great, moving current of the Vow, we leave behind our own calculation and conceit.

NOTES

[1] A Buddhist Churches of America (BCA) and Institute of Buddhist Studies (IBS) public lecture presented on August 14 & 16, 1998.

CHAPTER 8

SHINRAN'S VISION OF ABSOLUTE COMPASSION

—ALFRED BLOOM

Introduction

We can interpret religion from its most primitive to its most sophisticated and profound expressions as an endeavor to free people from the bondage of the unknown and from the enslavement of egoism. The history of Buddhism provides a significant illustration of this process. It is clear that the Buddhist insight into the workings of karma and the goal of nirvāṇa relieved ancient man of the anxieties concerning his life and destiny based in ancient Indian folk religion where man had to placate gods and fend off demons. Faith in Buddha enabled people to rise above the superstitions of their day. Those folk beliefs played no role in Buddhism. Unfortunately the institutionalization of Buddhism brought about the reinterpretation of those beliefs now in the service of Buddhism.

Within the Buddhist tradition we can observe, nevertheless, the attempt to relieve anxiety and fear in the story surrounding the Obon festival. Here we must call attention to ancient man's fear of evil spirits and avenging ghosts because of lack of proper treatment of the dead. These beliefs are still current today. However, in the story which relates the origin of Obon we find that the monk Moggallana, as a result of attaining spiritual insight, was able to see his mother suffering in the other world as a hungry ghost. He was disturbed and asked Buddha what he could do to save his mother. Buddha recommended gifts to the Order and the services of feeding the hungry spirits began.

What is important to note in this story is that Moggallana's mother was not bothering anyone even though she had not been properly treated by her son. Without spiritual insight from the practice of Buddhism he could not know what was happening to her. Buddhism is telling us in story that evil spirits, or spirits of the dead, cannot harm us, but we can help them. At that stage of intellectual and religious development, that would have been a great liberating message reflecting the compassion of Buddhism for the sufferings and fears of the masses. Unfortunately, again, in the course of the history of institutions, this legend focused anxiety on both the danger of the dead and appealed to one's guilt and anxiety concerning the future well-being of departed loved ones. A large part of the economic foundation of Buddhist temples came to be based on practices to relieve anxiety concerning the dead.

The point we wish to make is simply that religion has as its chief aim to dispel anxiety, to overcome fear, to provide strength and courage to face the challenges of existence. It should have no part in using anxieties and fear to maintain its hold over the life of the individual. Thus even in Buddhism, the concepts of heaven and hell, which have been used in tradition to secure adherence and to threaten unbelievers, have no part in the essential meaning and teaching of Buddhism.

The thesis of this paper is that it was not until Shinran that Buddhism attained a theoretical position where such concepts became irrelevant and meaningless as ways to stimulate religiosity and adherence to a particular teaching. There are no statements in Shinran's writings which indicate that one would go to hell because he did not believe or follow Shinran's teaching. Shinran dedicated himself to giving hope to those who thought they were hopeless. We can see this clearly if we compare Shinran's statements on human destiny with descriptions as to who goes to Avīci hell or with Nichiren who was quite clear that those who opposed his teaching were doomed to hell. When Shinran declares that even though he might be consigned to hell for reciting *Nembutsu*, he is reflecting, perhaps, Nichiren's insistence on *Nembutsu Muken Jigoku*, hell without interval, awaiting those who recite *Nembutsu*.

We cannot go into Shinran's own experience in detail, except to say that he realized his utter powerlessness to release himself from egoism and karmic bondage through the prescribed disciplines of traditional Buddhism. The more deeply he experienced his own imperfection and spiritual powerlessness, the more deeply he penetrated the meaning of Amida's compassion until he perceived that compassion, like truth or wisdom, could not be a relative quality, but had to be a totally embracing, absolute quality completely beyond any criteria or distinctions invoked by the moralism of ordinary society.

It is for this reason that Shinran's religious faith has been called "a religion beyond good and evil" and why he could state paradoxically that if it was easy for a good man to be saved, how much more the evil man.[1] As he notes, it is the general opinion of mankind that the good people have an advantage through their goodness over the evil person. Hence, the usual position is that if an evil man can he saved, how much more the good man. The two statements seem a hair's breadth apart, but actually they embody totally different understandings of the meaning of Buddha's compassion. The moralist view sees compassion in a relative way, correlated to the degree of goodness a person possesses. There is only a grudging recognition that even the evil person has a claim on compassion. In Shinran's view, compassion is absolute and may be claimed equally by the evil person, and perhaps even a little more so because the plight of the evil person calls forth the depth of Buddha's compassion.

In various ways throughout his writings Shinran gives expression to his awareness of the absoluteness of Amida's compassion, beyond quantity and criteria. He sees faith in the Vow as dispelling fear, particularly fears concerning the evils that we as human beings perform as a result of our passionate and imperfect natures. No evil we do separates us from Amida's compassion. We can illustrate the anxieties of guilt which Shinran addressed from the *Heike Monogatari*, a famous novel of the Kamakura period. There is an account of the visit of an aristocrat to Hōnen in repentance for his sins of killing in war. He states:

> My mind was clogged with the evil desire of killing others and saving my own life, so that no good thoughts could dwell in me ... So whatever shame may overwhelm me I know that it is but retribution for this deed. Therefore I would shave my head and go as a mendicant priest, practicing austerities and seeking only the Way of Buddha. But even if I could do this in the body, I cannot believe that my Heart would be changed; for whatever austerities I might practice would not be enough to attain salvation. Alas! When I think over the conduct of my past life, my guilt is greater than Mount Sumeru, while all my righteousness is less than a speck of dust; and if thus in vain I end my life, without doubt I shall be reborn in the Three Ways of Torment.[2]

It is common also in Christian circles that people believe they are too evil to be saved, or live in guilt and fear because of supposed evils they have done. Shinran's message must have been tremendously liberating for the people of his day as it may be in ours.

Shinran's interpretation of Buddhism combines the insights he received as a result of the long years of anxious spiritual search on Hiei, his association with Hōnen and his life among the common people during his teaching career. All his experiences enabled him to perceive the deeper nuances of compassion in Buddhist tradition. In order to make clear his position in the broadening perspective of compassion which he observed in Buddhist history, we shall survey briefly the background of his teaching within the context of the evolving Buddhist tradition.

I Compassion in Buddhist Tradition

As we are well aware, the bases of Buddhism are the qualities of Wisdom and Compassion in the Buddha. These aspects of Buddha are particularly emphasized in the Mahayana tradition. Thus for the Mahayanist the figure of the Bodhisattva replaces that of the Arhat as the symbol of spiritual life. The Bodhisattva begins his spiritual cultivation motivated by the search for his own salvation, and at the same time ends dedicated to the salvation of all beings. The deeper he probes wisdom, the more he finds the heart of compassion.

In the history of Buddhism there has been significant growth in the depth and scope of the meaning of compassion. In this development Pure Land Buddhism is remarkable for its focus on compassion as the motivating force of life. We observe this clearly in comparing Gautama Buddha and Bodhisattva Dharmakara.

In the case of Gautama, he engaged in religious discipline in order to liberate himself from the evils of finite life such as illness, old age, and death. Through this he came to understand the true nature of existence. His first impulse was to leave the world because his way was too subtle and difficult for the masses of people. He at first refused to teach, but an Indian god, Brahmā Sahampati, implored him to remain and work among the people. He conceded and stayed.

In the story of Dharmakara's career, we can see that he was motivated to take up his discipline after he observed the sufferings of the masses and hence dedicated himself to find a way to emancipate them. He contemplated for five kalpas in perfect sincerity and purity and practiced for innumerable kalpas in order to lay the basis for the Pure Land. He became Amida Buddha.[3]

Śākyamuni represents the typical Arhat approach. Dharmakara is the archetypical Bodhisattva. Many critics of Pure Land teaching claim that it replaces Śākyamuni with Amida. However, it was part of the Pure Land revolution to establish new symbols and images to dramatize the way of compassion. The gradual growth in popularity of Amida Pure Land Buddhism in China and Japan is due to the fact that it presented a comprehensive and universal ideal of compassion which gave hope to even the lowest and most sinful person. The system of 48 Vows included every contingency—even the salvation of women in the 35th Vow. The Vows evidence a solidarity among all beings since the Bodhisattva refuses to accept complete enlightenment unless all other beings can share it with him. It is a profound expression of the indivisibility of compassion.

However, there was development in the Pure Land tradition as it gradually overcame the essential moralism of traditional Buddhism. Initially, compassion was a relative quality and depended on the performance of various good deeds whether meditation or recitation of the name. Even though there was an easier way, it was necessary for the individual to be purified of his karmic evil. Amida Buddha was also one Buddha among other Buddhas offering various ways to enlightenment. With Shan-tao (善導, 613-681) the centrality of Amida becomes clear. Only those practices directed to him are most effective. Practices to other Buddhas are to be set aside. They are not wrong—they are unnecessary.

With Hōnen, Amida becomes the sole object of worship, no other Buddha should be addressed. Only the recitation of the name is effective in the last age in the decline of the Dharma (*Mappō*, 末法). Other practices are rejected as not being in harmony with Amida's Vow.

With Shinran a further step in understanding Amida took place which was one of degree, but also one of a kind. He exalted Amida Buddha as the expression of ultimate reality and his Vows as guarantees of salvation, rather than justification for particular practices.

II The Status of Amida Buddha in Shinran's Thought

In Shinran's thought Amida Buddha became the primary and ultimate symbol of reality and its essential compassionate nature. Amida was Reality. Shinran capped the evolution of Amida thought as it developed from the conception of Amida as a supplementary Buddha who could be worshiped and invoked along with other Buddhas and Bodhisattvas in the general Mahayana tradition to a superior Buddha in the Pure Land tradition, which singled Amida out as the most effective source of salvation for this age of decline, to the Supreme Buddha as the ultimate foundation of all reality and the basis of all compassion however it was expressed in Buddhist tradition.

The indication of this transition may be seen in Shinran's use of the term *kuonjitsujō* (久遠実成) which refers to the eternity of the Buddha, that is, Buddha has been Buddha from the most infinite past, there never being a time when he was not Buddha. This term or similar notations appear in Shinran's hymns and invite attention.

Wasan 88 in Shinran's *Jōdo Wasan* collection states:

Amida, the Buddha existing from the eternal past
(*kuonjitsujō Amida Butsu*, 久遠実成)
Pitying the common fools (in the world) of the five defilements,
Appeared in the Castle of Gayā
Manifesting Himself as Śākyamuni Buddha.[4]

Further, stanza 55 provides an interesting contrast in which Shinran juxtaposes the myth of the *Pure Land Sūtra* (*Amidakyō*) to the *Lotus Sūtra*. According to the *Pure Land Sūtra*, Amida became Buddha ten kalpas ago.[5] However, influenced by the *Lotus Sūtra*, Shinran declares that he is actually a Buddha of infinite duration in the past. Thus he writes:

Since Amida became Buddha,
Ten kalpas have passed. So (the sūtra) says.
But He seems to be a Buddha
Older than the innumerable mote-dot kalpas (*jinden kuongō*, 塵点久遠劫).[6]

Evidence for the influence of the *Lotus Sūtra* on Shinran's thought concerning the eternity of Amida Buddha can be found in his comment concerning the meaning of the innumerable mote-dot kalpas (*jinden kuongō*) found in an annotated copy of the *Jōdo Wasan*[7] made by Shinran. He employs a figure in which the age of the Buddha is compared to the amount of time that would pass were the universe to be ground into a powder like that used in ink and a grain was placed in each country in the three thousand-fold worlds of the Cosmos. As there are thousands upon thousands of lands, so there have been thousands upon thousands of kalpas since Amida became Buddha. This imagery was adopted from the *Lotus Sūtra*, chapter sixteen, where it is offered in slightly different form to emphasize the eternity of the Buddha Śākyamuni.[8] In contrast to the bare statement of only ten kalpas of the *Pure Land Sūtra*, Shinran sought a heightened perspective to emphasize that Amida Buddha's eternity, and hence absoluteness, transcends the human ability to calculate.

The term *kuonjitsujō* which Shinran employed was a technical term of Tendai Buddhism implying the ultimacy and eternity of Śākyamuni Buddha as taught in the *Lotus Sūtra*. According to this concept, a Buddha who had neither beginning nor end was more ultimate and spiritually significant than a Buddha who had a beginning but no end (*Mushi-mushū-butsu* 無始無終佛 versus *Ushi-mushū-butsu* 有始無終佛). Having taken over the principle of the *Lotus Sūtra* and applied it to Amida Buddha, Shinran could, therefore, declare that Śākyamuni Buddha was really a manifestation of Amida Buddha in *Wasan 88* quoted above.

In Shinran's effort to exalt Amida Buddha to the highest level of spiritual reality and conception, he also drew upon the distinction of two types of Law Body (*Nishuhosshin* 二種法身)[9] derived from T'an-luan's (Donran 曇鸞 476-542 C.E.) text *Ōjōronchū* (往生論註)[10] and the traditional Mahayana theory of *Trikāya* or three bodies of the Buddha.[11] The theory of two types of Law Body reflects the necessity to correlate the absolute and relative aspects of the nature and function of Buddhahood, while the idea of three bodies attempts to unify the metaphysical, mythological-devotional, and historical relations among the various conceptions of Buddha in Mahayana tradition. Both theories set forth the metaphysical and spiritual meaning of Buddhahood.

Shinran, therefore, employed the terms offered by Buddhist tradition in order to stress the fact that Amida Buddha expressed the fundamental reality of absolute compassion. Amida Buddha was for him the ultimate symbol to which all other Buddhist symbols become secondary or mere shadows. He set forth his view decisively in the *Yuishinshōmon'i*:

> Nirvāṇa is called extinction, non-action (unconditioned), ease, eternal bliss, the True State of things, True Thusness, One Thusness, Buddha Nature, hence, as Buddha Nature, Tathāgata. This Tathāgata fills the infinite world. Thus he fills the minds of the entire ocean of beings. It is taught that the plants, trees and land all become Buddha. Since all beings in their mind trust the Vow of the Law Body of Means, their entrusting mind is Buddha Nature. This Buddha Nature is the Real State of things; the Real State of things, hence the Law Body.
>
> However, in respect to the Buddha, there are two types of Law Body. One is the Law Body of the Real State of things and the other is the Law Body of Means. The Law Body of the Real State is without color or form. Our thought cannot attain to it and our words fail. When form is manifested from the One Thusness, we call it the Law Body of Means. Its form is called Dharmakara Bhikṣu and he aroused the forty-eight great Vows. The Bodhisattva Vasubandhu called the form which was manifested, having as its essence the Original Vows of Infinite Life and Light, the Tathāgata of Universal Unhindered Light. This Tathāgata we call the Tathāgata of the Recompensed Body, being recompensed through the karmic cause of his Vows. Thus we have come to call him Tathāgata Amida.[12]

If we scrutinize this statement closely in its terms and atmosphere, we see that for Shinran Amida is not merely a Buddha among Buddhas. He is a manifestation out of the heart of reality. He fills all and indwells all.

Although the above statement is unequivocal in asserting the ultimacy of Amida, it could be argued that such terms may apply to other Buddhas as well and they do not in themselves imply absoluteness. It is here that the application of the term *kuonjitsujō* to Amida gains its significance. According to Professor Tamura Yoshirō, the concept derives from the theory of the original-unpro-duced-enlightenment (*Hongaku* 本覚) taught in Tendai Buddhism.[13] Shinran, relying on this thought, considered Amida Buddha as *the* expression of the trans-historical Law Body of the Real State of things (*Dharmāta-Dharmakāya*, *Hosshō-hosshin* 法性法身). He thus gave a first theoretical foundation to Pure Land faith and experience, not only in terms of human need, but as a profound way to understand life and reality.

Conclusion

If we try to assess the meaning of these teachings in terms of our contemporary life, we must stress that the Pure Land tradition, and notably Shinran, was show-ing that despite the problems and sufferings of existence, there is hope. Com-passion is the essence of life and reality even when we are unaware of it. It fills the cosmos and it embraces without excluding any. In Shinran's stress on the fulfillment of Amida's Vow, we can see salvation is a present reality. We need no longer fear for our destinies because of our sins and our guilt. The dynamic, existential features of Shinran's thought have been frequently overlooked be-cause he is regarded as teaching otherworldliness which was characteristic of traditional Pure Land thought. In a truly functional way, however, Shinran turned the center of attention of religion from the future world to this world. Re-ligion became a matter of living *now*. Shinran wished to liberate man from his fears generated through centuries of traditional doctrine that failure to believe or practice properly would lead a person to damnation.

The logic of Shinran's understanding of the nature of Amida and the per-fection of his Vows leads to the conclusion that one is saved whether or not he consciously knows about it, or whether he is good or evil. For Shinran Amida's compassion is totally inclusive and universal. His view is expressed poetically in his *Kōsō Wasan*:

> By the benefit of the Unhindered Light,
> The virtuous, great Faith is obtained;
> Assuredly does our evil passion turn into Enlightenment
> As ice melts to water.

> Hindrances of evil become the substance of virtue.
> As with the example of ice and water:
> The greater the ice, the greater the water;

> The greater the hindrance, the greater the virtue.

> In the ocean of the inconceivable Name

Even the corpses of the evil ones and the Dharma-abusers cannot remain as such:
All rivers of evil entering the ocean
Become one taste with the water of virtue.

When many rivers of evil passion enter
Into the ocean of the Great Compassionate Vow
Of the Unhindered Light throughout the ten quarters,
They become one in taste with the water of Wisdom.[14]

We should note in this passage that Shinran extends the meaning of the statement by the patriarch T'an-luan concerning the paths of the Śrāvakas and Pratyekabuddhas, two early types of Buddhist devotees, to cover all evil persons and slanderers of Buddhist teaching who were virtually consigned to hell and excluded from the hope of salvation in Buddhist tradition.[15] Similar condemnation is suggested by the exclusion clause appended to the Eighteenth Vow of the *Larger Pure Land Sūtra.*[16] For Shinran, however, compassion could not be compassion in its deepest sense and exclude anyone. Thus he is quoted in the *Tannishō*:

> We should know that Amida's Original Vow does not discriminate whether one is young or old, good or evil, and that Faith alone is of supreme importance, for it is the Vow that seeks to save the sentient beings burdened with grave sins and fiery passions.
>
> Therefore, if we have Faith in the Original Vow, no other good is needed because there is no good surpassing the Nembutsu. Nor should evil be feared, because there is no evil capable of obstructing Amida's Original Vow.[17]

Since there are no qualifying criteria which control the arising and reception of faith, Shinran, in line with his awareness of the ultimacy of Amida Buddha and the fulfillment of his Vows, rejected all distinctions and conceptions employed in traditional Buddhism to describe Great Faith:

> As I contemplate the ocean-like Great Faith, I see that it does not choose between the noble and the mean, the priest and the layman, nor does it discriminate between man and woman, old and young. The amount of sin committed is not questioned, and the length or practice is not discussed. It is neither "practice" nor "good," neither "abrupt" nor "gradual," neither "meditative" nor "non-meditative," neither "right meditation" nor "wrong meditation," neither "contemplative" nor "non-contemplative," neither "while living" nor "at the end of life," neither "many utterances" nor "one thought." Faith is the inconceivable, indescribable, and ineffable Serene Faith. It is like the *agada* which destroys all poisons. The medicine of the Tathāgata's Vow destroys the poisons of wisdom and ignorance.[18]

According to Shinran, salvation is entirely a matter of the Vow. It does not hang on events and conditions of time and space, or the impositions of man and society. Salvation cannot rest on chance factors. Shinran makes it clear that the completion of the Vow requires nothing from the side of man, including the act of faith, as the causal basis for birth in the Pure Land. Otherwise the emphasis on the fulfillment of the Vow would be devoid of meaning and significance. Our residual karmic bondage may influence the point in our experience when we become aware of Amida's compassion, but it is not a factor in determining whether or not we actually receive that compassion.

We are suggesting that from the standpoint of the Vow all are equally saved even now, despite the presence or absence of the experience of faith itself. The reason for this is that salvation depends on the Vow and not on any finite condition.

Someone may ask then what is the point of being religious, if we are saved in any case? This is an important question. However, it reflects the virtually universal notion that religion is a means to an end. We get the benefit of salvation from being religious. For Shinran, however, religion becomes the way to express gratitude for the compassion that supports all our life. It is not a tool for ego advancement or gaining benefits.

The point of being religious for Shinran is that when we come to have faith in the Original Vow and live in its light, we truly become free to live a full and meaningful existence in this life. If there is some advantage over not being religious, it lies in the fact that people who are religious in the so-called self-powered way and the non-religious are filled with anxiety and fears or a sense of emptiness and meaninglessness in their lives.

Shinran's perspective permits a person to see deeply into his life to detect the springs of compassion which sustain it; it allows him to participate and associate with all types of people despite their unattractiveness or difficulty because he understands the potentiality that works in their very being. In perceiving the compassion that embraces all life, the man of faith can himself become an expression of that compassion touching the lives of others.

Though perhaps we have poorly expressed Shinran's vision of absolute compassion and traveled a complicated path of Buddhist philosophy and interpretation, we hope that we have not distorted too severely the fundamental intention of Shinran to enable people to live with meaning, depth and hope in this life, and leave matters of destiny up to the mystery of Amida's Vow.

NOTES

[1] *Tannishō* 3, Ryukoku Translation Series II (Kyoto: Ryukoku Translation Center, Ryukoku University, 1966), p. 22. (Hereafter other texts in this series are referred to as RTS.)

[2] A. L. Sadler, trans., *The Heike Monogatari*, in *Transactions of the Asiatic Society of Japan* (Vol. 46, pt. II, 1918), pp. 184-185.

[3] *Shinshū Shōgyō Zenshō* I (Kyoto, 1957), p. 7. (Hereafter referred to as SSZ.)

[4] *Jōdo Wasan*, RTS IV (Kyoto: Ryukoku University, 1965), p. 122.

[5] *Amidakyō*, SSZ I, p. 69.

[6] *Jōdo Wasan*, p. 87.

[7] SSZ V, p. 9.

[8] Leon Hurvitz, *Scripture of the Lotus of the Fine Dharma* (New York: Columbia University Press, 1976), pp. 130, 237-238 respectively. See *Jōdo Wasan*, RTS IV, p. 87, note 2.

[9] The two types of Law Body appear in T'an-luan's *Ōjōronchū* (SSZ I, pp. 336-337) when he discusses the meaning of the various descriptions of the Pure Land, Buddhas and Bodhisattvas. He states that there are two dimensions in each Buddha and Bodhisattva. One is the Law Body of True Reality (*Dharmatā-Dharmakāya, Hosshō-hosshin* 法性法身) which is defined as formless and indefinable. It is the realm of absolute principle. The second, and inseparable dimension, is the Law Body of Means (*Hōben-Hosshin* 方便法身) by which the ultimate reality takes a form in order to express and mediate compassion to ordinary people.

[10] SSZ I, 279-349.

[11] The Three Bodies of the Buddha (*Sanshin* 三身) are *Dharmakāya* (*Hosshin* 法身) or Law Body, the ultimate principle; *Sambhogakāya* (*Hōjin* 報身), or Body of Recompense which is the result for the sincere endeavor of the Bodhisattva and is based on the realization of the principle of cause and effect, whereby one enjoys the fruits of one's endeavors; and finally, *Nirmānakāya* (*Keshin* 化身) or Body of Transformation (or Manifestation) which refers to the various forms a Buddha may take to deal with beings.

[12] SSZ II, pp. 630-631.

[13] Tamura Yoshirō, *Kamakura Shinbukkyō Shisō no Kenkyū* (Kyoto: Heirakuji Shoten, 1966), p. 532.

[14] *Kōsō Wasan*, RTS VI (Kyoto: Ryukoku University, 1974), pp. 62-65.

[15] *Ibid.*, p. 64. The passage in T'an-luan's *Ōjōronchū* (SSZ I, p. 302) on which this stanza is based reads: "The 'ocean' refers to the fact that the Buddha's all-knowing Wisdom is deep, broad and endless, not leaving as they are the corpses of middle and lower sages (i.e., pratyekabuddhas and śrāvakas) of the Two Vehicles who perform miscellaneous good deeds. Thus it is likened to an ocean."

[16] SSZ I, p. 9. The Vow reads: "If all those beings hear that name, believe and rejoice even for one thought (moment), and sincerely transfer (the merit of the thought) desiring to be born in that Land, then they will obtain rebirth and abide in the state of non-retrogression. Only those are excluded who have committed the five deadly sins and slandered the *Dharma*." (Author's translation)

The five deadly sins include parricide, matricide, killing an arhat, shedding the blood of a Buddha, and destroying the harmony of the Sangha (See W. E. Soothill, and L. Hodous, *A Dictionary of Chinese Buddhist Terms* [Kaohsiung, Taiwan: Buddhist Culture Service, n.d.] p. 128a). The five deadly sins incur the penalty of perpetual hell (*Avīci*) where one suffers continually. They represent the most profound and serious sins contemplated in Buddhism (See H. Nakamura, *Bukkyōgo Daijiten* [Tokyo: Tokyo Shoseki Kabushiki-gaisha, 1975] I, p. 357). Those who slander the Dharma are also reborn in the hell of perpetual suffering and lack the basis for becoming Buddhas (H. Nakamura, *Bukkyōgo Daijiten*, II, p. 1322, *Mukenjigoku*).

[17] *Tannishō*, RTS II, p. 16.

[18] *Kyōgyōshinshō*, RTS V (Kyoto: Ryukoku University, 1966), pp. 113-114.

CHAPTER 9

RELIGIOUS TRANSFORMATION AND LANGUAGE IN SHINRAN

—DENNIS HIROTA

In the Pure Land Buddhist tradition, particularly as developed by Shinran (1173-1263), the religious path is integrated with language.[1] It is the "path of easy practice" (*igyōdō*), in contrast to the "path of difficult practice" (*nangyōdō*) or the "Path of Sages" (*shōdōmon*), precisely because it provides a way to enlightenment—or contact with the real—through and in the medium of language. In this, *Jōdo shinshū* ("the true essence of the Pure Land way") as articulated by Shinran differs from Buddhist traditions in which delusional thought and conceptualization are broken through by means of meditative practices and disciplines. Authentic engagement with the Pure Land path is not, however, simply an intellectual grasp or acceptance of the verbal teaching, but involves a shift in the awareness of language itself. We are moved from an appropriation of the teaching into our conventionally perceived universe to a realization of language as false and true in Shinran's senses. On the one hand, conceptions of self and world are seen to be shaped by the attachments and judgments of the egocentric self and become fabrications ("empty talk and gibberish"). On the other hand, "the Name alone is true and real."[2] It is accessible to our understanding, yet makes present that which transcends false conception, being characterized by the nondualities of word and reality and of act and word. To hear the Buddha's Vow as true language is to "realize shinjin" or attain the Buddha's mind. Thus, the teaching has a therapeutic function, illuminating the falsity of the thought and speech ordinarily generated by human beings, and at the same time, as true word, it enters and transforms their thought and speech.

The nature of the language of the path may be approached by distinguishing two phases in authentic engagement with it: the point of entrance into such engagement and its subsequent unfolding in the practicer's life. These two phases or dimensions correspond, in Shinran's terms, to realization of shinjin ("hearing the Name") and performance of practice ("saying the Name of the Tathāgata of Unhindered Light"). Shinran's assertion of the essential unity of these phases holds a critical place in his thought, for it was by delineating his conception of shinjin that he sought to clarify the fundamental nature of practice in Hōnen's teaching. Thus he states: "Saying the Name is the right act, supreme, true, and excellent. The right act is the nembutsu. The nembutsu is Namu-amida-butsu.

Namu-amida-butsu is right-mindedness."[3] Here, the equivalency of utterance, reality, word, and thought (shinjin) is asserted. Elsewhere he states regarding nembutsu: "'Thinking' and 'voicing' have the same meaning; no voicing exists separate from thinking, and no thinking separate from voicing."[4]

The transformative character of shinjin and nembutsu and their internal continuity—a thorny problem in traditional Shin scholastics—may be best understood by taking into account the linguistic dimension of the path, in which authentic engagement (hearing and saying the Name) functions as the locus of the simultaneous and inseparable presence of samsaric existence and true reality. Below, I will consider first the moment of hearing the Name as entrance into such engagement, then the development of this hearing as linguistic activity unfolding in the practicer's ongoing existence. These two phases are also depicted in the accompanying Diagrams I and II.

I Entrance into Authentic Engagement: Hearing the Name as the Transformation of Self

Shinran interprets the phrase "hear the Name" from the *Larger Sūtra* passage teaching the fulfillment of the Eighteenth Vow as signifying realization of shinjin; it expresses entrance into authentic engagement in linguistic terms, or entrance into a new realm of language, which implies a new mode of awareness. This awareness is not attainment of nondiscriminative wisdom in which the subject-object dichotomy that characterizes delusional thought and perception has been eradicated; nevertheless, a new, transformative paradigm of apprehension of self, world, and true reality emerges in which the subject-object dichotomy has lost its domination.

The new paradigm is characterized not by the centrality of an autonomous self as subject discerning and relating itself to the elements of the teaching (Amida, Name, Pure Land) as objects, but rather by the dual presence, emerging inseparably and in opposition, of self as false, samsaric existence and Vow or Name as true reality. Self and Vow together become present in this way at the very point that a boundary between them arises, as two faces of that boundary. Here, the motion of the self acting to possess the elements of the path is arrested; nevertheless, the person who realizes shinjin gains a new apprehension that occurs as the appearing of the boundary itself. This happens in two ways. On the one hand, the boundary arises as the horizon of the self, delimiting and defining one's entire existence and the dimensions of its possibilities. On the other hand, with the breakdown of the effort directed toward rectifying the self by assimilating what is true and good and expelling what is evil, this horizon takes form as, and thus manifests, an opposite movement—the approach to the self of inconceivable true reality emerging as the Name.

To delineate this new mode of awareness and the relationships that underlie it, it is necessary to cut across the subject-object cleavage of practicer and Vow that dominates initial, self-power engagement. This may be accomplished by considering the process of entrance in terms of negative and positive aspects that occur simultaneously.

(1) Dissolution of the Conceptual Frameworks of Provisional (Self-Power) Engagement

Provisional engagement is informed by the activity ("doubt") of an inner self that objectifies and judges the self, its world, and the teaching, seeking to enhance its own existence by achieving good and avoiding evil.[5] It is expressed in Shinran's writings as "belief in the recompense of good and evil and reliance on [one's own practice of] the root of good (nembutsu)." Here, two elements are implied: (1) the frameworks of ordinary thought—including causality and the discrimination of good and evil—within which the practicer as subject grasps the elements of the path and his or her involvement with them; and (2) the motive force or effort to incorporate what is good into the self and eliminate from the self and its world what is evil—expressed, in Shinran's words, as relying on the nembutsu as "one's own good act."

When the inner self that manifests itself as the imposition of these frameworks emerges not as the arbiter of true good and evil but rather as the reified activity of the fundamental blind passions of desire (appropriation of good) and aversion (eradication of evil) rooted in self-attachment, the means of judging the existence of the self and determining the path disintegrate. The stance of the absolutized self has been engulfed in the very evil it sought to differentiate and distance itself from; thus, the drive to establish one's existence through moral rectification is uprooted. With regard to the practicer, this aspect is the "overturning of the mind of self-power."

With the dissolution of the stance of the subject of provisional engagement that seeks to disengage itself from its own past and from the flux of existence in the world together with other beings, one's conception of oneself—as the objectified self acting to amend itself—loses its clear outlines. To employ the images of the teaching, one's existence becomes coextensive with time stretching back into the "beginningless past," and one's present bears the influence of the acts in other lifetimes, as other selves, in other circumstances of existence. The self becomes fluid, a tissue of acts permeating the temporal boundaries of this life, and is fused to the past through unknowable deeds that remain as traces in the present. Moreover, not only temporally, but "spatially" as well, the fixed boundaries of the objectified self and its separateness from the "outside" world melt, and there emerges an awareness of the self as floundering in an ocean of existence with other beings. With regard to the elements of the path, there is likewise a dissolution as the frameworks in which they had been grasped instrumentally cease to define them. When the thinking that had guided one's acts in establishing a relationship between oneself and Amida as person and Pure Land as goal loses its capacity even to determine what is good and effective for achieving its ends, the conceptions of Amida and Pure Land themselves are invalidated (in fact they correspond to no more than "transformed buddha-bodies and lands"), and the Name, above all, ceases to function as a means for invoking the Buddha or gaining merit for progress to the Pure Land. With the dismantling of the parameters of interpersonal or teleological relationships with the self, Amida's Vow can no longer be located in a linear, temporal past of this world—as a principle set in motion that one can bring one's life into accord with; further, the Pure Land cannot be located as an extension of the spatial coordinates of this existence. Buddha and Pure Land fulfilled through the Vow cease to be meaningfully conceived through calculative thinking.

(i) Boundary as Interfusion: Apprehension of Reality as Hearing the Name

Entrance into authentic engagement is the perforation and transformative relocation of the boundary of the self. This new boundary not only circumscribes the self, but also manifests the presence of that which stands beyond, transcending the self and its conceptual universe. The presence of this far side of the boundary is apprehended as the Name; that is, the arising of the horizon of the practicer's existence is itself also the hearing of the Name. This hearing is not one's perceiving and arrogating the path that stands apart from oneself; precisely such a subject-object relationship marks provisional, self-power engagement. Rather, it is the arising of the horizon that simultaneously divides and conjoins the polar opposites of false existence and true reality, so that both sides become loci of new apprehension.

The dissolution of the elements of the path as objectified by calculative thinking signifies their extrication from our usual frames of reference, but not a lapse into mere meaninglessness. This is because it is the teaching itself that moves the practicer toward the collapse of the "doubled" (self-judgmental) self, and because at the same time it provides—in the Name—the means for a new mode of apprehension. This is the meaning of Shinran's statements that shinjin arises from, and is given as, Amida's Vow. Thus, there is a circularity from the teaching to the realization of shinjin, and from realization of shinjin to a new understanding of the teaching, or to an apprehension of the language of the path as words made new.

Concerning the first phase of this reciprocal movement, the narrative of Dharmākara-Amida sets forth the bodhisattva's practice so that it stands in contrast with the efforts of beings. The acts of sentient beings and the acts of Buddha are represented as antithetical dimensions of blind passions and wisdom, falsity and true reality. Shinran further underscores this opposition by emphasizing, in the narrative, the purity of Dharmākara's practice in each of its moments. Thus, the fulfillment of the Vow does not stand simply at the conclusion of aeons of practice, but is brought into every moment of that practice, so that the Vow-narrative contracts into a mode of temporality removed from our usual conceptual frameworks. Here, the opposition between being and Buddha becomes one of temporal existence and that which transcends it at every point, or the life of the self within the world and that which pervades the life of the world as one.

This compression of the Vow's establishment and fulfillment into each moment of Dharmākara's practice has its parallel in the field of language. The Vow-narrative moves toward its own condensation into the Name of Amida, in the same way removing itself from our usual frameworks of understanding. It is not simply that the Name lies at the end of a long process leading to its establishment; rather, it is of the nature of the Vow that the Name embody all the elements of the entire narrative—aspiration for Buddhahood, aeons of practice, attainment of wisdom-compassion, liberation of all beings—which are together rooted in reality (formless dharma-body). It is for this reason that Shinran explains "hearing the Name" as hearing "how the Buddha's Vow arose—its origin and fulfillment,"[6] and also as occurring as "one thought-moment." These movements toward condensation, temporal and linguistic, fuse in the thought-moment of realization of shinjin. This hearing the Name and its instantaneity signify the total compression of the Vow, which is also the complete extrication of the path from a discursive grasp and any calculated process of attainment. The nembutsu ceases to be one's own good, being disentangled from causal frameworks that center on the acts of the self, and comes to be apprehended rather as a movement toward one. In Shinran's emphasis on the Name as Amida's call to beings and on the Seventeenth Vow that Buddhas throughout all time and the entire cosmos say and praise the Name, we find an image for this approach. It is precisely at the point where the horizontal, linear frames of reference condense that this Name emerges as the presence of reality beyond conceptual grasp.

(2) Dual Presence of Samsaric Existence and True Reality

The realization of shinjin may also be discussed in affirmative terms, as a mode of apprehension in which the existence of the self and true reality arise together to awareness, even while they lie beyond the thought and conception of the self possessed of blind passions and ignorance. This apprehension may be grasped as a double-sided re-delineation of the limits or boundary of one's own existence.

(i) **Boundary as Horizon: Apprehension of Self and World as Samsaric**

While on the one hand practicers are bereft of the power of self-definition and self-direction, having been forced to relinquish the absoluteness of their frames of reference, on the other hand, they have, from another perspective, overcome the fragmentation of the self—the incessant bifurcation into absolute subject and amenable object, together with the division of self from other beings and the world—and been enabled to apprehend their existence entire. For the self—whose center, as the judge of the worth and destiny of the self, has dissolved—to be apprehended whole is for the delimiting horizon of its own existence to arise. That is, the self at once loses its own definition as absolute and enduring and comes to apprehend itself as samsaric existence in entirety. These two aspects—dissolution and holistic apprehension—are inseparable and can arise only together.

Here, the existence of the self, conditioned by its history and its acts and circumstances, moves in inevitable circularity. It rises to self-awareness as samsaric only where it is thoroughly bounded and circumscribed temporally at every possible point. Though one had sought or assumed within that circle a stable, undistorted point of reference for determining one's existence, apprehension of the whole must include the relinquishment of the very possibility of any such stance. When the self is apprehended thus, all possibility of establishing a basis for one's own liberation must be abandoned. This is the meaning of overcoming the fragmentation of the self in its temporal aspect through the collapse of the doubled self.

There is also a "spatial" aspect, for it is precisely the arising of the horizon of the self and the collapse of the doubled, inner self that leads to the falling away of the distinction the self had sought to construct and enforce between its own existence and the world of existence together with other beings. This aspect is vividly expressed in Shinran's words in *Tannishō*, 5: "All sentient beings, without exception, have been my parents and brothers and sisters in the course of countless lives in many states of existence." He makes this statement in explaining his refusal to say the nembutsu for the repose of his parents. The basic reason is his incapacity to fulfill any good act whose merit he might turn over to others. This is an expression of his awareness of the horizon of his existence as wholly samsaric. He goes on, however, to stress the absurdity of blandly assuming that one can direct merit to one's ancestors—a powerful element of Japanese religiosity—by pointing out the interrelationships between oneself and all other beings, so that to save one's parents would be to save countless multitudes of living things. We see here the intimate link between the self-awareness of one's own existence as bounded and samsaric and the awareness of that existence—precisely in being samsaric—as intertwined with the existence of all beings. All living things come to manifest the possibilities and limits of one's own existence.

This is the perception underlying the expression, "this self possessed of blind passions, this world that is a burning house." It calls to mind the vision of Bodhisattva Dharmākara, who is enabled through the power of Lokesvararaja Buddha to survey all worlds and beings before establishing the Primal Vow. In fact, it points to the opposite side of the newly formed boundary of the self: the active face of reality that comes to pervade one's existence.

(ii) Hearing as the Crystallization of Reality in the Name

Where the path approaches to touch one's own existence (condenses into the Name), the horizon of the self arises and the hearing of the Name occurs. That the Name is heard, then, means that it is apprehended as the crystallization of the Vow-narrative, a gestalt in which wisdom-compassion is compressed. It is this apprehension that underlies Shinran's creation of altar scrolls in which sculpted or painted images of Amida Buddha are replaced by the written characters of the Name, in one of several versions, in a vertical line with a lotus pedestal beneath. Here, the Name has the character of form that is at the same time formless reality, of language that is pervaded by the silence of astonishment or inconceivability. On the one hand, it is true reality (wisdom-compassion, unhindered light) that has coalesced at the boundary of the self; on the other hand, it is itself the boundary of the self in karmic existence that has arisen through the falling away of calculative thought. Shinran states in a hymn:

> The light shines everywhere ceaselessly;
> Thus Amida is called Buddha of Uninterrupted Light.
> Because beings hear this power of light,
> Their mindfulness is enduring and they attain birth.[7]

To hear the Name is to hear or apprehend the power of light, and this light or hearing becomes enduring mindfulness in the hearer.

The Name can embody these movements—contraction and emergence—because of its dual character as true language or as word that is also silence. The movement of condensation occurs along the horizontal vector, when the entire span of the Vow-narrative, extricated from temporal, conceptual frameworks, fuses into and becomes present as one thought-moment. The movement of emergence occurs along the vertical vector at that very point of condensation, when the Name becomes the opposite face of the horizon of the self as samsaric existence.

Shinran's altar scrolls include another innovation in addition to the representation of Amida Buddha as Name: the inscription of scriptural texts above and below the central image. It may be said that text and Name stand not only in the circular relationship between teaching and realization mentioned above, but also in the dialectical one between horizontal and vertical that we have been delineating. The texts free themselves from conceptual grasp and condense into the Name, which is encountered as another face of the horizon of the self. At the same time, however, Shinran speaks of the "ultimate brevity *and expansion* of the length of time in which one attains the mind and practice that result in birth in the Pure Land."[8] Thus, the one thought-moment of hearing the Name unfolds in acts of language, which now newly articulate the nature of self and world in fulfilled engagement with the path. Let us consider this "expansion" next.

Diagram I. Entrance into authentic engagement

The classic formulation of a paradigm of Pure Land Buddhist religious awareness is Shan-tao's two aspects of deep mind. Traditional Shin discussions of it, however, tend to remain doctrinal and intellectualized because the shift into such awareness has not been explored. The entrance into authentic engagement set forth in this article, focusing on the domain of language (as Shinran does in *Tannishō*), may be diagrammed:

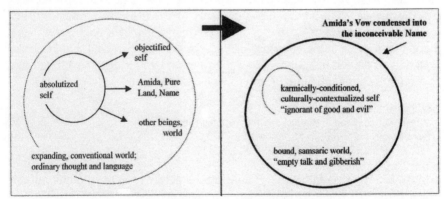

(a) Provisional engagement: doubled self of calculative thinking that assesses its own acts and its condition in the world: "Endeavoring to make oneself worthy", "reflecting knowingly on one's evil"; "making the nembutsu one's own good act"; "judging people as good and bad."

(b) Moment of entrance into authentic engagement: collapse of calculation simultaneous with the arising of the double-sided horizon of the world of the self and the Vow. The boundness of one's existence emerges interfused with the hearing of the Name as the presence of transcendent reality.

Realization of shinjin as the movement from (a) to (b) includes: 1. the dissolution of any stance for an inner, reified subject that can buttress itself by assimilating what it judges good and distancing itself from "evil" that threatens it; 2. the freeing of the path (Buddha, Pure Land, nembutsu) from objectification within the coordinates of conventional thought and self-serving efforts to appropriate and utilize it; 3. the arising of a holistic apprehension of the limits or horizon of one's existence together with other beings as a web of acts characterized by the passions of self-attachment and by the inescapable falsity of one's thoughts and perceptions shaped by ordinary language; 4. the presence to oneself of that which is real (as life, light), apprehended in the hearing of the Name.

The horizon (or dual presence of Name as compassionate reality and self and world as samsaric existence) depicted as holistic and instantaneously emerging in I (b) represents not an objective, doctrinally dictated barrier between being and Buddha but rather a fundamentally altered mode of existence and awareness. To depict this, it must be recast (as in Diagram II) to manifest the dynamics that evolve with regard to the practicer's life. Where calculative thinking collapses and the path condenses into the Name, all linear relations between one's acts and the Vow are severed by the radical disjunction between them. Here, there is no basis for genuine awareness of the path embedded in a subject-object dichotomy. The horizon itself, however, in its linguistic character as the Name, enters the practicer's awareness and holds together two transformative moments in which its dimension of polar opposition arises and simultaneously is overcome—allowing first interfusion [Diagram II (b^1)] and then interaction [Diagram II (b^2)] with Vow and world—without being dissolved. This is the basic model of shinjin as both salvific (attainment of transcendent reality) and interrelational (providing for a coherent apprehension of self, path, and world) in Shinran's writings.

II Human Existence as Authentic Engagement: Saying the Name as Transformation

Shinran speaks of hearing the Vow or Name as transformative. He states, for example, that when one "encounters" the Vow—entrusts oneself to its power—"all roots of good and all virtues" become "perfectly full in one's heart."[9] Further: "because one entrusts oneself to the power of Amida's Vow—this is the absence of calculation on the part of the practicer—one cuts off and abandons the five evil courses and becomes free of the four modes of birth naturally (*jinen*)."[10] When one hears the Name, one is "filled" with the Buddha's virtues (wisdom-compassion), so that bondage to samsaric existence is broken. From the perspective of the Name, the aspect of nonduality in the arising of the double-sided horizon dominates, for the "Name embodying the perfectly fulfilled supreme virtues is true wisdom that transforms our evil into virtue,"[11] or into itself. Shinran expresses this nonduality with regard to the practicer's condition also:

> The directing of virtue for our going forth is such
> That when Amida's active means toward us reaches fulfillment,
> We realize the shinjin and practice of the compassionate Vow;
> Then birth-and-death is itself nirvāṇa.[12]

Here we see the fundamental elements of the model of realizing shinjin that we have sketched above: that which is real touches human existence where the origin and fulfillment of the Vow coalesce as the Name and the path condenses into a single instant; here, word and reality are nondual. This occurs when hearing the Name is the collapse of the inner self that objectifies the self and the path. The bifurcation of the self through assuming the stance of an absolutized self of calculative thinking is overcome, and the distinction of self and path as subject and object falls away. Engagement with the teaching is liberated from ordinary discursiveness and self-objectification, and the Name becomes a transparency (light, wisdom), pervaded by a silence in which instrumentality is replaced by the presence of that which transcends conceivability. Thus, act and word are also nondual. The result is the emergence of the dual presence of practicer (samsaric existence) and true reality together with the transformation in which birth-and-death is itself nirvāṇa. Shinran uses the metaphors of the practicer being filled by the ocean of Amida's virtues or their blind passions flowing into and become one with the ocean of the Vow (mind of compassion) to express this.

There are several points to be noted concerning this transformation. First, it occurs without the conscious effort or even awareness of the practicer: "In entrusting ourselves to Amida's Primal Vow and saying the Name once, necessarily, without seeking it, we are made to receive the supreme virtues, and without knowing it, we acquire the great and vast benefit."[13] This attainment of supreme virtues is not brought about through the practicer's will or endeavor; rather, it occurs precisely where calculative thinking falls away and the elements of the path are removed from our usual frames of reference. Thus, it takes place instantaneously, apart from causal processes we might initiate; with utter decisiveness; and at a level deeper than ordinary awareness. For this reason, Shinran adopts the term *jinen* to characterize the dynamic of this transformation, explaining simply that, free of designs, "one is made to become so."

At the same time, however, the transformation does not remain confined to the one thought-moment of realization of shinjin or to an instant that transcends temporal existence:

> "To be made to become so" means that without the practicer's calculating in any way whatsoever, all his past, present, and future evil karma is transformed into good. "To be transformed" means that evil karma, without being nullified or eradicated, is made into good, just as all waters, upon entering the great ocean, immediately become ocean water.[14]

We see here that while transformation occurs with realization of shinjin, it encompasses, without negating, the practicer's entire temporal existence, including all the acts that make up ongoing life. Thus, two moments may be distinguished with regard to this transformation: the moment of realizing shinjin, when it fundamentally and irreversibly takes place ("virtues quickly and rapidly become perfectly full in the heart"[15]), and the moment of ongoing life when evil acts continue to be transformed into good while remaining evil. While the first moment of transformation permeates one's existence in its unconscious depths, the second suggests that, though not brought about by conscious endeavor, transformation is not wholly beyond the awareness of beings. Thus Shinran states that "constant mindfulness of the Primal Vow arises in persons of shinjin naturally (by *jinen*)."[16]

Transformation comprises these two moments because it is inseparable from the opposition that, together with the nonduality or simultaneity that does not nullify it, characterizes the arising of the double sided horizon of the self. Shinran speaks of transformation precisely because it is the arising of the horizon—with the attendant collapse of calculative thinking—that allows for the presence of reality to emerge. At the same time, it is not that reality is present prior to the arising of the horizon of the self (hearing the Name), nor can beings carrying on their ordinary lives directly realize the nonduality that marks the stance of the Name as wisdom or suchness: "We are full of ignorance and blind passions. Our desires are countless ... to the very last moment of life they do not cease." Here, the opposition of true reality and samsaric existence is also one of wisdom and ignorance. Nevertheless, the Name "breaks through all the ignorance of sentient beings and fulfills all their aspirations," and "the compassionate light of the Buddha of unhindered light always illumines and protects the person who has realized shinjin; hence the darkness of ignorance has already cleared." Shinran asserts that ignorance both remains and is dispersed.

This condition reflects the complex nature of the Name, which is reality that transcends conception and as such transforms practicers's existence without their knowing or seeking it, and which is also characterized by form and thus is accessible to conscious apprehension. The second moment of transformation signifies the functioning of the Name, with its two dimensions, to integrate the nonduality of reality with the practicers' ongoing existence so that it rises to conscious awareness. Thus, Shinran states that practicers "should truly receive the Name of the Primal Vow/ And never forget it, whether waking or sleeping." [17] To "truly receive (信受, *shinju*) the Name" is to realize shinjin; it is the crystallization of wisdom-compassion as the Name at the horizon of one's existence. Another face of this reception of the Name, however, is that one "never forgets it, whether waking or sleeping." The unfolding of the transformative moment into the whole of one's life is accomplished through the linguistic dimension of human existence. It is as and through word (Name) that reality continuously transforms the person's life. The Name possesses this power because it functions not simply as another word of conceptual thought, but more basically as a new, double-faceted paradigm of language underlying all linguistic activity and awareness.[18]

For Shinran, the conviction in one's own powers to determine finally what is good and what is evil is the motive force that lies at the core of a person's acts of self-attachment. It is what he calls calculative thinking or hakarai. Although, in Shinran's view, as long as we live, we will remain persons of blind passions, with waves of jealousy, anger, and desire rising in our hearts, with the realization of shinjin and the self-awareness of our conditionedness, such thoughts and emotions are defused and may gradually be deprived of their power to dominate us.

But if we are ignorant of good and evil, how are we to conduct our lives?

Just as persons of shinjin continue to live out the consequences of their acts, for the Buddha plays no role to either judge or forgive, and yet live each moment within the working of Amida's Vow, so they continue to live in the world of false discrimination and delusional attachments, and yet their awareness is pervaded by the Name of Amida. Thus, they do not draw the lines of good and evil, and seek to establish their good and eradicate their own and others' evil. It is stated:

> Even when our thoughts and deeds are evil, if we thereby turn all the more deeply to the power of the Vow, gentleheartedness and forbearance will surely arise in us naturally (*jinen*, i.e., through the spontaneous working of the Buddha's mind of wisdom-compassion).[19]

The realization of shinjin is the collapse of any stance for an absolutized subject to view, judge, and impose its will on itself and the world. This does not mean, however, that the world is perceived as a morally homogeneous flatland or that a person is merely passive. The terrain is newly marked, not by determinations of gain and loss or right and wrong that shore up the righteousness of the self, but by a heightened and acute sense of both pain and gratitude—the pain visited on other living beings and the expenditure of life-energy borne by the closely interwoven world that is the cost for one's own existence, and the joy in and gratitude for one's own life as the locus of the activity of wisdom-compassion that arises in one's acts from beyond the delusional horizons of the self. Out of such awareness emerges the vocation of the Pure Land Buddhist, which is the call to see and experience the self and the beings of the world anew, not objectified, but with ever greater breadth and clarity.

In terms of the teaching, this is to live by Amida's Name and light. The Shin Buddhist's job of work is to hear and say the nembutsu. This is for one's self and world to become manifest to the self; it is for one to come to speak what is true within ordinary words and to enact what is real within the contexts of daily life. The obligation of the Shin path is above all to know the self and world by the exercise of such awareness, for such knowing allows for the arising of a world of action in which the reified self is no longer absolute center.

Diagram II. Two inseparable moments of transformation in authentic engagement

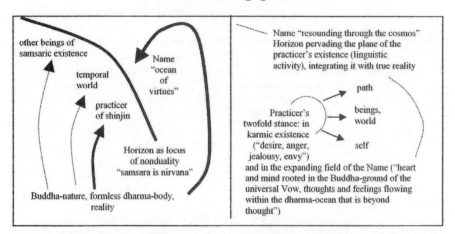

(b¹) The primary moment of transformation: arising of the double-sided horizon as the emergence of the nonduality of delusional existence and true reality. Word and reality are one ("From this oneness form was manifested") and act of hearing and reality are one ("shinjin is none other than Buddha-nature"). Here, the horizon as nondual reality further signifies that "Tathāgata pervades the countless worlds ... Thus, plants, trees, and land all attain Buddhahood."

(b²) Continuous transformation in the present: the horizon (self as blind passions/reality as Vow) arises anew as the saying of the Name —voiceless and voiced, unconscious and conscious—within the linguistically-shaped and karmically-bound acts that make up one's ongoing temporal existence. Thus, "the minds, good and evil, of foolish beings are immediately transformed into the mind of great compassion," and further, "the more ice of passions, the more water of enlightenment."

In Shinran's thought, the Name as true language (conception permeated by inconceivability, or "horizontal" and "vertical" planes interfused) harbors the nonduality of samsaric existence and true reality. Reality cannot be attained through a subject-object relationship (acquisition of the elements of the path), but neither can it be encountered by human understanding without engagement with the path (cannot be reached simply through reflection into the self or upon reality). The horizon arising as the Name, however, without allowing any objectification of reality, is itself also the presence of dharma-body that fills and unites oneself and all beings (b¹). The teaching as the unfolding of the Name, based on this simultaneous nonduality and polarity of practicer and Buddha, comprises a bridgework of dialectically interactive conceptual structures that discloses to apprehension the ineffable reality in its depths. Thus, Amida "gives" his mind to ignorant beings possessed of blind passions or "grasps" them with the light of wisdom; the "boundlessness ... and all-inclusiveness of the Tathāgata's virtues is likened to the unobstructed fullness of the ... ocean," and those virtues flood the practicers' hearts. Conversely, their "rivers of blind passions, on entering the ocean of the Vow ... become one in taste with that sea of wisdom"; "blind passions and enlightenment become one body and are not two."

This nonduality does not signify eradication of delusional thought or attainment of nondiscriminative wisdom; therefore Shinran states, with regard to Buddha, that Amida's light is "unhindered" by beings' passions, and with regard to beings, that they attain the Buddha's virtues without knowing or seeking it and that their evil is transformed into good without being nullified. In other words, nonduality underlies the double-sided horizon, but thought and perception remain linguistic and conceptual. Nevertheless, because of this dimension of nonduality, Shinran speaks of the "wisdom of shinjin" ("since Amida's Vow is wisdom, the emergence of the mind of entrusting oneself to it is the arising of wisdom") and "nembutsu that is wisdom" (*Hymns of the Dharma-Ages*, 34-35). In fact, it is through the Name in its character as linguistic act that integration of one's ongoing existence with true reality occurs. Passions still arise, but with the dissolution of calculative thinking that absolutizes the "inner" self, they are divested of the directedness and the driving force of the intellect, which functions instead to alleviate them. That is, the Name as the arising of the double-sided horizon comes to form the core of the practicer's words, which are transformed by it into false language (delusional thought and blind passions that harbor the inconceivability of the Name as the illumination of their own falsity and distorted perceptions of the world) and into true language (words with the power to presence and disclose the horizon's dimensions of polarity and nonduality to oneself and others) (b^2).

NOTES

[1] This article is a highly condensed summary of portions of a longer study, "Shinran's View of Language: A Buddhist Hermeneutics of Faith," *Eastern Buddhist*, 26:1 (Spring 1993), 50-93 and 26:2 (Autumn 1993), 91-130. For a version in Japanese, see my book, *Shinran: Shūkyō gengo no kakumeisha* (Kyoto: Hōzōkan, 1998).

[2] "For a foolish being of blind passions, in this fleeting world—this burning house—all matters without exception are lies and gibberish, totally without truth and sincerity. The nembutsu alone is true and real." See *Tannishō*, "Postscript," in Dennis Hirota, trans., *Tannishō: A Primer* (Kyoto: Ryūkoku University, 1982), 44, and D. Hirota et al., trans., *The Collected Works of Shinran* (CWS), (Kyoto: Jōdo Shinshū Hongwanji-ha, 1997), 1:679.

[3] *The True Teaching, Practice, and Realization of the Pure Land Way*, "Chapter on Practice," 12 (CWS 1:18; SSZ 2:8). Also see "Chapter on Practice," 77 (CWS 1:56; SSZ 2:35).

[4] *Notes on "Essentials of Faith Alone"* (CWS 1:468; SSZ 2:637).

[5] For a discussion of my distinction between initial or provisional engagement and fulfilled or authentic engagement, see my article, "Breaking the Darkness: Images of Reality in the Shin Buddhist Path," *Japanese Religions*, 16:3 (January 1991), 17-45. A version of this article

may also be found in D. Hirota, ed., *Toward a Contemporary Understanding of Pure Land Buddhism* (Albany, N. Y.: State University of New York Press, 2000), 33-72.

[6] "Chapter on Shinjin," 65 (CWS 1:112; SSZ 2:72).

[7] *Hymns of the Pure Land*, 12 (CWS 1:327; SSZ 2:487).

[8] *Passages on the Pure Land Way* (CWS 1:298; SSZ 2:445).

[9] *Notes on Once-Calling and Many-Calling* (CWS 1:487; SSZ 2:616).

[10] *Notes on the Inscriptions on Sacred Scrolls*, 37 (CWS 1:496; SSZ 2:580).

[11] *The True Teaching, Practice, and Realization of the Pure Land Way*, "Preface" (CWS 1: 3; SSZ 2:1).

[12] *Hymns of the Pure Land Masters*, 35 (on T'an-luan) (CWS 1:370; SSZ 2:505).

[13] *Notes on Once-Calling and Many-Calling* (CWS 1:481; SSZ 2:611). Also: "Though people of the diamond-like mind neither know nor seek it, the vast treasure of virtues completely fills them," (*Notes on Once-Calling and Many-Calling* [CWS 1:487; SSZ 2:617]).

[14] *Notes on "Essentials of Faith Alone"* (CWS 1:453; SSZ 2:623).

[15] *Notes on Once-Calling and Many-Calling* (CWS 1:487; SSZ 2:616).

[16] *Notes on "Essentials of Faith Alone"* (CWS 1:454; SSZ 2:623).

[17] *Hymns of the Pure Land Masters*, 96 (on Genshin) (CWS 1:386; SSZ 2:512).

[18] The thought of Ippen (1239-1289) affords an example of focus on the point of the arising of the Name (one "discards one's self-being and becomes solitary and single with Namu-amida-butsu"), so that "the nembutsu says the nembutsu", without the counterbalancing movement of the second moment of transformation. See Dennis Hirota, *No Abode: The Record of Ippen* (Honolulu: University of Hawaii Press, 1997), p. lxxi ff.

[19] *Tannishō: A Primer*, p. 40, and CWS 1:676.

CHAPTER 10

FREEDOM AND NECESSITY IN SHINRAN'S CONCEPT OF KARMA[1]

—UEDA YOSHIFUMI

(TRANSLATED BY DENNIS HIROTA)[2]

The concept of karma existed prior to the rise of Buddhism, and though quickly adopted into Buddhist thought, its precise role in the early tradition and its relationship to such concepts as the five aggregates and dependent origination remain topics of controversy among modern scholars. It may be said, however, that in Mahāyāna tradition, the major significance of karma lies in its expression of temporal existence from the stance of the no-self nature (anātmatā) of all things.[3] The bodhisattva, in realizing prajñāpāramitā, thoroughly breaks through discriminative thinking and comes to stand in suchness. At that time, he attains dharmakāya or "reality-body," but he does not simply remain in the realm of the formless, where the subject-object dichotomy has been completely obliterated. Dharmakāya holds within itself the nonduality of the karma-created (saṃskṛta) and the uncreated (asaṃskṛta), the temporal and the timeless, and thus develops from itself the subsequently attained nondiscriminative wisdom that, while never parting from suchness or the uncreated, sees and acts in the world of saṃsāra, working to save ignorant beings. The functioning of karmic causation is the foundation of the existence of the bodhisattva—who has transcended birth-and-death—in the realm of saṃsāra, and the self-realization of the karma-created (false discrimination, subjectivity and world) as karma-created is the content of, and inseparable from, nondiscriminative wisdom.

While in Mahāyāna thought in general the concept of karma is taken up from the stance of the transcendent, as an aspect of existence in the world of the enlightened being, in Shinran's thought—in his concepts of karmic evil (zaigō, tsumi) and past karma (shukugō)—it expresses rather the stance of the person who has awakened, through insight into the fundamental nature of human existence, to the impossibility of transcendence. Nevertheless, Shinran's concept of karma shares with that of Mahāyāna tradition the nature of being established in the immediate present, in which time is itself timelessness, as the content of the personal realization of Buddha's wisdom or of no-self in his case, as the content of the "nembutsu of wisdom" or "wisdom of shinjin."[4] Below, I will discuss the central elements of Shinran's concept of karma as an expression of religious awakening in his teaching.

I The Great Path of Unobstructedness

Shinran states: "The person of the nembutsu is [one who treads] the great path free of all obstruction" (*Tannishō* 7).[5] These words express the remarkable freedom of the person who has realized shinjin—the person whose blind passions have become one with the wisdom-compassion of Amida Buddha. Shinran goes on to explain, "The evil he does cannot bring forth its karmic results." Does this mean that the person of the nembutsu does not fall into karmic causation? Or is it an example of religious hyperbole, meant to be understood only figuratively?

Causation is a cornerstone of the Buddha's teaching. Śākyamuni states, "He who sees dependent origination (*pratītya-samutpāda*, i.e., causation) sees me (Buddha)." Even the enlightened one is subject to the law of action-recompense and cannot violate or circumvent it. Thus, Shinran uses the term "karmic power of the great Vow" to express the strength of Amida's salvific activity. This working is not simply a matter of Amida's will or compassion; mere aspiration to save others would be futile without the aeons of practice performed as Bodhisattva Dharmākara. The working of the Vow is manifested from dharmakāya as suchness, but without the creation of karma through practice, no means to save can be devised and no results achieved.

If even Buddha must realize that all volitional acts fall within the working of action-consequence, what does it mean that the evil acts of the person of the nembutsu "cannot bring forth their karmic result"? It does not mean that a person eradicates his karmic evil through saying the Name, for Shinran rejects such practice as based on attachment to one's own powers. Neither can it be taken to mean that, because birth into the Pure Land in the future is assured, *ultimately* his evil acts will not have the effect of continuing samsaric existence. There is nothing to imply that this freedom belongs only to the future, and elsewhere Shinran states, "We have been able to encounter the moment when shinjin, firm and diamond-like, becomes settled ... so that we have parted forever from birth-and-death" (*Kōsō wasan* 77).[6]

In addition to this assertion of the radical freedom of the person of shinjin, there is another notable passage treating karma in *Tannishō*:

> Good thoughts arise through the prompting of past good; evil comes to be thought and performed through the working of evil acts (karma). These words were among those spoken by the late master: "You must realize that there is never [any act]—even so slight as a particle on the tip of a rabbit's hair or sheep's fleece—that is not evil that we commit and [the working out of] past karma (*shukugō*)." (*Tannishō* 13)

According to this passage, in all our activity—our thoughts and feelings, words and deeds—we do not commit good and evil according to our own judgments and decisions, but merely obey the working of our past acts. Shinran here attributes absolute control over the conduct of our lives to karmic causation, implying a complete denial of moral responsibility and freedom of will in the present. Surely such an awareness of karma might be called fatalistic, for in the thorough necessity of all our acts, whether good or evil, the present self is completely powerless.

Moreover, the karma from our past that rules our lives is always evil. In the first sentence of the passage quoted above, evil indicates the opposite of good, but in the words of Shinran that follow, both "good thoughts" and "evil acts"—good and evil as determined in the moral and ethical dimensions of human life—are "evil that we commit and caused by past karma." "Evil" in the latter sense encompasses both good and evil as we normally consider them; that is, even acts we usually deem good are seen as rooted in evil.

Karma, as a general Buddhist term, denotes both good and evil acts. According to the law of karmic causation, past acts, whether good or evil, become causes manifesting their effects in the present, and likewise, present acts become causes of results that will appear in the future. Good causes necessarily result in good and evil in evil: this necessity between cause and result is the essential characteristic of karma. For Shinran, since he states that both "past good" and "evil acts" are in fact evil, necessity leads entirely from evil as cause to evil as result. "Good thoughts" that arise through the prompting of past good are also included in the statement, "There is never [any act] ... that is not evil that we commit and [the working out of] past karma." This necessity from evil to evil lies at the heart of Shinran's concept of karma. According to it, we lack the potential to do anything that is not evil. If whatever we do—even acts we consider to be good and virtuous—is in fact evil, then whatever our subjective thoughts, in reality we have no moral freedom of choice. We can do no other than evil.

For Shinran, evil is not foremost an issue of social life, but rather of a person's attainment of Buddhahood. In order to realize enlightenment, one must perform various religious practices to rid oneself of false thinking and the blind passions that arise from it. The person bound about by his passions, however, cannot keep from committing acts that they motivate and cannot, therefore, realize Buddhahood. Any act other than practice that makes Buddhahood possible—however virtuous according to our usual standards—is evil from the stance of Buddha. If it does not bring one closer to enlightenment, then it only involves one further in endless birth-and-death. Shinran terms the good we do in our daily lives "good acts variously poisoned" by falsity and passions. Even the human capacity to love, which sometimes seems a gift that brings a person to transcend himself, is seen to harbor egocentricity at its core, and only the Buddha's "heart of great compassion is replete and thoroughgoing" (*Tannishō* 4). Perhaps the clearest expression of the extent to which Shinran's concept of evil encompasses all aspects of life may be seen in his statement, "Not wanting to go quickly to the Pure Land, or becoming forlorn with thoughts of death when even slightly ill, is also the activity of our blind passions" (*Tannishō* 9). When a person in sickness comes to realize that death is near, it is natural however good or evil he may be that he should feel loneliness and pain at parting from life. Even such natural human feelings Shinran labels "blind passions." In its depths, then, the evil we commit transcends the realm of human interaction, and extends to the very limits of human existence.

Shinran states, on the one hand, that as a human being one is so bound by one's past acts that all that one does in the present is defiled by evil, whatever one's conscious intentions; and on the other, that as a person of the nembutsu, one has broken free from the bondage of such karma, so that the evil one has done cannot bring about its retribution. Moreover, these two assertions do not concern two different kinds of people—for example, those who have not yet realized shinjin and those who have; nor do they describe two stages in the religious life of a single person, such as before and after the realization of shinjin. Both these statements apply to the same person—the person who has realized shinjin—simultaneously. Both articulate the nature and content of his religious awakening. How are we to understand this absolute bondage simultaneous with absolute freedom? First, let us consider Shinran's understanding of the basic elements of the concept of karma, temporality, and causality.

II Temporality: Karma is Always Past Karma

In Shinran's concept of karma, all that we do, think, or feel is instigated by past action; in other words, all that we are in the present has been determined by the past. What does this mean for the future? Most Buddhist and Shin scholars state that the concept of karma differs from a kind of fatalism in that one can freely exert one's will in determining the course of the future, so that it is possible, through effort in the present, to anticipate betterment. Though this may be acceptable in general Buddhist thought, it does not represent Shinran's thinking. Whatever we may seek to do in the present, our future is determined, and there is no room whatever for any change or improvement through our present activity. Our acts, whether morally good or evil, are all seeds that send us to hell, and there is nothing we can do to change this and direct ourselves toward attainment of Buddhahood.

According to the general Buddhist concept of karma, all the painful or happy circumstances that we experience in this world are the results of past volitional acts; only our present good and evil thoughts are not caused by past karma. Acts are classified into good, evil, and neutral, with the first two types bringing recompense. The pleasant and painful circumstances in the present are the results of past good and evil acts, but they themselves are karmically neutral with regard to the future. Concerning karmic causation, "Causes are good or evil; results are neutral": this is an ironclad rule in both the Hīnayāna and Mahāyāna traditions. Shinran, however, teaches not this general Buddhist insight, but rather that the good and evil we commit in the present are brought about by past karma. This clearly departs from the fundamental Buddhist concept of causes as good and evil but results as karmically neutral.

That our physical, mental, and verbal acts in the present are all induced by past karma means that not only the present but the future also is determined by the past. In the general Buddhist concept of karma, the present holds both the results of the past and the causes of the future. If, however, the present thoughts and actions that become the cause of the future are all determined by past acts, then not only the present but even the future is encompassed within past karma. There is no power in the present to give birth to the future.

Fundamentally, the future is distinguished from the past in its potentialities in contrast to the determinedness of the past, but if the present is completely conditioned by the past and there is no possibility in the present newly to give rise to the future, the present holds no meaning as the present and, accordingly, the future also lacks the significance of the future. Not only the present, but even the future into its furthest reaches is controlled by past karma and lies within its determinedness, and good or evil acts performed in the present lack the power to alter this. Thus, only the acts committed in the past possess the original significance of karma as an act—a free exercise of will—influencing later life and circumstances. By contrast, acts committed in the present or the future do not possess the significance of new karma. Since there is no creation of karma in the present, there is no present as we usually think of it.

Ordinarily we conceive time as existing objectively as a regular, linear progression that transcends our subjectivity. It forms a framework within which we and all things exist, and all our thoughts and acts arise within it. From the Buddhist perspective, however, such time, like the other aspects of the dichotomized, objectified world that we see standing apart from us, is the product of false thinking based on egocentric discrimination. If we seek to grasp time at its very ground-source—time in which we as true subjectivity are actually living—we must abandon objectified concepts of time. The self as true subjectivity takes now—the immediate present—and actual existence to be identical; objective time cannot enclose it. In other words, our true subjectivity cannot be illuminated through such concepts of time. The self that exists within conceptualized time is not the actually living and thinking self, but nothing more than the objectified self or subjectivity. Linear time advancing mechanically and inexorably apart from ourselves is merely a conception of genuine time, a shadow projected by it. Actual time is that time in which the subjectivity itself stands. There is no framework existing beforehand; rather, time is established and moves moment by moment through the activity of the subjectivity. Our thoughts, words and deeds do not occur within time; rather, time is established where the three modes of activity take place. Where acts are being performed is the present, where they have ended is the past, and where they have yet to begin is the future.

If the present is robbed of all sense of our performing acts, there is nothing to be called present karma, and the present cannot be established. Without the present, nothing different from the past can be created; hence, the progression from the present into the future becomes a continuation of the past, and the future also fails to be established. In this concept of past karma, present and future are meaningless; the past alone dominates all. For all eternity there is only the past. Further, where there is no meaningful present and future and all is merely the burden of the past, neither can there be a past in the ordinary sense. The pastness in Shinran's concept of karma—the endless future being controlled by the past—is not a past relative to present and future, but is eternal, pervading the temporality called past, present, and future; it is beginningless and continues endlessly. It is, in other words, samsaric existence that is essentially unchanging however far one goes into the past or future. The eternalness of past karma is none other than this samsaricness. In this way, Shinran's concept of past karma expresses the temporal dimension of the total lack of any condition for salvation in human beings.

III Karmic Causality and Free Will

The concept of karma is commonly understood to teach that one reaps the fruits of one's own acts. Through good acts one obtains favorable life-conditions, through evil acts one undergoes pain. As the subject of moral freedom, one accepts as one's own responsibility that present pain is the consequence of evil karma created through one's decisions and acts of will in the past and, at the same time, seeks to accumulate good karma in the present in order to gain happy conditions in the future. This popular conception of the working of karma may not be mistaken with regard to Buddhism in general, but, as we have seen, it differs from Shinran's understanding.

At the foundations of the popular conception of karma lies the subject that exercises free will. An example of this thought may be seen in *Dhammapada*, which belongs to early Buddhism:

> An evil act that has been committed, like milk, does not congeal immediately. It is like fire covered with ash; smoldering, it accompanies the foolish one. (71)

> The foolish person commits evil acts but is unaware; dull and ignorant, he suffers according to his own acts, just as though burnt by fire. (136)

It is not clear whether such sayings are spoken with focus on the past, present, or future. They may be taken as teaching the relation of past to present, or again of present to future. But their general intent concerns the present; it is the message that we should refrain from evil acts and strive to perform good:

Like the wealthy merchant with few companions who shuns dangerous roads, like the person who, cherishing life, shuns poison, so you should shun evil acts. (123)

Be prudent in speech, control your will, and do not commit evil with the body. Purify these three kinds of activity. [In this way] you will attain the path taught by the sages. (281)

Shinran, however, states, "Good acts are not necessary ... nor is there need to despair of the evil one commits" (*Tannishō* 1). Our moral decisions in the present are irrelevant; good and evil are not at issue. In fact, there is no question of the nature of the acts we perform, and no room for any intervention of personal effort and ideals. As we have already seen, both the "good" and "evil" committed in the present are prompted by past evil acts. The karmic evil of the self is fathomless and forms the core of the self itself. However we might strive, it is impossible for us to improve our circumstances in the future. This concept of past karma is established in the realization that the self as the subject of free will cannot extricate itself from falsity, delusional thinking, and fierce attachment to an unreal self, and that it is powerless in any efforts to awaken to true reality.

Since good and evil thoughts in the present all arise determined by past karma, our decisions and efforts in the present—and, indeed, the subject of free will seeking to suppress evil and nurture good thoughts—are completely bereft of meaning. This denial of the self of free will applies to the past also, for any point in the past when an act was performed was, at that time, the present, and was already conditioned by what preceded. Past karma has been accumulated from the depths of the past, and together with ignorance extends back into the beginningless past. Hence, our good and evil acts in the past were also prompted by past karma that existed from before, not the free will of our subjectivity. However far back we go, no acts escape the fundamental character of dependence on preceding evil past karma. The unfolding of this abysmal pastness expresses in temporal terms the delving into the depths of the self. This negation of the self and its potential for good in the past and present reaches, of course, into the future as well. In this way, the concept of past karma denies the validity of the self-determining ego and its attachment to its own goodness and moral judgment throughout the past, present, and future.

In the case of reaping the fruits of one's own acts, karmic causality functions as the basis for the continuity of the freely acting self as temporal existence. The present forms the nexus of the past and future, and there the subject of free will stands, acting as the central axis of causality. Facing the past, the person sees good and evil acts as the causes of the happy or painful results of the present, and facing the future, he sees pain and pleasure as the result of present good and evil acts. What integrates and sustains these two aspects of causality—from past to present and from present to future—and forms their pivot is the subject existing and freely exercising its will in the present. On the basis of these two aspects of causality, time as past, present, and future is established.

In Shinran's thought, however, the causal relationship of karma is single: from past to present *and* future. Here, causality has a twofold significance. Negatively, it breaks through the common notion of "reaping the fruits of one's own acts" based on the subject performing acts of moral judgment and free will in the present. It is the past, not the present, that forms the center of causality. The ego-self in the present, as the result of past karma, is dominated completely by the working out of past acts and possesses no freedom. However far back into the past one goes, it is impossible to say "I do this" in the sense of the self acting freely according to one's own intents. The focal point of causality in past karma is not the subject of personal will. Rather, past karma transcends the time termed past, present, and future in the direction of the past, and thereby transcends the self as temporal existence. There is a similarity here with the concept, or realization, of original sin in Christianity. While original sin is founded on the common ancestor of all individuals, however, the concept of past karma points directly to the individual himself. Herein lies its positive significance. Although past karma transcends the self as the subject of free will, it works to bind the self to its own past acts; hence, its significance as the acts of one particular individual is never lost. In past karma as "karmic evil that I have performed," "I" points not to a freely acting subject, but rather to the bonds of one's own karmic evil. Since one is brought to act through the past karma one bears, there is no act one commits that does not arise from one's own karmic evil.

Causality in Shinran's concept of past karma, then, is related not to the self as the subject performing acts in the present, but rather to the self as the bearer of karmic evil from the past. Its fundamental nature is not temporality, as in the case of the two aspects of causality in general Buddhist thought, but rather the bond between oneself in the present and immeasurable karmic evil in the past. Thus, its significance lies not in the moral action of the self committing good or evil, but rather in the awakening to the self as karmic evil.

IV Transformation: Karma is No-Karma and No-Karma is Karma

The person who has realized shinjin is fettered by his past evil and, at the same time, is free and unobstructed, for his past acts cannot bring forth their results. This does not mean that he stands apart from the working of causation. To borrow phrases from the Zen kōan of Hyaku-jō and the fox, "he does not obscure karma" (*fumai inga*)—he abides in its working and is clearly aware of this—and yet "he does not fall into karma" (*furaku inga*). Shinran articulates the nature of karma as experienced by the person of shinjin through the concept of "transformation":

> Without the practicer's calculating in any way whatsoever, all his past, present, and future karmic evil is transformed (*tenzu*) into good. To be transformed means that karmic evil, without being nullified or eradicated, is made into good, just as all waters, upon entering the great ocean, immediately become ocean water.[7]

Our karmic evil remains just as it is, and at the same time it is transformed into the Buddha's virtues; hence, we are bound to the world of birth-and-death, and yet we do not experience the unfolding of our karma as bondage, but rather as the free activity of wisdom-compassion in genuine self-awareness. Freedom here is not a matter of being able to exert our egocentric will. Such freedom is in reality the constraint of blind passions and false self, what Jaspers calls "self-will" (*Ich Will*) or "apparitional freedom" (*Scheinfreiheit*). True freedom lies rather where the demands of ignorant self-will fall away in the awakening to the working of karma; hence, Shinran states, "It is when one simply leaves both good and evil acts to karmic recompense and entrusts wholeheartedly to the Primal Vow that one is in accord with Other Power" (*Tannishō* 13). Here, the natural working of karmic causation (*gōdō jinen*), by which we live leaving all to karmic recompense, and the natural working of the power of the Vow (*ganriki jinen*), by which we tread the path of necessary attainment of enlightenment guided by the Buddha's wisdom, function as a single natural working.[8] True freedom—the power to act in accord with things as they truly are—can only be the activity wisdom-compassion taking what stands opposed to itself (necessary working of karmic evil) as itself. As D. T. Suzuki states, "Karma is no-karma and no-karma is karma."[9]

The awareness that karma renders us incapable of doing other than evil —that all our thoughts, whether normally judged good or evil, arise through the prompting of immense karmic evil from the past—is not fatalistic, for it is not attained through intellectual reflection, as an objective truth about the world around us, but only through the wisdom of Buddha unfolded in us in the realization of shinjin. Thus, it does not spawn resignation or passivity; rather, vital and positive life is born from it, for awareness of one's karmic evil is also awareness of one's salvation, and is established only as the Buddha's wisdom-compassion taking the defiled as itself. In abandoning one's clinging to a relative freedom, which is in fact subjugation to evil, one becomes aware that the necessity of evil is encompassed by the freedom of wisdom-compassion. As the T'ang dynasty Pure Land master Shan-tao teaches, the deep mind of shinjin has two aspects: that with regard to the practicer or self (*ki no jinshin*), in which one realizes that there is no condition within oneself for release from saṃsāra, and that with regard to dharma or Primal Vow (*hō no jinshin*), in which one entrusts oneself to the necessary attainment of birth through Amida's wisdom-compassion. These are two faces of a single religious awakening.

The transformation of karma is, at its core, the transformation of awareness. It is the awakening of the true subjectivity free of egocentric will or, in general

Buddhist terms, the realization of no-self. Shinran clearly expresses this transformation in the following verse:

1) When, into the vast ocean of Amida's Vow of wisdom,
The waters of the foolish beings' minds, both good and evil,
Have returned and entered, then immediately
They are transformed into the mind of great compassion.
(*Shōzōmatsu wasan* 40, SSZ II, p. 520)

Shinran annotates this verse: "'Transform' means that the evil mind becomes good." "Evil mind" refers to blind passions and embraces both the good and evil, morally and ethically judged, mentioned in the verse. "Good" refers not to moral goodness, but to complete freedom from blind passions. It is "the mind of great compassion" or, in the verses quoted below, the "ocean water of virtues" and "ocean water of wisdom." Transformation is not, however, simply a conversion of blind passions into enlightenment; hence, Shinran also uses the expression "become one taste":

2) The ocean waters of the inconceivable Name are such
That even the corpses of grave offenders and slanderers of dharma do not
    remain as they are;
When the myriad rivers of all evils have returned,
They become of one taste with the ocean water of virtues.
(*Kōsō wasan* 41)

3) When, to the ocean waters of the great compassionate Vow
Of unhindered light filling the ten quarters,
The streams of blind passions have returned,
They become one taste with the ocean water of wisdom.
(*Kōsō wasan* 42, SSZ II, p. 506)

Our blind passions are transformed into great compassion—they become wisdom-compassion—and in the mind that results, blind passions and wisdom are of "one taste." If blind passions have become wisdom, however, there should be only wisdom; it should not be necessary to speak of the two as becoming "one taste." We see here that the mind in which blind passions and wisdom-compassion have become one has two aspects. First, it is the Buddha's "good" mind. Our "good and evil" mind, on returning to and entering the ocean of the Vow, becomes the "mind of great compassion," which is also great wisdom. Second, this good mind is not good alone, but at the same time embraces within itself the "evil mind," the blind passions. Thus the two—wisdom-compassion and blind passions—while they stand opposed as pure and defiled, form the single "good" mind, which is shinjin, or the mind that is true, real, and sincere (*makoto no kokoro*).

This self-contradictory structure of transformation on the one hand together with oneness that includes duality on the other is also clarified by Rennyo. He states, concerning the aspect of becoming one (transformation):

> Already the practicer's mind of evil is made the same as the Tathāgata's good mind. This is what is meant when it is said that the Buddha's mind and the mind of the foolish being become one.
>
> (*Gobunshō* II, 10; SSZ III, p. 440)

Our minds become the same as Amida's good mind; nevertheless, our blind passions do not simply disappear or change utterly into wisdom-compassion. To clarify this point, Rennyo states:

> Amida Buddha mends sentient beings. "To mend" means that, while leaving the mind of the sentient being just as it is, Amida adds the good mind (Buddha's mind) to it and makes it good. It does not mean that the mind of the sentient being is completely replaced, and is distinguished and taken in as Buddha-wisdom only.
>
> (*Go-ichidaiki kikigaki* 64, SSZ II, p. 548)

Here, there is both wisdom and blind passions. The mind of the foolish being, before becoming one with the Buddha's mind, is blind passions, and on realizing shinjin, it changes into the same mind as the Buddha's. This transformed mind, however, has not ceased to be blind passions, for it holds within itself the mind of the foolish being. For this single mind, blind passions are not something other than itself. That is, the good mind (*shinjin*) that is the same as the Buddha's mind, established through the Buddha's mind and the mind of the foolish being becoming one, has awakened to itself as blind passions and karmic evil. Stated conversely, the mind that has been able to awaken to itself as blind passions is the same good mind as the Buddha's. To know oneself as blind passions is to become one with the Buddha's mind.

The following two verses articulate the whole of what we have seen above: Buddha's mind and the mind of the foolish being becoming one, and the complex structure of the one mind the good mind thus established.

> 4) Through the benefit bestowed by unhindered light,
> One realizes the shinjin of vast transcendent virtues:
> Unfailingly the ice of blind passions melts
> And immediately becomes the water of enlightenment.
>
> (*Kōsō wasan* 39)

> 5) Obstructing evils have become the substance of virtues;
> It is like the relation of ice and water:
> The more ice, the more water;
> The more hindrances, the more virtues.
>
> (*Kōsō wasan* 40, SSZ II, pp. 505-506)

Through the working of the Vow, we realize shinjin, and our blind passions become the Buddha's mind of great wisdom and great compassion (verse 4). In this mind, blind passions and the good mind make up one whole (verse 5: our "obstructing evils have become the substance of virtues"), but they do so while standing in a relationship of mutual opposition ("the more hindrances, the more virtues"); hence, our passions, just as they are, have become one with great wisdom and, in addition, through the working of that wisdom, they are gradually transformed like ice melting to become water. *Tannishō* 16 also speaks of this interaction after the realization of shinjin:

> If shinjin has become settled, birth will be brought about by Amida's working, so there must be no designing on our part. Even when our thoughts and deeds are evil, then, if we thereby turn all the more deeply to the power of the Vow, gentleheartedness and forbearance will surely arise in us through the working of jinen.

Through the working of wisdom-compassion, our blind passions are transformed into the same good mind as the Buddha's; this occurs at the moment of realizing shinjin and, further, continues to occur throughout life. This is the path of perfect unobstructedness.

V The Emergence of the Authentic Present

Realization of shinjin takes place in "one thought-moment" (*ichinen*), which Shinran explains as "time at its ultimate limit" (*Once-calling and Many-calling*, p. 32). This one thought-moment, like other moments, occurs within samsaric time, but in it, the mind of blind passions becomes one with the transtemporal mind of the Vow. Hence, that which is timeless fills this moment of the practicer's life, and for him samsaric time reaches its end: "We have parted forever from birth-and-death." Perhaps the most illuminating discussion of the structure of this one thought-moment is that of Prof. Nishitani Keiji in "The Problem of Time in Shinran."[10] Nishitani delineates the religious nature of this moment as the emergence of true existence, unfolding it as the place of the simultaneity of 1) the time in which Amida fulfilled the Primal Vow to save all beings throughout history—this is the past prior to any being, further back in the past than any point in the historical past, 2) the time of the establishment of the Pure Land, which is the future for each being, however far into the future it exists, and 3) the historical present of the realization of shinjin. These three times, while remaining distinct and sequential as past, present, and future, are brought into simultaneity in the practicer of shinjin through the working of the Primal Vow. Further, in the religious existence of shinjin, the practicer delves into the depths of the present moment, which, as the place of simultaneity, opens bottomlessly into the transtemporal that penetrates it and makes it the true present. It is such reflection that is expressed in Shinran's statement, "When I consider deeply the Vow of Amida, which arose from five kalpas of profound thought, I realize that it was entirely for the sake of myself alone!" (*Tannishō*, "Postscript"). This nonduality or simultaneity of the temporal (historical time of the practicer) and the transtemporal (working of Buddha) is the focus of Nishitani's article.

From the perspective of our concerns here, however, it must be added that the content of the practicer's reflection inevitably involves past karma. Shinran's statement above continues: "How I am filled with gratitude for the Primal Vow, in which Amida settled on saving *me, though I am burdened thus greatly with karma.*" To delve into the depths of the present in shinjin is none other than to delve back into the immense burden of karmic evil one has borne for beginningless kalpas into the distant past, and also to realize that this karma will continue to disclose itself in the future. "Our desires are countless, and anger, wrath, jealousy, and envy are overwhelming, arising without pause; to the very last moment of life they do not cease, or disappear, or exhaust themselves" (*Once-calling and Many-calling*, p. 48). Thus, "When the karmic cause so moves us"—when past karma functions as the cause or condition for some act—"we will do anything" (*Tannishō* 13).

Passage of time is ordinarily experienced as a progression from past into present and present into future; as potentiality, it flows out of the future and recedes into the past. For the person of shinjin, however, the course of time is not merely linear, but cyclical and repetitive—not merely historic, but samsaric—for he realizes that the working of evil past karma constrains him and deprives him of all possibility for new and free activity. His heart and mind, as great compassion established through the transformation of his blind passions, has broken free from birth-and-death, but since this mind (the good mind) includes blind passions within itself, even though he has entered the timeless ocean of the Vow and gained immeasurable life, simultaneously he lives samsaric time and has, in fact, for the first time genuinely awakened to the nature of his existence as blind passions and karmic evil. This awakening corresponds to deep mind with regard to self, which is essentially the realization that "hell is to be my home whatever I do" (*Tannishō* 2). This necessity of karmic evil is apprehended temporally as all-prevailing pastness. The relative past and present, and thus future also, conceived in terms of acts performed according to our will, are not actual time, but time encompassed within the pastness of karma. Karma, as primal, fundamental evil, transcends the good and evil acts that constitute relative existence and possesses temporal absoluteness. Thus, when past karma is seen to be evil, evil is understood to form the root-foundation of the person as relative existence. All acts of good or evil throughout the past, present, and future—that is, human life as temporal existence—through being dominated by past karma, are evil from their source. For this reason, Shinran, from his stance within the realization of shinjin, teaches not the creating of karma in the present, but only karmic recompense.

At the same time, however, the fulfillment of salvation is also seen in terms of an encompassing pastness in the establishment and fulfillment of the Primal Vow to save all beings. Dharmākara has become Amida Buddha, and the Name,

Namu-amida-butsu, in which each being is already included and called to as "Namu," pervades the ten quarters. The realization of this pastness "further back in the past than any point in the past" corresponds to deep mind with regard to dharma or Vow. The prevailing pastness of karmic evil (samsaric existence of the sentient being) and the pastness of the fulfillment of the Vow (Amida Buddha) are established for the practicer only in self-contradictory fusion and interpenetration with each other; this fusion takes place in the present as genuine time, and its first emergence is the thought-moment of the realization of shinjin, in which the mind of the being and the mind of Buddha become one.

The person who has realized shinjin, looking to the past, finds both the fulfillment of the Primal Vow and the depths of his past karmic evil; at the same time, he apprehends his future as the certain plunge into hell, and as the Pure Land. The futurity as the Pure Land differs from the future within samsaric time, which is in fact no more than repetition of the past. It is genuine futurity or freedom, which means that in it bondage to temporal existence as birth-and-death has been broken and the oppressive burden of the past has been lifted. The future that is apprehended as the Pure Land, then, is transtemporal; it cannot be confined to the future of samsaric time. In every present moment of the life of shinjin, obstructing karmic evil is transformed into virtue, and the two aspects of the future fuse into one. For this reason, Shinran speaks of realization of shinjin as itself the immediate attainment of birth occurring in the present.[11] While the Pure Land remains the future, the person of shinjin immediately attains birth, and while to the very last moment of life anger and envy arise without pause, he has parted forever from birth-and-death and his heart "sports in the Pure Land."

The fulfilled Pure Land is the land of immeasurable light and the fulfilled Buddha—Amida, or the mind of the Vow—is the Buddha of inconceivable light; both are in essence boundless light or wisdom that surpasses conceivability and transcends time. While the karmic past gives rise to samsaric time, that which transcends time—immeasurable light, or the ocean of the Vow—as the pastness of the Vow's fulfillment, penetrates and fuses with samsaric pastness to form the genuine present of the practicer of shinjin, and as the futurity of the Pure Land, it imparts to each present moment of the life of shinjin its character as authentic time. The eternal (timelessness) does not stand solely beyond samsaric time in the future, but fuses with the present; the present (hence the relative past and future also) is not merely impermanent or temporal, but is established on the foundation of the timeless that pervades it. True time—not an objectified reflection of time, but time that encompasses the subjectivity—is established only as the interpenetration of time and timelessness. It is here—where the past is, on the one hand, samsaric existence burdened by karmic evil and, on the other, the fulfillment of the Primal Vow; where the present is the fusion of these two kinds of past in the realization of shinjin; and where the future is both bondage that leads inexorably to hell and freedom in which that bondage has been broken through—that the true subjectivity of no-self, which is free of egocentric will, lives and thinks and acts. Past and present, while remaining distinct, are one;

further, present and future, while distinct, are one. This is the temporal aspect of the mutual opposition of sentient being and Buddha simultaneous with their identity, or of the grounding of karma in the working of the Primal Vow.

The present of the person of shinjin, as both past and future, necessity and freedom, holds at once the two contradictory aspects of deep mind, for leaving both good and evil (temporal existence) to karmic recompense—awakening to the karmic evil that pervades the past, present, and future—takes place in the realization of shinjin. Samsaric pastness (necessity), while remaining necessity, gives itself up totally and comes to stand within the future (freedom): "The heart of the person of shinjin already and always resides in the Pure Land" (*Letters*, p. 27). Each moment of his life may be envisioned as a point on the circumference of a circle. Every act up until death is dominated by the past, and this domination moves him along the circle of samsaric time, in which nothing new can arise. Simultaneously, however, he is encompassed by the Vow, and through the Vow's power, he is brought beyond the circle into a trajectory directed to the genuine future, which is the Pure Land. Each moment is transformed (*tenzu*), so that every new present possesses the newness or originality that cannot arise from karma. In the life of shinjin, each day is new and fresh. The future in such life lies not along the circumference of samsaric time, but in the constant transformation by which the direction of karma-ridden time is broken and the practicer is brought to face the Pure Land. Thus, in the interpenetration of time and timelessness in shinjin, we come to know true and real time—the self-aware, impermanent existence that is living and, accordingly, that is dying. Although samsaric time merely stretches out endlessly, the time of the subjectivity, while it flows, does not flow, and while it moves, is still. It is time, and it is eternity or timelessness. Life and death do not simply stand in mutual opposition; within life there is death, within death there is life. Such life is true life, such death true death.

VI Radical Shame: The Awakening to Karmic Evil

Shinran terms effort to desist from evil and perform good *hakarai* ("deliberation," "calculation," "contrivance"), referring to the working of intellect and will, in all its facets, to attain salvation. He states:

> Sages of the Mahāyāna and Hīnayāna and all good people, because they take the auspicious Name of the Primal Vow as their own roots of good (i.e., say the nembutsu out of their own judgment and will to do good), are incapable of awakening shinjin, of understanding Buddha-wisdom, and of understanding the [Buddha's] establishment of the cause [of birth in the Pure Land].
>
> (*Kyōgyōshinshō*, "Chapter on Transformed Buddha and Land," SSZ II, 165-166)

Those who strive to be virtuous, believing themselves capable of doing good and shunning evil, are engaged in *hakarai* or designing born of attachment to their own worthiness and capabilities; hence, shinjin cannot open forth in them and they cannot understand the Buddha's wisdom. To become free of attachment to one's own powers (self-power) and to entrust oneself to the Primal Vow are no more than different expressions for the same thing.

> As long as there is self-working, it is not Other Power, but self-power ...
> Self-working is the *hakarai* of the person of self-power.
>
> (*Goshōsokushū* 10, SSZ II, p. 712)

Moreover, "Other Power means to be free of any form of *hakarai*" (*Letters*, p. 39). As long as *hakarai* remains, one does not entrust to the Primal Vow. Further, it is because one does not grasp the nature of past karma that this *hakarai* does not fall away.

Only when a person knows that he cannot do other than evil, however much he might strive to do good, does he realize that he lacks any means to extricate himself from samsaric existence; his judgment and will being poisoned by self-attachment, nothing remains to him but utter entrusting of himself to the Primal Vow. It may be thought that realization of shinjin involves a decision or personal commitment; Shinran's expressions reveal it in negative terms, not as a "leap of faith," but simply as the thorough dissolution of *hakarai*. Further, among early Shin Buddhists, there were those who felt that it was natural for the genuine practicer to fear committing evil; such an attitude is criticized in *Tannishō* 13 as "the thought of one who doubts the Primal Vow and fails to understand the working of past karma in our good and evil acts." If the karmic conditions exist, we cannot avoid evil however we may strive to. When we grasp the nature of our karmic past, it becomes impossible for us to believe that a person must despair of his evil; finding ourselves powerless, we cannot but abandon our self-will and "leave both good and evil to karmic recompense."

Hakarai includes both the will to cease from evil and do good and the discrimination that judges. Both aspects are accompanied by our feelings and emotions. In terms of human intellect, *hakarai* is ignorance of genuine good and evil. Although burdened with karmic evil, we are not aware of its working; believing ourselves capable of choosing good over evil, we value as essentially worthy our aspirations to perform good as best as we can. To become free of *hakarai*, then, is to awaken to our karmic evil and to our actual ignorance of good and evil. Shinran states:

> I know nothing of what is good or evil. For if I could know thoroughly, as is known in the mind of Amida, that an act was good, then I would know the meaning of "good." If I could know thoroughly, as Amida knows, that an act was evil, then I would know "evil." But in a foolish being full of blind passions, in this fleeting world—this burning house—all matters without exception are lies and gibberish, totally without truth and sincerity. The nembutsu alone is true and real.
>
> (*Tannishō*, "Postscript")

In the realization of shinjin, a person awakens to his own ignorance; thus, one aspect of shinjin is wisdom: "When one has boarded the ship of the Vow of great compassion … the darkness of ignorance is immediately broken through" (*Kyōgyōshinshō*, "Chapter on Practice," 78).

Karmic evil, however, cannot rise to self-awareness by itself, and the intellect alone cannot discern its own profound ignorance. For a person to realize that, though he had assumed he could choose between good and evil, in fact he cannot, he must first distinguish intellectually between good and evil. Animals and infants, who cannot make this distinction, can have no awareness of karmic evil. In addition, the will must be exerted in action.[12] Shinran states, after instructing a disciple to kill in order to attain birth in the Pure Land:

> "If we could always act as we wished, then when I told you to kill a thousand people in order to attain birth, you should have immediately gone out to do so. But since you lack the karmic cause enabling you to do this, you do not kill even a single person. It is not that you keep from killing because your heart is good. In the same way, a person may wish not to harm anyone and yet end up killing a hundred or a thousand people." Thus he spoke, referring to our belief that the good of our hearts and minds is truly good and the evil truly evil, not realizing that Amida saves us through the inconceivable working of the Vow.
>
> (*Tannishō* 13)

The phrase, "If we could always act as we wished," means "if it were in our power to act according to our *hakarai*." That we do not kill means not that we will not kill because we are good; rather, we cannot carry it out merely because we lack the karmic conditions. When this is realized, it is clear that though we considered ourselves good and morally upright, in fact we cannot genuinely be called good. Acts that we judged intellectually to be good are not really so.

Our intellectual judgment of good and evil and our conviction that we can accomplish good through our will (even if not perfectly, at least to some extent) is *hakarai*. As long as we remain in the stance of *hakarai*, we cannot know that "Amida saves us through the inconceivable working of the Vow." Unless this *hakarai*—this resolve to make ourselves morally and spiritually worthy—reaches a total impasse and all room for design and effort vanishes, entrusting to the Primal Vow will not arise. When we have exerted all our will and intellect in seeking what is good and true, and thus reached our limits—if we have earnestly listened to the teaching—a conversion or turnabout occurs. This is an awakening, a returning. Shinran calls it "the equal of perfect enlightenment" (*tōshōgaku*). Here, our intellect, will, and feelings are transformed into true wisdom that knows—and great compassion that grasps—karmic evil as itself.

It is commonly said that being human inextricably involves evil. This view does not, however, constitute realization of oneself as a "person in whom karmic evil is deep-rooted and whose blind passions abound" (*Tannishō* 1). Realization of karmic evil is not accompanied by feelings that evil is "natural" or "unavoidable"; rather, it is felt to be deeply shameful. This shame is not a form of regret that includes feeling that one can reform in the future. Rather, all expectation of moral or spiritual progress is gone; there is nothing but shame and lament. Regret or remorse tends to arise in the ethical and moral dimensions of human existence. The shame born of awakening to one's karmic evil goes deeper, to the roots of one's personal existence itself, and belongs to religious life; in this sense, it is radical and pervasive. Shinran states:

> With our snake's or scorpion's mind of wickedness and cunning,
> It is impossible to perform good acts of self-power;
> And unless we entrust ourselves to Amida's directing of virtue,
> We will surely end without shame, without self-reproach.
>
> (*Shōzōmatsu wasan* 99, SSZ II, p. 528)

To reflect on one's own evil and be filled with regret is still to be "without shame," which is impossible without wisdom. If to feel regret means to pass judgment in the present on an act committed in the past, then the past act may be seen as evil, but the present is no longer so. From the perspective of karmic evil, however, not only the past but the present also is evil, and the future holds no possibility for anything but evil. Simple repentance over a single past act is meaningless. In the consciousness of karmic evil, there remains no room for remorse, but only the realization that one is a "being possessed of blind passions" or "deep-rooted karmic evil."

An example of such realization may be seen in the *myōkōnin* Shichisaburō of Mikawa province. When he discovered that he had been robbed of some firewood, feelings of gratitude toward the thief arose in him. He understood the theft to be the result of his having stolen from the thief in the past. Thus, he was moved to profound shame for his past offense, and further, realizing that the person had come to take back stolen property because he, Shichisaburō, had no idea of how to return it, he wanted to thank him. He did not merely accept the theft because it was retribution for his own past misdeed; in fact, he did not see the act as a theft. Through it he was awakened to his own karmic evil, and since this awareness was the activity of great compassion in him, he felt joy rather than resignation, gratitude rather than vindictiveness. The self that takes an egocentric perspective and self-love as its fundamental nature had been transcended, as had the objectively moral or ethical stance that judges the thief as a criminal.

In the belief that we merely reap the fruits of our own acts, there is only causality and no transcendence of it; there is never more than saṃsāra, and no salvation. Shichisaburō's subjectivity, however, is no-self in which egocentric will has fallen away and religious love emerges as gratitude toward the thief. As Shinran states, "Obstructing evils"—karmic recompense—"have become the substance of virtues." With a subjectivity in which blind passions that arise moment by moment are transformed into no-self through genuine self-awareness—through the mind of Buddha—the person of shinjin acts in accord with his nature and circumstances, manifesting the working of compassion in the occurrences and interactions of ordinary life. In awakening to his karmic evil, he carries on his life subject to causality and, further, has transcended it. Thus Shinran states that he "constantly practices great compassion" (*Kyōgyōshinshō,* "Chapter on Shinjin" 65).

NOTES

[1] Author's Note: This article is based on *Bukkyō ni okeru gō no shisō* (Kyoto, 1957), pp. 7-39; its present form and much of the detail in content, however, have emerged from discussions with the translator.

[2] The original text has been adapted and edited in translation.—*Trans.*

[3] Various concepts are used in the history of Buddhist thought to express no-self. Among them, the five aggregates in early Buddhism and emptiness in the *Prajñāpāramitā Sūtras,* while including temporal implications, do not give direct expression to the element of time. The temporal side of emptiness was clarified by Nāgārjuna through the concept of mutual dependence, by which he showed theories of time as linear succession to be untenable. In terms of the relationship of action and recompense, there can be neither simple continuity nor interruption, neither permanence nor impermanence. The positive implications of karma for the bodhisattva's temporal existence were articulated in the early Yogācāra of Maitreya, Asanga, and Vasubandhu through the concept of the simultaneous, reciprocal causation of *ālaya-vijñāna* and defiled dharmas. See my *Bukkyō ni okeru gō no shisō,* pp. 42-79.

[4] Shinjin 信心 is the "true, real, and genuine mind" (*makoto no kokoro*) in which a person's mind and the mind of Buddha have become one without their duality and mutual opposition being eradicated. This term expresses the core of Shinran's religious awakening.

[5] Quotations from *Tannishō* are from Dennis Hirota, trans., *Tannishō: A Primer* (Kyoto: Ryūkoku University, 1982); portions have been adapted.

[6] In *Shinshū shōgyō zenshō* (hereafter as SSZ; Kyoto: Ōyagi Kōbundō, 1941), p. 510.

[7] Ueda Yoshifumi, ed., *Notes on "Essentials of Faith Alone": Yuishinshō mon-i* (Kyoto: Shin Buddhism Translation Series, Hongwanji International Center, 1979), pp. 32-33. Many of the quotations from Shinran in this article are from other volumes of this series: *Letters of Shinran: Mattōshō* (1978; hereafter as *Letters*), *Notes on Once-calling and Many-calling: Ichinen-tanen mon'i* (1980), and *The True Teaching, Practice and Realization of the Pure Land Way: Kyōgyōshinshō* (Volume 1, Chapters on Teaching and Practice, 1983; Volume II, Chapter on Shinjin, 1985). Portions have been adapted.

[8] For a discussion of the working of *jinen,* see my article, "The Mahayana Structure of Shinran's Thought," Part II, *Eastern Buddhist,* Vol. XVII, No. 2 (Autumn 1984), pp. 51-52.

[9] *The Essence of Buddhism* (Kyoto: Hozōkan, 1968), pp. 30-32.

[10] In *Eastern Buddhist,* Vol. XI, No. I (Mav 1978), pp. 13-26.

[11] For a discussion of the two meanings of "birth" in Shinran, see my article, "The Mahayana Structure of Shinran's Thought," Part I, *Eastern Buddhist,* Vol. XVII, No. I (Spring 1984), pp. 71-78.

[12] For a discussion of the process of realizing shinjin, see my article, "How is Shinjin to be Realized?" *Pacific World* (Institute of Buddhist Studies, Berkeley), New Series, No. 1 (1985), pp. 17-24.

CHAPTER 11

THE JOY OF SHINRAN: RETHINKING TRADITIONAL SHINSHŪ VIEWS ON THE CONCEPT OF THE STAGE OF THE TRULY SETTLED[1]

—MURAKAMI SOKUSUI

(TRANSLATED BY EISHO NASU)

I

For many years, I have been mulling over an unsettled question relating to the traditional manner of explaining Shinran's concept of attaining the truly settled stage in the present life (*genshō shōjōju*). In order to identify the problem clearly, let me present a few passages from some well known Shinshū exegetical works. First, let us examine a passage from the *Shinshū yōron* (The Essence of the Shinshū Teaching) discussing Jōdo Shinshū's theory of benefits (*riyakuron*), a passage which deals with the teaching of "dual benefits" in the present life and in the future life (*gentō ryōyaku*).

> For Shinshū followers, one anticipates realizing ultimate nirvāṇa in the Pure Land. In the present life, we are initiated into the truly settled stage (*shōjōju*), which is endowed with the hope of realizing ultimate nirvāṇa. This hope eliminates all feelings of frustration about unsettledness in the future and is characterized as the hope springing from the great settled mind (*dai anjin*) of the settled anticipation (*ketsujō yōgo*) for the certain realization of future birth in the Pure Land. We become confident about the ultimate achievement of our lives to be realized in the Pure Land of the other shore (*higan*), and thus we are able to live our present lives with the settled mind of total confidence (*anjin ryūmyō*) and full of hope.[2]

The ultimate nirvāṇa of enlightenment is the benefit realized in the Pure Land in the future. The truly settled stage is the benefit realized in the present life and makes one "filled with the hope of realizing nirvāṇa in the Pure Land," which is "the hope springing from the great settled mind of the settled anticipation for the certain realization of future birth in the Pure Land."

This type of explanation of the attainment of the truly settled stage in the present life naturally leads to the following kinds of interpretations.

> A: "To save" means to save someone from his/her dissatisfactions and deficiencies in the present life. Therefore, in terms of time, salvation is located in the future and the

priority of salvation should be found in the future. In a sense, this is one of the natural characteristics of the concept of salvation itself. In soteriological religions, salvation must be perfect: as long as the physical body exists, we cannot accomplish this perfection in the present life ... Although it may not manifest consciously, hope for this future provides those who aspire to be born in the Pure Land with a great resource for living in the present. Therefore, as a soteriological religion, [Shinshū] affirms the position that the priority of salvation should be found in the future.[3]

B: We need to pay special attention to this concept [of attaining the stage of truly settled in the present life] because it teaches us that the brightness of the future and our hope for the future in fact sustain our present lives. Shinran teaches us how to live in the present life based on his affirmation of the superiority of salvation in the future. Brightness in one's present life comes not only from the present life itself. We also experience how much the bright hope for tomorrow brightens up our present lives.[4]

These interpretations of Shinran's teaching on the stage of the truly settled represent a future-centric logic in which present existence is governed by future hope. According to this understanding, one is to feel fulfilled and secure in the present life through the confidence that one will certainly be born in the Pure Land and attain nirvāṇa in the future.

Yet, if Shinran's conception of attaining the truly settled stage in the present life is to be understood in this manner, how are we to respond to the following critiques?

A: There are some people who teach about salvation in Jōdo Shinshū in a future-centric manner without giving it much thought. But I disagree with them. For example, we often hear that "Shinshū followers' religious life is just like Saturday night. On Saturday night, we feel joyful because we know that tomorrow is Sunday. Likewise, the present life is joyful because we know that we are going to be born in the Pure Land when we die ... " However, in reality, "tomorrow" is not Sunday but more like Monday. In the afterlife in the Pure Land, there awaits more work that will make us busier than in this life. It is a grave mistake to believe that it will be an easy time in the Pure Land after death ... If it were Saturday night now, we might wish for Sunday to come sooner. However, in the case of birth in the Pure Land, if you wish to go to the Pure Land quickly, we might wonder if we weren't free of blind passions.[5] That is very unrealistic.[6]

B: Since I am not sure whether the Pure Land really exists, I do not have any illusory yearning for birth in the Land of Utmost Bliss in the afterlife. If my life depended on such thoughts, my present life would certainly be filled with anxiety until I die, because my anxiety could not be eased until I actually got there and saw that the Pure Land existed.[7]

C: Shinran was a truly honest person and never discussed anything with confidence until he had experienced it. Therefore, he could not talk about the afterlife as if he had already seen it, because he had yet to experience it.[8]

Now I want to stress that I am not against the traditional Shinshu doctrine of the dual benefits in the present and future lives (*gentō ryōyaku setsu*). Shinran's view of the attainment of the truly settled stage in the present life and realization of nirvāṇa in the afterlife (*tōrai metsudo*) is clearly delineated in several Shinshū scriptures.[9] I am very well aware that Shinran himself explains that the meaning of the truly settled stage is "to have become one who will unfailingly attain Buddhahood" and "to become settled as one who will definitely be born in the Pure Land."[10] The problem is whether it is true that Shinran's joy of becoming a person of the truly settled stage is based in anticipation for birth in the Pure Land in the future. If Shinran's concept of attaining the truly settled stage in the present life means to live in hope with anticipation for future birth in the Pure Land, the primary benefit of the Shinshū teaching in this life would be simply the *anticipation* for the attainment of Buddhahood through birth in the Pure Land in the afterlife. The attainment of the truly settled stage in this life, then, becomes merely a secondary by-product.[11] If this were true, no matter how greatly the significance of the present life is emphasized in Shinshū teaching, we must accept the criticism that Shinshū is a religion whose primary focus is in the afterlife. We must also face the related criticism that aspiration for birth in an uncertain Pure Land is nothing but a quest for a shadowy illusion. However, I would like to raise the question of whether Shinran's understanding of the joy of attaining the truly settled stage was really such a future-centric idea.

II

To examine Shinran's understanding of the joy of attaining the truly settled stage, I will review how he describes this joyfulness in his major work, the *True Teaching, Practice, and Realization of the Pure Land Way* (*Ken Jōdo shinjitsu kyō gyō shō monrui*, hereafter *Kyōgyōshinshō*). Shinran's first reference to joy is found in the preface (*sōjo*) to the text.

> How joyous I am, Gutoku Shinran, disciple of Śākyamuni! Rare it is to come upon the sacred scriptures from the westward land of India and the commentaries of the masters of China and Japan, but now [*ima*] I have been able to encounter them. Rare is it to hear them, but already [*sude ni*] I have been able to hear. Reverently entrusting myself to the teaching, practice, and realization that are the true essence of the Pure Land way, I am especially aware of the profundity of the Tathāgata's benevolence. Here I rejoice in what I have heard and extol what I have attained.[12]

In the separate preface (*betsujo*) to the Chapter on Shinjin, Shinran explains the source of his joyfulness.

> As I reflect, I find that our attainment of shinjin [*shingyō*] arises from the heart and mind with which Amida Tathāgata selected the Vow, and that the clarification of true mind has been taught for us through the skillful works of compassion of the Great Sage, Śākyamuni ... Here I, Gutoku Shinran, disciple of Śākyamuni, reverently embrace the true teaching of the Buddhas and Tathāgatas and look to the essential meaning of the treatises and commentaries of the masters. Fully guided by

the beneficent light of the three sūtras, I seek in particular to clarify the luminous passage on the "mind that is single" ... Mindful solely of the depth and vastness of the Buddha's benevolence, I am unconcerned about being personally abused.[13]

In the section known as the Turning and Entering through the Three Vows (*san-gan tennyū*), Shinran explains the tenor and expression of that joy.

Nevertheless, I have now [*ima*] decisively departed from the "true" gate of provisional means and, [my self-power] overturned, have entered the ocean of the selected Vow ... Having entered forever the ocean of the vow, I now realize deeply the Buddha's benevolence. To respond with gratitude for the supreme virtues, I collect the crucial passages expressing the true essence of the Pure Land way, constantly saying, out of mindfulness [the Name that is] the inconceivable ocean of virtues. Ever more greatly rejoicing, I humbly receive it.[14]

And in the postscript (*gojo*) of the *Kyōgyōshinshō*, he tries to convey the depth of his feeling.

How joyous I am, my heart and mind being rooted in the Buddha-ground of the universal Vow, and my thoughts and feelings flowing within the dharma-ocean, which is beyond comprehension! I am deeply aware of the Tathāgata's immense compassion, and I sincerely revere the benevolent care behind the masters' teaching activity. My joy grows ever fuller, my gratitude and indebtedness ever more compelling.[15]

The joyfulness Shinran expresses in these passages is based on his realization that "now" (*ima*) he has "already" (*sude ni*) encountered the teaching of Amida's Primal Vow. It is the joy of taking refuge in the Ocean of Amida's Vow (*gankai*), not an expression arising from anticipation for his future birth in the Pure Land.

On the other hand, there are also passages in which Shinran seems to express joy for his anticipated birth in the Pure Land, as in the conclusive exaltation (*kettan*) in the section discussing the significance of the Great Practice (*daigyō shaku*).

Thus, when one has boarded the ship of the Vow of great compassion and sailed out on the vast ocean of light, the winds of perfect virtue blow softly and the waves of evil are transformed. The darkness of ignorance is immediately broken through, and quickly reaching the land of immeasurable light, one realizes great nirvāṇa.[16]

However, it should be recognized that the main point of this passage is becoming a being who has "boarded the ship of the Vow of great compassion."[17]

In a similar vein, Shinran seems to discuss the joyful anticipation of the moment of death (*rinjū no ichinen*) in the section "On Being the Same as Maitreya" (*bendō Miroku shaku*) in the Chapter on Shinjin.

Because sentient beings of the nembutsu have perfectly realized the diamond-like mind of crosswise transcendence, they transcend and realize great, complete nirvāṇa on the eve of the moment of death.[18]

Yet when we consider the sentence preceding this passage—"Because Mahāsattva Maitreya has perfectly realized the diamond-like mind of the stage equal to enlightenment, he will without fail attain the stage of supreme enlightenment beneath a dragon-flower tree at the dawn of the three assemblies"[19] —we see that Shinran wrote the passage to demonstrate the superiority of the nembutsu practice and not to express joy for the anticipation of birth in the Pure Land at the moment of death. Shinran's intention becomes even clearer when we read the next sentence of the passage.

> Moreover, the people who have realized the diamond-like mind are the equals of Vaidehī and have been able to realize the insights of joy, awakening, and confidence. This is because they have thoroughly attained the true mind directed to them for their going forth, and because this accords with [the working of] the Primal Vow, which surpasses conceptual understanding.[20]

Shinran's focus is thus on the attainment of the three insights of joy, awakening, and confidence in the present life just as Vaidehī attained them.

In fact, Shinran admits in a number of his writings that he feels not joy but reluctance when anticipating the death that will lead to birth in the Pure Land. In the same chapter of the *Kyōgyōshinshō*, Shinran laments that he feels "no happiness at coming nearer the realization of true enlightenment."[21] In Chapter Nine of *A Record in Lament of Divergences* (*Tannishō*), Shinran is remembered as saying:

> It is hard for us to abandon this old home of pain, where we have been transmigrating for innumerable kalpas down to the present, and we feel no longing for the Pure Land of peace, where we have yet to be born. Truly, how powerful our blind passions are! But though we feel reluctant to part from this world, at the moment our karmic bonds to this Sahā world run out and helplessly we die, we shall go to that land.[22]

Instead of intimating any hope for the anticipated birth in the Pure Land, Shinran honestly discloses to us that such hopefulness never arises in his heart.

What, then, is the source of joy for Shinran? In the same chapter of the *Tannishō* Shinran goes on to describe just what the wellspring of joy is.

> What suppresses the heart that should rejoice and keeps one from rejoicing is the action of blind passions. Nevertheless, the Buddha, knowing this beforehand, called us "foolish beings possessed of blind passions"; thus, becoming aware that the compassionate Vow of Other Power is indeed for the sake of ourselves, who are such beings, we find it all the more trustworthy ... Amida pities especially the person who has no thought of wanting to go to the Pure Land quickly. Reflecting on this, we feel the great Vow of great compassion to be all the more trustworthy and realize that our birth is settled.[23]

Shinran's joy derives from nothing other than his immediate experience, "now" (*ima*), encountering "the great Vow of great compassion" (*daihi daigan*) of Amida who "pities especially the person who has no thought of wanting to go to the Pure Land quickly." Therefore, in the first chapter of the *Tannishō*, Shinran places greater emphasis on "being brought to share in the benefit of being grasped by Amida, never to be abandoned" (*sesshu fusha*)[24] than on the realization of birth in the Pure Land.

At the risk of sounding repetitious, let me remind the reader that I am not suggesting that Shinran rejects the concept of birth in the Pure Land. My purpose here is to pinpoint where in the texts Shinran discusses joyfulness and what he says the source of joy is. Traditional Shinshū scholarship circumscribes the stage of the truly settled as no more than a causal stage for the attainment of Buddhahood, despite Shinran's strong emphasis on its presentness. Certainly there is no doubt that it is one stage of a bodhisattva; and, of course, the practitioner's realization of ultimate nirvāṇa is to be achieved after birth in the Pure Land. However, it does not necessarily follow that anticipation for birth in the Pure Land is the concrete content of joy experienced by Shinran. As clearly shown in the above citations, Shinran's joy is founded in the one thought-moment of realization of shinjin (*gyakushin no ichinen*)—the moment when Shinran realized that he was "brought to share in the benefit of being grasped by Amida, never to be abandoned." This interpretation of Shinran's conception of joy is further strengthened and clarified by reference to the following passage.

> Thus, when one attains the true and real practice and shinjin, one greatly rejoices in one's heart. This attainment is therefore called the stage of joy ... Even more decisively will the ocean of beings of the ten quarters be grasped and never abandoned when they have taken refuge in this practice and shinjin. Therefore the Buddha is called "Amida Buddha." This is Other Power.[25]

Although Shinran has yet to attain buddhahood, his salvation has already been accomplished at the moment of attaining the true and real practice and shinjin. If we imagine that Shinran still yearns for the future Pure Land at this point, we would have to do so based on the assumption that Shinran still had feelings of emptiness and that his life was yet to be truly fulfilled. This is clearly not the case.

Although Shinran has attained shinjin, he was still an ordinary being filled with blind passions. On this point, Shinran states:

> Concerning the term [to] *cut off* [blind passions]: because we have awakened the mind that is single, which is directed to us for our going forth, there is no further state of existence into which we must be born, no further realm into which we must pass. Already the causes leading to the six courses and the four modes of birth have died away and their results become null. Therefore we immediately and swiftly cut off birth-and-death in the three realms of existence.[26]

For Shinran, the existence or non-existence of blind passions is no longer of any concern. Shinran even says that "If we had the feeling of dancing with joy and wished to go to the Pure Land quickly, we might wonder if we weren't free of blind passions."[27] The life of an ordinary being filled with blind passions is not to be considered empty. Any feelings of emptiness Shinran had were satisfied by Amida's great Vow of great compassion which is completely trustworthy —not by a longing for the future attainment of Buddhahood through birth in the Pure Land. Shinran does not say that, because Amida promises birth in the Pure Land in the *future*, his attainment of the truly settled stage makes him joyful *now*. Rather, he says that, because he has attained the truly settled stage *now*, his attainment of birth in the Pure Land in the *future* becomes necessary. Shinran makes this point in the Chapter on Realization.

> When foolish beings possessed of blind passions, the multitudes caught in birth-and-death and defiled by evil karma, realize the mind and practice that Amida directs to them for their going forth, they immediately join the truly settled of Mahayana. Because they dwell among the truly settled, they necessarily attain nirvāṇa.[28]

This is similarly stated in the *Hymn of the Pure Land* (*Jōdo wasan*).

> Those who attain true and real shinjin
> Immediately join the truly settled;
> Thus having entered the stage of nonretrogression,
> They necessarily attain nirvāṇa.[29]

And, in the *Notes on "Essentials of Faith Alone"* (*Yuishinshō mon'i*), we find, "To return is to attain the supreme nirvāṇa without fail because one has already entered the ocean of the Vow."[30] It is clear that Shinran's priority is on encountering the teaching of the Primal Vow and not on the future attainment of nirvāṇa. In fact, for Shinran, "It is not attainment of the unexcelled, incomparable fruit of enlightenment that is difficult; the genuine difficulty is realizing true and real shinjin [*shingyō*]."[31] The most significant issue for Shinran is realizing shinjin. Once one realizes shinjin, one's attainment of the fruit of enlightenment becomes a necessary event.[32]

There are many other examples similar to these passages in Shinran's writings. For example, in the *Notes on the Inscriptions on Sacred Scrolls* (*Songō shinzō meimon*), Shinran describes the easiness of attaining nirvāṇa.

> *To go is easy*: When persons allow themselves to be carried by the power of the Primal Vow, they are certain to be born in the land that has been fulfilled through it; hence, it is easy to go there ... Through the karmic power of the great vow, the person who has realized true and real shinjin naturally is in accord with the cause of birth in the Pure Land and is drawn by the Buddha's karmic power; hence the going is easy, and ascending to and attaining the supreme great nirvāṇa is without limit. Thus the words, *one is drawn there by its spontaneous working* (*jinen*). One is drawn there naturally by the cause of birth, the entrusting with sincere mind that is Other Power.[33]

The important issue is to be carried by the power of the Primal Vow—to attain true and real shinjin. Birth in the true fulfilled land (*jippōdo*) is simply a natural result of the karmic power of the great Vow. Those famous words of the *Tannishō*—"I have no idea whether the nembutsu is truly the seed for my being born in the Pure Land or whether it is the karmic act for which I must fall into hell"[34]—reveal Shinran's firm conviction of his birth through total entrusting in the Primal Vow, so much so that his birth in the Pure Land in the future is not even an issue. If his joy arose from his hope for future birth in the Pure Land, shinjin and nembutsu would be merely instruments or methods for birth and not unconditionally free from human value judgments. Shinran goes so far as to state, "I am incapable of any other practice, so hell is decidedly my abode whatever I do,"[35] revealing that for him birth in the Pure Land in the afterlife was simply an inconceivable event. Utter joy stems instead from encountering the inconceivable Vow "now."

Shinran's joy of encountering the teaching of the Primal Vow is most clearly reflected in his notes "On Jinen Hōni" which is composed toward the end of his life.

> Amida's Vow is, from the very beginning, designed to bring each of us to entrust ourselves to it—saying "Namu-amida-butsu"—and to receive us into the Pure Land; none of this is through our calculation. Thus, there is no room for the practicer to be concerned about being good or bad. This is the meaning of *jinen* as I have been taught.[36]

III

This problem concerning Shinran's conception of joy is closely related to doctrinal discussions on the relationship between shinjin and aspiration for birth in the Pure Land (*yokushō*). In traditional Shinshū studies, scholars have taken up this problem under the rubric of such topics for discussion as truth and expediency in the three vows (*sangan shinke*), aspiration for birth in the Pure Land in the three vows (*sangan yokushō*), and the relationship between shinjin and aspiration (*shingan kōzai*).

In the *Larger Sūtra*, shinjin, practice, and its benefits appear in all three vows for the cause of birth in the Pure Land, namely the Eighteenth, Nineteenth, and Twentieth Vows of Dharmākara Bodhisattva.[37] Shinran understands that each of these is independently vowed to establish the cause for sentient beings' birth in the Pure Land. The differences among the three form the basis for Shinran's exegesis of self power and Other Power. The first significant difference is that, in the Eighteenth Vow, shinjin precedes practice (*shinzen gyōgo*); while in the Nineteenth and Twentieth Vows, practice precedes shinjin (*gyōzen shingo*). Based on this difference, Shinran understands that shinjin in the Nineteenth and the Twentieth Vows is established through sentient beings' practice and identifies this as the shinjin of self power (*jiriki no shin*) in which practitioners aspire to attain birth in the Pure Land through the virtues created by their practices. On the other hand, the shinjin of the Eighteenth Vow, which precedes practice, is the shinjin of Other Power (*tariki no shin*) responding to Amida's commands (*chokumei*) without doubt and in joyful entrustment (*mugi aigyō*). The practice that follows shinjin is defined as the easy practice of enduring shinjin (*shin sōzoku no igyō*). The second difference among the three vows concerns the listing of the three minds. Two of the three minds—sincere mind (*shishin*) and mind of aspiration for birth (*yokushō*)—appear in all three vows. However, the middle of the three minds is different in each vow: in the Eighteenth Vow entrusting (*shingyō*) is listed as the second of the three minds; in the Nineteenth Vow it is aspiration (*hotsugan*); and in the Twentieth Vow it is directing virtues (*ekō*). Shinran's interpretation of this difference is that, although the three vows all mention the mind aspiring for birth, in the Nineteenth and the Twentieth it is the self power mind of aspiration for birth. In the Eighteenth Vow, however, the mind aspiring for birth is to be taken as a synonym for shinjin or entrusting mind (*shingyō*). Therefore, it is interpreted as the mind of settled anticipation (*ketsujō yōgo*) for birth in the Pure Land.[38]

In other words, the mind of aspiring for birth in the Nineteenth and Twentieth Vows identifies the mind of practitioners who abhor their lives in this world of defilement and aspire for the land of purity. It is the mind of practitioners who desire to abandon this world and seek to fill up their feelings of emptiness in the present life with the hope for future birth in the Pure Land. They recognize the defilement of the world they live in yet are unable to recognize their own falsity and insincerity. Shinran realizes that those practitioners misapprehend both the nature of practice and their own motives to believe that they can attain birth in the Pure Land by relying on the root of goodness produced by their own self power practice. No matter how strongly they aspire for birth in the Pure Land, and no matter how much they accumulate roots of goodness, their self power efforts can never free them from anxiety in the present life or provide the strength for living in the present world.

The mind of aspiration for birth in the Eighteenth Vow is traditionally defined as the mind of settled anticipation for birth in the Pure Land. However, if we discuss it without reference to the reality of the present, it simply becomes a future goal. The stronger we wish for the realization of the ideal future, the emptier our present lives become—no matter how firmly settled is our mind for anticipating the realization of future birth in the Pure Land. Even though future birth in the Pure Land is guaranteed, it does not save us from suffering in the present life. Such convictions about future birth are, after all, not so different from the shinjin of self-power in the Nineteenth and Twentieth Vows.

When Shinran realized that Amida's light of wisdom crushed the faults of his incomplete understanding of the Buddha's wisdom (*furyō bucchi*) created out of his reliance on his self power mind of aspiration for birth (*jiriki yokushō shin*), he had the religious experience of "being overturned and entering into the realization of shinjin through the three vows" (*sangan tennyū*). It was then that, for the first time, he realized the mind of entrusting (*shingyō*) without any hindrance of doubts (*gigai muzō*). At that point, his own falsity and insincerity were crushed, and he realized that he was a man "incapable of any other practice."[39]

In the Eighteenth Vow, entrusting (*shingyō*) is to be established as the negation of the self-power mind of aspiration for birth, or the self-power mind hoping for future birth. From the standpoint of the Eighteenth Vow, the present life is not abhorrent simply because one exists in a defiled world; rather, shinjin makes us realize our own insincerity in negating the present reality as abhorrent. When the mind that is attached to self power has been crushed by the light of the Buddha's wisdom, then the present reality which we find difficult to accept is transformed into a positive one in which we can recognize its significance as it is. The mind of aspiration described in the Eighteenth Vow, which is the mind of settled anticipation for birth, is only possible at the moment of shinjin, when the mind is brightened by the Buddha's wisdom and entrusts Amida Buddha's command (*chokumei*).

In the Nineteenth and Twentieth Vows, the mind of aspiration for birth is the aspiration of the "self" (*ware*) toward "tathāgata" (i.e., the Pure Land). When one realizes that this "self" is an ordinary sentient being destined to fall into avici hell (*hitsuda muken*), the direction of aspiration toward the Pure Land is overturned, and one realizes the proper perspective, which is instead that "tathāgata" is directed toward "self." This is the mind of aspiration in the Eighteenth Vow.[40]

> Finally, "aspire for birth" is the command of the Tathāgata calling to and summoning the multitude of all beings ... [H]e took the mind of directing virtues as foremost, and thus realized the mind of great compassion. Accordingly, the Buddha directs this other-benefiting, true and real mind of aspiration for birth to the ocean of all beings. Aspiration for birth is this mind of directing virtues. It is none other than the mind of great compassion; therefore, it is untainted by the hindrance of doubt.[41]

In this realization of shinjin, tathāgata and the Pure Land do not exist in the future but have already come to exist in this present life. They have existed since the time of the absolute past and will exist into the absolute future as an uninterrupted force working in this present reality. The Pure Land realized in shinjin is not a Pure Land waiting in the afterlife. As T'an-luan says, "the name of the land performs the work of the Buddha. How can we conceive of this?"[42] Since one becomes aware of this Pure Land through shinjin in the present—in the "now" (*ima*)—one's salvation is accomplished here, and one receives the benefit of Amida's light once grasped never to be abandoned (*sesshu fusha*).[43] At the moment shinjin is realized, there is no other future life to wish for any longer. For the person of shinjin, there is no need for the welcoming at the moment of death (*rinjū raigō*) in the future time. Therefore, Shinran in one of his letters teaches:

The practicer of true shinjin, however, abides in the stage of the truly settled, for he or she has already been grasped, never to be abandoned. There is no need to wait in anticipation for the moment of death, no need to rely on Amida's coming. At the time shinjin becomes settled, birth too becomes settled.[44]

Although the term "aspiration for birth" (*yokushō*) is used in the context of birth in the Pure Land, it is "now" when we entrust (*shingyō*), and the aspiration is nothing other than the mind of entrusting. Therefore, the term "aspiration for birth" needs to be understood as a synonym for entrusting mind (*shingyo*) in the context of the "now."

In doctrinal discussions on the relationship between shinjin and aspiration (*shingan kōzai*), the term aspiration as used in the Eighteenth Vow has traditionally been interpreted as a synonym for entrusting mind. The term "entrusting mind" is used to signify Amida's command at present, and the term "aspiration for birth" implies the land that is included in Amida's command but is yet to be presented. However, although it is called "the land yet to be presented," it should not be understood in terms of a conviction or wish to be born in a Pure Land existing in an imaginative future time. If we interpret the phrase "the land yet to be presented" as the Pure Land in the temporal future, the joy of shinjin would be equivalent to the mind of settled anticipation (*ketsujō yōgo*). If that were the meaning of the truly settled stage (*shōjōju*), we should rather say that the entrusting mind is a synonym for the mind of aspiration for birth and not vice versa. Since we say that the mind of aspiration is a synonym for the entrusting mind, the joy of shinjin should not be understood as the mind of settled anticipation for future birth. The mind of settled anticipation is established at the moment of realization of the entrusting mind. Shinran's experience of salvation and joy should be understood as realized at the one thought-moment of shinjin (*shin no ichinen*), when he was awakened to be embraced by the benefit of "once grasped never to be abandoned."

IV

According to the presuppositions underlying traditional doctrinal discussions on the meaning of the truly settled stage (*shōjōju*), the concept of birth in the Pure Land (*ōjō*) is understood strictly as to "leave here and be born [in the Pure Land] on the pedestal of the lotus flower,"[45] following Hōnen's teaching. If we are bound by this definition, then interpreting the concept of birth in the context of the present life becomes a radical exercise that some see as distorting the fundamental paradigm of the Pure Land teaching. However, as Ueda Yoshifumi has suggested many times, we must recognize that Shinran employs the concept of birth in the Pure Land with a broader vision beyond the traditional definition of birth as simply a matter of the afterlife.[46] This is evident in Shinran's teaching, such as "becom[ing] established in the stage of the truly settled" is the meaning

of *attaining birth*, [47] and "when a person realizes shinjin, he or she is born immediately."[48] Although I employ the concept of birth in the context of the present
life, I am not saying that ordinary beings become extraordinary or change their
nature in any way. Nor does this shift in viewpoint imply that sentient beings
will attain enlightenment in the present life. Thus there is no need to fear that it
might be confused with the teaching of the Path of Sages. I am well aware of the
dangers of suggesting that enlightenment is attained in the present body and of
Shinran's criticism of such a position in chapter fifteen of the *Tannishō*.

> On the assertion that one attains enlightenment even while maintaining this bodily
> existence full of blind passions. This statement is completely absurd.[49]

If we understand the concept of birth in the Pure Land as leaving here and
being born in the Pure Land, the land is reduced to a place existing in the future
as a kind of continuation of our present lives in this world. Furthermore, if we
continue in this line of thinking, we must necessarily make a split between life
in this world and life in the coming world, taking this world as a defiled land
and the other world as pure. In this context, salvation occurs only after birth into
the Pure Land in the afterlife. Attaining the truly settled stage in the present life,
too, simply becomes a reflection in the present world of our future salvation in
the afterlife. But we must remember that Amida's salvation has been proffered
since the time of innumerable kalpas past and extends into the infinite future.
The Pure Land of Bliss is the land of eternal existence. The Tathāgata, however,
does not quietly preside in that eternal land and wait for us to attain birth. According to T an-luan's explanation of the significance of Amida's accomplishment of the Primal Vow:

> His Vow gave rise to the Power; the Power fulfils the Vow. The Vows have not been
> in vain; the Power is not empty. The Power and Vows work in complete harmony, and
> are not in the least discordant with each other; hence "accomplishment."[50]

Due to Amida's Primal Vow, the Tathāgata never stops working. Shinran understands that, according to his pledge, the Tathāgata has made Śākyamuni
expound the *Larger Sūtra* and causes sentient beings to practice, entrust and
realize. Teaching, practice, entrusting, and realization are all the contents of
Amida's directing his virtues in the aspect of going forth (*ōsō*). Therefore, in the
Chapter on Teaching, Shinran says, "in the aspect of going forth, there is the true
teaching, practice, shinjin, and realization."[51]

The Pure Land is the land of eternity. However, simply because we are going
to the Pure Land in the afterlife we should not assume that the Pure Land exists
only in the future and has nothing to do with our present lives. Our salvation in
the Pure Land does not start in the future. In the *Kyōgyōshinshō*, Chapter on the
True Buddha and the Land, Shinran prefers the word "infinite light" to "infinite
life" in describing the nature of the Pure Land,[52] which implies that Shinran

understands the unhindered working of Amida as destroying the blind passions of sentient beings without interruption.[53] Traditional scholarship also agrees that the True Buddha and the Land are "the peaceful and spontaneous wonderful fruition" and "the root of embracing and awakening all beings in the ten directions." The Tathāgata "exists and expounds the Dharma right now." The Pure Land is also the Pure Land in which "the name of the land performs the work of the Buddha."

In Vasubandhu's *Treatise on the Pure Land* (*Jōdoron*), this eternal Tathāgata and the Pure Land are explained as "the manifestation of true merit." T'an-luan interprets the meaning of "true" here as "neither inverted nor false" (*futendō fukogi*). He explains that it is not false because "it leads sentient beings to ultimate Purity."[54] The Tathāgata and the Pure Land have always existed and transformed sentient beings living in the three realms of impurity by assimilating them into the pure nature of the Tathāgata and the Pure Land.

According to Shinran, the "manifestation of true merit" is "the sacred Name that embodies the Vow,"[55] and "directing of virtue" is "Amida's giving the Name that embodies the Primal Vow to sentient beings throughout the ten quarters."[56] The virtues of the Tathāgata and the Pure Land are directed to sentient beings in the concrete form of the single Name. Therefore, a contact point between, on the one hand, the eternal and true Tathāgata and the Pure Land, which are beyond the paradigm of time, and, on the other hand, us, who live in the paradigm of temporality, is only possible in the "present" when we hear the Name and entrust in it. At the one thought-moment of shinjin, we take refuge in the eternal ocean of the Primal Vow. Shinran teaches that this is the only chance for our salvation to become complete—not before or after. The benefit given at the moment of shinjin is the truly settled stage. Shinran places the benefit of the truly settled stage into the ten benefits given in this life (*genshō jūyaku*).[57] However, within these ten there is no benefit of the *hope* of settled anticipation of future birth. Once we realize shinjin, our attainment of birth in the Pure Land happens naturally. Therefore, Shinran says in the *Hymns of the Pure Land Masters* (*Kōsō wasan*):

> Since shinjin arises from the Vow,
> We attain Buddhahood through the nembutsu by the [Vow's] spontaneous working.
> The spontaneous working is itself the fulfilled land;
> Our realization of supreme nirvāṇa is beyond doubt.[58]

And in the *Hymns of the Dharma-Ages* (*Shōzōmatsu wasan*):

> The directing virtue embodied in Namu-amida-butsu
> Is, in its benevolent working, vast and inconceivable;
> Through the benefit of the directing of virtue for going forth,
> We have already entered (*enyū seri*) the aspect of directing of virtue for returning to this world.[59]

If we simply believe that directing virtue for returning to this world begins only in the afterlife by following a strict dichotomy that this world is for the present life and the Pure Land is for afterlife, then we cannot understand the significance of Shinran's hymn that tells us "we have already entered the aspect of the directing of virtue for returning to this world." We can understand the hymn only when we realize that at the moment of shinjin we have already taken refuge in the Pure Land of eternity.

Taking another tack, one may attempt to associate the relationship between the attainment of nirvāṇa in the Pure Land and the attainment of the truly settled stage in the present life with the idea that "hope for the future sustains our present lives." However, a bit of rhetorical magic lies hiding in this idea. Behind the statement that future hope sustains present life there is an assumption that time flows as an uninterrupted continuum like a river running without interruption. In respect to the concept of birth in the Pure Land, this statement also assumes two separate realms—this world and the coming world (the afterlife). While perhaps the future world is arguably in the process of becoming this world, the future world cannot immediately become this world. Even though we may have "hope of settled anticipation (*ketsujō yōgo*) for birth in the Pure Land, which is the hope of the great settled mind (*dai anjin*) for the truth certainly to be realized," within such a dichotomous interpretation the present world is reduced to nothing but empty human life. To the contrary, we must realize that, when this world is truly fulfilled, we naturally know that the coming life is fulfilled.[60]

Finally, I would like to point out that there is a problem with the analogy comparing time in this world to a Saturday spent anticipating Sunday. The joy of Saturday is based on experiences of actually having enjoyed Sundays in the past. On the other hand, birth in the Pure Land is something we have never experienced. The only person who can truthfully use such an analogy is one who has received in the present life the benefit of having been embraced and never forsaken. An experience of the eternal, an experience of "attaining shinjin," must have occurred first. Only when one attains shinjin does the path of birth in the Pure Land at last become clear. From this standpoint, as Rennyo says, "as for nirvāṇa, we are grateful knowing that Amida will save us."[61] Feelings of gratitude for Amida's salvation naturally inspire us into the anticipation of that salvation, causing us to say," "we are grateful knowing that Amida will save us" and not vice verse (i.e., it is not that anticipation leads to gratitude). It is in this sense that aspiration for birth becomes a synonym for entrusting mind. Therefore, the proposition "hope for the future sustains our present lives" is to be rejected as a viable interpretation of Shinran's concept of attaining the truly settled stage in the present life. We must remember that, for the majority of modern people (with very special exceptions), this kind of interpretation brings no hope for salvation at all.[62]

NOTES

[1] Translator's Note: This is a translation of "Shinran no yorokobi," in *Zoku Shinran kyōgi no kenkyū* (Kyoto: Nagata Bunshōdō, 1989), pp. 91-109, by the late Prof. Murakami Sokusui, Ryukoku University, Kyoto, Japan. This essay originally appeared in *Ryūkoku daigaku ronshū* 400/401 (1973). Unless otherwise noted, all of the quoted passages have been translated into English by the translator. Minor editorial changes and revisions are made in the texts and notes according to the journal's editorial guidelines and conventions of academic publication in English. Additional notes are inserted occasionally to help readers identify the original texts and their English translations if available. Any errors are solely the responsibility of the translator.

[2] Ryukoku University, ed., Shinsh*ū yōron* (Kyoto: Hyakkaen, 1953), pp. 143-144.

[3] Kiritani Junnin, *Shinran wa nani wo toita ka* (Tokyo: Kyōiku Shinchōsha, 1964), pp. 50-52..

[4] *Ibid.*, p. 242.

[5] *Tannishō*, in *The Collected Works of Shinran* (hereafter, CWS) (Kyōto: Jōdo Shinshū Hongwanji-ha, 1997), p. 666.

[6] Katō Kyōjun, *Wakaki sedai no Tannishō* (Kyoto: Hyakkaen, 1958), pp. 83-89.

[7] Honda Kenshō, *Tannishō nyūmon: Kono ranse wo ikinuku tame no chie* (Tokyo: Kōbunsha, 1964), p. 69.

[8] *Ibid.*, p. 112. I would like to remind the reader that my citing of the *Tannishō nyūmon* does not mean that I necessarily agree with all of the author's views in the text.

[9] The concept of dual benefits appears, for example, in the *Rokuyōshō* by Zonkaku: "Question: As for the benefits of attaining the truly settled stage and of attaining of enlightenment, are they dual benefits or a single benefit? Answer: They are dual benefits. The truly settled stage is the attainment of the stage of non-retrogression [in the present life]. Enlightenment is the attainment of nirvāṇa [in the afterlife]" (*Shinshū shōgyō zensho* [hereafter, SSZ], vol. 2, [Kyoto: Ōyagi Kōbundō, 1941], p. 321). In Rennyo's *Letters* (1-4), we also find the following: "Question: Should we understand [the state of] being truly settled and [that of] nirvāṇa as one benefit, or as two? Answer: The dimension of 'the awakening of the one thought-moment' is that of '[joining] the company of those truly settled.' This is the benefit [we gain] in the defiled world. Next, it should be understood that nirvāṇa is the benefit to be gained in the Pure Land. Hence we should think of them as two benefits" (Minor Lee Rogers and Ann T. Rogers, *Rennyo: The Second Founder of Shin Buddhism* [Berkeley: Asian Humanities Press, 1991], p. 152).

[10] *Notes on Once Calling and Many Calling*, in CWS, p. 475, notes 4 and 7. For the original Japanese text, see *Ichinen tanen mon'i*, in SSZ, vol. 2, pp. 605-606.

[11] By using the word "primary" (*daiichigi*), I mean that it is "central" (*chūshin*) but not "ultimate" (*kyūkyoku*). Therefore, here "secondary" (*fukujiteki*) means "subordinate" (*jūzokuteki*).

[12] CWS, p. 4; SSZ, vol. 2, p. 1.

[13] CWS, p. 77; SSZ, vol. 2, p. 47.

[14] CWS, p. 240; SSZ, vol. 2, p. 166.

[15] CWS, p. 291; SSZ, vol. 2, p. 203.

[16] CWS, p. 56; SSZ, vol. 2, p. 35.

[17] In a hymn praising Shan-tao (87), however, Shinran says:

> Casting off long kalpas of painful existence in this world of Sahā,
> We live in expectation of the Pure Land, the uncreated;
> This is the power of our teacher, Śākyamuni;
> Let us respond always in gratitude for his compassion and benevolence.
> (*Hymns of the Pure Land Masters*, in CWS, p. 383; SSZ, vol. 2, p. 511)

In this hymn, Shinran seems to express hope for the anticipated birth in the Pure Land. However, this hymn is based on passages in Shan-tao's *Panchou-tsan (Hanjusan)*.

> Attainment of deliverance from the
> Suffering of many kalpas in the Sahā World
> Is especially due to the benevolence of the
> Great master Śākyamuni.
> (*Hanjusan*, translated by Hisao Inagaki, in *Ryūkoku daigaku ronshū* 434/435
> [1999]: pp. 108-109)

> How can you expect to reach the Treasure Land now?
> It is indeed due to the power of the
> Great Master of the Sahā World [Śākyamuni].
> (*Ibid.*, p. 98)

Also, we need to pay attention to the hymn that precedes the above hymn:

> Had we not received the power of the universal Vow,
> When could we part from this Sahā world?
> Reflecting deeply on the Buddha's benevolence,
> Let us think on Amida always.
> (CWS, p. 383; SSZ, vol. 2, p. 511)

In this hymn, Shinran is emphasizing that "receiving the power of the universal Vow" is the most important factor for birth.

[18] CWS, p. 123; SSZ, vol. 2, p. 79.

[19] *Ibid.*

[20] *Ibid.*

[21] CWS, p. 125; SSZ, vol. 2, p. 80.

[22] CWS, p. 666; SSZ, vol. 2, p. 778.

[23] CWS, p. 665-666; SSZ, vol. 2, p. 777.

[24] CWS, p. 661; SSZ, vol. 2, p. 773.

[25] *Kyōgyōshinshō*, Chapter on Practice, in CWS, p. 54; SSZ, vol. 2, p. 33.

[26] *Kyōgyōshinshō*, Chapter on Shinjin, in CWS, p. 115; SSZ, vol. 2, p. 74.

[27] *Tannishō*, in CWS, 666; SSZ, vol. 2, p. 778.

[28] CWS, p. 153; SSZ, vol. 2, p. 103.

[29] CWS, p. 341; SSZ, vol. 2, p. 493.

[30] CWS, p. 454; SSZ, vol. 2, p. 624.

[31] *Kyōgyōshinshō*, Chapter on Shinjin, in CWS, p. 79; SSZ, vol. 2, p. 48.

[32] Also in the *Passages on the Pure Land Way* (*Jōdomon ruiju shō*), Shinran says that "it is impossible to realize pure shinjin, impossible to attain the highest end. This is because we do not depend on Amida's directing of virtue for our going forth and because we are entangled in a net of doubt" (CWS, p. 299; SSZ, vol. 2, p. 445).

[33] CWS, p. 496-497; SSZ, vol. 2, p. 563.

[34] CWS, p. 662; SSZ, vol. 2, p. 774.

[35] CWS, p. 662; SSZ, vol. 2, p. 774.

[36] CWS, p. 427-428; SSZ, vol. 2, p. 530.

[37] Shinran cites the three vows in the Chapter on Shinjin (18th Vow) and the Chapter on Transformed Buddhas and Lands (19th and 20th Vows) in the *Kyōgyōshinshō* as follows: "If, when I attain Buddhahood, the sentient beings of the ten quarters, with sincere mind entrusting themselves, aspiring to be born in my land, and saying the Name perhaps even ten times, should not be born there, may I not attain the supreme enlightenment. Excluded are those who commit the five grave offences and those who slander the right dharma" (18th Vow, in CWS, p. 80; SSZ, vol. 2. p. 48-49); "If, when I attain buddhahood, the sentient beings of the ten quarters—awakening the mind of enlightenment and performing meritorious acts—should aspire with sincere mind and desire to be born in my land, and yet I should not appear before them at the moment of death surrounded by a host of sages, may I not attain the supreme enlightenment" (19th Vow, in CWS, p. 208; SSZ, vol. 2. p. 144); "If, when I attain Buddhahood, the sentient beings of the ten quarters, on hearing my Name, should place their thoughts on my land, cultivate the root of all virtues, and direct merits with sincere mind desiring to be born in my land, and yet not ultimately attain it, may I not attain the supreme enlightenment" (20th Vow, in CWS, p. 229; SSZ, vol. 2. p. 158).

[38] For a more detailed discussion of this issue, see Murakami Sokusui, *Shinran kyōgi no kenkyū* (Kyoto: Nagata Bunshōdō, 1968), pp. 301-310.

[39] *Tannishō*, in CWS, 662; SSZ, vol. 2, p. 774.

[40] Murakami, *Shinran kyōgi no kenkyū*, p. 12.

[41] Chapter on Shinjin, *Kyōgyōshinshō*, in CWS, p. 103-104; SSZ, vol. 2, p. 65.

[42] Hisao Inagaki, trans., *T'an-luan's Commentary on Vasubandhu's Discourse on the Pure Land* (Kyoto: Nagata Bunshōdō, 1998), p. 233; SSZ, vol. 1, p. 324.

[43] Shinran provides a note explaining this phrase: "*setsu* [to grasp] means to pursue and grasp the one who seeks to run away" (CWS, p. 347).

[44] *Lamp for the Latter Ages* (*Mattōshō*), in CWS, p. 523; SSZ, vol. 2, p. 656.

[45] *Kango tōroku*, vol. 6, in the SSZ, vol. 4, p. 393.

[46] See Ueda Yoshifumi, "Shinran no ōjō shisō," Parts 1 and 2, *Shinran kyōgaku* 13 (1968): pp. 97-117; 14 (1969): pp. 105-128.

[47] *Ichinen tanen mon'i*, in CWS, p. 475; SSZ, vol. 2, p. 605.

[48] *Yuishinshō mon'i,* in CWS, p. 455; SSZ, vol. 2, p. 625.

[49] CWS, p. 674; SSZ, vol. 2, p. 786.

[50] Inagaki, *T'an-luan's Commentary*, p. 251; SSZ, vol. 1, p. 331.

[51] CWS, p. 7; SSZ, vol. 2, p. 2.

[52] CWS, p. 177; SSZ, vol. 2, p. 120

[53] In the *Lamp for the Latter Ages*, Shinran comments: "The statement, 'they attain nirvāṇa,' means that when the heart of the persons of true and real shinjin attain the fulfilled land at the end of his or her present life, that person becomes one with the light that is the heart of Tathāgata, for his reality is immeasurable life and his activity is inseparable from immeasurable light" (CWS, p. 541; SSZ, vol. 2, p. 675). See also Ōe Junjō, *Kyōgyōshinshō kōjutsu* (Kyoto: Nagata Bunshōdō, 1964), p. 274.

[54] Inagaki, *T'an-luan's Commentary*, p. 135; SSZ, vol. 1, p. 285.

[55] *Songō shinzō meimon*, in CWS, p. 501; SSZ, vol. 2, p. 583.

[56] *Ichinen tanen mon'i*, in CWS, p. 474; SSZ, vol. 2, p. 605.

[57] *Kyōgyōshinshō*, Chapter on Shinjin, in CWS, p. 112; SSZ, vol. 2, p. 72.

[58] CWS, p. 382; SSZ, vol. 2, p. 510.

[59] Modified, CWS, p. 411; SSZ, vol. 2, p. 522.

[60] A similar critique can also be applied to Kiritani Junnin's interpretation in *Gendai ni wasurararete iru mono* (Sapporo: Kyōiku Shinchōsha, 1961), pp. 26-31.

[61] See *Rennyo Shōnin goichidai kikigaki*, Chapter 19, in SSZ, vol. 3, p. 537.

[62] In addition to the works referred in the notes, this paper has also been generally informed by the following works:

Ueda Yoshifumi, "Kako genzai mirai ga towareru toki," in *Jōdo Shinshū wo rikai suru tameni*, edited by Dendōin Kenkyūbu (Kyoto: Hongwanji Shuppan Kyōkai, 1972).

Fugen Daien, *Saikin no ōjō shisō wo megurite* (Kyoto: Nagata Bunshōdō, 1972).

Kiritani Junnin, "Genjitsu kyūsai no rikai," in *Ōhara sensei kokikinen: Jōdokyō shisō kenkyū*, edited by Ōhara Sensei Kokikinen Ronbunshū Kankōkai (Kyoto: Nagata Bunshōdō, 1967).

Shigaraki Takamaro, "Shinran shōnin ni okeru genshō shōjōju no igi," *Ryūkoku daigaku ronshū* 365/366 (1960): pp 150-164.

Sasaki Tetsujō, *Shūgi yōron* (Kyoto: Hyakkaen, 1960).

III.   MODERN ISSUES IN SHIN THOUGHT

CHAPTER 12

SHINRAN AND AUTHORITY IN BUDDHISM

—GALEN AMSTUTZ

Master Genkū—the eminent founder who had enabled the true essence of the Pure Land way to spread vigorously [in Japan]—and a number of his followers, without receiving any deliberation of their [alleged] crimes, were summarily sentenced to death or were dispossessed of their monkhood, given [secular] names, and consigned to distant banishment. I was among the latter. Hence, I am now neither a monk [*hisō*], nor an individual in ordinary worldly life [*hizoku*]. For this reason, I have taken the term Toku ["stubble-haired"] as my name.[1]

Jōdo Shinshū Buddhism—the largest of the traditional Japanese Buddhist institutions—is still widely misperceived. The one dominant impression of Shin is that it is the Buddhism for those who are not disciplined enough to participate in the "real," i.e. renunciant (or at least meditative) Buddhist practices which define "normative Buddhism." The reasons for the development of this misleading impression are remarkably complex.[2] Yet the essential issue in Shinran's thought and in the subsequent Shin tradition has always been obvious: not an inferiority complex towards monastic Buddhism, but an articulation of a radically independent sense of self-legitimating Buddhist experience, a puristic Mahāyānist "suddenness."

Shinran's teaching was a comprehensive, systematic reformulation or renarrativization of the Pure Land mythos based on a rearticulated "leap" notion of authority. The question of authority has been so visceral that Shinran's rhetoric has historically been difficult for people outside the Shin tradition to grasp (including other Japanese Buddhists). A high degree of noncommunication has ensued.[3] Yet Shinran's ideas[4] can be summarized clearly as a logical triangle with three conceptual clusters: enlightenment as *ekō*; the idea of Buddhist practice as *akunin shōki* awareness; and the institutional transcendence of the lay-monk polarity in the *hisō hizoku* principle.[5]

The *ekō* ("turning of merit") cluster was fundamental. Shinran's basic insight was that enlightenment had to happen in the final analysis by itself, by some process coming as it were from "outside" the ego. The term *ekō* contained two meanings: the spontaneous religious transformation he called absolute "yielding" or "entrusting" (*shinjin*) in relation to the deity of the Amida Buddha (symbolizing perfect enlightenment), and the revalorization of the concepts "Pure Land" and "entrusting" so that they meant perfect enlightenment and basic earthly enlightenment respectively. The deep linkage between these two aspects of *ekō* was in the fundamental relaxation of "normal" human ego effort. For Shinran, spontaneous "entrusting" was the only way enlightenment could come about. In terms of his linguistic reformulation, *shinjin* was a reliance on "that power" (*tariki*), most accurately a reference to the power of the Eighteenth Vow of Amida laid out in the Larger Pure Land Sūtra as interpreted idiosyncratically by Shinran. In one sense the Vow as understood by Shinran was the declaration of a logical tautology, asserting that the only condition for perfect enlightenment after death (i.e., rebirth in the Pure Land) was a basic enlightenment experience in life; in another, more powerful sense the power of the Vow also lay in the sug-gestion that the Amida Buddha quite independently of human institutions had a certain dynamic energy, an ability to transfer merit (*parināmanā*) or to spon-taneously work to effect enlightenment in human minds. In short, *ekō* implied the notion of *paramārthasatya* (*shintai*, the truth of supreme enlightenment) as an active agent. The Eighteenth Vow or the "working of the Amida Buddha" via *ekō* did not involve monasticism, meditation, texts, other Buddhist deities, and any ritual practices understood as able to cause enlightenment intentionally; all of these miscellaneous practices were lumped together under the classifica-tion of self-power (*jiriki*), for Shinran's *ekō* involved giving up the idea that intentional practices had instrumental value in the final analysis.[6] The practice of vocal nembutsu was also redefined and revalorized, becoming not only the sole meaningful ritual but also no more (and no less) than the expression of thanksgiving that the deity of Amida Buddha was constantly engaged in bring-ing enlightenment about in the course of ordinary human life.[7]

Shinran's *ekō* concept at first looks unconventional, but it was simply a re-statement of traditional Mahāyāna themes. One such theme was the traditional Mahāyāna dialectic of the interrelationship and overlap between the realms of enlightenment and ignorance. Shinran's thought, like all Mahāyāna thought, expressed the ultimate identity of opposites combined with the paradoxical transformation of those opposites into one another; *shinjin* was merely an al-ternate term for the realization of this dual simultaneous saṃsāra-and-nirvāṇa position.[8]

Even more importantly, Shinran's idea of *ekō*, although it had no precedent in conventional Pure Land interpretation, was but a recapitulation in the Pure Land rhetorical context of one of the most ancient problems of Indian thought, that of the "leap" to religious transformation. The monistic religious rhetorics which dominated traditional Buddhism contained irresolvable logical contradic-tions because they could not explain the gap between the ordinary experience of reality and the Higher Reality, or else, they resorted to some conceptual de-vices (such as levels of reality in various Indian systems) which functioned as dualistic explanations anyway. Indeed, the theories of the most important Indian traditions in general—including both Nāgārjuna and *bhakti* schools—ultimately admitted of no clear formal causal relationship (*ajātivāda*) between the state of

ignorance and the state of enlightenment;[9] the idea that the fruit of enlightenment at the end of the path of practice (*mārga*) must be "instantaneously," i.e.,
noncausally, realized became a universal (if implicit) assumption.[10] Although in
normal institutional practice this situation never caused significant doubts about
the centrality of classical Buddhist monastic life's ritual and mythos, it raised
many persistent logical problems about the exact status of the path in relation
to the leap.[11]

Shinran's minimalism restated the spontaneist, *ajātivāda* truism utilizing a
bipolar (rather than a monistic) rhetoric. It explicitly postulated a gap between
the ideal reality of *paramārthasatya* and the problematic ordinary reality of ego
and attachment. For Shinran, it was only as ego and attachment were dissolved
and broken down by the activity of *paramārthasatya* (Amida Buddha), which
came as it were from "outside" the troubled ordinary mind, that this boundary
was softened. Classical Shin doctrine presented this dichotomy as never being
fully overcomeable in a living person anyway—no human experience could become so fluid as to be entirely at one with the perfect *pratītyasamutpāda*—but
what could be achieved, in the state of Yielding or "right assurance," was an understanding that one had gotten close enough to enlightenment in life that one's
unwanted karmic continuation would cease at death.[12] In any case, by (provisionally) situating "enlightenment" and "human ignorance" as separate spheres,
the logical problems of self-reference which monistic conceptualization entailed
(as in Ch'an/Zen) were eliminated.

The idea of reliance on an "external" deity—in Shinran's case Amitābha—
was normal in Mahāyāna religious life. For example, the texts of Bhāvaviveka,
a sixth century Madhyamaka thinker, showed that the concept of emptiness and
the concept of the Buddha were inseparable, and that to "see" the philosophical
idea was the same as seeing "the Buddha" and vice versa. Not only was emptiness associated with a specific form of sensory perception, but visual power
yielded concrete visions of the Buddha's physical form which might be merged
with intellectual understanding in a single philosophical and devotional act.[13]
While the gap between worshiper and Buddha who is worshiped was ultimately
broken down in nonduality, that nonduality was inseparable from the "dualistic"
experience of concrete manifestation via deity. Out of this combination of self-
reliance and dependence on Buddhas and bodhisattvas arose the special irony
characteristic of the more sophisticated Mahāyāna literature: to be truly independent was to realize one's dependence on others, especially spiritual beings
manifesting emptiness.[14]

Shinran's idea of reliance was more abstract than that of classical Indian or
Chinese Buddhism. A strong element of visionary experience had manifested
itself in Shinran's own youthful experience, and the principles of his doctrines
were partly discovered in transcendental encounters with Buddhist deities or
texts. However, once Shinran's mature doctrine was established, the importance
of classical visionary experience dropped away and played little part in the later

mainstream teaching.[15] Shinran's interpretation of the Pure Land mythos had a relatively modern character because it short-circuited the mediating feature of conventional Buddhist religiosity which had consisted of the supernormal bodhisattvas and visionary experience. Although the mythic framework had been set up by the efforts of the bodhisattva Dharmākara in the immemorial past, Shinran's own interpretation of *shinjin* went directly to the "formless" or "non-cognitive" realm of *paramārthasatya* as active agent, thus bypassing the deities and altered states traditionally cultivated by specialists.[16] Through *ekō*, ultimate enlightenment (the Amida) communicated with the world of the human directly, changing the Amida from a more or less physical, concretely visual-ized deity to a relatively abstract representation of perfected *pratītyasamutpāda*. Shinran's Amida was no longer an object either "interior" or "exterior," but was still a transforming "force" still somehow "other" by virtue of the gap between ignorance and enlightenment.[17]

Having done away with the usual intentional and visionary traditions, prac-tice for Shinran consisted instead on the recognition of the bipolarity of the states of ignorance and enlightenment in everyday life, i.e. the push and pull of human ignorance and Amida's light.[18] This theory of practice constituted the second cluster, *akunin shōki* awareness. The "evil person" (*akunin*), defined according to Shinran's special dyadic view, was inherently the true object (*shōki*) of the activity of the Amida. However, Shinran's rhetoric of the power of the vow and the final "leap" to basic satori was deceptive in that it concealed how much a definite disciplinary regime was built into the approach, although it was distinc-tively nonmonastic and mundane. Thus, rather than relying on precepts, visual-ization, and meditation, Shinran's approach relied on critical introspective study of the operations of the ego in ordinary daily life and on an eventual recognition of the polar relationship between the suffering produced by these ego operations and the liberation produced by the intervention by the *paramārthasatya*/Amida (from "outside" as it were) into the ordinary ego frame.[19]

Though independent of tantrism as such as practiced in China and Japan, a relationship existed between Shinran's mild-mannered, mundane introspective study of ego and the more exotic transgressive practices of tantric Buddhism. In each case, the world of ignorance was examined and exploited as part of a systematic scheme to lift and direct attention to the presence of other liberatory possibilities. In the case of Shin, one major aspect of this approach was the ac-ceptance of sexuality in normal life, or at least a marginalization of renunciant sexual control as a main issue.[20]

Shinran's ideas about enlightenment via *ekō* and correct practice as *akunin shōki* awareness culminated in the denial of the essential meaningfulness of the monk-lay categories in the obtaining of enlightenment.[21] This was the third clus-ter, the *hisō hizoku* (neither monk nor lay) principle. Conventional Buddhism had already implicitly agreed that enlightenment involved a "leap" whose exact karmic preconditions were not precisely knowable, but conventional Buddhism had generally accepted without question the mythic models of monasticism or the charismatic teacher in a legitimating lineage. (Indeed, classical monastic Buddhism tended to presuppose a necessary homology between its experiential and institutional dichotomies, that is, the experiential dichotomy between wisdom and ignorance must normally be correlated with the institutional distinction between monk and lay.) Shinran's doctrine rejected the institutional dichotomy while preserving the experiential one. This modification of the institutional theory in Buddhism had major repercussions. According to Shinran no person or lineage could mediate the working of the Buddha in another (as distinguished, however, from being able to provide a correct religious description of the *tariki* enlightenment process). Thus, even more than in monastic lineage traditions, Shinran's theory emphasized the individual as the independent locus of enlightenment with minimal conventions.

Buddhism could still be embodied in a community of followers and in a teaching leadership, but not a monastic community and not a monastic leadership. The working principle instead became equal followership (*dōbō*) among persons linked by acceptance of the *tariki* theory, replacing the kinds of hierarchy presumed in traditional forms of Buddhist institutionalization. The model for a Buddhist community which emerged from Shinran's thought was so different from the models of monastic Buddhism that it initiated an entirely different politics: it allowed the development of a new kind of Buddhist organization based on an underlying egalitarian principle. Furthermore, putting enlightenment theoretically beyond the control of any specific teacher or any specific instrumental practices generated a flexible inclusivity; followers had to agree on the *tariki* principle and on the authority claim of the Honganji family to maintain the proper teaching about it, but did not have to agree on much else.

The denial, or marginalization, of conventional monastic status meant the marginalization of the semantic field associated with either asceticism in the traditional institutions or guru-disciple relationships in tantric Buddhism, especially magic and thaumaturgy (such as conventional merit transfer from monks to ancestors). This shift especially involved a denial of the uses of magic and thaumaturgy by states or aristocrats for private purposes and a rejection of the use of Buddhism as an instrument of political control over the people. Magic and thaumaturgy had been networked with *kami* and with *honji suijaku* concepts in ways linked to the political power establishment. The rejected field of conventional monastic Buddhist semantics also included a range of pollution-purity concerns which were connected to the maintenance of the oppressive social statuses of women and eta.[22]

Shinran did not attack the traditional mythos of Buddhism so much as go completely around it and ignore it in favor of an independent approach. Criticism of monasticism was implicit, but Shin (like Nichiren in yet another way) had such a self-sustaining mythos of its own that its propositions did not depend on, and were ultimately not defined by, the contrasts with monasticism.

The three interlocking clusters of ideas in Shinran's thought were accompanied by a stylistic shift in the presentation of Buddhism, toward a simplification of ritual, text, and iconography. Nevertheless, Shin shared the general features of Mahāyāna tradition with the monastic schools: philosophy, ritual, chanting and music, architecture, textual study, moral seriousness (even if the formal attitude toward the monastic precepts was different), religious education, and karma theory. Indeed what remained striking was not how much Shinshū differed from other kinds of Buddhism, but how much it paralleled them. Furthermore, even without a sophisticated understanding of Buddhist *śūnyatā* philosophy on the part of a follower, Shinran's rhetoric distinctively inculcated strong emotional, ethical, and political ideas: the *ekō* concept yielded a mood of universal hope and, for lack of a better word, "piety"; the practice of *akunin shōki* awareness taught humility and self-criticism; and *hisō hizoku* gestured toward an absolute idea of underlying human spiritual equality. These emotional, ethical, and political ideas together bonded into a powerful new moral field, a field which transcended the old concept of Buddhist practice as a gradual progress to rebirth as monk after many karmic cycles.

Of course, even though Shinran's thought was rooted in traditional Mahāyānist understandings about the spontaneity of enlightenment, in many respects it was also so creatively unconventional, its legitimating claims so formally tenuous, and the political authority implications so serious, that the doctrines were open to many criticisms. These became as much a part of the tradition as Shinran's ideas themselves. Two major issues stood out: Shinran's difficulties with achieving conventional textual legitimation, and the misleading outward appearance of the *akunin shōki* rhetoric which accompanied *ekō*.

Shinran exaggerated the formal validity of his legitimating claims. The traditional Honganji lineage notion that Shinran reflected Hōnen's original intent has always been doubtful: the Pure Land tradition closest to Hōnen was probably Benchō's *Chinzei-ha* and its teachings about the literal *nembutsu*, the conventional Pure Land, and the residual monastic path. However, the most fundamentally problematic issue was Shinran's technique of using the Buddhist scriptures to justify his ideas. Successful normal interpretation required meeting the expectations of received Buddhist conventions: texts had to be acceptable, word definitions and usage had to be acceptable, and a schematic conceptual structure had to be set up and aligned with traditional Buddhist concerns. Instead, Shinran imposed his *ekō* ideas on his materials and reorganized the conventional terms to fit his purposes.[23] Indeed, Shinran generated his dry and nonvisionary rhetoric of Buddhist enlightenment by stringing together conceptual and linguistic bits from a body of Buddhist rhetoric which was in fact largely visionary; this process required a particularly creative recombinant hybridization of inherited East Asian Buddhism. The idiosyncratic intellectual discourse which resulted was highly rational, sophisticated, and systematic on its own terms, and yet was at the same time forced and artificial with respect to its original source texts.[24]

Consequently, Shinran's handling was simply not persuasive to the normal, i.e. monastic, community.

The most confusing aspect of Shinran's rhetoric was the embedded language of the "easy" path of yielding to Amida as opposed to the "difficult" path of the monastic sages. Language subordinating Pure Land to monastic Buddhism had naturally been built into Pure Land rhetoric from India onwards and was part of its received conceptual structure. In Shinran, the easy path language was merged with what appears to be Shinran's own distinctive personal language of self-abnegation.

> I know truly how grievous it is that I, Gutoku Shinran, am sinking in an immense ocean of desires and attachments and am lost in vast mountains of fame and advantage; so that I rejoice not at all at entering the stage of the truly settled [*shinjin*] and feel no happiness at coming nearer the realization of true enlightenment. How ugly it is! How wretched![25]

Modern commentators especially have latched onto this passage to show that as an individual Shinran was lacking in self-confidence or self-respect and that somehow this individual failure is the key to the tradition.[26] However, while to some extent Shinran (like any Buddhist intellectual) was clearly an individual with a profound sense of self-analysis, treating the self-reflection passages in isolation radically ignores the impersonal larger context of Shinran's language. In actuality, the statements on self-reflection were part of the comprehensive interpretation systematically reconstructed around *ekō, hisō hizoku* and particularly the regime of *akunin shōki* practice. Since *akunin shōki* represented a particular kind of sophisticated mythic approach, the language of self-abnegation had a strongly rhetorical quality and served as a structural aspect of Shinran's bipolar Buddhist conceptualization. When Shinran used the character *gu* ("foolish") famously to describe himself in the *Kyōgyōshinshō* and some other works, it was in the sense of "precept breaker," thus establishing his nonmonastic Buddhist mythos.[27] The explicit language of self-criticism or self-abnegation actually occupied only a small portion of Shinran's doctrinal corpus.[28]

Overall, Shinran's writing was quite preponderantly sūtra-based Mahāyānist language manipulated at both popular and technical levels. He was not a confessional writer, but a systematic mytho-philosopher. No unambiguous evidence exists that Shinran thought of his approach as inferior to the monastic one. Some of Shinran's original remarks, as well as the attitude of the later tradition, suggest that he even directed a certain amount of sarcasm towards monasticism which is concealed behind the surface rhetoric of "easy" and "difficult."

> [I]f you imagine in me some special knowledge of a way to birth other than the nembutsu or a familiarity with the writings that teach it, you are greatly mistaken. If that is the case, you would do better to visit the many eminent scholars in Nara or on

Mt. Hiei and inquire fully of them about the essentials for birth. I simply accept and entrust myself to what a good teacher told me, "Just say the Name and be liberated by Amida"; nothing else is involved. [29]

It may be assumed that Shinran was aware that he was issuing a challenge to the mythos of monastic Buddhism and its authority.[30]

This ex-insider's conflicted relationship with normal Buddhist authority and its mytho-philosophical conventions may be the real key to Shinran. Above all, nothing about the subsequent history of the Shin tradition suggested a weak sensibility lacking in energy or activity. Shinran's successors and the larger Shin doctrinal tradition which grew out of the original work stressed positive Shinranian themes of the inclusiveness of the *tariki hongan* (*Main Vow of the other-power*) and the construction of the universal *kyōdan* (community of the teaching). This community became the largest, richest, most independent, and most active in traditional Japan. Thus, far from being simply a "failed monk," behind the masks of technical interpretation and his own self-deprecation, Shinran may be construed as being one of the most shrewdly and profoundly rebellious individuals in East Asian history.

NOTES

[1] Yoshifumi Ueda, ed., *The True Teaching, Practice and Realization of the Pure Land Way: A Translation of Shinran's Kyōgyōshinshō*, 4 vols. (Kyoto: Shin Buddhism Translation Series, Hongwanji International Center, 1983-1990), vol. 4, p. 613 (slightly altered for clarity).

[2] See Galen Amstutz, *Interpreting Amida: Orientalism and History in the Study of Pure Land Buddhism* (Albany: SUNY Press, 1997).

[3] Zen schools, for example, often criticized the Shin tradition for its laxity in monastic practices, borrowing the Pure Land rhetoric of "easy practice" out of its Shin context; this ignored Shin's overt theoretical rejection of monastic authority, as well as the rhetorical aspect of the opposition of "difficult" and "easy." Scholars in the academic monastic traditions rarely even engaged Shin; those that tried, such as Kegon's Hōtan (1651-1736), could find the *Kyōgyōshinshō* impossible to understand (Kiritani Junnin, *Kyōgyōshinshō ni kiku*, 3 vols. [Tokyo: Kyōiku Shinchōsha, 1979], vol. 1, p. 21).

[4] Summaries of Shinran's thought include Yoshifumi Ueda and Dennis Hirota, *Shinran: An Introduction to his Thought* (Kyoto: Hongwanji International Center, 1989), Dennis Gira, *Le Sens de la Conversion dans l'Enseignement de Shinran* (Paris: Editions Maisonneuve et Larose [Collège de France, Bibliothèque de l'Institut des Hautes Études Japonaises, 1985]), Alfred Bloom, *Shinran's Gospel of Pure Grace* (Tucson: University of Arizona Press, 1965), or Alicia and Daigan Matsunaga, *Foundations of Japanese Buddhism*, Vol. II, The Mass Movement (Los Angeles: Buddhist Books International), pp. 95-106.

[5] Shinran's original ideas were presented, even at their most "popular," in a form of technical Buddhological writing related to *p'an chiao* (J., *hankyō* [*kyōsōhanjaku*]), the East Asian

Buddhist tradition of justifying a presentation of Buddhist doctrine in terms of rankings or modulations of the accepted textual tradition. (On *p'an chiao*, see Kenneth Ch'en, *Buddhism in China* (Princeton: Princeton University Press, 1964), pp. 181-182, 303-311, 318-319; see *kyōsōhanjaku* in Kaneko Daiei *et al.*, eds., *Shinshū shinjiten* [Kyoto: Hōzōkan, 1983], pp. 108-109.) The pervasive relation to *p'an chiao* first meant that Shin doctrine was specially concerned about only a very narrow issue, the authority question of *ekō*. Second, it meant that it was inseparably tied to longstanding features of Pure Land rhetoric and was embedded in the Sino-Japanese Mahāyāna philosophical tradition; it presupposed a shared philosophy and sensibility. But presentation of Shinran's doctrines in his own *p'an chiao* style—in other words, in terms of his own *Kyōgyōshinshō* schematizations and even their popularizations in the wasan and other works—is noncommunicative to any but an informed Buddhist audience.

[6] "Yielding to the Buddha" (*shinjin*) in Shinran's Pure Land language was the same as the forty-first and higher bodhisattva ranks in conventional monastic schemata. (Like earlier Buddhist concepts of *sraddhā* ("faith"), Shinran's *shinjin* had no meaning outside of its unique context (viz., the idea of "conversion"; see Gira)). Theories about the rapid realization of Buddhahood had already emerged with Saichō and Kūkai, where *sokushin jōbutsu* meant a stage of basic satoric realization in this life; thus the concept was long current. (Paul Groner, "Sokushin jōbutsu Traditions at Mt. Hiei," in George J. Tanabe, Jr., and Willa Jane Tanabe, eds., *The Lotus Sūtra in Japanese Culture* [Honolulu: University of Hawaii Press, 1989], pp. 53-74.)

[7] The interpretation of *nen* was the traditional crux. Conventional monastic Pure Land teachings understood this to mean a range of practices; popular Pure Land and some of Hōnen's followers took it to mean physical vocalization of the name of the Buddha; Shinran took it to mean the involuntary satoric *shinjin* transformation itself, only secondarily (and ritually) expressed in the vocalization of the Buddha's name.

[8] Ueda Yoshifumi, "The Mahayana Structure of Shinran's Thought, Part I," *The Eastern Buddhist* vol. 17, no. I (Spring 1984), pp. 57-78 and "The Mahayana Structure of Shinran's Thought, Part II," vol. 17, no. 2 (Autumn 1984), pp. 30-54. But as Ueda notes (Part II, p. 54) the trend in Shin rhetoric after Shinran was to speak monotonously of the *shinjin* experience as a promise of "rebirth" or karmic liberation into the supreme enlightenment, rather than to explore the Mahāyānist complexities of the saṃsāra/nirvāṇa simultaneity or to pursue the clarification of relationships with other kinds of Buddhist rhetoric. The specialized narrowness of the Shinshū *p'an chiao* academic tradition and its political emphasis has made Shinran's thought seem more intellectually naive than it was.

[9] Karl H. Potter, *Presuppositions of India's Philosophies* (Englewood Cliffs, NJ: Prentice-Hall, 1963), pp. 236-254.

[10] David Seyfort Ruegg, *Buddha-nature, Mind and the Problem of Gradualism in Comparative Perspective: On the Transmission and Reception of Buddhism in India and Tibet* (London: School of Oriental and African Studies, University of London, 1989), pp. 6-8, 141-182.

[11] See Ruegg and the essays in Peter N. Gregory, ed., *Sudden and Gradual: Approaches to Enlightenment in Chinese Thought* (Honolulu: University of Hawaii Press, 1987). The disputes over the conceptualization of the path and the mārga-enlightenment relationship eventuated most prominently in the sudden and gradual controversies associated with Ch'an and in the famous Ch'an-Tibetan debate studied by Ruegg.

[12] Strangely, this particular configuration of Buddhist myth had never previously appeared in Asian Buddhism in spite of the pervasive prior awareness of the idea of the active bodhisattva or buddha, the idea of *parināma[nā]* (merit transfer from a bodhisattva) and the generic awareness that final enlightenment must of necessity be instantaneous.

[13] Malcolm David Eckel, *To See the Buddha: A Philosopher's Quest for the Meaning of Emptiness* (San Francisco: Harper, 1991), pp. 3-4; see also Eckel, "Gratitude to an Empty Savior: A Study of the Concept of Gratitude in Mahāyāna Buddhist Philosophy," *History of Religions*, vol. 25, no. 1 (1985), pp. 57-75.

[14] An important part of Bhāvaviveka's rhetoric was even given over to the concept of "previous vows" (*pranidhāna*), by which the Buddha expressed his activity to rescue humankind (Eckel, *To See the Buddha*, pp. 17-18, 51-61, 68-83, 147-48). Thus gratitude to an "empty" deity, the symbolized "otherness" of perfect emptiness, saturated Mahāyāna. (Cf. George R. Elder, "'Grace' in Martin Luther and Tantric Buddhism," in Houston, G. W., ed., *The Cross and the Lotus: Christianity and Buddhism in Dialogue* [Delhi: Motilal, 1985], pp. 39-49; Elder discusses how tantric Buddhism also can externalize the Buddha's action as "grace.") These ideas originated separately from the Pure Land mythos per se.

[15] The Heian genre of *ōjōden* (records of visionary encounter with Amida) tended to fade in importance after the Kamakura period. (See Frederic J. Kotas, "Ojoden: Accounts of Rebirth in the Pure Land," [University of Washington Ph.D. dissertation 1987], pp. 198-199.)

[16] Shinran's *tariki* system paid less attention to the visionary details of the mythic *sambhogakāya* or to the physical, concrete engagement with a visionary deity via traditional practices of visualization *samādhi* or even oral nembutsu. Conventionally the Pure Land was a *hōdo* or "recompensed" land, one of the regions of existence where the *sambhogakāya* or enjoyment body of the Buddha manifested itself, for this was the aspect of the Buddha most associated with the tradition of visionary contact; on the other hand, supreme perfect enlightenment or *dharmakāya* had been something more transcendent, beyond and above the *hōdo* Pure Land. Shinran collapsed the conventional categories so that Pure Land was both *hōdo* and supreme *dharmakāya* in one. This shift retained the bipolarity between ignorance and enlightenment but obviated the visionary.

[17] The terminology which Shin retained for its own working iconography of Amida images was not *sambhogakāya*, but *hōben hōshin* (*upāya* dharma-bodies), i.e. provisional representations of the supreme ultimate (but not the same as *sambhogakāya*).

[18] Shinran's understanding of karma was subordinated to his overall ideas of *ekō* and *akunin shōki*. (Leslie Kawamura, "Shinran's View of Karma," in Ronald W. Neufeldt, *Karma and Rebirth: Post Classical Developments* [Albany: State University of New York Press, 1986], pp. 191-202, and Ueda Yoshifumi, "Freedom and Necessity in Shinran's Concept of Karma," *The Eastern Buddhist* N.S. vol. 19, no. 1 [Spring 1986], pp. 76-100.)

[19] Shinran's teaching was distinguished by the absence of anything that could be called *śamatha* (concentrative meditation). If nembutsu recitation in other Pure Land teachings or in Zen-oriented systems was primarily a form of concentrative meditation, Shinran's idea of becoming aware of the dyadic relationship of ego and enlightenment was more like *vipasyanā* ("insight meditation"). (On the ambiguity of the uses of *śamatha* in traditional Buddhism, see Ruegg.)

[20] But here too there was a difference with specialist tantric practice: where tantra developed

complex and dramatic ritual procedures to merge with the deities and break the boundaries of ignorance, Shin practice remained mundane, using daily life as the object of its special kind of *vipasyanā*. Although the idea was not theoretically developed in traditional Shin doctrine, some scholars have suggested that these tantra-like themes of enlightenment-in-"transgression" played a role in Shinran's marriage, which was more complex than its surface character (violation of the monastic precepts) would suggest. (Minamoto Junko, "On Shinran's Marriage," *Young East* N.S. Vol. 10 [Summer 1984], p. 3, pp. 3-8.)

[21] Hosokawa Gyōshin, "Shinran no 'Mukai myōji no biku' ni tsuite," in Chiba Jōryū and Hataya Akira, eds. *Shinran shōnin to Shinshū* (Kyoto: Yoshikawa Kōbundō, 1985), pp. 29-41, discusses Shinran in detail as a "preceptless monk" or "monk in name only." Shinran has been compared to Vimalakīrti (see Miyai Yoshio, *Nihon jōdokyō no seiritsu* [Tokyo: Seikō shobō, 1979], pp. 201-240, or Mikiri Jikai, "Yuimakyō ni mirareru kairitsu," in Sasaki Kyōgō, ed. *Kairitsu shisō no kenkyū* [Kyoto: Heirakuji shoten, 1981], pp. 329-341), but even the *Vimalakīrti Sūtra* (*Yuimakvō*) supports the precepts. Since the Shin teaching is neither monastic nor guru-initiated, it is not clear (despite its fund of practical social wisdom) that the Shin is really describable as a traditional bodhisattva path. (Yün-hua Jan, "The Bodhisattva Idea in Chinese Literature: Typology and Significance," in *The Bodhisattva Doctrine in Buddhism* [Waterloo, Ontario: Canadian Corporation for Studies in Religion by Wilfrid Laurier University Press, 1981], pp. 125-152; in the same volume, Hisao Inagaki, "The Bodhisattva Doctrine as Conceived and Developed by the Founders of the New Sects in the Heian and Kamakura Periods," pp. 165-192; and Leslie S. Kawamura, "The Myōkōnin: Japan's Representation of the Bodhisattva," pp. 223-237.) Shinran's own view was made clearest in the *Tannishō*: "In the matter of compassion, the Path of Sages and the Pure Land path differ. Compassion in the Path of Sages is to [intentionally] pity, sympathize with and care for beings. But the desire to save others from suffering is vastly difficult to fulfill. Compassion in the Pure Land path lies in saying the Name [in *shinjin* celebration], quickly attaining Buddhahood, and freely benefiting sentient beings bearing a [*tariki*] heart of great love and great compassion. [Because] in our present lives, it is hard to carry out the [intentional bodhisattva] desire to aid others however much love and tenderness we may feel; hence such compassion always falls short of fulfillment" (Dennis Hirota, trans., *Tannishō: A Primer: A Record of the Words of Shinran Set Down in Lamentation Over Departures from his Teaching* [Kyoto: Ryukoku University, 1982], p. 24; slightly altered for clarity).

[22] *Eta* is the untouchable, outcast group in Japan.—*Ed.*

[23] The notion that Shinran's "leap" ideas could be read into any of the seven "patriarchs" he selected for his mythos was implausible. (According to Shinran's theory, the elements of *tariki* teaching had been found in seven of the major earlier teachers: Nāgārjuna, Vasubandhu, Tan-luan, Tao-ch'o, Shan-tao, Genshin, and Hōnen.)

[24] The approach had a Rube Goldberg quality, and like a Rube Goldberg invention required a certain suspension of disbelief. Shin apologists even in English have too often maintained a disingenousness about this relationship and presented the difficult *p'an chiao* texts as if they were intelligible at face value. This remains one of the barriers to the intelligibility of Shinran's language outside of the Shin community. (See Luis O. Gómez, "Shinran's Faith and the Sacred Name of Amida," *Monumenta Nipponica* vol. 38, no. 1, esp. pp. 81-84.) Where this problem has been recognized, it has been addressed mainly in the limited terms of how Shinran's readings of the source texts diverged literally from the normal readings. (See e.g., Ueda, *Kyōgyōshinshō* for notes on Shinran's variant readings.)

[25] As translated in Ueda, *Kyōgyōshinshō*, vol. II, p. 279; cf. Suzuki, D.T. trans. and commentary, *The Kyōgyōshinshō: The Collection of Passages Expounding the True Teaching, Living, Faith and Realizing of the Pure Land* (Kyoto: Shinshū Ōtaniha, 1973), p. 140. Cited for example in Takahatake Takamichi, *Young Man Shinran: A Reappraisal of Shinran's Life* (Waterloo, Ontario: Canadian Corporation for Studies in Religion by Wilfrid Laurier University Press, 1987), p. 102, or Bloom, p. 29.

[26] See especially Shinran's invented term for himself, Gutoku. Suzuki, for example, posed this as consisting of two Chinese characters meaning literally "ignorant" and "bald-headed." This suggested Shinran's unworthiness to be in the monastic priesthood, his commonness, his stupidity. (Suzuki, *Kyōgyōshinshō*, pp. 140, 212; viz. also see paradigmatic treatment by Bloom, pp. 28-30.)

[27] Bandō Shōjun, "Shinran no kairitsukan," in Sasaki Kyōgō, ed. *Kairitsu shisō no kenkyū* (Kyoto: Heirakuji shoten, 1981), pp. 555-579. More accurately than Suzuki, Ueda and Hirota gloss the meaning of the character "Toku" in the name Gutoku as short-haired, stubble-headed, or badly-shaven. The term was used to describe the hair of monks who had let it grow out longer than appropriate; thus it was a term of derision for those who broke the precepts. (*Shinran: An Introduction to His Thought*, p. 34.) In the terms of his own *tariki* thought, Shinran's self-appellation of Gutoku is best considered a complex irony directed not only at himself but at the monastic institution.

[28] The Gutoku passage cited is the only statement like it in the *Kyōgyōshinshō*; a few other statements along these lines appear in the *Tannishō*, a posthumous work by one of Shinran's followers which is thought to record some of his oral teaching. However, almost all of the language of self-criticism or despair in Shinran occurs in the *wasan* verse set *Shōzōmatsu wasan* (verses on the *mappō* decline of the dharma), where the overt subject is the decline of monastic Buddhism, which accentuates the need for Shinran's *ekō* theory. Thus almost every such passage can be assimilated to Shinran's impersonal *tariki* theory. In a very few places the personal voice of Shinran seems to appear, for example, his reflection on his own egoistic desire to be a teacher (Ryukoku University Translation Center, *Shōzōmatsu Wasan: Shinran's Hymns on the Last Age* [Kyoto: Ryukoku University Press, 1980], no. 116, p. 120).

[29] Hirota, *Tannishō*, pp. 35-36; slightly altered.

[30] Takahatake, pp. 5-6, 89. The first words in the *Kyōgyōshinshō* are *hisokani omonmireba* and *tsutsushinde*: "I reflect within myself [*hisokani omonmireba*]: The universal Vow difficult to fathom is indeed a great vessel bearing us across the ocean difficult to cross ... . Reverently [*tsutsushinde*] contemplating the true essence of the Pure Land way ... " (Ueda, *Kyōgyōshinshō*, vol. 1, p. 57, 63; Kiritani, vol. 1, pp. 76, 102). However, *hisokani* ("keeping it to oneself") and *tsutsushinde* ("with restraint, with self-control, fearing danger") can also be rendered as "carefully," "circumspectly" or "cautiously"; such renderings would be in consonance with the original political environment which faced Shinran. Of course, later interpretation, especially as routinized in the Tokugawa period, tried to emphasize the innocuousness of the *tariki* theory of authority.

CHAPTER 13

SHINRAN AND MODERN INDIVIDUALISM

—GERHARD SCHEPERS

Individualism has long ceased to be a phenomenon characteristic only of Western societies, as the stereotypes of East and West would like it to be. It likely never was the sole prerogative of the West anyway. Economic progress, worldwide communication, and modern life styles have advanced the tendency towards individualism everywhere in the contemporary world. Japan is, of course, no exception. The impact of this can be seen in various ways in the religious world. Growing independence of thought and critical awareness often lead to a rejection of traditional forms of religion and even religion as such. However, as a result of global interchange between cultures and societies, there is also a growing appreciation of the myriad religious traditions in the world, and of the different cultural elements and modes of living or thinking which they invoke. This has also led to more pluralism within the single traditions and thus to more space and movement for individual choice among different value systems.

On the one hand, these tendencies may lead to a growing egocentrism and isolation of the individual. With regard to American society, Robert N. Bellah has pointed out that religion tends to become more and more individualistic and private and that, in the end, individuals may formulate their own private religion.[1] On the other hand, confused by the complexity of modern life and without a firm basis to support them as independent individuals, many people turn back to traditional, pre-modern forms of religion or to religious fundamentalism. The latter seems to provide solid ground for the individual but, at the same time, it rejects individual freedoms and spurns many other elements of modern society. Can religion not have a more positive function with regard to the problems of the contemporary world? Is the consciousness of the individual and individualism's conceptual framework not deeply rooted in religious traditions? In the following, I will try to show that a religious basis for modern individualism can be located not only in the Judaeo-Christian tradition, but also in Japanese religion, namely in Shinran.

I The Religious Basis of Individualism

In the Western tradition, the growing emphasis placed on the individual and on personal responsibility has been, since the time of the Old Testament, closely

155

related to religious experience. This emphasis was developed especially by the prophets in the context of a deep awareness of their own sinfulness.[2] In Christianity, it has been based on two elements of faith that mutually condition each other: an awareness of deep personal sinfulness similar to that in the Old Testament and, at the same time, faith in God's love that accepts and saves each individual human being.[3] Other cultural factors have also contributed to the emergence of the modern individual in the West: Greek thought, Roman civilization, particularly Roman law, and the spirit of independence of the Germanic nations could be mentioned here. Since medieval times we observe a deepening self-consciousness of the individual. This is no more apparent than in Luther, who rose up to defend his personal belief against Pope and Emperor, the supreme religious and secular authorities of the time. Luther's emphasis on faith alone, on the hopelessness of the human situation as long as one relies on one's own efforts, as well as other elements in his life and thought bear a close and compelling resemblance to elements in Shinran. This has been pointed out by a number of scholars. Related to this deepened religious consciousness of the individual is a concomitant development in European thought since the Middle Ages, the growing critical consciousness that has advanced modern science and philosophy with their secular and often anti-religious tendencies.

With regard to the situation in Japan, Tesshi Furukawa deplores the fact "that in Japanese society the individual has never been firmly established in his own proper right. [4] Here, there is surely a considerable difference to the development witnessed in European society. Consciousness of the individual is, however, not lacking in the Japanese tradition. Among religious thinkers in Japan, Shinran is probably the one who has most strongly and convincingly emphasized the importance of the individual. Best known in this context is his word, quoted in the epilogue of the *Tannishō*: "When I carefully consider the Vow ... I find that it was solely for me, Shinran, alone!"[5] Yasutomi Shinya rightly speaks of the discovery of the self in Hōnen and Shinran and of its close relation to the idea of salvation in Jōdo Buddhism.[6] Ienaga Saburō also emphasizes the emergence of a faith that is based on the independence of the individual as an important new achievement of Kamakura Buddhism.[7] It is remarkable that this emphasis on the individual appears to be based on a structure of faith that resembles the Christian, in spite of differences such as the concept of sin.[8] In Shinran, there is profound awareness of the hopeless condition of human beings and of their inability to free themselves from evil, blindness, and passions through their own efforts. At the same time, the deep faith given by Amida assures salvation when all individual efforts are abandoned. Could not this trust and faith of Shinran also provide a basis for the modern individual when confronting the problems of today's world?

In faith, Shinran knew that he was unconditionally accepted by Amida as the individual being he was in spite of imperfections. From the point of view of this absolute faith and trust in Amida, all ethical, social, or political values and institutions are relativized. This is the basis for Shinran's spirit of criticism. Occasionally, this encompasses religious and political institutions, as in the well-known passage at the end of the *Kyōgyōshinshō*, where he vehemently blames "the emperor and his retainers" for "going against the dharma and justice" in their attempt to suppress Hōnen's teachings.[9] Furthermore, Shinran's realization of his own vanity leads to solidarity with even the lowest members of society and to an emphasis on the equality of all men and women, high and low, as expressed in the term *dōbō*. Implied in this is the discovery of something universally human that transcends national and cultural boundaries.[10] What this could mean to our present age is pointed out by Katō Chiken in his interpretation of Kiyozawa Manshi. He stresses that Manshi's idealism, which is based on Shinran's thought, shows the Japanese a way towards modernization and internationalization of religion.[11]

It seems to me that Shinran's thought could prove to be one of the few traditional religious beliefs in Japan, if not the only one, that, while preserving the continuity of tradition, can provide a basis for the individual in order to face the challenge of modern society. In a quite remarkable way, Shinran has been able to develop new and even revolutionary insights and concepts within the traditions of both Mahayana Buddhism and his own Japanese culture. These insights are still relevant in contemporary society.

II The Importance of Shinran in Present-day Japan

The relevance of Shinran in Japan today is supported by statistical data which I have collected from Japanese media by using the databases of several leading newspapers.[12] Combined with other data on Japanese religion they reveal a relatively widespread interest in Shinran and the Jōdo Shinshū in Japan today, especially when compared to other religious thinkers and traditions.

A significant finding emerged when comparing the contents of all articles on the four major schools of Japanese Buddhism in the *Asahi Shimbun* in 1990. Almost half of those on the (Jōdo) Shinshū belonged to a category virtually non-existent in the case of articles on other schools of Buddhism. This category comprises articles concerning problems of inner reform of the Jōdo Shinshū, self-criticism, discussion of actual social problems or criticism and protest with regard to social, political and other issues. This indicates that, for the wider public, only the Shinshū seems to contain a considerable potential for criticism and reform, whereas the other traditional religions and the so-called "New Religions" (*Shinkō Shūkyō*) tend to be quite conservative.

A second indication of the influence of Shinran's thought in Japan today is evidenced by the extensive literature on him, ranging from popular works to highly specialized scholarly investigations. The records of the National Diet Library show that about 700 books on Shinran have been published since 1969, and well over 3000 on the Shinshū. In addition, there are several thousand articles on Shinran or the Shinshū published during the same period. The wide-spread interest in Shinran and the Shinshū tradition is demonstrated by the large number of publications outside the Shinshū context. Even in popular magazines, Shinran's personality and thought are frequently examined. It is apparent that many Japanese sense the significance of Shinran's thought for modern society and the modern individual. This relevance has been pointed out by scholars and intellectuals both inside and outside the Shinshū tradition.

In this century, Shinran appears to have been especially popular during times of crisis after the two world wars. After the First World War there was the overwhelming success of Kurata Hyakuzō's reading drama "The Priest and His Disciples" which appeared in 1918 and caused a flood of Shinran biographies. The main reason for the impact of these publications can be found in Shinran's personality. His humbleness and strength, his compassion and determination, his life as a pious and scholarly priest and, at the same time, as a layman with a family, his strength of faith and service even to the lowest members of society, all deeply impressed his contemporaries and many others since his day. Without the charisma of Shinran's personality the influence of his thought, however cru-cial, would undoubtedly be much more limited. The extent to which he is still alive in modern Japan is remarkable. In the Shinshū, neither Rennyo nor any other successor could replace him as spiritual leader, and his popularity goes far beyond the limits of this school.

In times of crisis and change, when the individual in modern society feels at a loss and forlorn or suppressed, many can draw strength from the experience of faith of Shinran. He was in a distressful situation when arbitrarily exiled to Echigo, but was able to overcome it through the strength of his trust and faith given by Amida which then proved to be a reliable basis for the rest of his life. In this context, I found an interesting article in the *Asahi Shimbun* (February 17, 1989) entitled "The History of Suppression is Sad." There, a parallel is drawn between the fate of the well-known philosopher Miki Kiyoshi and Shinran. Miki was drafted into service (which was actually a penal service) on a ship that left the port in 1942 on the same day, February 18, on which Shinran, in 1207, ar-rived in his exile in Echigo. Later, Miki was arrested as a Communist sympa-thizer and died in prison. The last essay that he wrote there was on Shinran.

Miki is one of those intellectuals who "rediscovered" Shinran for the many disturbed individuals who inhabited the rootless landscape of the immediate postwar period. At that time, criticism of traditional Japanese society and the search for new values made the ideas of Marxism attractive to many Japanese intellectuals. It is astonishing that, in this context, a medieval Buddhist thinker, Shinran, was given special attention. Discussion of Shinran's thought after the war was initiated by the Marxist historian Hattori Shisō.[13] Hattori emphasizes the revolutionary significance of Shinran's thought, that he stood on the side of the people and rejected the idea of the "preservation of the nation" (*go-*

koku) which had been a central function of Japanese Buddhism.[14] Ienaga, who modified Hattori's interpretation,[15] regards Shinran as the apex of the history of thought in Japan. He mentions especially Shinran's emphasis on the individual and the precedence of faith over secular power in Shinran, by which the state and other worldly authorities are relativized.[16] Other scholars have similarly tried to reinterpret Shinran's thought, emphasizing the social and political critique contained in his works as it relates to the human condition of modern society.

Shinshū scholars had no reason to argue against the significance thus attributed to Shinran within the history of Japanese thought. They had sufficient reason, however, in many cases to argue against some of the new interpretations of Shinran. Their criticism ranges from rejection to a careful study and critical evaluation of these approaches. The whole discussion has greatly enhanced research on Shinran and has led to a new, more balanced, and historically founded view of Shinran and his place in the history of thought. Against Hattori and others, most Shinshū scholars rightly point out that the critical and even revolutionary elements in Shinran cannot be understood correctly if they are not seen in the context of his basic religious experience, his absolute trust and faith in Amida's vow as the only way to salvation.

III Future Prospects

It is astonishing, but likely unavoidable given the structure of traditional Japanese society, that there is such a contrast between, on the one hand, Shinran's original religious impulse and its social and political implications and, at the same time, the feudal structure that has characterized the Shinshū over long periods of its history. However, what is most remarkable here is the fact that the critical spirit of Shinran has indeed survived in the Shinshū tradition; it could become the basis of criticism and reforms within this school and even in sociopolitical contexts. In the Ōtani Sect, this is demonstrated particularly by the reform movement started by Kiyozawa Manshi, the impact of which can still be felt today. It led to remarkable democratic reforms within the sect and to the founding of the *Dōbōkai Undō* in 1961 (paralleled by the *Mon Shintokai-Zukuri Undō* in the Honganji Sect). The *Dōbōkai Undō* aims at the return to Shinran's thought and his religious experience as the basis for a new religious awareness in modern society, emphasizing the role of the individual believer. While such tendencies are not necessarily supported by all and sometimes even regarded with suspicion, as far as one can see, they have led to an active concern for social and political issues among many members of the sect. In any case, it seems to me that the Shinshū is the only major Buddhist tradition in Japan that can play a critical and positive role in modem society. This is corroborated by the sustained attention given to this aspect of the Shinshū in Japanese newspapers.

The re-evaluation of Shinran's thought after the war by scholars and intellectuals with widely different ideological backgrounds has demonstrated Shinran's relevance in modern society and for the modern individual. It seems to me, however, that the emancipatory potential of his thought is not yet fully realized. This is especially true of his emphasis on the individual, quite remarkable within the history of Japanese thought. It can be understood only on the basis of his deep trust and faith in Amida.

NOTES

[1] See Robert N. Bellah, et al.: *Habits of the Heart: Individualism and Commitment in American Life* (Berkeley, Los Angeles, and London: University of California Press 1985), pp. 219-249, esp. pp. 220ff.

[2] See Gerhard Schepers, "The Christian Concept of Sin," *Humanities* (ICU) 10 (1975), pp.75-77.

[3] *Ibid.*, pp. 80-86.

[4] Tesshi Furukawa, "The Individual in Japanese Ethics," *The Japanese Mind*, ed. by Ch. A. Moore (Tokyo: Tuttle, 1973), p. 239.

[5] Ryukoku Translation Center, trans. and annotated, *The Tanni Shō* (Kyoto: Ryukoku University, 1963) (=Ryukoku Translation Series, vol. 2), p. 79.

[6] Yasutomi Shinya, "Shinran to kiki-ishiki. Shūkyō-teki shutai no keisei." *Ōtani Gakuhō* 65.4 (1986), pp. 71ff.

[7] Ienaga Saburō, "Watakushi ni totte no Shinran," *Zoku-Shinran o kataru* (Tokyo: Sanseido, 1980), p. 23ff.

[8] See G. Schepers, "Shinran's View of the Human Predicament and the Christian Concept of Sin," *Japanese Religions* 15.1 (1988), pp. 1-17.

[9] *Teihon Shinran Shonin Zenshū* (TSSZ), ed. by Shinran Shonin Zenshū Kankōkai, 9+1 vols. (Kyoto: Hōzōkan 1969-1970), 1.380.

[10] Cf. Ienaga Saburō, "Watakushi ni totte no Shinran," p. 20.

[11] Katō Chiken: *Ika ni shite shin o eru ka: Uchimura Kanzō to Kiyozawa Manshi* (Kyoto: Hōzōkan, 1990), pp. 191-257.

[12] See G. Schepers, "Shinran's Thought in Present-Day Japan," *Humanities* (ICU) 25 (1993), pp. 99-103 (a later version of this paper will be published in *The Impact of Traditional Thought on Present-Day Japan* [Monographien aus dem Deutschen Institut für Japanstudien der Philipp-Franz-von-Siebold-Stiftung, vol. 81] [München: Iudicium Verlag, 1994]).

[13] Cf. Hattori Shisō, *Shinran nōto* (Tokyo, 1948 [rpt. Fukumura Shuppan, 1970]), and *Zoku Shinran nōto* (Tokyo, 1950 [rpt. Fukumura Shuppan, 1970]).

[14] Hattori Shisō, *Shinran nōto, passim.*

[15] Ienaga Saburō, *Chūsei Bukkyō shisō-shi kenkyū*, 1947 (rpt. Kyoto: Hōzōkan, 1955), pp. 201-209.

[16] Ienaga Saburō, "Watakushi ni totte no Shinran," p. 9.

CHAPTER 14

SHINRAN AND HUMAN DIGNITY: OPENING AN HISTORIC HORIZON[1]

—FUTABA KENKO

(TRANSLATED BY KENRYU T. TSUJI)

I Shinran's Concept of Ōjō (Rebirth)

What new thought did Shinran introduce to human history? To answer this question we are immediately reminded of his teaching of the salvation of the evil person and his opening of the doors of the Buddha-Dharma to all peoples. However, what we are asking here is: how did his path of salvation and his teaching of rebirth for the common person, who was considered as lowly as rocks, roof tiles and grains of sand, actually affect the behavior of people in the course of history.

Ōjō means to be reborn into the Pure Land, commonly interpreted as the rebirth of a person after his death into the realm of perfect happiness that transcends history. After the middle of the Heian period (794-1185) many books such as *Rebirth into the Pure Land*, and *A Chronicle of Rebirth*, a book relating the lives of people who desired rebirth, were published. All these books dealt with people who desired rebirth into the Pure Land after death.

It is clear that Shinran taught rebirth into the Pure Land. In his most important treatise, *Teaching, Practice, Faith and Enlightenment*, he wrote that faith was the true cause of rebirth into the Pure Land. In the well known tract *Tannishō* he said,

> When we have faith that rebirth into the Pure Land is attained ... The noble resolution of each of you in crossing the boundaries of more than ten provinces without regard to your life was solely to hear the way of rebirth in the Land of Bliss. You would, however, be greatly mistaken if you suspect me of knowing some other way of rebirth than Nembutsu or that I possess some other scholarly knowledge.

It is clear, therefore, that Shinran's teaching of rebirth into the Pure Land does have aspects of rebirth after death.

This aspect became more pronounced when Shinran's teaching became known as the way of rebirth into the Pure Land. Rennyo, the eighth descendant of Shinran, greatly increased the number of Shinshu followers by popularizing the teaching. In his letters to them he wrote,

> As I deeply contemplate the nature of human existence, I realize that enjoyment of human life is as momentary as the flash of lightning or a drop of morning dew. Even if one were to enjoy the ultimate luxuries of life, such enjoyment lasts only for a period of fifty or a hundred years. If the winds of transciency should blow upon him, he will suffer the pains of illness and eventually pass away. In death one can neither depend on his wife or children nor on his wealth and treasures. One must traverse alone the path over the mountain of death and cross the river of no return. Therefore, what one must seriously seek is the after-life and wholeheartedly trust in Amida Buddha. Embracing a firm faith in Amida Buddha one must be reborn in the Pure Land of Peace.

Rennyo considered the after-life to be of supreme importance and encouraged all to seek rebirth in the Pure Land, for after all, the present life was a dream, an illusion. Through the years Rennyo's philosophy of rebirth was accepted as Shinran's traditional teaching and was transmitted to the present day. Even today in the proclamation by Konyo Shonin we find the following words:

> This is the Buddha-Dharma. When we single-mindedly trust in Amida Buddha for our salvation in the after-life, abandoning doubt and all self-centered practices, in that single act of faith we will be embraced by Amida who will never cast us away. Our rebirth is assured now—we will complete our rebirth in the after-life in the western Pure Land and will become free from eternal suffering.

If Shinran's religion of rebirth in the Pure Land was solely for the purpose of finding peace and bliss in the after-life, it could offer no practical meaning for this present life. Therefore, it could give no new direction to human conduct to change the course of history. There are some modern historians who state that Shinran's religion of Other Power rose from the ground of human despair and therefore could do nothing for the real world; nor should it do anything for the world.

I call this grave misconception of Shinran's teaching of rebirth in the after-life "the burial of Shinran." My reason is that I do not think that the main object of Shinran's teaching was simply rebirth in the Land of Bliss. When Shinran taught rebirth in the Pure Land, he proclaimed the attainment of Buddhahood as the ultimate objective, which was for the purpose of saving all sentient beings from suffering through the work of Great Compassion. Therefore, the purpose of rebirth in the Pure Land in the after-life was not for the self-enjoyment of a blissful state but to become a Buddha and return to the world of suffering to exercise Great Compassion for the enlightenment of all sentient beings. At the very beginning of his major work entitled, *Teaching, Practice, Faith and Enlightenment*, Shinran stated, "When I carefully consider Jōdo Shinshū it has two kinds of movement—the phase of going and the phase of returning." When Shinran thought of the Pure Land, he visualized the dynamic world of Buddha's

Compassion which did not exist independent from the suffering of sentient beings. The general framework of his teaching was that we attained Buddhahood in the after-life (a state free from the limitations of human existence) and returned to this world. Thus it was clear that the main purpose of rebirth was to return and practice Great Compassion. Shinran's ultimate concern was the exercise of the compassionate power in the present life, which was "empty, vain and false." To disregard this phase of the great return, which was of paramount importance to his teaching, and depicting Shinran as a person living in despair, is alienating him completely from the real world of human life. This is what I mean by "burying Shinran."

What Shinran meant by faith (*shinjin*) was a faith that was a gift granted from the power of the Primal Vow (*Teaching, Practice, Faith and Enlightenment*). Thus faith, the awakening to the true mind of Amida, was given to all sentient beings. To receive this faith was none other than to accept "the benefit of practicing Great Compassion." Shinran said,

> The True Buddhahood. The Mind Aspiring for Buddhahood is the Mind to Save Sentient Beings. The Mind to Save Sentient Beings is the Mind which embraces sentient beings to make them attain Birth in the Pure Land of Peace and Bliss ...
>
> This Mind (Faith) is the Great Bodhi-Mind; this Mind is the Great Compassionate Mind. This Mind arises from the Wisdom of Infinite Light...
>
> The Ocean-like Vow being equal, our aspiration is equal. The aspiration being equal, the Great Compassion is equal. The Great Compassion is the right cause for the attainment of Buddha's Enlightenment.

The attainment of faith meant to be endowed with the great Bodhi mind, which was the power of Great compassion that surrounded all sentient beings and actualized their rebirth into the realm of Buddhahood or the Pure Land. Shinran realized this faith in which he was embraced in Amida's Primal Vow, here and now, and practiced great compassion from this ground of Amida's Primal Vow.

In recent years there have been attempts to extricate the historical and realistic Shinran—who has been buried too long under the traditional teaching of rebirth into the Pure Land in the afterlife. Even today this task remains incomplete.

This tradition completely neglected Shinran's Buddhist position of the negation of the self and his criticism of the religious society which revolved around the monastic life. It was this tradition that buried Shinran under the mass of secular morality. The most representative school within this tradition promulgated the idea that Shinran's teaching constituted a belief of rebirth in the Pure Land in the after-life and mere subservience to the prevailing social code of ethics in this life. Rennyo's interpretation of Shinran was typical of this tradition. What was Shinran's place in history, how did he view society and the world in which he lived? These questions were completely neglected.

In the last century, Manshi Kiyozawa (1863-1903), a priest of the Ōtani denomination of Jōdo Shinshū, rediscovered Shinran. He said that the ultimate religious experience was to become one in this present life with the absolute unlimited being. Here he experienced complete satisfaction and overcame the notion of rebirth in the Pure Land in the after-life. He said that so long as there was spiritual satisfaction, evil, poverty and other social ills posed no problems. The problem with such a person who entrusted himself to an absolute unlimited power and lived solely in the peace that transcended this world, was that he had nothing to contribute to human history. Therefore he had no criticism against the ethico-religious and political system of Shintoism which negated human personality.

In the so-called period of Taishō democracy there emerged a person known as Naotarō Nonomura. In a book entitled *A Critique of Jōdo Teaching*, he stripped from Shinran's religion the teaching of rebirth into the Pure Land and tried to probe the essence of Jōdo doctrine. Rebirth in the Pure Land, he said, was merely an Indian myth and Shinran only used this verbal symbol to teach the truth of religion. Nonomura further stated that the essence of Shinran's religion was to transform the person gripped by self-attachment and free from this self-attachment. His theory was brilliantly presented but gained neither the support of his contemporaries nor their successors. The Jōdo Shin Buddhist Sangha could not understand him and finally expelled him. Shinran and his doctrine of rebirth in the Pure Land was closely related with the essence of his religion and could never be taken lightly. This relationship has yet to be thoroughly investigated and still remains a question for present day Jōdo Shin followers.

Nonomura made a brilliant critical analysis of the Jōdo teaching. He made an important point by stressing that Shinran's teaching was to release the individual from his self-attachment. But he did not go far enough in elaborating on one's mission in history. He stopped at the point of the individual's release from self-attachment which was a transcendental experience, but did not go one step further to criticize the ego-centered power of the state and its institutionalized morality. He did not question Shinto as the state religion but simply accepted the authority of the state and its morality. Therefore, he could not align himself with Shinran's position in criticizing the state and the morality of the times. He also buried Shinran.

The collapse of nationalism after World War II brought on a reexamination of Shinran's position in history. The peculiar viewpoint of present day nationalism sees Japanese Buddhism as a state religion and equates the laws of Buddha to the laws of the nation. Some consider Shinran's Buddhism also a state religion for he was said to have recited the Nembutsu for the good of the imperial household as well as its subjects. If so, why was Shinran persecuted and treated as a criminal and exiled by the government? Why did Shinran himself defy the government and say, "I disobey both the laws of the Emperor and the laws of the nation, and differ with opinions" (*Teaching, Practice, Faith and Enlight-*

enment). Why did he resent the injustice of the authorities? These questions remain unanswered by these proponents.

In the postwar period the historian Hattori Yukifusa (1901-1956) attempted to clarify Shinran's place in history by denying the existence of the patriotic Shinran who was buried under the secular and national systems. His thesis prompted much debate among the scholars. Although he made many people aware of Shinran's place in history, the general public did not take notice. Let us now reexamine this important subject in the following pages.

II Shinran in History

As I have mentioned above, the way of faith as expounded by Shinran was not to seek peace and happiness for oneself in the after-life. It was the way of becoming a Buddha to lead all sentient beings to Buddhahood out of great compassion. Faith (*shinjin*) for Shinran was the realization of the true mind of Buddha which was completely free from all ego-centeredness. This faith was none other than the transcendental wisdom given equally to all sentient beings from the absolute Compassion of the Buddha.

When the Nembutsu originated in man's ego-centeredness, it operated only for the purpose of self-profit. This activity was of course contrary to the Buddha-Dharma and ceased to be Buddhism. The Nembutsu Faith was the manifestation of the mind of great compassion which had the power to sever all ties of self-attachment. The Nembutsu was not a means to gain benefits for oneself. The Nembutsu itself gave ultimate value to human life. In describing the process of the attainment of faith Shinran wrote that the ego-centered mind was awakened to the true mind of Buddha which was working unceasingly to enlighten all beings.

In Shinran's passage which I quoted above, he stated that the mind of faith given to us by Amida Buddha was a mind of great compassion that leads us to Buddhahood and at the same time leads others to Buddhahood. Thus the Buddha mind that was transferred to Shinran at once gave birth to a new personality which was now committed to fulfill the work of great compassion in the world of suffering. For Shinran, to be surrounded by Buddha's compassion was not to wait for rebirth in the Pure Land in the after-life. The decision to take refuge in the Buddha was in itself a result of the work of Amida's Primal Vow. At the moment he became aware of Amida's Compassion surrounding him, he became identified with this power of compassion and he assumed a new identity which now worked to fulfill the work of Buddha's Compassion. This was what rebirth in the Pure Land meant for Shinran.

The power of Absolute Truth transformed Shinran's ego-centered mind and now made him one with Amida's Primal Vow of Great Compassion. Thus anyone who awakened to Amida's Primal Vow immediately assumed a new personality that was imbued with Amida's compassion and worked for the enlightenment of others.

Such an individual also became more acutely conscious of the depth of his own ego-centeredness. The wisdom of the Primal Vow also was the wisdom that made him clearly see the evil side of his imperfect human existence and awakened in him the never ending desire for its transformation. It became natural for him to confront the problems of his society and the world and to work for its solutions with new religious insights.

What problems then did Shinran face in history? The new Shinran, who was awakened to the Primal Vow of Amida, found a world that was suffering from human injustice. He, therefore, confronted this injustice and worked for the establishment of equality in human society.

Shinran's master, Hōnen, taught the exclusive practice of Nembutsu which was the way for all people to be born equally into the realm of Buddhahood. Amida's Primal Vow was the power that enlightened all people equally. Because of this truth he encouraged all to recite the Nembutsu. Equality meant that the wise and the ignorant were equal. So were the good and evil. Any discrimination against the ignorant and the evil could not possibly be called equality. Therefore, Amida brought forth the way of Nembutsu that could be easily recited by all. Hōnen proclaimed his teaching in the following words:

> The Nembutsu is easy and therefore can be recited by all. Other practices are difficult and cannot be followed by all. Why do we call it the Primal Vow of Amida? Because it offers rebirth to all sentient beings by discarding the difficult way and adopting the easy way.
>
> If building statues and temples were the way to Buddhahood, then there is no hope for the poor. Moreover, the rich are few and the poor are many. If the wise and the talented were the objects of salvation by the Primal Vow, the ignorant would have no hope of rebirth. Moreover the wise are few and the ignorant are many. If only those who listen to and observe the Dharma often were the objects of the primal Vow, there is no hope for those who rarely listen and observe. Moreover, those who often listen to the Dharma are scarce and those who rarely listen are many. If those who uphold the precepts were the object of the Primal Vow, there is no hope for those who break the precepts or those who have no precepts at all. Moreover, those who observe the precepts are few and those who break the precepts are indeed many.
>
> Know, therefore, that it is the same with all other practices. You must never doubt this. If all the practices listed above were necessary to become the object of the Primal Vow, then those who attain rebirth are few and many are those who cannot attain rebirth. Therefore, Amida Buddha when he was the Bodhisattva Dharmākara in the infinite past was moved by compassion to save all beings equally and did not make the carving of statues and the building of temples prerequisites for rebirth required by the Primal Vow. Amida made the sole practice of the Nembutsu recitation the essence of the Primal Vow.

Hōnen viewed all people as equal and further emphasized that all people attained Buddhahood equally. What significance did this new teaching have on society? It goes without saying that the poor, the ignorant, the undisciplined, and the precept breakers all belonged to the lowest strata of society. Those in the position of power and the landowners were never considered evil even when they heavily over-taxed the laborers. Those who did not give up the harvests of their labors to the authorities were considered evil. Not only that, they were punished by the gods and abandoned by the Buddhas and Bodhisattvas. The poor and the uneducated who opposed the establishment could receive neither the blessing of the gods nor the salvation offered by the Buddha and the Bodhisattvas. However, if all these common people were saved equally by the Nembutsu they would fear neither the punishment of the gods nor the abandonment by the Buddhas. Thus if all were saved by the Nembutsu, it constituted an extremely dangerous teaching, threatening the power of the authorities by encouraging the practice of evil. Therefore, the imperial court and the newly established Kamakura government had to clamp down harshly on the Nembutsu movement. Jōkei, a typical example of the old Buddhist school, attacked the Nembutsu followers by accusing them of disobeying the gods, disrupting the nation and tearing apart the system that had conveniently equated the nation's law with the Dharma of the Buddha.

The governing authorities had been using Buddhism and Shintoism as watchdogs to keep the people in check. Now the exclusive practice of Nembutsu gave the people an opportunity to free themselves from the bonds of this servitude, discover their human dignity and strive for its complete fulfillment.

Disobedience to the authorities led to both Hōnen's and Shinran's exile in 1207. Jōmon, Chōsai, Kōkaku, Hyōku, Kōsai, Shōku were also exiled and Sai'i, Shōgan, Jūren and Anraku were executed. The Nembutsu was banned. Now, Shinran in exile could expend all his energies showing the way of Buddhahood to the poor, the underprivileged, the uneducated and especially those who were considered evil. Shinran gave hope to people who found a new life in the Primal Vow of Amida Buddha because he taught the way of Buddhahood for all the ignorant and evil people. From this ground of universal salvation he criticized a society that tried to establish an exclusive world built on power, knowledge, and wealth.

Shinran wrote, "Lords and vassals who opposed the Dharma and justice bore indignation and resentment (to the Nembutsu teaching)." All persons with faith in the Nembutsu tried to establish a world in which every person would be equal in realizing his humanity. Any government that tried to destroy this world could be none other than enemies of the Dharma and human justice.

What was behind this authority that opposed the Dharma and human justice? As Jōkei said, the power behind this authority was a system that equated the rule of the temporal ruler with the eternal Dharma and the basis of this system was the unification of religion and politics.

From ancient times the supreme authority of the Japanese nation was ordained in this unique system. In the ancient book of *Kojiki* was written, "Our Mikado is the Ruler of all under heaven, and with the one hundred and eighty gods of heaven and earth performs the sacred rites of spring, summer, autumn, and winter." Thus the emperor was the chief officiant of the festivals and his political authority was derived from this religious position. The laws of the country were therefore based upon a system in which religious authority of the emperor was identified also with his political authority. This was a theocratic system.

All the Shinto shrines in the nation came under the jurisdiction of the emperor and his subjects without exception were forced to observe the festivals. In every town and village the people were organized around the shrines to uphold the laws of the land. The people had no freedom and were the instruments of the state. The emperor was sanctified and became a living god. The people were thrown into degradation and their individual freedom was usurped. They were firstly and lastly tools of the state. Praying to the gods meant obedience to the political authorities and the people could not escape this system. Those who did not pray to the gods were punished according to laws of the state and further incurred the wrath of the gods.

This unification of religion and politics (church and state) was revived after the Meiji Restoration. The emperor ruled his subjects as a living god and under his authority a government was organized that had absolute religious and political powers. Any person who did not bow before the emperor or worship the gods was considered disloyal to the crown and was subjected to great pressure. Such oppression occurred even within our recent memory. This kind of oppression has continued through Japanese history from the distant past to the present. Even the modern government is organized under this system. In the middle ages governors were dispatched to strategic locations around the country and these lords governed their domain under this religious-political authority.

The unity of the Buddha's Dharma and the emperor's law was justified under the system of the unification of religion and politics. Such a system was the Buddhist edition of the oneness of church and state.

Buddhism, a universal religion offering enlightenment to all peoples equally, was degraded and became a secular force when it was identified with a political system. This system further caused confusion by not differentiating the Buddha from the Shinto gods. The Buddha was the same as the Shinto gods to be prayed to for selfish needs and the Buddha-Dharma became just an instrument to satisfy one's greed. However, the faithful followers of the Nembutsu refused to yield to this system and worship the gods. Jōkei, therefore, attacked the Nembutsu devotees as disloyal subjects who broke the law. The imperial court and the military rulers suppressed the traditional Buddhist movement and the Nembutsu followers because they feared the disruption of their religious-political authority.

The persecution of the Nembutsu followers became very severe. During the Kenchō period (1249-1256) the governing authorities from the lord of the manors and his administrators down to the village chiefs all persecuted the Nembutsu Sangha which was organized by Shinran during his twenty years in the Kantō area. This happened twenty years after Shinran's return to Kyoto.

The Nembutsu followers were accused by the authorities as immoral people who feared no punishment even when they committed evil. Therefore, it was only natural for the authorities to use this reason to ban the Nembutsu movement. Śākyamuni called such authorities people who had neither the eyes to see the truth nor the ears to hear the voice of the Dharma. These people who wallowed in their power and were intolerant of any other religious faith were people to be pitied. Shinran also said that Nembutsu followers should have compassion on their persecutors and embrace the hope that they, too, might someday awaken to the truth. It was a fervent hope that they would be delivered from the illusion of grandeur based upon a temporal power and realize true human dignity founded on the mind of the Buddha. Shinran saw the fallacy of a system that equated the Buddha and the Bodhisattvas with its gods and taught, "In the *Nirvāṇa Sūtra* it says—those who take refuge in the Buddha will be worshiped by the gods of heaven."

The Nembutsu followers who parted from a social system established by the authoritarian government of the imperial court and the warrior class proceeded to create their own society founded on the principle of equality of all peoples. Thus was opened a new community founded on a principle quite contrary to that of the traditional society that denied human freedom. This was a community that transcended even the instability, divisiveness and suffering of the new Sangha.

Towards the end of the Kenchō era (1256) the persecution of the Nembutsu followers was intensified with greater force. In order to escape from this intolerable condition Shinran's eldest son, Zenran, abandoned the Nembutsu practice that did not pay homage to the Shinto gods and encouraged the followers to submit to the authorities. When Shinran discovered what Zenran was doing, he had no choice but to banish him from his family in 1256. He then advised his followers to move to another area if they could not endure the persecution; there should not be any compromise whatsoever with a system that did not recognize human freedom. Any power structure that trampled on human dignity was absolutely contrary to the Nembutsu way which proclaimed equality of all human beings. To align themselves with this kind of establishment was undermining the historical significance of the Nembutsu.

Shinran's Nembutsu which proclaimed universal enlightenment for all people could not possibly be equated with a religion, whose main purpose was only to satisfy one's greed. For after all, the Nembutsu Sangha stood for the establishment of the equality and the dignity of all human beings. Shinran's burning faith prompted him to free the farmers who suffered from the exploitation of the political-religious government that justified the use of force to achieve their ends. Shinran tried to reform a society, built on an outdated feudal system ruled by an emperor with divine rights and the subsequent military government ruled by the warrior class, and create a society founded on Truth.

Those who recited and practiced the Nembutsu broke the law of the land and were considered unpardonable evil criminals. In the eyes of the authorities, Shinran and the farmers who followed him had broken the law of Nembutsu prohibition.

The Nembutsu devotees were awakened to their own evil nature by Amida's Light of Wisdom but for the authorities it was another matter. The Nembutsu devotees were evil because they were lawbreakers. However, from the standpoint of Amida Buddha both the Nembutsu devotees who had awakened to their own evil nature and the authorities, who lived under the illusion of their goodness, were to be saved equally. If these authorities could be saved by Amida's Compassion, how much more so the Nembutsu devotees, hence, the ringing words of the *Tannishō*, "Even a good person is saved by Amida Buddha, how much more so the evil person." In teaching the way of salvation for the evil person Shinran offered the people suffering under the yoke of despotism a bright hope for a new free society.

So far we have examined how Shinran's teaching was virtually buried under the heavy notion of salvation in the afterlife and have rediscovered the real purpose of his teaching. His was a powerful message based on the Primal Vow of Amida Buddha, offering enlightenment to all beings equally. Shinran tried to build a society on this basic principle.

Shinran's faith involved a drastic transformation of the self-centered heart that awakened to Amida's Heart of Great Compassion working tirelessly to bring enlightenment to all beings. Thus, in faith the human heart became identified with the Primal Vow of Amida Buddha and human beings became the vehicle of Amida's great compassionate activity. To make all human beings equally realize their true humanity was the work of Amida's Primal Vow. This work only was the true good. On the other hand, any person or system that interfered with this process could only be a false good. The religious political system of Shinto and the identification of the Buddha-Dharma with the emperor's law advanced by some Buddhists closed the doors to the establishment of equality and dignity of the human person. It was Shinran's unique teaching that offered salvation to all these people considered evil by the establishment.

Any morality that disregards the human person cannot but be, as in Shinran's words, vain, empty, and false.

> I know neither good nor evil. The reason is that when I know good which appears good in the mind of Amida, only then can I say I know good; and when I know evil which appears evil in the mind of Amida, only then can I say I know evil. This is because we are being possessed of passions and our world is impermanent like a house on fire. All things are vain and empty and are not true in themselves. The Nembutsu alone is true.
>
> (*Tannishō*)

The only way in which human beings could truly know good and bad was when they judged good and bad from the standpoint of Amida's mind. Shinran felt that he could judge good and bad only from this position. Shinran categorically denied all other positions and he could not permit the existence of an evil system that trampled on the dignity of the human person and denied him the possibility of fulfilling his true human potential:

> One must seek to cast off the evil of this world and to cease doing wretched deeds; this is what it means to reject the world and to live the Nembutsu.
>
> *(Mattōshō)*

This was Shinran's moral stance. Shinran stated,

> If, therefore, we have faith in the Primal Vow, there is nothing that can surpass the Nembutsu; there is no need for fear of evil because there is no evil that obstructs the power of Amida's Primal Vow.
>
> *(Tannishō)*

Since Shinran's morality was based on the transcendental foundation of Amida's Primal Vow, it was beyond any temporal morality enforced by the government. Thus, nothing surpassed the true good of the Nembutsu that guided all peoples equally to the way to Buddhahood. And there was nothing to be feared, for Shinran's moral standard was based on the Infinite Compassion of Amida Buddha. The supreme purpose of Shinran's morality was to realize the ultimate good of Amida Buddha and to work for the actualization of Amida's Great Compassion.

It has long been thought, however, that Shinran's teaching was simply to follow the prevailing moral standards of the nation and at death be born in the Land of Bliss, finally enjoying the peace and bliss of the Pure Land. This view of Shinran relegated his teaching to the after-life and buried him in the secular morality of the establishment.

The ultimate objective of Shinran's Nembutsu (*shinjin*) was to realize Buddhahood and live dynamically in the flow of history in harmony with Amida's Primal Vow. Thus, he opened a world where all peoples could live equally in truth. He took issue with any social condition that obstructed the realization of human dignity the complete fulfillment of the human person in the way of the Buddha.

NOTES

[1] This translation by Rev. Kenryu T. Tsuji is the first chapter of a book entitled, *All of Shinran* (*Shinran no Subete*), edited by Kenko Futaba, former President of both Ryukoku University

and Kyoto Women's College. Professor Futaba's chapter is entitled, "Shinran's Opening of an Historic Horizon" (Shinran no hiraita rekishiteki chihei). Professor Futaba passed away in July, 1995.—*Ed.*

CHAPTER 15

TOWARDS A SHIN BUDDHIST SOCIAL ETHICS

—AMA TOSHIMARO

(TRANSLATED BY ROBERT F. RHODES)

I The Need for a Shin Buddhist Social Ethics

Social ethics does not refer to personal morality, but rather deals with the question of a person's role in, and responsibility towards, social problems, and how one can best engage oneself in society in order to create a better world. This was not a problem in the pre-modern age when society and the state were accepted as "given," and when people were generally content with keeping their position in society as good subjects. It was only when the ideal of a nation state came into existence that social ethics became a topic of serious debate, as people were then able to participate in the creation of the nation and society as equal members of their country.

In Japan, social ethics became an important issue only in 1945 when, with her defeat in World War II, the imperial system collapsed and a new Constitution, based on popular sovereignty, was adopted. In this sense, "social ethics" is a fairly new concept in Japan, which became an issue, first and foremost, at the level of the ordinary citizen, as it still is today, where active participation in political, economic, educational, and environmental problems—all of which substantially affect daily life—was required as morals for citizenship.

Under such circumstances, why is it necessary to stress the need for a social ethics based on Shin Buddhism? As stated above, such ethics is a matter of individual concern with one's relationship to society, and therefore, it may be argued that it is sufficient for a Shin Buddhist to participate in society at the level of an ordinary citizen. However, it is important to note that behind this argument lies the notion that religion belongs to a transcendental realm beyond the affairs of this secular world, which must be considered carefully.

Therefore, I should like to suggest the following three reasons as an answer to the question above. First, Shin Buddhism, historically, has often been engaged in society in a misguided way. Second, religion presents a perspective which, by making all things in this world relative, serves to deepen and enrich civic social ethics. Third, there is a general misunderstanding of the central teaching of Other Power (*tariki* 他力) which has prevented the followers from active participation in social matters.

First, the Shin Buddhist institutions actively supported the modern imperial nation. Not only did Higashi and Nishi Honganji provide financial assistance when the Meiji government was established, but they also sought to create, up to the time of Japan's defeat in 1945, "loyal subjects" needed by the imperial government. Particularly during times of war, they took the lead in preaching that the duty of a Shin Buddhist was to die gloriously on the battlefield, and therefore urged the simple believers to march off to combat.[1] Furthermore, the abbots of both Honganjis took imperial princesses as their wives and thus established close ties with the imperial family, which further served to provide an important emotional support for the imperial system, especially as these abbots were regarded as living buddhas. Of course, in that age, Japan needed nationalism if she was to remain an independent country. During the early Meiji period (1868-1912), the Shin Buddhist institutions had suffered a severe blow from the anti-Buddhist persecution and therefore, it may be understandable that they became entangled with nationalism in order to re-establish themselves. However, the path they took led them far away from the Buddhist teachings, as in glorifying war to such an extent, they justified the slaughter of humanity in the name of compassion, the fundamental teaching of Buddhism. This was nothing more than casuistry. Even after the war, many priests and lay Buddhists still blamed everything on "the trend of the times" and so refused to confront their war responsibilities.[2]

Therefore, how should we, who wish to live our lives on the basis of a Shin Buddhist faith, understand these past actions perpetrated in its very name? What, after all, is the basis of social action in Shin Buddhism? When we consider these questions, those of us who follow such a faith cannot leave the question concerning social ethics unanswered.

Second, as religion transcends the secular realm, it provides us with a perspective from which everything in this world can be relativized, which makes it possible to perceive various contradictions and conflicts within society with sufficient objectivity. As a result, religion can serve to resolve these problems. A good example is the anti-war peace movement led by Vietnamese Buddhists during the Vietnam War. Though I do not wish to go into details here, suffice it to say that South Vietnam was turned into a battlefield as a result of ideological conflicts, and that Vietnamese Buddhists refused to support either of these ideological positions, and instead, took the sufferings of their fellow human beings upon themselves, treating their pain as their own. By devoting themselves single-heartedly to non-violence and the spirit of compassion, these Buddhists were able to work towards the ending of the war, unlike the politicians.[3]

What is particularly important to note here is that, through their experience, these Vietnamese Buddhists expanded the idea of *duḥkha*, the fundamental principle of Buddhism, to encompass not only personal suffering but also that which has its roots in the structure of society itself. In this way, they attempted to work actively towards the eradication of suffering which arises from social and political problems.[4] This became the core idea of the socially-engaged Buddhism that subsequently appeared in various parts of Asia, and marks the appearance of a "Buddhist social ethics" which is clearly distinct from that of a civic-oriented one.[5]

Among Japanese Buddhists also, before thinking about social ethics as just concerning citizens or a people of a particular country, there are growing attempts to ask how they, as Buddhists, can participate in society on the basis of their own faith.[6] In particular, since the 1960s, there has been a move towards democratization within Higashi Honganji (Shinshū Ōtani-ha) and as part of this attempt, there has arisen a need to define an image of an ideal society or form of social participation, based on the teaching of Shin Buddhism.[7] The recognition that there is a pressing need to construct such a social ethic is spreading among Shin Buddhists.

Let us now turn to the third reason why there is a necessity to address the issue of a Shin Buddhist social ethics. Among Shin priests and lay people, there is a particular reluctance to engage in social problems from the standpoint of their faith. One reason for this may be traced back to the fact that the need for "social ethics" has not yet been fully accepted in Japanese society as a whole. However, I feel that the major reason seems to be the mistaken understanding of the characteristic of the Shin Buddhist doctrine of Other Power, which refers to the power of Amida Buddha's Vow, guaranteeing the attainment of Buddhahood by ordinary beings. Unfortunately, reliance on Other Power has often been misunderstood to mean that one must refrain from active decision-making, even when confronted with the problems of daily life. The Shin teaching of entrusting oneself to Amida came to be understood, in practical terms, to "leave everything up to others" and hence, instead of working voluntarily to change the actual world, the ideal Shin Buddhist way of life was defined as accepting reality "as it is" and going along with the flow of events. This, however, is a mistaken understanding of Other Power, as even though this is essential in order for ordinary people to become buddhas, we must still do our best to live our daily lives to the utmost. That is what life is all about! The only thing that Other Power guarantees is the attainment of Buddhahood. It will not resolve the contradictions, conflicts, and discord in our daily life. Shin Buddhists often fail to see this, and as a result, they are prevented from looking squarely at social suffering and so have remained unable to practice the compassion, required of all Buddhists. Therefore, in order to dispel this mistaken view, we need to clarify the significance of social ethics in Shin Buddhism.

II The Problem of the Two Truths

In the previous section, I pointed out that Shin Buddhism has a history of being closely allied to the state—one which was based on the divine right of the emperor. The ideological basis of this attitude towards the state was set forth in the doctrine of the Two Truths (*shin-zoku nitai* 真俗二諦), which, when we think about Shin Buddhist social ethics, is necessary to consider first.

These Two Truths are Absolute Truth (*shintai*) and Worldly Truth (*zokutai*). In Shin Buddhism, the former referred to its teaching of attaining Buddhahood by being born in Amida Buddha's Pure Land, while the latter was understood to refer to secular order and morality. However, these Two Truths were turned into a doctrine for regulating Shin Buddhists' activities in society, which, simply put, required the followers to observe social order, cultivate social virtues, and become people useful to the state—all in the name of Worldly Truth.

This doctrine developed from the principle that "the king's law is fundamental (*ōbō ihon* 王法為本)", preached by Rennyo 蓮如 (1415-1499), the eighth abbot of Honganji, who required his followers to respect this in order to protect them from the harsh persecution of the daimyō (feudal lords), although he still regarded faith (*shinjin*) as of primary concern.[8]

Under the Tokugawa feudal system, it was not faith but loyalty to the political system that became the main requirement, and the doctrine of the Two Truths was used to inculcate an obedient dutiful way of life useful to the rulers. However, after the collapse of the shogunate in 1868, Buddhism was actively persecuted by the new Meiji government, and as we saw above, this crisis led the Buddhist institutions to adopt a very nationalistic stance. Through this process, this doctrine gradually became the dominant ideology, and eventually came to hold a central place in the modern Shin Buddhist doctrinal system. For example, in the Temple Law of the Denomination (*Shūsei jihō* 宗制寺法) compiled by both Higashi and Nishi Honganji as their supreme laws after the Meiji Restoration, it was declared to be their orthodox teaching.

According to the temple law of Higashi Honganji, having faith in birth in the Pure Land was defined as the Gate of Absolute Truth. The law further stated that:

> To revere the emperor, to observe the laws, to refrain from violating the rules of society, to refrain from causing discord in human relations, and by such means applying oneself diligently to one's occupation and helping the nation prosper—this is the Gate of Worldly Truth.

Moreover, the two gates were said to support and augment each other.[9]

In Nishi Honganji, Absolute Truth was said to be "hearing the Buddha's Name in faith, and repaying the (Buddha's) great compassion in one's mind," while Worldly Truth was defined as "treading the human path and observing the king's law." Here once again, the two gates were said to support and augment each other.[10]

There are at least two problems with this doctrine. First, it rejects the supremacy of faith advocated by Hōnen 法然 (1133-1212), Shinran 親鸞 (1173-1262) and their followers, and instead gives priority to observing an ideology of morality which serves to uphold the state. Although both Absolute and Worldly Truths were said to support and augment each other, the relationship between the two was not explained sufficiently. The observance of secular morality proclaimed, for example, in the Imperial Rescript on Education (Worldly Truth), cannot be deduced from the act of uttering the nembutsu with faith in Amida Buddha's Original Vow (Absolute Truth). Nor is there any necessary connection between the Shin Buddhist teaching and acting as loyal subjects. In spite of this, the Shin Buddhist institutions taught their believers the need to become loyal subjects, observing such ordinances as the Imperial Rescript on Education.[11]

Second, there is the problem that Shin Buddhists exhibited little doubts about submitting themselves to the social order and secular morality with which they were confronted, let alone criticize them. While there were people who benefited from maintaining the order, there were also many who were oppressed by it, or were unjustly deprived of their human rights under it. In other words, attempts to maintain or strengthen social order often tend to cover up the contradictions and injustices inherent within it, and the doctrine of the Two Truths assisted in such concealment.

Seen from another angle, it is clear that this doctrine did not arise naturally from the fundamental teachings of Shin Buddhism, but was created in order to muster Shin believers, socially, in a systematic attempt to protect the Shin Buddhist institutions. Moreover, the widespread support of this doctrine by both Shin believers and people in general was made possible by the strong nationalistic sentiment in Japan during this time so that Shin Buddhism failed to protect its autonomy and hence, was swallowed up by nationalism.

III The Basis of a Shin Buddhist Social Ethics

Let us carry our analysis a little bit further as there is a need to explain why it was possible for the doctrine of the Two Truths to develop in Shin Buddhism, and unless this point is clarified, it is possible that similar misguided attempts to mobilize believers socially, in the name of Shin Buddhism, may recur in the future.

Paradoxically, the answer to the above question lies in the way the nembutsu of the Original Vow was taught. As stated above, Hōnen only emphasized how ordinary beings could attain Buddhahood, without teaching the necessity of adopting a special set of morals distinctive to nembutsu practitioners and hence, the way in which each of them led their life was left up to them. He states, "As for the way in which to lead your life, you should live it by reciting the nembutsu. You should abhor and reject all things that obstruct the nembutsu, and refrain from doing them."[12]

Why, then, did Hōnen refrain from teaching morals and a particular way of life to his followers? To put it briefly, it was because he understood humans as being inextricably bound by their "karmic conditions (*gō-en* 業縁)."[13] Here "karma (*gō*)" means "actions" while "conditions (*en*)" refer to their "indirect causes," which humans have no way of completely knowing. While the cause-and-effect relationships that we can understand appear to us as inevitable, "conditions (*en*)" in these relationships can only be seen as "chance," and such "chances" control human actions. Furthermore, the karmic conditions of each person are different and therefore, even though everyone may be required to follow a uniform way of life, it is impossible to do so in actuality. Even morality may be useless in some cases, as for example, a person who has been taught not to kill, and who in fact would not kill even an insect, would kill enemy soldiers when sent off to the battlefield. It is impossible to foretell what a person may do depending on their karmic conditions, which is why Hōnen taught that we need to ultimately rely upon the nembutsu of the Original Vow. This is truly a penetrating insight into our karmic conditions.

However, it must be said that this insight was lacking in the doctrine of the Two Truths, in which there was no apprehending of sorrow where the world of religion becomes real to us only when we realize our ultimate moral inability. The doctrine was, for all practical purposes, just a moral theory, but was ironically forced upon a way of life which had been left up to each nembutsu practitioner since the time of Hōnen. As well as this, the ethos of submission to authority which had been fermenting since the Tokugawa period, made the people accept the doctrine uncritically, as it was set forth by the chief abbot himself.

In the teaching of the nembutsu of the Original Vow, as Hōnen had taught, the question of how to lead one's life was left up to the judgment of each individual nembutsu practitioner and therefore, any attempt to create a new Shin Buddhist ethics must start from this point. Basically, each practitioner has to discover their own way to lead their life depending on their situation. At first sight, this may seem passive and vague, but actually it is a way of life in which priority is given to the autonomous decision-making power of each individual, which needs to be regained as it is the basis of, and the prerequisite for, any possible Shin Buddhist social ethics.

As stated above, under the imperial system, the Higashi Honganji institution sought to muster its believers for nationalistic political purposes by using the doctrine of the Two Truths. Yet we must not forget that there was a person within its ranks who attempted to go beyond all this and tried, like Hōnen and Shinran, to uphold the supremacy of faith. Similarly, the institution also gave birth to a nembutsu practitioner who refused to ignore the sufferings of his fellow believers and stood up fearlessly for the cause of social justice. Although both their activities were far outside the mainstream of Shin Buddhist history, the construction of a Shin Buddhist social ethic must begin by reviving their hopes and visions. These two people are Kiyozawa Manshi 清沢満之 (1863-1903)

and Takagi Kenmyō 高木顕明 (1864-1914) and therefore, in the pages below, I should like to briefly discuss their understanding of ethical values in society.

IV Kiyozawa Manshi and his Faith-centered Religion

Kiyozawa Manshi was a scholar who created, for the first time in Japan, an academic religious philosophy based on the study of western philosophers like Hegel. Also, as a priest in Higashi Honganji, he was influential both in modernizing its institution and in interpreting Shinran's thought in a modern way.

Among Kiyozawa's many achievements, the most noteworthy was the fact that he succeeded in going beyond the doctrine of the Two Truths. In his essay, "The Relationship between Religious Morality and Common Morality," the last work he published before his death, he proclaims religious values to be absolute.[14] According to Kiyozawa, the reason why Worldly Truth is preached alongside Absolute Truth in Shin Buddhism is to demonstrate to nembutsu practitioners how difficult it is to lead a life in accordance with secular morality (that is to say, Worldly Truth). For this reason, even while emphasizing this Truth, it only spoke of the "king's law and benevolence," or "humanity, justice, courtesy, wisdom and sincerity" or secular "codes," without going into details about what each signified. In other words, for those whose minds had not yet settled in faith, Worldly Truth was taught in order to lead them to "religion" by making them realize their inability to live a moral life. Similarly, for those who had already attained unwavering faith, the same Truth served to make them realize even more acutely the impossibility of living a moral life and thereby allowing them to rejoice all the more in having attained faith in the Other Power.

To sum up, for Kiyozawa, the doctrine of the Two Truths serves merely to demonstrate the following points: (1) that, once one has attained faith, there is no need to be dismayed even if one cannot live morally and (2) that, once one realizes that one cannot live a moral life, one becomes even more grateful for having attained faith (in Amida Buddha, who specifically promises to save even the most degenerate human being). Therefore, Kiyozawa argues that, even though one may have to cast morality aside in order to lead one's life in faith, it cannot be helped. This statement, which signifies his abandonment of morality, shows his success in stating that religious values are absolute. It is identical, in content, to the proclamation made by Hōnen and Shinran in the 13th century, concerning the supremacy of the nembutsu of the Original Vow.

As mentioned before, this essay was published in 1903. We may add that the Imperial Rescript on Education had already been promulgated in 1890 and that greater stress was being placed on the inculcation of the need to become good subjects of the emperor by leading moral lives. When we understand the historical context, we can see how critical Kiyozawa was of the Japanese society of his time:

... the Shinshū worldly truth teaching is not something which sets out to impose prescriptions on human behavior ... For that reason it is a great misperception to think the worldly truth teaching exists in order to compel people to uphold standards of human behavior or by extension to benefit society and the nation. If the worldly truth teaching were expounded in connection with the laws of the king or the precepts of benevolence and humanity, as a matter of course it would be conducive to the performance of [these duties] to some degree. In fact [such concerns] are an appendant phenomenon. The essential point of the teaching is to show that one is unable to carry out [these duties] ... Despite the fact that the essential thrust of the doctrine is religious, it is its appended moral elements that seem to be valued most highly; a strange set of circumstances indeed![15]

In this way, Kiyozawa politely consigned the orthodox Shin Buddhist doctrine of the Two Truths to oblivion.

Several years earlier in 1892, he attempted to construct the foundations of a Shin Buddhist social ethics in his *Skeleton of a Philosophy of Religion*, where he defines religion as a faculty, found within finite human beings, which seeks for the Infinite. Furthermore, Kiyozawa distinguishes two ways in which the finite can attain to the Infinite. The first is the method of developing the Infinite which resides within the finite, while the second is through the Infinite reaching out and embracing the finite and bringing it into itself. Kiyozawa called the former the "Self-exertion Gate" and the latter the "Other-power Gate."

I should like to note the following point that Kiyozawa makes here. In the Other-power Gate, as the difference between the finite and the Infinite becomes apparent, not only do people revere the Infinite, but they also show greater concern for the ethical relationships among finite beings themselves, and as a result, strive to put into practice the "right path of the human world (*jinsei ni seidō* 人世の正道)." As he says:

(In the Other-power Gate), when one attains the Settled Mind (*anjin* 安心) the distinction between the finite and the Infinite becomes vividly clear. It becomes truly clear that the finite exists within the realm of the Infinite. At that point, one realizes for the first time that the finite is truly finite. For this reason one apprehends, on the one hand, one's religious connection to the Infinite, and, on the other hand, one's moral connection with other finite beings, and recognizes the distinction between so-called "religion" and "morality." One then comes to exert oneself in the practice of the right path of the human world in the ethical realm.[16]

The distinction between religion and morality is clearly recognized for the first time when one gains faith in the Other-power Gate, and as a result, the freedom to put the "right path of the human world" into practice without fear or anxiety about the consequences. This must be the starting point of the social ethics we are considering here. It may be noted that the term "right path of the human world" is rendered as "the progress and improvement of the world" in the English translation of the *Skeleton*.[17] Although the term "social ethics" is not used here, this rendering clearly indicates the nature and direction of social engagement based on a Shin Buddhist faith, which becomes even clearer when considering how Kiyozawa himself subsequently participated actively in the movement to reform the Higashi Honganji institution.[18]

For example, in his essay entitled "The Present Benefits of Buddhism" published in 1896, he writes that finite beings, even while remaining in the finite state, can apply themselves in the world "actively and vigorously."[19] Furthermore, he unequivocally states that an active and vigorous life is a "great source of welfare in the human world" and that only those who have faith in the Other-power Gate are able to devote themselves wholeheartedly to it.

Kiyozawa's movement to reform Higashi Honganji was forced to disband soon after it created a nationwide organization. One may say it was a setback and defeat, but from Kiyozawa's point of view, it provided an opportunity to appeal for the necessity of reform beyond the boundary of Higashi Honganji and to society as a whole, which was a development and enrichment of the social ethics of Other-power Buddhism. This is clearly indicated in the editorial placed at the beginning of Issue 14 of the journal, *Kyōkai jigen* 教界時言 (Timely Words for the Buddhist World), which Kiyozawa published with his colleagues in the reform movement. Here, he went beyond calling for the reform of Higashi Honganji, and proclaimed his intention to embark on such a movement encompassing all of Japanese society.

> To begin with, to reform the administration of Ōtani-ha [i.e. Higashi Honganji] is not our only goal. As ordinary Buddhists, we wish to engage in discussion worthy of Buddhists. As ordinary men of religion, we wish to set forth views worthy of such people. As ordinary citizens, we wish to set forth intentions worthy of citizens and serve to promote the culture of the Japanese empire. We have already proclaimed this in the first issue of this journal. In the ten-odd months since we began publication, the situation, both within and outside Higashi Honganji, has undergone rapid change. It is now impossible to limit our journal solely to matters pertaining to the reform of its administration. Therefore, from this issue on, the *Kyōkai jigen* will work for the reform of the Buddhist world in general along with that of the Ōtani-ha administration. As well as this, we shall call for improvements in the political, legal, educational and academic realms, and we hope that, while doing this, we shall not be remiss in reviewing anything connected with religion.[20]

In the subsequent issue of *Kyōkai jigen*, Kiyozawa published an essay titled "Buddhists, Why Do You Lack Self-Esteem?"[21] in which he emphasized that a Buddhist must simultaneously live in two worlds, namely the religious and the secular. Religious people tend to concentrate on giving themselves up to the transcendent world beyond daily life. However important though this might be, they must not forget the existence of the everyday world—a world of human relationships dominated by "unmistakable distinctions of self and others, intimate and distant relationships." Kiyozawa argues that, being confronted with such a world, religious people need to involve themselves in it in a practical way, and stresses the necessity of living resolutely in the everyday world on the basis of Other-power faith.

Towards the end of his life, Kiyozawa gave the name *seishin shugi* 精神主義 (literally "spirit-ism") to this way of life which stressed, above all, the need to establish one's life on a "perfectly firm ground," sustained by the Absolute/Infinite.[22]

Kiyozawa further explains this way of life as the "logical path by which the 'spirit'(*seishin*, or the Other-power faith) develops," which cannot be ignored when thinking about a Shin Buddhist social ethics. According to this passage, the *seishin* develops throughout life in stages, a process that can be clearly seen. Kiyozawa, above all, emphasized doing this by establishing oneself in the Other Power in the everyday world which is, to repeat his words above, dominated by "unmistakable distinctions of self and others, intimate and distant relationships." He did not consider faith as just having peace within one's own mind which merely keeps oneself locked up in a narrow, fixed world, but rather spiritual awareness only comes alive in "practical actions (*jikkō* 実行)" based on Other-power faith, which must also include social ethics.

Then, of what does such a social ethics consist? Though Kiyozawa has already provided us with several suggestions, it was Takagi Kenmyō who actually put them into practice.

V The Social Ethics of Takagi Kenmyō

As is well known, the Meiji Constitution contained a clause which stated that the emperor was "sacred and inviolable" and in order to back up such a claim, the government incorporated the crime of High Treason (*taigyaku-zai* 大逆罪) into the criminal law in 1908, which held that anyone who harmed, or attempted to harm, the emperor or his direct descendents would be put to death. It just so happened that in May 1910, some workers in a lumber mill in Nagano prefecture were arrested for the illegal possession of explosives. In the course of interrogation, it was discovered that they had been planning to assassinate the emperor, and because of this, they were tried for the above crime. Yamagata Aritomo, who held the reins of government in those days, decided to use this opportunity to eradicate socialists and anarchists whose influence had been growing in Japanese society. The prosecution concocted a story about their plotting to assassinate the emperor with the prominent socialist Kōtoku Shūsui 幸徳秋水 (1871-1911) as their ringleader. This government fabrication became known as the "High Treason Incident,"[23] in which Takagi Kenmyō was implicated.

Takagi, himself, was born on May 21, 1864, as the son of a confectioner in Aichi prefecture, and after graduating from a school in Nagoya belonging to Higashi Honganji, he became a priest. In 1897, he was sent to Jōsenji 浄泉寺 in Wakayama prefecture, and two years later became its head priest. Many of the members of this temple lived in *hisabetsu buraku* 被差別部落 (socially discriminated communities), and suffered from poverty and discrimination. Deeply moved by their plight, Takagi became a leader of their liberation movement. He also worked actively for the abolition of state prostitution, and bitterly opposed the Russo-Japanese War when it broke out. As can be clearly seen from his essay entitled "My Socialism"(*Yo ga Shakaishugi* 余が社会主義),"[24] Takagi's actions were a form of social practice based on his Shin Buddhist faith. However, because he was on close terms with the socialists, he was unfortunately drawn into this "High Treason Incident."

For this reason, on January 18, 1911, Takagi was sentenced to death along with twenty-three other people. Among them, twelve were actually put to death, while the rest, including Takagi, had their sentences commuted to life imprisonment. He was sent to a prison in Akita prefecture, where he hanged himself on June 24, 1914, at the age of 51. Shinshū Ōtani-ha (Higashi Honganji) defrocked Takagi on the very day of his sentencing. However, with the spread of the Dōbōkai movement (同朋会, Association of Fellow Believers) within the denomination in the 1960s, Takagi's importance was re-evaluated and finally, on April 1, 1996, the denomination officially reversed their previous decision, and thereafter he was fully reinstated.[25] Higashi Honganji not only restored Takagi but also declared it would do its utmost to carry on his work, which bodes well for the future of Shin Buddhism, since an important guiding principle for its ethics is clearly revealed in Takagi's deeds.

Basically, Shin Buddhist social ethics is not anything that can be expressed through general plans or slogans, but rather something that those who have attained *shinjin* will undertake, based on their own decision in accordance with the particular circumstances in which they find themselves. As noted above, each human being is distinct as each carries karmic conditions peculiar to that particular person and therefore, they cannot be lumped together, as it were, and treated as if they are all the same. However, should there be a common element in Shin Buddhist social ethics, it is that it accords with Amida Buddha's compassion. In this respect, Takagi practiced compassion with a pure heart.

In "My Socialism," he relates how he attained peace and happiness upon receiving Amida Buddha's compassion, whereupon his life was completely transformed, enabling him to abide in the desire to "do what the Buddha wishes me to do, to practice what he wishes me to practice, and make the Buddha's will my own will." The Other-power faith transformed all of his previous thoughts and prompted in him "great determination." In this way, Takagi "opened himself up (*tainin* 体認)" to Amida Buddha's mind of compassion, and became very determined to put it into practice, which he did by embarking on a movement to bring about "progress (*kōjō shinpo* 向上進歩)" and "community (*kyōdō seikatsu* 共同生活)," sustained by "compassion directed equally towards everyone." In Takagi's words, our desire is neither to receive medals nor to become generals or nobles. We wish to bring about "progress" and "community" through energy and labor sustained by faith.

Then, what exactly are "progress" and "community"? The former consists of realizing peace through thoroughgoing opposition to war and elimination of social inequality and discrimination, while the latter refers to life free from the "struggle for existence," where labor is used only for producing sustenance so that the cultivation of one's spiritual life can be actualized without any problems. What Takagi expressed is profound, all the more so as he stated what he believed simply. What is worthy of being called "progress" and "community" still remain weighty questions, even after passing through the dark history of the modern world. What choices should we, who lead our lives on the basis of Other-power faith, make in order to bring about these two ideals? This is indeed the problem of a modern Shin Buddhist social ethics.

Conclusion

Seen in this way, it can be said that both Kiyozawa Manshi and Takagi Kenmyō unflinchingly directed their gaze on the problems of modernity and sought to express compassion, the life-force of Buddhism, in new forms. As their examples illustrate, compassion in modern society cannot simply remain a personal virtue, but rather, it needs to become the guiding principle within laws and institutions to be truly effective.[26]

Whether an individual can be compassionate or not depends on circumstances; some people may become so upon gaining *shinjin*, while others may remain selfish as before. It basically depends upon that individual's karmic conditions. However, to repeat the point again, it is inevitable in this modern world that a person's life is profoundly affected by laws and institutions and therefore, compassion, too, must not be limited to being merely a personal virtue but rather become a potent force for transforming society. It may take various forms, but Takagi's goals of "progress" and "community" provide us with important guidelines when thinking about any Shin Buddhist social ethics.

As long as Buddhism is a religion of compassion, I believe that there can be no such thing as Shin Buddhist faith indifferent towards what is happening in the actual world. Faith, sustained by compassion, is naturally sensitive to the contradictions and absurdities in contemporary society and hence, by placing greater importance on the cultivation of such sensibilities, we shall surely be able to enrich this Other-power faith.

REFERENCES

Akegarasu Haya 暁烏敏, 1904. "Shussei gunjin ni atauru sho 出征軍人に与うる書 (Letter to a Soldier Going Off to the Front Lines)," in *Seishinkai* (精神界), vol. 4, no. 4, 1904.

Ama Toshimaro 阿満利麿, 1994. *Kokka shugi wo koeru: Kindai nihon no kenshō* 国家主義を超える：近代日本の検証 (*Beyond Nationalism: An Inspection of Modern Japan*). Tokyo: Kōdansha.

——, 1999. *Hito wa naze shūkyō wo hitsuyō to suru no ka* 人はなぜ宗教を必要とするのか (*Why Do People Need Religion?*). Tokyo: Chikuma Shobō

Blum, Mark. trans., 1989. "The Relationship between Religious Morality and Common Morality" by Kiyozawa Manshi. *The Eastern Buddhist*, vol. 22, no. 1 (Spring 1989), pp. 96-110.

Fairbank, John K., Edwin O. Reischauer and Albert M. Craig. eds. *East Asia: The Modern Transformation*. Boston: Houghton Mifflin.

Fukuma Kōchō 福間光超, Sasaki Kyōshō 佐々木孝正 and Hayashima Yūki 早島有毅, eds. 1983. *Shinshū shiryō shūsei* 真宗史料集成 (*A Collection of Shin Buddhist Documents*), vol. 6 Kyoto: Dōbōsha 同朋社.

Honganji Shiryō Kenkyūjo 本願寺史料研究所, ed. 1969. *Honganji shi* 本願寺史 (*History of Honganji*) vol. 3. Kyoto: Jōdo Shinshū Hongwanji-ha 浄土真宗本願寺派.

Ichikawa Hakugen 市川白弦, 1970. *Bukkyōsha no senso sekinin* 仏教者の戦争責任 (*The War Responsibilities of Japanese Buddhists*). Tokyo: Shunjūsha. Reprinted in *Ichikawa Hakugen Chosakushū* 市川白弦著作集, vol. 3. Kyoto: Hōzōkan, 1993, pp. 5-216.

——, 1975. *Nihon fashizumu-ka no shūkyo* 日本フアシズム下の宗教 (*Japanese Religion under Fascism*). Tokyo: Enuesu shuppan エヌエス出版. Reprinted in *Ichikawa Hakugen Chosakushū*, vol. 4. Kyoto: Hōzōkan, 1993, pp. 3-361.

Izumi Shigeki 泉恵機, 1995. "Takagi Kenmyō no jiseki ni tsuite 高木顕明の事積について (On Takagi Kenmyō's Achievements)," *Shindo* 身同 no. 14 (August 1995). Kyoto: Shinshū Ōtani-ha Dōwa Suishin Honbu 真宗大谷派同和推進本部, pp. 59-81.

——, 1996a. "Takagi Kenmyō no gyōjitsu 高木顕明の行実 (The Life of Takagi Kenmyō)," *Shinshu* 真宗 (March 1996). Kyoto: Shinshū Ōtani-ha Shūmusho 真宗大谷派宗務所.

——, 1996b. "Takagi Kenmyō ni kansuru kenkyū: Shiryō oyobi ryaku nempu ni tsuite" 高大明に関する研究 (A Study concerning Takagi Kenmyō: On the Sources and Brief Chronology)," *Ōtani Daigaku Shinshū Sōgō Kenkyūjo Kenkyū Kiyō*, vol. 14.

——, 1997. "Takagi Kenmyō kenkyū no genjō to hōkō: Takagi Kenmyō kenkyū 高木顕明研究の現状と方向—高木顕明研究 (1) (The Present State and Direction of Research on Takagi Kenmyō: Studies on Takagi Kenmyō [1]), *Shindō*, no.16.

Kasahara Kazuo 笹原一男 and Inuoe Nobuo 井上鋭夫, eds. 1972. *Rennyo/Ikkō ikki* 蓮如──一向一揆, Nihon shisō taikei. Tokyo: Iwanami Shoten.

Kiyozawa Manshi 清沢満之, 1892. *Shūkyō tetsugaku gaikotsu* 宗教哲学骸骨 (*Skeleton of a Philosophy of Religion*). Kyoto: Hōzōkan.

──, 1893. *Skeleton of a Philosophy of Religion*. Translated by Zenshirō Noguchi. Tokyo: Sanseidō 三省堂.

──, 1896. "Bukkyo no genri 仏教の現利 (Present Benefits of Buddhism)", in *Mujintō* 無盡燈, vol. 2, no. 9.

──, 1897. "Honshi no shōrai 本誌の将来 (The Future of this Journal)," *Kyōkai jigen* 教界時言, no. 14.

──, 1898. "Bukkyōsha nanzo jichō sezaruka 仏教者蓋自重乎 (Buddhists, Why Do You Lack Self-Esteem?)," *Kyokai jigen*, no. 15.

──, 1901. "Seishinshugi 精神主義 (Spiritual Awareness)," *Seishinkai* 精神界 vol. 1, no. 1. Reprinted in *Kiyozawa Manshi Seishinkai ronbunshū* 清沢満之「精神界」論文集, ed. by Ōtani Daigaku Shinshū Sōgō Kenkyūjo. Kyoto: Heirakuji Shoten, 1999, pp. 3-6.

──, 1903. "Shūkyōteki dōtoku (zokutai) to futsū dotoku tono kōshō 宗教的道徳 (俗諦) と普通道徳との交渉 (The Relationship between Religious Morality and Common Morality)," *Seishinkai*, vol. 3, no.5. Reprinted in *Kiyozawa Manshi Seishinkai ronbunshū*, pp. 159-172.

Moriya Tomoe 守屋友江, 1996. "Kindai Nihon ni okeru bukkyō no jiko kaikaku: Kiyozawa Manshi no kyōdan kaikaku undo近代日本における仏教の自己改革: 清沢満之の教団改革運動 (Self-Reformation of Buddhism in Modern Japan: Kiyozawa Manshi's Religious Reform Movement)," *Shūkyō kenkyū* 宗教研究 (Studies in Religion), no. 310.

──, 1999. "America bukkyo no tanjō: Imamura Yemyō ron アメリカ仏教の誕生—今村恵猛論 (The Birth of American Buddhism: A History of Acculturation of Japanese Buddhism with Special Reference to Bishop Yemyō Imamura)." Doctoral Thesis Meiji Gakuin University, 1999.

──, 2000. *Yemyō Imamura: Pioneer American Buddhist*. Honolulu: Buddhist Study Center Press.

──, 2001. *America bukkyo no tanjō: 20 seiki shotō niokeru nikkei shūkyō no bunka hen'yo* アメリカ仏教の誕生—20世紀初頭における日系宗教の文化変容 (*The Birth of American Buddhism: Cultural Transformation of Japanese American Religion in Early Twentieth Century*). Hannan daigaku sōsho 阪南大学叢書 64. Tokyo: Gendai Shiryō Shuppan 現代史料出版.

Nhat Hanh, Thich. 1967. *Vietnam: Lotus in a Sea of Fire*. New York: Hill and Wang.

──, 1987. *Interbeing: Commentaries on the Tiep Hien Precepts*. Berkeley: Parallax Press.

Queen, Christopher and Sallie B. King, eds. 1996. *Engaged Buddhism: Buddhist Liberation Movements in Asia*. Albany: State University of New York Press.

Shinshū Kyōgaku Kenkyūjo 真宗教学研究所, ed. 1975. *Kyōka kenkyū* 教化研究 No. 73-74: "Shiryō: Bakumatsu ishin no shūmon to kokka 資料: 幕末維新の宗門と国家 (Source Materials: The Denomination and the State in the Closing Years of the Tokugawa Shogunate and the Meiji Restoration)." Kyoto: Shinshū Ōtani-ha Shūmusho 真宗大谷派宗務所.

Takagi Kenmyō 高木顕明, 1904. "Yo ga shakaishugi 余が社会主義 (My Socialism)," in Takagi Kenmyō Tsuitō Shūkai 高木顕明追悼集会, ed., *Enshōki kiroku* 遠松忌記録 (*Record of the Memorial Service for Enshō [Tagaki Kenmyō]*). Hikone, Shiga Prefecture: Fusanbō 風山房, 1998, pp. 19-25.

Wagatsuma Sakae 我妻栄, ed. 1969. *Nihon seiji saiban kiroku: Meiji, go* 日本政治裁判記録: 明治-後 (*Records of Japanese Political Trials: Meiji Part two*). Daiichi Hōki 第一法規.

NOTES

[1] Let me give one example from "Letter to a Soldier Going Off to the Front Lines" by Akegarasu Haya 曉烏敏 (1877-1954): "Before you defeat the enemy country, you must defeat the enemy in your heart: the voice that says 'I want to return alive.' You must consider this voice as the devil's temptation ... Please fight courageously and when you return ... come back as white bones" (Akegarasu, 1904).

[2] Ichikawa Hakugen 市川白弦 (1902-1986) is one of the few Japanese Buddhists who have consistently pursued the problem of war responsibilities of Japanese Buddhism and Japanese Buddhists since the end of the war in 1945. His works like *The War Responsibilities of Japanese Buddhists* (1970) and *Japanese Religion under Fascism* (1975) are important for Buddhist social ethics. For details, see Thich Nhat Hanh, 1967.

[3] Cf. Thich Nhat Hanh, 1987.

[4] On engaged Buddhism see, for example, Queen and King, eds., 1996.

[5] As one such attempt, there is *Āyus* アーユス (The International Buddhist Association Network), a Japanese inter-denominational Buddhist NGO (non-governmental organization). URL: http://www.ayus.org/.

[6] The Constitution of Shinshū Ōtani-ha gives the "actualization" and "realization" of a "society based on Buddhist fellowship" (*dōbō shakai* 同朋社会) as the denomination's goal.

[7] For example, in his *Ofumi* (Letters), Rennyo states as follows: "You should put priority on the king's law and hide the Buddha's law from sight. In society, you should put priority on benevolence, and refrain from slighting other Buddhist denominations. Moreover, you should not treat the gods rudely" (Kasahara and Inoue, eds. 1972, p. 71).

[8] Shinshū Kyōgaku Kenkyūjo, 1975, p. 131.

[9] Honganji Shiryō Kenkyūjo, ed., 1969, p. 181.

[10] One section of the Imperial Rescript on Education reads as follows: "Should emergency arise, offer yourself courageously to the State; and thus guard and maintain the prosperity of Our Imperial Throne coeval with heaven and earth. So shall ye not only be Our good and faithful subjects, but render illustrious the best traditions of your forefathers" (Translation taken from Fairbank, Reischauer and Craig, 1965, p. 276). The Rescript was issued in 1890. Nearly twenty years before that, in 1871, Kōnyo 広如, the then chief abbot of Nishi Honganji, stated as follows in his last testament (*Ikun* 遺訓), "Everyone born in the emperor's land is indebted to the emperor ... .Do not err concerning the teaching of the Two Truths. In this life, remain loyal to the emperor" (Fukuma, Sasaki and Hayashima, eds., 1983, pp. 197-98).

[11] Hōnen, "Shonin densetsu no kotoba (諸人伝説の詞)" in *Wago Tōroku* 和語灯録 (Writings in Japanese) vol. 5. *Shōwa Shinsan kokuyaku daizōkyō* 昭和新纂国訳大蔵経, Jōdoshū seiten 浄土宗聖典, Tōhō Shoin 東方書院, 1928, p. 258.

[12] Concerning the following discussion on karmic conditions, see Ama, 1999.

[13] This article is found in Kiyozawa, 1903. For an English translation, see Blum trans., 1989.

[14] Blum trans., 1989, pp. 106-108, slightly modified.

[15] Kiyozawa, 1892, p. 100.

[16] An English translation of the *Skeleton* was prepared by Noguchi Zenshirō 野口善四郎 on the occasion of the World Parliament of Religion held in Chicago in 1893. See Kiyozawa, 1893. As Kiyozawa himself apparently made numerous corrections to Noguchi's draft translation, the English translation can be seen as reflecting Kiyozawa's views quite faithfully. The translation "the progress and improvement of the world" is found on p. 75.

[17] On the relationship between the movement to reform Higashi Honganji and the development of Kiyozawa's thought, see Moriya, 1996.

[18] Kiyozawa, 1896.

[19] Kiyozawa, 1897.

[20] Kiyozawa, 1898.

[21] Kiyozawa, 1901.

[22] Wagatsuma, 1969 is a useful reference for understanding the general outline of the "High Treason Incident." On its relationship to Buddhism, see Ama, 1994.

[23] This article is contained in the present volume (Chapter 16).—*Ed.*

[24] I must add here that the re-evaluation of Takagi's deeds and official reinstatement are due largely to the research of Prof. Izumi Shigeki 泉恵機 of Ōtani University, who has put much effort into rediscovering Takagi's life and work for the present generation.

[25] Although I was not able to treat him in this paper due to the limitation of space, Imamura Yemyō 今村恵猛 (1867-1932), the second chief missionary of the Honpa Hongwanji (commonly known as Nishi Honganji) also worked to incorporate compassion into laws and institutions. He is an important example of a person who practiced Shin Buddhist social ethics. Imamura lived around the same time as Kiyozawa and Takagi, and for this reason, too, his work needs to be considered in detail. On Imamura's work, see Moriya, 1999, Moriya, 2000, and Moriya, 2001.

CHAPTER 16

MY SOCIALISM[1]

—TAKAGI KENMYŌ (ENSHŌ)[2]

(TRANSLATED BY ROBERT F. RHODES)

Preface

My socialism does not derive from that of Karl Marx. Nor does it follow from Tolstoy's pacifism. I do not seek to interpret it scientifically and propagate it throughout the world, like Mr. Katayama,[3] Kosen,[4] or Shūsui.[5] However, I have a faith that is mine alone, which I have put down on paper as I intend to put it into practice. Though my friends, the readers, may oppose my position and subject it to laughter, what follows is something of which I am firmly convinced.

Main Discourse

I do not feel that socialism is a theory, but rather a kind of practice. One person says that it is a prophetic call for social reform, but I think socialism is the first step (towards such a reform). Thus we hope to put it into practice as extensively as possible. I think we need to reform the social system rapidly, and change the social structure completely from the ground up. Yet another person is propagating socialism as a political theory. However, I consider socialism to be related much more deeply to religion than to politics. In proceeding to reform society, we have to, first of all, begin from our own spirituality. Hence I should like to set forth the gist of my faith and practice just as I understand it, without borrowing from past systems of those socialists who are my so-called elders.

I shall discuss socialism by dividing it into two parts. The first is the object of faith while the second is the content of faith. The first (part on the) object of faith will be further divided into three sections: (1) the doctrine, (2) the teacher, and (3) society. Next, the second (part on the) content of faith will also be further divided into two sections: (1) the revolution of thought, and (2) practical action.

What, then, do I mean by the doctrine, which is the first (topic concerning) the object of faith? It is Namu Amida Butsu. "Namu Amida Butsu" is an Indian word, and it is truly the saving voice of the Buddha, which shines like a light in a dark night, protecting us with absolute equality. Even though it is working to provide peace and comfort to intellectuals, scholars, government officials and the wealthy, Amida's main concern is with the common people. (Namu Amida Butsu) is the mighty voice that grants happiness and comfort to ignorant men and women.

Expressed in Japanese, (Namu Amida Butsu) is the voice calling on us not to worry because the transcendental being of universal good called Amida Buddha will save us, and to have no fear because he will protect us. Ah! It's Namu Amida Butsu that gives us strength and life!

It is truly the absolute transcendental compassion. It is the Buddha's universal love. We can only be appalled by those who delight in hearing that (Namu Amida Butsu) is a command to killing. This evidently goes to show that only a few people in our country have understood either religion or Namu Amida Butsu.

In short, I think that Namu Amida Butsu refers to peace and comfort as well as salvation and happiness provided equally to all. How can we misunderstand this Namu Amida Butsu to be a command to subjugate the hated enemy?

I have heard Dr. Nanjō[6] speak several times (where he exhorted his audience by saying) "if you die, You will go to the Pure Land, so (don't worry about your life and) attack the enemy!" Did he stir up feelings of hostility (in his audience)? (If so) isn't this pitiful?

Second, the teacher (人師 *ninshi*) [meaning the "teacher of human beings"] refers to my ideal person. First is Śākyamuni. Each of his words and phrases reflects his theory of individualism. But what about his life? Casting away his royal rank, he became a mendicant monk (沙門 *shamon*, Skt. *śramana*), all for the purpose of removing suffering from and giving happiness to people. He spent his entire life with only three robes and a begging bowl, and died under the bodhi tree. At the time of his death, even birds and animals wept in sorrow. Wasn't he a great socialist of the spiritual realm? [Though his socialism is not identical in theory with that of the Heiminsha (平民社, "Society of Commoners")[7] or that of the followers of *Chokugen* (直言, "Straight Talk").[8]] He thought little of social rank or status. (Through his teachings), he reformed part of the social system of his time. Indeed, there is no question that he succeeded in changing a number of things.

Although I could name a number of teachers in India and China, I shall not mention them here. In Japan, people like Dengyō 伝教 (767-822),[9] Kōbō 弘法 (774-835),[10] Hōnen 法然 (1133-1212),[11] Shinran 親鸞 (1173-1262),[12] Ikkyu 一休 (1394-1481),[13] or Rennyo 蓮如 (1415 -1499)[14] all reserved their deepest sympathy primarily for the common people. In particular, when I remember that Shinran spoke of "fellow practitioners walking together in the same direction (*ondōbō ondōgyō* 御同朋御同行)" and stated that "the venerable titles of monks and priests (*sōzu hosshi* 僧都法師) are used for serfs and servants,"[15] I realize that he was really not only deeply sympathetic towards the common people, but that he was also, without doubt, a socialist who realized a life of nondiscrimination in the spiritual realm. [However, even this is different from the theory of present-day socialists.] In light of these points, I declare Buddhism to be the mother of the common people and the enemy of the nobility.

Third is society, which refers to the ideal world. What do you all think? I consider the Land of Bliss (i.e. the Pure Land) to be the place in which socialism is truly practiced. If Amida is endowed with the thirty-two marks,[16] the novice bodhisattvas who gather (in the Land of Bliss) are also endowed with the thirty-two marks. If Amida is endowed with the eighty minor marks,[17] the practitioners (in the Land of Bliss) are also endowed with the eighty minor marks. If Amida enjoys delicious meals of a hundred flavors, sentient beings (of the Land of Bliss) also enjoy delicious meals of a hundred flavors. If Amida is the "sublime unity of the accommodated body and the fulfilled body" (*ōhō myōki* 応報妙帰),[18] then the practitioners are also the "sublime unity of the accommodated body and the fulfilled body." (Those born in the Land of Bliss) gain supernatural powers identical with those of Amida Buddha—including the ability to see anything at any distance, the ability to hear any sound at any distance, the ability to go anywhere at will, the ability to know the thoughts of others, the ability to recollect their own former lives and of others—and, realizing that "the Buddha mind is the mind of great compassion," become beings who continually fly to other lands in order to save people with whom they are karmically related. This is why it is called the "Land of Bliss." In truth, socialism is practiced in this Land of Bliss.

We have never heard that beings in the Land of Bliss have attacked other lands. Nor have we ever heard that they started a great war for the sake of justice. Hence I am against war (with Russia).[19] I do not feel that a person of the Land of Bliss should take part in warfare. [However, there may be those, among the socialists, who advocate the opening of war.] [This refers to Mōri Saian 毛利柴庵 (1871-1938)].[20]

I shall now discuss the first section of the content of faith: the revolution of thought. Specialists (of Shin Buddhist doctrine) wrangle over this point, speaking of "taking refuge (in Amida Buddha) in one instant of thought" (*ichinen kimyō* 一念帰命) or "the practitioner's faith" (*gyōja no nōshin* 行者の能信).

As I have stated above, when we come to seek the ideal world upon receiving instructions from teachers like Śākyamuni, and reflect deeply within our minds by hearing the voice of the savior Amida calling to us, we then gain peace of mind, feel great joy and become vigorous in spirit.

This is truly so. We live in a country where the common people in general are sacrificed for the fame, peerage and medals of one small group of people. It is a society in which the common people in general must suffer for the sake of a small number of speculators. Are not the poor treated like animals at the hands of the wealthy? There are people who cry out in hunger; there are women who sell their honor out of poverty; there are children who are soaked by the rain. Rich people and government officials find pleasure in treating them like toys, oppressing them and engaging them in hard labor, don't they?

The external stimuli being like this, our subjective faculties are replete with ambition. This is truly the world of defilement, a world of suffering, a dark night. Human nature is being slaughtered by the devil.

However, the Buddha continually calls to us: "I shall protect you, I shall save you, I shall help you." People who have discovered this light have in truth gained peace and happiness. I believe that they have been released from the anguish that makes them turn away from the world and have gained hope.

Our thoughts cannot but change completely: "I will do what the Buddha wishes me to do, practice what he wishes me to practice and make the Buddha's will my own will. I will become what the Tathāgata tells me to become." This is the time of great determination!

Second, practical action. Since the revolution in thought discussed above is the result of a profound empathy with the Buddha's universal love, we need to open ourselves up (*tainin* 体認) to the Tathāgata's mind of compassion. ["Open ourselves up" or "bear with patience" (*tainin* 耐忍)? Perhaps it is better to use the expression "truly recognize" (*tainin* 諦認) here, rather than "bear with patience."][21] We must practice it. Even a haughty seventy-year old marquis who has received the Grand Order of the Chrysanthemum cannot be called an ideal human as long as he treats a pretty seventeen or eighteen-year old like a toy. Even though a general may have been victorious in war, if he pays no attention to (the number of) soldiers dead or wounded, he is not worth a penny to us. A person who beats a child just for peeping into a nobleman's house is truly despicable.

No, we do not wish to become recipients of the Grand Order of the Chrysanthemum, generals or noblemen like them. We are not laboring in order to become such people. The only thing I wish to accomplish through my great energy and human labor is progress (*kōjō shinpo* 向上進歩) and community life (*kyōdō seikatsu* 共同生活). We labor in order to produce and we cultivate our minds so that we can attain the Way. But look at what's happening! We cannot help but lament when we hear that religious functionaries are praying to gods and Buddhas for victory. Indeed, a feeling of pity arises in my heart and I am sorry for them.

We must take our stand within this world covered over by darkness, and propagate the saving light, peace and happiness (of Namu Amida Butsu). Only then can we fulfill out great responsibility. My friends! Pray recite this "Namu Amida Butsu" with us. Cease taking pleasure in victory and shouting "banzai." This is because "Namu Amida Butsu" is the voice that leads everyone equally to salvation. My friends! Pray recite this "Namu Amida Butsu" with us, cast off your aristocratic pretensions and cease looking down upon the common people. This is because Namu Amida Butsu is the voice expressing sympathy with the common people. My friends! Pray recite this "Namu Amida Butsu" with us, remove all thoughts of the struggle for existence from your minds, and exert yourselves for the sake of community life. This is because people who recite Namu Amida Butsu are included among the inhabitants of the Land of Bliss. Inasmuch as this is what the nembutsu signifies, we must proceed from the spiritual realm and completely change the social system from the ground up. I am firmly convinced that this is what socialism means.

In closing I wish to cite a passage from one of Shinran Shōnin's letters which is (often) quoted in pro-war arguments and ask my friends, the readers, to see if it advocates the opening of hostilities or whether it is a gospel for peace.

The *Go-shōsoku-shū* 御消息集 (*A Collection of Letters*), first column, right-hand section of the fourth page (the first part is abridged), states:

> In the final analysis, it would be splendid if all people who say the nembutsu, not just yourself, do so not with thoughts of themselves, but for the sake of the imperial court and for the sake of the people of the country. Those who feel uncertain of birth should say the nembutsu aspiring first for their own birth. Those who feel that their own birth is completely settled should, mindful of the Buddha's benevolence, hold the nembutsu in their hearts and say it to respond in gratitude to that benevolence, with the wish, "May there be peace in the world, and may the Buddha's teachings spread!" (End of quote)[22]

Alas, this is an example of the old adage that "fear makes us see monsters in the dark."[23] Although the passage above is a gospel for peace, have people mistaken it for the sound of a bugle commanding us to attack the enemy? Or did I mistake the bells and drums of battle for injunctions for peace? I shall leave it up to my friends, the readers, to decide.

However, I am fortunate in that I hear both bugles and bells of battle as gospels for peace. Many thanks. Namu Amida Butsu.

REFERENCES

Hirota, Dennis, et al. 1997. *The Collected Works of Shinran*, 2 vols. Kyoto: Jōdo Shinshū Hongwanji-ha.

Takagi, Kenmyō Tsuitō Shūkai 高木顕命追悼集会, ed. 1998. *Enshōki kiroku* 遠松忌記録 (Record of the Memorial Service for Enshō [Takagi Kenmyō]. Hikone, Shiga Prefecture: Fūsanbō 風山房, 1998. (Includes a text of "My Socialism" as well as the following: Ama Toshimaro 阿満利麿, "Enshōki kinen kōen 遠松忌念講演 [Commemorative Lecture for Takagi Kenmyō's Memorial Service]," pp. 3-18).

Yoshida Kyūichi 吉田久一, 1959a. "Uchiyama Gudō to Takagi Kenmyō no chosaku," 内山愚童と高木顕明の著作 (The Writings of Uchiyama Gudō and Takagi Kenmyō), *Nihon rekishi*, 131 (May 1959), pp. 68-77.

——, 1959b. "Kōtoku jiken to bukkyō 幸徳事件と仏教 (The Kōtoku Affair and Buddhism)" in his *Nihon kindai bukkyōshi kenkyū* 日本近代仏教史研究 (Studies in the History of Modern Japanese Buddhism). Tokyo, Yoshikawa Kōbunkan, 1959, pp. 434-548.

Besides the works above, the following are useful sources for Takagi's life and thought:

Higashi Honganji 東本願寺, 2000. *Takagi Kenmyō: Taigyaku jiken ni renzashita nembutsusha* 高木顕明 –大逆事件に連座した念仏者 (Takagi Kenmyō: A Nembutsu Practitioner who was Implicated in the High Treason Incident). Shinshū Booklet 真宗ブックレット 8. Kyoto: Higashi Honganji.

Shinshū Ōtani-ha Dōwa Suishin Honbu 真宗大谷派同和推進本部, ed. 1995. *Shindō* 身同, no. 14 (August 1995). Special Issue on the High Treason Incident. Includes the following articles:

(1)   Yamaizumi Susumu 山泉進, "Taigyaku jiken towa nani ka 大逆事件とは何か (What is the High Treason Incident)," pp. 15-30.

(2)   Hakka Akihito 八箇亮仁, "Taigyaku jiken to tokushu buraku 大逆事件と特殊部落 (The High Treason Incident and Tokushu Buraku)," pp. 31-45.

(3)   Ishikawa Rikizan 石川力山, "Taigyaku jiken to bukkyō: Uchiyama Gudō no jiken renza to Sōtōshū no taiō 大逆事件と仏教—内山愚童の事件連座と曹洞宗の対応 (The High Treason Incident and Buddhism: Uchiyama Gudō's Implication in the Affair and the Response of the Sōtō School)," pp. 46-58.

(4)   Izumi Shigeki 泉恵機, "Takagi Kenmyō no jiseki ni tsuite 高木顕明の事積について (On Takagi Kenmyō's Achievements)," pp. 59-81.

Takagi Michiaki 高木道明, 1970. "Taigyaku jiken to buraku mondai: Takagi Kenmyō no hito to shisō 大逆事件と部落問題—高木顕明の人と思想 (The High Treason Incident and Buraku Problem: Takagi Kenmyō's Life and Thought)." *Buraku mondai kenkyū* 部落問題研究 28 (December 1970), pp. 19-33.

Yasutomi Shinya 安富信哉, 1999. "The Opening of the Spirit of Dharmākara: The Case of Reverend Takagi Kenmyō, a Shin Buddhist Priest of the Meiji Period." *The Pure Land*, 16 (December 1999), pp. 122-130.

NOTES

[1] *Yo ga shakaishugi* (余が社会主義). This essay is one of two pieces of Takagi Kenmyō's extant writings, which was discovered by Yoshida Kyūichi among Takagi's confiscated

papers and published for the first time in Yoshida 1959, listed in the bibliography above. According to Takagi's own note attached to the paper, "This draft was completed in the ... month of Meiji 37 (1904)." The translation is based on the amended text found in Takagi Kenmyō Tsuitō Shūkai, ed., *Enshōki kiroku*, pp. 19 -25, also listed above. Parentheses in the translation indicate words added by the translator, while square brackets indicate passages found in brackets in the original text.—*Ed.*

[2] Enshō (遠松) is Takagi's pen-name, taken from the name of his temple, Enshōzan Jōsenji 遠松山浄泉寺.

[3] Katayama Sen 片山潜 (1859-1933), an influential socialist activist and leader of the Japanese trade union movement.

[4] Refers to Sakai Toshihiko 堺利彦 (1871-1933), also known as Sakai Kosen 枯川, a leading socialist who started the *Heimin shinbun* with Kōtoku Shūsui in 1903. Although the text has "古川" it should read "枯川."

[5] Refers to Kōtoku Shūsui 幸徳秋水 (1871-1911).

[6] Nanjō Bun'yū 南条文雄 (1849-1927). A scholar and priest of the Ōtani branch of Jōdo Shinshū. He was one of the first to undertake the study of Sanskrit Buddhist texts in Japan. From 1903 to 1923, he served as president of Ōtani University,

[7] A socialist organization created by Kōtoku Shūsui and Sakai Toshihiko in 1903, which published the weekly *Heimin shinbun* 平民新聞 (*Commoner's News*). However, the newspaper was forced to close down in 1905 due to government repression and lack of resources.

[8] Another socialist weekly, which took the place of *Heimin shinbun* after its closure. In eight months this newspaper was also banned by the government.

[9] Refers to Saichō 最澄, the founder of the Tendai school. The imperial court posthumously granted him the title of Dengyō Daishi 伝教大師 (Master who Transmitted the Teachings).

[10] Refers to Kūkai 空海, also known as Kōbō Daishi 弘法大師 (The Master who Spread the Dharma). Founder of the Shingon school.

[11] Founder of the Jōdo school.

[12] Hōnen's disciple and the founder of the Jōdo Shin school.

[13] A popular Rinzai Zen monk known for his eccentric behavior.

[14] The eight abbot of Honganji of the Jōdo Shin school.

[15] Paraphrase of the second and third lines of the 12th verse of *Gutoku hitan jukkai* 愚禿悲嘆述懐 (*Gutoku's Lament and Reflection*) which is part of Shinran's *Shōzōmatsu wasan* 正像末和讃 (*Hymns of the Dharma-Ages*). Cf *The Collected Works of Shinran*, vol. 1, p. 423.

[16] Thirty-two distinguishing marks which all Buddhas are said to possess on their bodies.

[17] Eighty minor physical characteristics which all Buddhas are said to possess.

[18] All Buddhas are said to possess three bodies: (1) the accommodated body (*nirmāṇa-kāya*, 応身), or the body with which Buddhas manifest themselves to save sentient beings, (2) the fulfilled body (*saṃbhoga-kāya*, 報身), or the body which Buddhas receive as the result of their past practices, and (3) the Dharma body (*dharma-kāya*, 法身), or the body of Buddhas

identified with the Dharma itself. In Pure Land Buddhism, there was a major controversy over whether Amida Buddha should be understood as the accommodated or fulfilled body. On this point, Shinran states as follows in the preface to the Chapter on True Realization in the *Kyōgyōshinshō*: "Amida Tathāgata comes forth from suchness and manifests various bodies—fulfilled, accommodated, and transformed" (*The Collected Works of Shinran*, vol. 1, p. 153).

[19] The Russo-Japanese War (lasted from February 1904 to September 1905).

[20] Journalist and priest of the Shingon school. Publisher of the newspaper *Muro shinpō* 牟婁新報.

[21] This is Takagi's editorial note to himself.

[22] *The Collected Works of Shinran*, vol. 1, p. 560.

[23] A well-known phrase from the *Lieh-tzu* 列子.

CHAPTER 17

ETHICS IN AMERICAN JŌDO-SHINSHŪ: TRANS-ETHICAL RESPONSIBILITY

—KENNETH K. TANAKA

Preface

This paper is an attempt to explore the possibilities of the nature and role of "ethics" in American Jōdo Shinshū. Although ethics in recent years has attracted growing scholarly as well as popular interest, the topic remains virtually unexplored awaiting further studies from doctrinal, historical and other approaches.[1] The nature of this paper is primarily pastoral, for it advocates a personal view regarding the need as well as the kind of ethics in response to the religious environment of contemporary American society. As an introductory foray into a vast and complex topic, my objectives would be accomplished if this paper succeeds in generating questions and further investigations of this vital area of Jōdo Shinshū studies.

I The Term "Ethics"

For purposes of this investigation, ethics will be defined as "the correct set of actions, dispositions, attitudes, virtues, and ways of life that characterize an ideal person or society."[2] What then is the relationship between ethics to religion? This basic question is certainly subject to various opinions, but the general consensus, at least conceptually, regards the two as distinct. Soren Kirkegaard's famous category of human experience into the religious, ethical and aesthetic supports the validity of this distinction,[3] and the *Encyclopedia of Religion* also echoes this view as it defines:

> Religion involves beliefs, attitudes and practices that relate human beings to supernatural agencies or sacred realities. It addresses what has been called the problem of interpretability, which includes such persistent questions as the ultimate nature and purpose of the natural world and the meaning of death and suffering.[4]

In contrast, ethics is concerned primarily with regulating the conduct of individuals in communities and aims to settle interpersonal and social disputes and clarify issues that affect the quality of life in our world according to certain currently acceptable standards of behavior.

In this paper, I propose to use the term "soteriological" (or "spiritual") for what has been referred to above as "religion." This choice is intentional for, in my view, it helps to clarify the nature of ethics in relation to Jōdo Shinshū in America. There are two general views of "religion" in relation to ethics: 1. religion excludes ethics and 2. religion includes ethics. In other words, it involves the question as to whether "ethics" should be subsumed under the category of religion or lie outside of it. The difference of opinion on this issue is reflected in the writings of modern Shinshū scholars on other issues and constitutes one of the underlying themes that this paper indirectly attempts to address.[5]

I subscribe to the second position, that religion includes ethics. I have, therefore, adopted the term "soteriological" to refer to what "religion" normally refers, and elevated "religion" to a more inclusive meaning. Hence, in this paper, "religion" subsumes the "soteriological" and the "ethical" as its two major components.

Needless to say, ethics constitutes an enormously complex subject. It applies to a broad spectrum of concerns wherever human conduct is involved, and particularly when it involves controversy and ambiguity as to its "correctness" as, for example, abortion and euthanasia. In addition, these ethical issues entail, from a standpoint of formal inquiry, such questions as authority, motivation, retribution and redemption. In the case of abortion, the authority for the "pro-life" proponents rests with their reading of the Bible, while the "pro-choice" advocated appeal to women's civil rights. Motivations that mold the actions of the advocates on both sides are numerous and often complex, but invariably involve at its core what each side determines to be their inviolable authoritative basis as noted above. The last two of the four issues, retribution and redemption, may involve the citing of scriptural bases, for example, the appealing to the fear of eternal damnation by the pro-life advocates on one hand and the love of Jesus for the pro-choice supporters on the other.

Ethicists speak about two kinds of classical approaches to ethics, "deontological" and "teleological." The deontological approach understands morality as primarily in terms of duty, law, or obligation. The concern in this approach focuses on right versus wrong. The deontological approach sees Christian ethics in terms of the Ten Commandments or the revealed word of God as law to be followed. In contrast, the teleological approach sees morality as a means for realizing what lies at the end as the ultimate goal. This approach is concerned less with the question of right but more with relationship to the goal. In the Christian tradition, for example, the teleological position understands the culmination of moral life as the union with or participation in God, which becomes the good and the end of the moral life.[6]

For sake of a more neutral and less Christianized set of terms, I will in this report employ "obligatory ethics" for deontological and "goal-oriented ethics" for teleological.

II Nature of Ethics in General Buddhism

Buddhist scriptures are replete with categories of discipline and conduct (in the broad sense as expressed by such terms as *śiksā, śīla, bhāvanā, mārga, patha*) which are ethical in nature. For the laity, there are the Five and Eight Precepts, and the Ten Wholesome Acts. The novices adhere to the Ten Precepts. For the monks there are the 37 Wings of Enlightenment, which includes the Eightfold Path. In addition, the full Pratimokṣa Rules contain 227 or 250 specific precepts for the monks with an even larger number of precepts for the nuns. The Pāramitā Perfections in the Mahayana tradition play a crucial role in its soteriological scheme.

Even in the Pure Land Buddhist tradition with its image as the caretaker of the less capable, the ethical precepts abound with such categories as the Five Pains, Five Grave Offenses, Four Heavy Transgressions, Ten Wholesome Acts, Three Pure Acts, and the Vilification of the Dharma. Vasubandhu's Five Contemplative Gates and Zendō's (Shan-tao) Five Correct Practices are indicative of the concern for proper conduct and practices among the patriarchs of the spiritual lineage of Jōdo Shinshū. Even Hōnen, whose advocacy of the exclusive Nembutsu practice lead to the abrogation of discipline among his followers, was widely respected for leading a strict traditional monastic life. Similar assessment can be made about his spiritual teacher, the eminent Chinese Pure Land master Zendō.

According to Tachibana and Saddhātissa, two representative modern writers on Buddhist ethics, it appears appropriate to characterize ethics in Buddhism as falling primarily under goal-oriented ethics rather than obligatory.[7] The *Dhammapada*'s famous instruction states, "Not to commit evil, perform good. And to purify one's own mind, that is the teaching of the Buddha." This simple didactic phrase, in my view, succinctly conveys the nature of good and bad in Buddhism as primarily a means for the realization of soteriological emancipation. This is evident in the monastic precepts (*śīla*) which comprise one component of a balanced method of cultivation together with wisdom (*prajñā*) and mental concentration (*samādhi*; *dhyāna*). The precepts are aimed at contributing to the overall welfare of the spiritual seeker in the ultimate realization of wisdom or emancipation.[8] The meaning of the term for "moral conduct" (*śikṣāpada*; *sikkhāpada*) can be interpreted as "step or process" (*pada*) for "learning or cultivation" (*śiksā*); the meaning of process is endowed in other buddhist terms for cultivation, *mārga* (road) and *patha* (path).

Further, this goal-oriented character of ethics has as its primary objective the realization of spiritual life, not the maintenance of social order and harmony more in the category of obligatory ethics. This emphasis does not totally deny the existence of regulations for the latter purpose but they were ancillary or regarded as natural conduct of the enlightened.[9] Certainly the Pratimokṣa Rules that govern the communal and personal lives of the monastic community contain numerous rules that insure communal order, but even these were instituted with the explicit aim of fostering soteriological goals. The ancillary nature of these ethical regulations is historically attested as they did not constitute the "original" core teaching of the Buddha but were gradually added as problems and needs arose with the growth in the bourgeoning Buddhist communities. This utilitarian nature differs markedly from the Ten Commandments, which as a covenant between God and the Jewish tribe played much more of an essential role in their spiritual life.

III   The Soteriological Character of Shinran's Thought

I believe scholars and teachers would be in full agreement with the view that the goal-oriented ethics evidenced in other Buddhist teachings play no role in Shinran's thought. This stems from his unique doctrinal position of absolute Other Power which expunges any belief in the human ability to produce enlightenment on its own. The single, direct cause for enlightenment lies not with the seeker but in the Primal Vow of Amida Buddha as expressed in Chapter One of the *Tannishō*:

> Thus, entrusting yourself to the Primal Vow requires no performance of good, for no act can hold greater virtue than saying the Name. Nor is there need to despair of the evil you commit, for no act is so evil that it obstructs the working of Amida's Primal Vow.[10]

In this radical shift in the soteriological paradigm, the practices (*gyō*; *bhāvanā*) lie not within the realm of human capability but in the domain of Amida Buddha. Shinjin faith is all that is required, and even this is said to be the mind endowed by Amida.

The "antinomian" doctrine is further buttressed by the view that the very people who are incapable of performing any good deeds are the rightful object of the Primal Vow:

> Even a good person can attain birth in the Pure Land, so it goes without saying that an evil person will.[11]

Shinran's total rejection of anything resembling goal-oriented ethical efforts finds expression in his relentless attack of self-power (*jiriki*). As the Shinshū doctrine of the "progression through the three Vows" (*sanganten-nyū*) succinctly reveals, Shinran rejected the sundry virtuous practices of the *Contemplation Sūtra* and the recitative Nembutsu of the *Smaller Sūtra* as provisional teachings to be discarded for the highest teaching of the Primal Vow in the *Larger Sūtra*.

For Shinran, therefore, ethics as we saw in general Buddhism plays no role in realizing its soteriological transformation, Shinjin. This does not, however, fully resolve the issue of how to interpret Shinran's fervent and dauntless exhortation to accept the Pure Land teaching or to lead a spiritual life. Such messages, typical of any person committed to soteriological concerns, can be construed as "ethical" in the broad sense of the term. This shall be posed as one of the topics for future examination.

IV Ethics in Shinran's Thought

Shinran, however, was not totally oblivious to ethical issues, once beyond the boundaries of the two types of ethical categories discussed above. His assumption rests on the view that a spiritual person will try naturally to lead an ethical life. The very experience of Shinjin propels one to want to be ethical as expressed in one of his pastoral letters:

> When people come to have faith in the Buddha deep in their heart, they genuinely renounce this life, they lament their transmigration in Saṃsāra, they have deep faith in Amida's Vow, and they delight in saying Amida Buddha. If these people truly desire not to commit the evil deeds that they may be inclined to do, it is an indication of their renunciation of this world.[12]

Through the transformative experience of faith or Shinjin, one's natural inclination is to refrain from acts which would hurt others. Such a person would exhibit greater humility and engage in activities that transcend selfish predilections and self-aggrandizement. Shinran elsewhere wrote that the person of Shinjin would "thinking of the Buddha's benevolence, devote himself to the Nembutsu in order to respond with gratitude for that benevolence, and should hope for peace in the world ... "[13] Imbued with this deep sense of gratitude one spontaneously works for peace in the world.

Although Shinran did not advocate a particular set of ethics, he on the other hand never condoned unethical behavior. But his deeply soteriological teaching of absolute Other Power accentuated misunderstanding among some of his disciples. In the famous discussion in Chapter 13 of the *Tannishō* known in Shinshū as "licensed evil" (*zōakumuge*, "committing evil without obstruction"; *hōitsu muzan*, "self-indulgence without remorse"; *honganbokori*, "flaunting Amida's Vow"), Shinran criticizes the incorrect understanding of some Nembutsu followers who commit unethical acts in the belief that the Vow is unobstructed by evil deeds.

> There was in those days, a person who had fallen into a mistaken understanding. He asserted that since the Vow was made to save the evil person, one should purposely choose to do evil, taking it as the cause of birth. When rumors of misdeeds gradually reached Shinran, to end adherence to that wrong understanding he wrote in a letter: "Do not take a liking to poison just because there is an antidote."[14]

Here, Shinran proscribes the purposeful committing of unethical acts in "presuming" upon the Vow. Although the Vow ultimately does not exclude the perpetrator from enlightenment, Shinran never encouraged his followers to purposely commit evil in order to be saved.

Elsewhere, in one of his letters, Shinran is critical of those who speak ill of teachers and equates such action with the committing of the most serious Buddhist offense. In an expression of his unabashed human emotion, he appears personally offended by a disciple for his unethical conduct:

> People who look down on teachers and who speak ill of the masters commit slander of the dharma. Those who speak ill of their parents are guilty of the five grave offenses. We should keep our distance from them. Thus, since Zenjō-bō, who lived in the northern district abused his parents and slandered me in various ways, I had no close feelings for him and did not encourage him to come to see me.[15]

V Obligatory Ethics in Post-Shinran Shinshū History

The exigencies of a fledgling religious body led Shinshū leaders to enforce increasing adherence to moral conduct, which, in my view, can be categorized as obligatory ethics. Finding itself in an often hostile and unsympathetic religious setting, the emerging Shinshū groups expended inordinate amounts of energy in maintaining an image that would not jeopardize their precarious status. We see in the following few examples some common main themes that were to characterize the ethical concerns throughout the approximately two-hundred years (1263-1499) of the formative period up through Rennyo's time: 1) not to criticize other schools and their teaching, 2) to show respect for secular rulers and 3) to maintain a low profile.

The following, as aptly translated by Prof. James Dobbins, is an oldest surviving set of congregational regulations dated 1285, only 23 years after Shinran's death.[16]

1. As followers of the exclusive practice, do not denigrate other Buddhas or Bodhisattvas, or people of other persuasions and practices.

2. Do not indulge in arguments with people of other persuasions and practices.

3. Do not be slack in your respect for rulers and parents.

4. Do not denigrate the *kami* just because you say the *Nembutsu*.

5. Do not enter the *dōjō* laughing or whispering or with an air of haughtiness.

6. Do not give your teacher a bad reputation by preaching heresies (*jagi*) and by wrongly calling them the single-minded and exclusive teaching.

7. Do not punish disciples, simply because you are the teacher, without establishing what is right and wrong.

8. Do not denigrate your religious teacher or your fellow believers.

9. Whenever there are falsehoods spoken between fellow believers who appeal to you for

judgment, listen to what is right and wrong on both sides, and show them what is correct and what is not.

10. On the day of Nembutsu worship when you meet for services, do not do such things as eat fish or fowl.

11. Men and women should not sit together when they perform the Nembutsu, since it will be a disruption.

12. Do not act as a merchant of horses or human beings, for it is known to be disreputable.

13. In selling something, do not lie and charge even a single *mon* of money in excess, and, if you do, return the difference.

14. Do not indulge in illicit sexual relations with another person's wife, and do not slander others by saying they do.

15. As Nembutsu adherents, when you drink liquor, do not get drunk and lose your senses.

16. As Nembutsu adherents, do not steal or gamble.

17. Do not do such things as envy those who are superior or belittle those who are inferior.

The items listed above are prohibited. Abide by these seventeen correct regulations. Adherents of the Nembutsu, the exclusive and single practice, should admonish each other in them. [If people violate them,] then even if they are called fellow believers or religious companions, you should expel them from the congregation, and you should not sit with them or join them. In witness to the aforesaid regulations.

1285. 8. 13

Zen en
(signature)

Many of the same themes are also evident in Rennyo's letter entitled the "chapter on the manner of conduct" (*okite no shō*):

If we have listened seriously to the meaning of the Faith of the Other-Power of our school and have received Faith, we must place the essence of this Faith deep within our hearts and not expound it to others not of our sect. Furthermore, wherever we may be, in the alley-ways, avenues, in our village, and elsewhere, we must not openly boast of the virtues of our Faith without discretion as to those who may be present. Also, do not be disobedient to the district and local officials of government saying, "I have attained 'true Faith,'" but accept more and more of our civic responsibilities.

We must not insult the various deities and Bodhisattvas of the other schools as they are all embraced within the six characters, "Na"-"Mu"-"A"-"Mi"-"Da" and "Butsu."

In particular, while actively abiding by the laws of society outwardly and holding fast to the Faith of Other-Power inwardly, we must live our lives based on the common mores.

It must be understood that all the foregoing are points concerning the manner of conduct as established by our Jōdo Shinshū Sect.[17]

At the heart of these admonitions was the religious institution's relationship with the rest of society. This relationship, traditionally called the "two truths of the absolute and the secular" (*shinzoku nitai*), pre-occupied the minds of all Shinshū thinkers and leaders including Kakunyo, Zonkaku, and Rennyo. They attempted to reconcile the two realms in one form or another, which Prof. T. Shigaraki has categorized into five possibilities:

1. the absolute and the secular are one truth;
2. they are parallel truth;
3. they are mutually related;
4. the absolute influences the secular;
5. the secular truth is skillful or compassionate means.

In all five cases, Prof. Shigaraki points out, Shinran's advocacy of the absolute or soteriological truth was consistently compromised and often relegated to a subservient position.[18] Further, these above regulations exhibit a growing legislative tone as well as instruction for punitive actions as, for example, when Zen'en states, "[if people violate them,] ... you should expel them from the congregation." Rennyo, too, expressed threats of expulsion:

> If by some remote chance there are followers who do not adhere to these principles [of the three articles],[19] they should be removed from the list of bona-fide members of the Founding Shonin's School for a long time.[20]

After Rennyo's death, the family council (*ikkeshū*) comprised by Rennyo's close family members came to wield extraordinary powers, including the power of excommunication (*hamon*) and in times of warfare even the threat of execution (*shōgai*).[21]

VI Reasons for Ethics in Contemporary American Shinshū

I wish to approach this section by reiterating my opinion that for Shinshū to emerge as a viable and relevant force in modern America, the teaching must integrate the ethical concerns with its soteriological dimension. In so suggesting, it is not my intention to compromise the primary and foremost goal of Shinran's teachings, which as discussed above, is soteriological in nature. Further, this ethics must be in accord with the character and nature of Shinran's teachings.

The support for my view lies in part in the emerging character of religion in contemporary America. For many people, especially the young, the function of social welfare and concern for social issues carry a much greater degree of importance in religion. The pragmatic American character expects the religious teachings to actively respond to their "worldly," social, and personal concerns. This speaks well for religion in America for it reflects a yearning to make it play an enhanced role in one's life. It does not, as is sometimes asserted, constitute a dilution or a compromise of the true intent of religion, the spiritual life.

As we examined above, Jōdo Shinshū as a religious institution actively addressed ethical issues throughout its long history in Japan. However, in the modern period particularly in the Meiji period, which molded the initial character of Shinshū in America, Shinshū followers, as with other Buddhists, turned mostly to non-Buddhist values for their ethical authority and inspiration. Inspired at its core by Japanese Confucian values and colloquially called "*jōshiki*" (common sense), it provided clear structured modes of behavior in relating to the rest of society. A Shinshū follower, thus, looked internally to Shinshū teaching for soteriological reliance but turned externally beyond the Shinshū framework for ethical guidance (as promulgated by Rennyo above), a pattern in keeping with the traditional Shinshū application of the "two truths of the absolute and the secular" (*shinzoku nitai*).

Given this historical background, it is my assessment that the transplanting of Jōdo Shinshū in America entailed primarily the soteriological dimension but only secondarily the ethical. Hence, the ethical concerns for Shinshū followers in America were guided largely by a world-view of combined secular Japanese and American values. However, today, new demands are being made as its constituency shifts to those whose Japanese secular values are virtually non-existent, including both the younger generation of traditional Japanese-American members and the new converts. In addition, there is the emerging expectation of a more "relevant" religion as American society grapples with more complex and diverse issues which traditional secular values associated with Shinshū are unable to adequately address.

Further, it is my observation that the ethical issues interest a larger number of people than do the soteriological. Even in the Shinshū tradition, with its promise of universal salvation, its leaders including Shinran and Rennyo have lamented the rarity of people of true Shinjin. Shinran acknowledges the veracity of the Larger Sūtra statement, "Going is easy, but no one is there [in the true Pure Land]." Rennyo complained about the lack of interest and feedback by the audience to his series of summer sermons, likening his seemingly fruitless efforts to "a bee stinging the antler of a deer"![22] There is no reason to feel that the contemporary American situation is any different. However, there are reasons to feel optimistic, for as alluded to above, the American level of respect and confidence in religion remains relatively high in serving their social and personal needs. In this kind of religious climate, it seems incumbent upon Jōdo Shinshū from a pastoral and propagational standpoint to offer a clearer set of ethical guidelines to which a large number of people are predisposed to respond, in contrast to a far smaller number inspired strictly by the soteriological message.

In fact, Shinshū in America has had a legacy of interest in ethical concerns, particularly on the continental United States since the Second World War, with the beginning of the takeover of leadership by the English speaking second generation. The service books today associated with the Buddhist Churches of America contain liturgical messages of an ethical nature, the "Golden Chain" being the prime example. Also included are the "Jōdo Shinshū Creed," "Six Pāramitās" and "Eightfold Noble Paths." Some have criticized this as deviation from the Other Power teaching and advocate their elimination, but their tenacious presence, I believe, speaks to a deeper and pervasive need on the part of the current members. They serve a vital function of providing ethical guidelines for the socialization of the young. But their popularity equally extends to adults who find them easier to understand and palatable for application in their daily lives. These ethical teachings, as different from the soteriological, in a very curious way seem to satisfy their perception of Buddhism as a "way of life" (a refrain heard not infrequently among American Jōdo Shinshū members).

The above phenomenon is not confined only to the traditional members of American Shinshū institution, but reflects a shifting attitude of the pervasive secularized view of religion in what some have called a "post-traditional world." One of its characteristics is the focus on the here and now, where their concern is far less with the life after death but this life. This has come about, in part, by greater confidence and freedom on the part of the individuals to determine the course of their lives, including their religious beliefs and practices. This, in turn, has been made possible in the United States by the relative economic prosperity and absence of any disruptive major war since the end of World War II.

VII Trans-ethical Responsibility: Assumptions

In Shinshū, motive for action, including the uttering of the Nembutsu and carrying out of ethical instructions, has traditionally been explained as a "response in gratitude to the debt we owe Amida" (*button hōsha*). With the realization of the unexpected and undeserved gift of Shinjin, one is spontaneously moved to act out of sheer joy and gratitude. As one awakens to the compassionate forces that embrace one's life, that very realization functions as the vital source which generates that person's activities to pay back the world.

However, this traditional explanation presupposes that the person has realized Shinjin awakening, but would not be adequately applicable to others without such a realization. Shinran recognized two categories of people, for in his *Goshōsokushū* he states:

> The person who feels that his attainment of birth is not settled should, to begin with, say the Nembutsu in aspiration for birth. The person who feels that his attainment of birth is definitely settled should, thinking of the Buddha's benevolence, devote himself to the Nembutsu in order to respond with gratitude for that benevolence, and should hope for peace in the world and the spread of the Buddha Dharma.[23]

Given Shinran's recognition of the existence of a category of people without Shinjin, I wish to propose what I call "trans-ethical responsibility." It begins to address two unresolved issues: 1) ethical guidelines for those without Shinjin and thereby not yet fully inspired by the spirit of *button hōsha* and 2) more concrete guidelines for those with Shinjin in dealing particularly with complex, controversial ethical topics. The prefix "trans" in "trans-ethical responsibility" can be understood to mean either "to transcend" or "to transform." Both meanings are incorporated since trans-ethics simultaneously transcends the ordinary sense of ethics and transforms the self-perception (though not the nature) of the person involved.[24]

Trans-ethical responsibility of Shinshū transcends the other two kinds of ethics. Given the absolute Other Power teaching, we saw above that neither the goal-oriented nor obligatory approaches to ethics applied. Rather this trans-ethics falls under the third approach which the modern ethicists have recently begun to speak about, one based on responsibility.[25] Unlike the legislative and absolutist character of obligatory ethics, this approach is more voluntary and flexible in nature. It, further, does not suffer from the limitations of a utilitarian attitude that is inherent in goal-oriented ethics. In other words, this third form of ethics is unconditional in terms of its motivation and expectation which emanate out of one's internalized voluntary sense of responsibility.

VIII Process of Religious Education

The transformative dimension of trans-ethics functions to transform the person to become more involved in the reflective process of a soteriological quest. Through this ethical involvement, one is gradually illuminated by the principles and inspirations of a higher soteriological life. In one sense, through the trans-ethical participation one is confronted with the expectations and guidelines which were unknown, or at best ambiguous, to one preoccupied with the secular, ego-centric norms. One will likely experience personal struggles as one attempts to work through the conflict between the ethical ideals and the realities of one's selfish propensities. This gap can serve as a "mirror" for the person to come to a better appreciation of Shinran's admission about himself as one hopelessly defiled and filled with evil thoughts. Such introspective assessment of one's nature stems only from a higher soteriological set of ideals, not from the conventional worldly expectations where self-centered values remain the norm. Views such as this have previously been articulated by Shinshū teachers including Bishop Seigen Yamaoka and, as we see below, by Prof. Yoshifumi Ueda and Prof. Shōgyō Gustavo Pinto.[26]

Perhaps, trans-ethical responsibility may also begin to address, in part, a perennial Shinshū "dilemma" from the standpoint of religious education, that is, the question of "what to do?" Prof. Ueda has expressed this concern:

> Shinran speaks often of the nature and significance of his religious awakening, so even those who have not experienced that realm as deeply can have some grasp of it.

But as for the precise process by which he attained it, he is almost totally silent. In this, he differs remarkably from the founders of other Buddhist traditions … Thus, it is unclear what we must do to rid ourselves of calculation or doubt [as admonished by Shinran]. This is a difficult problem. But even if a perfectly adequate answer cannot be given, surely Shin scholars should seek to deal with it. Merely saying that it is important to listen to the teaching is not enough.[27]

It must be stressed that this ethical form is not being submitted as a means for realizing Shinjin, for that would turn into a blatant form of self-power (*jiriki*) which Shinran vehemently rejected. Perhaps, a distinction needs to be made between "self-power" and "self-effort." What Shinran rejected was the former, the idea of taking personal credit for one's realization but never the latter, a sincere effort on the part of the seeker to inquire and to understand. Further, this is in general accord with the American penchant for active individual self-effort in their religious life as aptly expressed by Prof. Pinto:

Effort is everything in our world. The west believes in making things happen; not in allowing things to happen naturally and spontaneously. We were educated to trust the power of the will. "Where there is will, there's the way." This is our conscious and unconscious motto. We think we have to do it, to make it happen, to produce it, to build it, to conquer and win over the obstacles. The western modern world is the result of a *jiriki*-oriented mind …

The West came to meet Buddhism through the path of *jiriki* because we are a *jiriki*-oriented civilization. But as much as we may try and fight, all our efforts will be insufficient and we discover that the final answer to Buddhism to man's quest cannot be reached by effort and discipline alone. This does not mean that effort and discipline are useless or unnecessary. If for no other reason, it is through them that we arrive at the realization that there is some other dimension of being. The emphasis on self-power forces us, sooner or later, to the discovery of Other-power. Finally, a state of exhaustion comes to the ego-centered effort and this allows us to realize Other-power as source and basis of existence. Where we imagined self-power, there was in reality Other-power. In other words, apparently two powers but truly One Power. And if we understand self-power as an Upaya (*hōben*) then it would be a most didactic coincidence that the West came into contact with Buddhism through sects that emphasize *jiriki*. At the same time, it is predictable that, slowly, interest would be aroused in schools like Jōdo Shinshū, in which Buddhism is seen from the standpoint of Other-power as One-power. In this way, history has been an able and wise master for the West.[28]

In this way, a large number of followers whose soteriological interest is faint may find relevancy in the Shinshū teaching as it addresses the more immediate ethical issues that preoccupy their lives. Often the idea of the "progression through the three Vows" (*sangantennyū*) is cited as a model for religious educational process, but this in my view applies to those already fully committed and engaged in the path for the realization of their soteriological goal. Hence, trans-ethical responsibility embraces a larger number and at a more rudimentary level in the religious path. It should further free us, particularly in the area of social welfare, from the self-imposed belief that since our ego-centered nature prevents us from fully helping others we can only wait until our return from the Pure Land after having attained enlightenment. This is a view traditionally supported by a *Tannishō* passage:

> Compassion in the Pure Land path is saying the Name, quickly attaining Buddhahood, and freely benefiting sentient beings with a heart of great love and great compassion. In our present lives, it is hard to carry out the desire to aid others however much love and tenderness we may feel; hence such compassion always falls short of fulfillment. Only the saying of the Name manifests the heart of great compassion that is replete and thoroughgoing.[29]

The intent of this passage, in my view, was to extol the superiority of the Pure Land Path over the Path of the Sages, to highlight the limitations on our ability on account of our self-centered human nature, and to urge the soteriological life. But it would be a misreading of the passage to regard this as a justification for apathy and non-involvement on account of our limited ability to benefit others. Certainly, in practical terms, we cannot help as fully as we wish. In spite of this, however, a genuine concern and compassion for the suffering or difficulties in the world would lead us to contribute a share of the responsibilities facing humankind to improve the quality of life on this earth.

IX Suggested Guidelines for Trans-ethical Responsibility in American Jōdo Shinshū

Needless to say, these express the view of one individual and are not intended to speak for any group or to be regarded as mandatory for anyone associated with the Jōdo Shinshū faith. I have concentrated on our four major American contemporary ethical topics: abortion, social welfare, capital punishment, and environment. After each point, ( ) denotes the topics among the four that are most impacted and [ ] indicates parallel sources in existing Shinshū statements and creeds in service books.

1) I believe that the world-universe in which we find ourselves, despite its downsides and tragedies, is fundamentally compassionate. This vision finds expression in the *Larger Sūtra*'s Monk Dharmākara whose selfless sacrifices aspired to spiritually nourish and liberate all sentient beings. (all four issues) [Jōdo Shinshū Creed (*kyōsho*) & Daily Aspirations (*seikatsu-shinjō*)]

2) The universe comprises an interconnected network in which I play a vital role. I as a member of this community must do my share to contribute to its welfare. We cannot wishfully depend on some "transcendent beings" to bail us out from the grave environmental, medical, and social crises that

now stare us in the face. (social welfare, environment) [Jōdo Shinshū Creed, Daily Aspirations, Golden Chain, Pledge]

3) In making my contribution to the world, I should not be motivated by a desire to be a "good person" or feel righteous that I have done a "good deed." It is because what I give back to the world pales in comparison to what I have received from the world. Plus, given my ego-centered proclivities, a "good" deed today will quickly be snuffed out tomorrow, or even the next moment, by acts driven by selfish motives. Shinran speaks to this: (social welfare) [Jōdo Shinshū Creed]

> Difficult is it to be free of evil nature
> The heart is like snake and scorpion
> Good acts also are mixed with poison—
> They are but deeds vain and false.
> (*Hitan jukkai san*, SSZ 2, p. 527)

4) I believe that criminal offenses are the result of causes and conditions reflecting the socio-economic environment of the offender. Though the offender must bear the responsibility for his actions, I as a member of the society should contribute to rectifying the underlying social problems as well as in rehabilitating the offender. Further, I should not feel righteous in looking down upon these people, remembering Shinran's words quoted in the *Tannishō*: (capital punishment)

> It is not that you keep from killing because your heart is good. In the same way, a person may wish not to harm anyone and yet end up killing a hundred or a thousand people. (p. 33)

5) I believe that there are no absolutes in matters of the conventional world. Crucial issues, in particular, involve complex sets of factors and yield no ready-made black and white, clear-cut answers. (abortion)

6) If at all possible, utmost effort must be made to preserve and foster life, and not to take life. (abortion, capital punishment) [first of the Five Precepts/ Six Pāramitās]

7) If I must terminate life, utmost care should be taken to be well informed about the subject matter. The decision-making must include a serious consideration for the welfare of all whose lives would be impacted, for a person is inevitably involved in a much wider interconnected set of relationships. (abortion, capital punishment, environment)

8) Whatever decision I make, I must be willing to bear my share of the responsibility for its consequences and not to shift blame or responsibility onto others. (abortion, capital punishment, environment) [Jōdo Shinshū Creed]

9) I do not make as my ultimate aim in life to accumulate wealth, gain fame, or garner power. (social welfare, environment) [Jōdo Shinshū Creed, Daily Aspirations, Golden Chain]

10) I strive to live simply and to share my energy, time, and resources for the betterment of the world. (social welfare, environment) [Jōdo Shinshū Creed, Daily Aspirations, Golden Chain]

11) I strive to refrain from idle talk and purposely creating discord among people and speaking ill of others without any constructive intention. (social welfare) [Jōdo Shinshū Creed]

12) I do not feel any need to consult or petition supernatural forces in order to satisfy worldly objectives or to allay fears and anxieties stemming from such forces. I, therefore, do not allow such activities as horoscope, fortune-telling, "superstitious" beliefs to serve as a guiding force in my life. [Jōdo Shinshū Creed]

NOTES

¹ See Alfred Bloom, "Ethical Perspectives in Shinran's Teachings," *Gankai* (Nov., 1980); Ronald Nakasone, "The Sacrifice of Baby Faye, Another Look: A Buddhist Sketch to Decision Making," *Pacific World* n.s. 2 (1986): 18-21; Friedrich Fenzl, "The Social Meaning of Shinran's Teaching for Our Time," *Pure Land* n.s. 3 (Dec., 1986): 29-34; John Ishihara, "A Shin Buddhist Social Ethics," *Pure Land* n.s. 3 (Dec., 1987): 14-33; Mark Blum, "Kiyozawa Manshi and the Meaning of Buddhist Ethics," *Eastern Buddhist*.21-1 (Spring, 1988): 61-81.

² Mircea Eliade, ed. *Encyclopedia of Religion*, 16 vols. (New York: MacMillan, 1987), Vol. 3, p. 340b. This source makes a distinction between ethics and morality. Morality is the correct set of actions, dispositions, attitudes, virtues, and ways of life that characterize an ideal person or society. On the other hand, ethics operates on the level of the scientific and the theoretical to explain morality in a thematic and systematic manner. Ethics is, hence, regarded as the study, and morality is the object of study.
  However, in contemporary colloquial usage, ethics is not only the "study of morality" but virtually identical to morality as defined above. This "blurring" of distinction manifests, I believe, in the contemporary coterminous use of "ethics and morality." This paper will adopt this expanded meaning of "ethics," which includes the meaning of "morality."

³ See *Ibid.*, Vol. 10, p. 92. While tension between religion and ethics was noted as early as the Greeks, the major separation took place during the Enlightenment Period, when ethical

authority based on human reason posed an alternative to the biblically inspired ethics.

[4] *Ibid.*, Vol. 10, p. 93b.

[5] For example, Sasaki Shōten's article has raised controversy in Japan for advocating a more inclusive *Shinshū* teaching that take into account the ordinary human concerns of "folk religion" and not simply be confined to pristine doctrine. See his article, "Shinshū and Folk Religion: Toward a Post-Modern Shinshū 'Theology'," *Nanzan Bulletin,* trans by Jan Van Bragt 12 (1988): 13-35.

[6] *Encyclopedia of Religion*, Vol. 3, p. 341a. They also speak about a third kind of ethics, "responsibility," but not being "classical" I shall treat it separately below.

[7] S. Tachibana, *Buddhist Ethics* (1926. Reprint. London: Curzon Press, 1975), p. 271; Hammalawa Saddhātissa, *Buddhist Ethics: The Path to Nirvāṇa* (1970. Reprint. London: Wisdom Publication, 1987), pp. 13, 99.

[8] Saddhātissa, *Buddhist Ethics*, pp. 56-57.

[9] *Ibid.*, p. 99. Saddhātissa qualifies that ethics does serve this secondary purpose as well.

[10] Dennis Hirota, trans. *Tannishō: A Primer* (Kyoto: Ryūkoku University Translation Center, 1982), p. 22.

[11] *Ibid.*, p. 23.

[12] *Mattōshō*, SSZ-2: 682, trans. James Dobbins, *Jōdo Shinshū: Shin Buddhism in Medieval Japan* (Bloomington and Indianapolis: Indiana University Press, 1989), pp. 55-56.

[13] *Goshōsokushū*, SSZ 2: 697.

[14] Hirota, trans. *Tannishō*, pp. 33-34.

[15] Yoshifumi Ueda, *et. al.*, trans. *Letters of Shinran* (Kyoto; Hongwanji International Center, 1978), pp. 58-59.

[16] Dobbins, *Jōdo Shinshū*, p. 67.

[17] *Shinshū Seiten*, pp. 301-302.

[18] See Bloom, "Shin Buddhism in the Modern Ethical Context," p. 301.

[19] 1. Not to teach false doctrine deviating from the teaching of the founder; 2. Not to discuss the teaching in public openly and without discretion; and 3. When asked by others of your sectarian affiliation, tell them that you are a follower of the Nembutsu teaching but not to mention specifically that you belong to the school founded by Shinran. Shinshū *Seiten*, pp. 351-352.

[20] *Ibid.*, p. 352.

[21] Dobbins, *Jōdo Shinshū*, pp. 152-153.

[22] Reference to Shinran is found in Y. Ueda, *et. al.* trans. *Notes on the Inscriptions on Sacred Scrolls* (Kyoto: Hongwanji International Center, 1978), p. 38. Reference to Rennyo appears in *Shinshū Seiten*, p. 387.

[23] *Goshōsokushū*, SSZ 2: 697.

[24] I owe my use of the term "trans-ethics" to David Matsumoto's thesis, "Transmorality in the Teaching of Jōdo Shinshū" (M.A. thesis, Institute of Buddhist Studies, 1984), pp. 137-138. I have adopted the same use of the meaning "to transcend" but not of "to transform." In his

use, the object of the "transformation" is the traditional understanding of ethics, while in my use the object is the way one perceives oneself.

[25] *Encyclopedia of Religion*, Vol. 3, p. 341a.

[26] Haruo Yamaoka, *Compassion in Encounter* (San Francisco: Buddhist Churches of America, 1970), pp. 9-16. See below for Ueda and Pinto references.

[27] Yoshifumi Ueda, "How is Shinjin to be Realized," translated by Dennis Hirota, *Pacific World* n.s. (1985): 17, 20.

[28] Shōgyō Gustavo Pinto, "From Self-Power to Other-Power," *Pure Land* 3 (1986): 136-138.

[29] Hirota, trans. *Tannishō*, p. 24.

IV. HISTORICAL AND COMPARATIVE PERSPECTIVES

CHAPTER 18

SHINRAN'S INDEBTEDNESS TO T'AN-LUAN

—BANDŌ SHŌJUN

I Shinran's Position in Pure Land Tradition

The significance of Hōnen's appearance in Japanese Buddhism lies in his epoch-making task of achieving the independence of the Pure Land School, which had long been regarded merely as a by-stream of Mahayana Buddhism. From various Buddhist disciplines he adopted the Nembutsu practice, insisting that in the latter days of the Dharma, Nembutsu practice is the only way through which all people, men and women, young and old, noble and mean, may equally be saved by virtue of the great saving power of Amida's Original Vow. As his teaching spread rapidly to all parts of Japan, a strong reaction to it arose. Myōe Shōnin (1173-1232) of the Kegon Sect was a representative of the older sects. He published a work entitled *Zaijarin* ("Smashing a Heterodox Dharma-Wheel"), in which he severely criticized Hōnen's radical standpoint. By and large, his criticisms against Hōnen centered round the question of *bodhicitta*. Myōe held that whereas the position of *bodhicitta* (man's aspiration for Enlightenment) in the Way of the Buddha is crucial, Hōnen totally neglected its importance, replacing it by Nembutsu, and therefore that Hōnen's doctrine could not possibly be called Buddhism. As Myōe was one of the most revered Buddhist priests of his time, a strict follower of Buddhist discipline himself and free from any sectarian or political prejudices, the penetrating question he raised was thought deserving of serious consideration. As Hōnen passed away immediately after he was released from exile on the island of Shikoku, it was only natural that Shinran, who inherited Hōnen's teaching, should have felt obliged to answer Myōe's crucial question. The situation in which Shinran thus found himself became one of the main motives for his *Kyō-gyō-shin-shō*.

According to the Mahayana conception of a bodhisattva (*bodhi-citta* inspired man; a seeker of Enlightenment), arising of *bodhi-citta* is regarded as the starting point of the bodhisattva's career. There is no bodhisattva apart from *bodhicitta*: *bodhicitta* is what makes a man a bodhisattva. In Nāgārjuna's *Mahā-prajñā-pāramitā-śāstra* is a statement, "When *bodhicitta* arises in man, at that very moment he attains Enlightenment." The first movement of bodhicitta in man's mind is a crucial moment, at which a bodhisattva is born out of an ordinary man. A bodhisattva is a man who is *bodhi*-centered, and no longer ego-centered. His mind is now oriented towards benefiting others rather than himself; he is ever ready to devote himself for the benefit of all the other beings, even at the cost of his own life. A bodhisattva embodies altruism. He identifies his own destiny with that of all sentient beings to the extent he feels, in Vimalakīrti's words, "A bodhisattva is sick because all sentient beings are sick." Therefore the appearance or presence of *bodhicitta* should be the central concern in all ages for all people who would call themselves Buddhists, not to mention the eminent figure Myōe of the Kamakura Period. It was no wonder, therefore, that Hōnen's insistence upon the Nembutsu practice as the only means for securing the ideal of universal salvation should have aroused in the minds of his contemporaries a grave doubt as to the authenticity of his doctrine. It was under such circumstances the question was raised as to whether the Nembutsu teaching expounded by Hōnen denied *bodhicitta* or not. Shinran's life-long task was to inquire into what Hōnen had actually intended to reveal, and to express his own conviction in his own terms. His main work *Kyō-gyō-shin-shō* is none other than the outcome of his spiritual inquiries into the teaching of salvation through Nembutsu alone.

Shinran's *Kyō-gyō-shin-shō* is made up of six chapters. It is written in Chinese. It was customary for Buddhist scholar-priests at that time to write in Chinese since all the sources from which they quoted were Chinese. In view of the fact that Shinran left a number of writings in Japanese, clearly meant for the generally illiterate common people, it may safely be said that his main work was addressed to his contemporary scholar-priests who were able to read classical Chinese. He purposely accommodated himself to this style of writing in order to appeal to the understanding of the educated Buddhist circle of his age to make his standpoint more readily understandable. In any case, there is no doubt that Chinese in his time was not only literary and formal but a means of communication and a common language among intellectuals. He entitled his main work, "A Collection of Important Passages Revealing the Truth of the Pure Land Teaching, Practice, and Attainment." In spite of this title, we find in this work a lengthy volume on "Faith" in its own right which is divided into two parts. He, nevertheless, did not mention "Faith" in the title of his work. Herein also we find a clue to his motive of addressing it mainly to learned Buddhists such as Myōe, for he was fully aware of his position and of his responsibilities to his age, since "Teaching, Practice, and Attainment" are traditional categories of the way of a Bodhisattva. Namely, a Way-seeker is first of all expected to listen to the "teaching," and then "practice" it faithfully, so as to reach the final "Attainment" or Enlightenment. Shinran tried to transcend tradition by first accommodating himself to it.

In order to show that Pure Land Buddhism is truly Mahayana and not his own arbitrary invention, in his main work, *Senchaku Hongan Nembutsu Shū*, Hōnen quotes extensively from a number of sūtras and commentaries in addition to the Five Eminent Pure Land masters. Shinran followed the pattern of his predecessors in his main work, in which he mentions the Seven Pure Land Patriarchs including Hōnen. How highly both Hōnen and Shinran regarded the tradition, rather than neglecting it, may be seen from the above-mentioned facts. One important fact to be remembered in this connection is that in the *Kyō-gyō-shin-shō* Shinran's own words amount to no more than one tenth of the whole volume, showing that Shinran thereby intended to make the centuries-old tradition speak for itself. Both Hōnen's *Senchaku Hongan Nembutsu Shū* and Shinran's *Kyō-gyō-shin-shō* adopt the form of *monrui* (collected passages), derived from Sung Dynasty China, which serves to demonstrate that one's opinions are not arbitrary but are based upon scriptural evidence. As it is customary for Buddhist scholars to argue in a dual form of theoretical reasoning and textual evidence, *monrui* was the form commonly adopted by Buddhist scholars, progressive and conservative.

Though Shinran was traditional in his outward forms, his thought was, in reality, drastically revolutionary. His way of reading scriptural texts was highly characteristic of this. For example, he construed a passage in the Larger *Sukhāvatī-vyūha Sūtra* related to "merit transference" (*pariṇāma*) to refer to Amida and not man as had been interpreted by all his predecessors. Shinran was firmly convinced that his way of reading best revealed the profound implications of the text. In the selected texts of the *Kyō-gyō-shin-shō* we find not a few similar examples.

Indeed, Shinran wrote the *Kyō-gyō-shin-shō* out of devotion to Hōnen, his spiritual master, as an expression of his gratitude for the latter's religious guidance. It is also true that it was Shinran's formal answer to the established sects with his scathing criticisms of heretical views outside as well as inside of the Pure Land School. But it is above all the first systematic exposition of Pure Land teaching ever attempted. Shinran's mission after his master's death was to make explicitly clear the quality of Nembutsu "Faith" accorded by Amida and not created by man. This quality of Nembutsu "Faith" was expressed by Shinran as being *tariki ekō* 他力回向 ("accorded by the Other Power" or "motivated by Amida"). In this way Shinran proceeded to demonstrate the fact that Nembutsu "Faith" is none other than the genuine *bodhicitta*, because of its freedom from man's agency motivated by self-will (*jiriki*). In the following, I should like to delineate in what manner Shinran tried to demonstrate the intrinsic nature of "Faith" implied in Nembutsu practice, with special regard to his indebtedness to T'an-luan's thought.

II Shinran and T'an-luan

Throughout his life Shinran was possessed of four names: Hannen 範宴, Shakkū 綽空, Zenshin 善信, and Shinran 親鸞. He named his first son Zenran 善鸞. Seeing these names, we are naturally reminded of the Seven Pure Land Patriarchs to whom, by his own acknowledgment, he was indebted for the formation of his thought. They are: Ryūju 竜樹 (Nāgārjuna), Tenjin 天親 (Vasubandhu) of India; Donran 曇鸞 (T'an-luan), Dōshaku 道綽 (Tao-ch'o), Zendō 善導 (Shan-tao) of China; Genshin 源信, and Genkū 源空 (Hōnen) of Japan. Apart from "Hannen," the names of Shinran and his son are formed from characters used in the names of those eminent masters. However, when we focus our attention on the two characters that form the name Shinran 親鸞, we realize that they derive from Tenjin and Donran, and this not without reason in view of the fact that in *Kyō-gyō-shin-shō* Shinran shows his special reverence for T'an-luan by designating him as a bodhisattva. Shinran was strict in his use of the three Chinese characters which denote "to say or state": 言 [*notamawaku*], 曰 [*iwaku*], and 云 [*iwaku*] using言, for sūtras, 曰 for commentaries and 云 for sub-commentaries. Despite the fact that T'an-luan's commentary on Vasubandhu's *Treatise on the Pure Land* (which is a commentary on the Larger *Sukhāvatī-vyūha Sūtra*) is a sub-commentary, to which he should have applied the character 云, he used the character 曰, which is only used for a commentary. Thus it is clear that Shinran equated the value of T'an-luan's thought as expounded in his main work, *Jōdo Ronchū* (*Wang-shēng-lun Chu*) with the thought expressed in Vasubandhu's *Treatise on the Pure Land*, upon which T'an-luan commented. Elsewhere in the *Kyō-gyō-shin-shō* we notice Shinran extensively quoting from T'an-luan's *Jōdo Ronchū*; the chapter on "Faith" in particular is occupied mostly by quotations from the *Jōdo Ronchū*. Above all, we find that at the very beginning of the *Kyō-gyō-shin-shō* Shinran introduces the key term of *ekō* in its dual aspects, going and returning, which is none other than Shinran's inheritance from T'an-luan. All these facts are clear evidence that T'an-luan's position in Shinran's thought is predominant. Undoubtedly in Shinran's case, the name does show reality.

It was Hōnen who designated the three sūtras and one commentary as the most revealing of the truth of salvation through Nembutsu. They are the Larger *Sukhāvatī-vyūha Sūtra*, the *Meditation Sūtra*, the Smaller *Sukhāvatī-vyūha Sūtra*, and T'an-luan's *Jōdo Ronchū* (Commentary on Vasubandhu's *Treatise on the Pure Land*). Vasubandhu's *Treatise on the Pure Land* is a product of his devotion to Amida Buddha and is characteristic of his systematic representation of the Pure Land, the detailed description of which is found in the Larger *Sukhāvatī-vyūha Sūtra*. It might be said that both Hōnen and Shinran are indebted to Vasubandhu and T'an-luan for a full appreciation of the purport of the Larger *Sukhāvatī-vyūha Sūtra*. While Shinran was among the disciples of Hōnen at Yoshimizu in Kyoto, he made an assiduous and extensive study of those scriptures. Among the documents now preserved by Nishi Honganji in Kyoto is a one-volume copy of the *Meditation Sūtra* and Smaller *Sukhāvatī-vyūha Sūtra* that was apparently used by Shinran at Yoshimizu. Tiny characters are written on the page margins, and among them is found the name of *Jōdo Ronchū*, clear evidence that in his early thirties Shinran was already acquainted with T'an-luan's thought. Therefore, it is highly probable that Shinran was introduced to T'an-luan by his master Hōnen. After Hōnen's death, it was mainly through the guidance of T'an-luan's thought that Shinran succeeded in making clear what was left unclarified by his master as to the true significance of "Faith" in Nembutsu practice originally expounded in the Larger *Sukhāvatī-vyūha Sūtra*. Before going into an analysis of Shinran's indebtedness to T'an-luan, let us consider two important factors: the nature of Shinran's life-long mission, and T'an-luan's contribution to Pure Land Buddhist thought.

III The Roles of Shinran and T'an-luan

As the founder of an independent Pure Land sect, Jodo Shu, Hōnen occupies a prominent position in the history of Japanese Buddhism. The leader of a newly established sect, he was naturally preoccupied with the task of defending the doctrine of his sect as well as his political stand besides being engaged in his authentic mission of expounding among the masses the doctrine of salvation through Nembutsu only. He had to face violent attacks from conservative minds belonging to traditional sects jealous of his popularity. However, for his successor, Shinran, it was only natural that the nature of his mission should differ somewhat from Hōnen's. After Hōnen's death, there appeared among his disciples a variety of views or different interpretations of his teachings. Some insisted that for a man to be saved, incessant recitation of Nembutsu was necessary, while others insisted that faith mattered rather than the reciting act. Shinran thus keenly felt the need for clarifying the true meaning of Hōnen's Nembutsu teaching. The *Kyō-gyō-shin-shō* is nothing less than the fruition of Shinran's lifelong endeavor. It might be said that Shinran's task consisted of the critical examination of the quality of "Faith" in Nembutsu practice.

It is certain that Hōnen's definition of Nembutsu was comprehensive. Therefore his Nembutsu was inclusive of all levels, motivated by *tariki* or by *jiriki*. Hence his disciples' confusion regarding "Faith," with all manner of interpretations presented. In Hōnen's eyes, there were two categories of practice: Nembutsu and all other miscellaneous practices. In his main work, he declared that all practices other than Nembutsu are not efficacious for attaining salvation in this latter age of Dharma, since they are not in accordance with the spirit of the Original Vow of Amida. His typical attitude toward the problem of Buddhist practice was obviously that of "Either-Or." This attitude is widely known as Senchaku 選択 (to select and to discard). In his lifetime, critical examination of Nembutsu had not been thoroughly undertaken. This task was consequently taken up by Shinran.

There are two main Pure Land streams in China, Shan-tao's (613-681 C.E.) and Hui-yuan's (334-416 C.E.). The former is based upon the *Meditation Sūtra* and the latter upon the *Pratyutpanna-samādhi Sūtra*. T'an-luan, Hōnen, and Shinran belong to the former stream. Although Nembutsu recitation is common to both traditions, the former saw a harmonious unity of the thoughts of Non-being (*prajñāpāramitā* philosophy based upon the principle of *śūnyatā*) and Being (Yogācāra or *vijñaptimātratā* philosophy based upon the principle of *prajñapti* or phenomenal being), while the latter was more inclined to emphasize the principle of *śūnyatā*. Therefore the ultimate source of their teaching differed: for the former it was the three Pure Land sūtras and T'an-luan's *Jōdo Ronchū*, for the latter it was the *Prajñāpāramitā* sūtras. The former spread among the common people while the latter remained confined to a small minority.

T'an-luan was most instrumental in clarifying and systematizing the doctrinal points in the former tradition of unifying the principles of Being and Non-being. His contribution to Pure Land thought in general is so enormous that it is extremely difficult for us properly to assess it. However, the following points may be mentioned as they seem to have special bearing on Shinran's thought: (1) A harmonious combination of Nāgārjuna's *śūnyatā* philosophy and Vasubandhu's *Vijñaptimātratā* philosophy, (2) the concepts of *jiriki* and *tariki*, (3) the idea of *ekō*. In the following let us examine, mainly from the above-mentioned points, Shinran's indebtedness to T'an-luan's thought.

(1) Unity of Being and Non-being

The state of enlightenment is beyond man's descriptive power. Yet nothing is more real or affective than enlightenment, for once we are actually faced with a man of enlightenment, his spiritual radiance is unmistakably felt and its effect is overpowering. Since ancient times, this indescribable experience of enlightenment found various ways of expression. An Upanishadic philosopher refused to express it in terms other than "*n'eti, n'eti*." Nāgārjuna contended that the ultimate reality can only be expressed in negative terms, and revealed his famous categories of eightfold negation. In the Upanishadic tradition itself, however, there did appear the attempt to express the transcendental experience of salvation or deliverance (*vimukti* or *mokṣa*) in such positive terms as *sacchidānanda* (*sat*, substance; *cit*, consciousness; *ānanda*, joy). These terms may be said to be aspects of the experience of *mokṣa*. In the Mahayana *Mahāparinirvāṇa Sūtra*, along with a number of negative expressions, we find an equal number of positive expressions of the state of enlightenment: "refuge," "cave," "light," "lamp," "Other Shore," "Peaceful Place," "Serenity," "vastness," and so forth. The term "Pure Land" is obviously one such expression, that points ultimately to the state of enlightenment, or *nirvāṇa*. In other words, "Pure Land" is a positive concrete expression of "*nirvāṇa*." The reason the term "Jōdo" (Pure Land) has survived to this day may be due to the Chinese mentality which favors concreteness over abstraction. Vasubandhu was the first in the history of Buddhism to show the structure of the Pure Land. This he did in terms of 29 categories, a result of his encounter with the Larger *Sukhāvatī-vyūha Sūtra*. He did not come to this sūtra out of mere intellectual curiosity. He existentially encountered the spirit expounded in this sūtra upon his conversion. This encounter constituted the motive for his Treatise on the Pure Land, at the very beginning of which we find his famous words of confession in praise of Amida: "O, Bhagavat, I take single-hearted refuge in the Tathāgata of unobstructed light penetrating through ten directions!" As is known, a detailed description of Amida's land of bliss (*Sukhāvatī*) is unfolded in the Larger *Sukhāvatī-vyūha Sūtra*. From devotion to Amida, Vasubandhu attempted to systematize the main features of the Pure Land that are described in detail in the *Larger Sūtra*. He classified all Pure Land constituents into three categories: land, buddhas, and bodhisattvas. The first refers to the place itself, and the second and the third refer to the beings who dwell therein. As to each category, he mentions 17 qualities (*guṇas*) for the land, 8 for the buddha, and 4 for the bodhisattvas. Altogether he mentions 29 qualities for the whole of the Pure Land, thereby delineating the Pure Land's content. T'an-luan inherited Vasubandhu's Pure Land ontology. This was accepted in turn by Shinran.

Vasubandhu's inclination towards something concrete and objective, as is exemplified by his acceptance of the substantive description of Pure Land in the *Larger Sūtra*, may easily be understood by looking into his philosophical background. Although Nāgārjuna's Mādhyamika philosophy refuses to represent *nirvāṇa* in positive or material terms, Vasubandhu's Yogācāra philosophy makes allowances for doing so. This accounts for the basic feature of Pure Land Buddhism which, embracing the Yogācāra standpoint through Vasubandhu, has held a wide following among the common people in the course of history, in sharp contrast to Zen Buddhism which, adhering throughout to Mādhyamika philosophy, has remained a religion for a relatively small minority.

On the other hand, T'an-luan, with a background of Mādhyamika philosophy, attempted to re-interpret Vasubandhu's interpretations of the Pure Land. Thus the unity of two opposing philosophical streams comes to be realized in the thought of T'an-luan. T'an-luan had submerged himself in the study of Mādhyamika philosophy with Nāgārjuna's *Mūlamadhyamakakārikā, Dvadaśani-kāya-śāstra, Mahāprajñāpāramitopadeśa*, and Āryadeva's *Śataśāstra* before his conversion to Pure Land Buddhism. If supra-experiential reality is to be expressed, it must inevitably take the form of "Being." This "Being" may be said to be the essence of the so-called "mythology." Mādhyamika philosophy refused to resort to the *upāya* of mythology. T'an-luan found himself in a position to deal with the "mythological expressions" resorted to by his predecessor, Vasubandhu. Thus, it could be said that he performed the task of demythologizing the Pure Land so as to bring all those who are faced with this mythology into direct contact with its inner spiritual meaning on an experiential level. T an-luan executed this epoch-making task resolutely, and the result of his efforts bore fruit in his *Jōdo Ronchū*.

It is noteworthy that T'an-luan, who had once encountered the depths of Mādhyamika philosophy, is seen positively affirming the "Being" of the Pure Land with its various adornments. T'an-luan says:

> Since Suchness is the state in which all illusions have disappeared, Dharmakāya is formless. Because of its very formlessness it can take all conceivable forms. Therefore, all the adornments of the Pure Land with various qualities are Dharmakāya itself [*Taishō*, vol. 40, p. 841b].

These lines have a Lao-tzean tone. It is quite obvious that here T'an-luan is seeing oneness amidst diversity. After touching upon the relationship between the oneness of Enlightenment and the diversity of the adornments of Pure Land specified by Vasubandhu, T'an-luan says:

> Buddhas and Bodhisattvas are made up of two-fold Dharmakāya: Dharmakāya in its aspect of suchness, and Dharmakāya in its upāya aspect. Out of the former the latter appears. By way of the latter is the former realized. Though distinct from each other, these two aspects of Dharmakāya are inseparable. Though they are one, they should never be confused [*Taishō*, vol. 40, p. 841b].

T'an-luan is trying to say that although buddhas and bodhisattvas are mentioned together with the land among the 29 adornments of Pure Land as if they were separate entities in their own right, they are simply a part of Dharmakāya itself. In other words, he points to the fact that they are authentic manifestations of the same Enlightenment that constitutes the essence of the Pure Land. To T'an-luan's enlightened eye the diversity is by no means a hindrance to his vision of the true essence of the Pure Land.

With regard to the Pure Land expressed in objective terms, T'an-luan declares:

> The so-called Pure Land is none other than a path which leads ultimately to Buddhahood; it is a supreme *upāya* [*Taishō*, vol. 40, p. 842a].

Shinran quotes these statements in the Chapter on Attainment of the *Kyō-gyō-shin-shō*. Therefore, as the other important statements, these may be taken as Shinran's own views.

We cannot help but be amazed at the boldness of these words. For when we hear the word *upāya*, we are unreasonably annoyed by a suggestion of something adulterated or superficial. But essentially *upāya* is not a synonym for falsehood. Rather it belongs, in its essence, to truth. In other words, *upāya* is none other than the dynamic aspect of truth. The activity of transcendental wisdom (*prajñā*) itself is *upāya*. However what interests us most in this context is that T'an-luan did not hesitate to make such a statement. Through this statement it is apparent that he wanted to express the essentially non-dual relationship between *nirvāṇa* or ultimate state of enlightenment and the so-called Pure Land. For he was firmly convinced that once one is in touch with *upāya*, somehow or other he is already in contact with truth because of the intrinsic solidarity of the two. To attempt to objectify what can never be objectified—this is one of the characteristics of Pure Land Buddhism.

As to the soteriological problems, T'an-luan makes, among others, the following statements:

> Among a number of passages in the Mahayana sūtras and commentaries, we often see the statement, "Sentient beings are after all 'non-arising' just like vast space." Why is it, then, that Vasubandhu Bodhisattva spoke of "desiring birth [in the Pure Land]"?
>
> All such things as the substance of sentient beings as imagined by an ordinary man, and the substance of "birth-and-death" as seen by an ordinary man, are in the last analysis unreal, like the hair of a tortoise or vast space. What is meant by "Birth" that was sought for by Vasubandhu Bodhisattva is "dependent arising," and so it was only tentatively so called [*Taishō*, vol. 40, p. 827b].

In these lines T'an-luan is discussing in the form of question and answer the question of who it is that desires birth in the Pure Land. By his question and answer T'an-luan suggests that there is no substance in the abstract concept of "sentient beings" who are supposed to be leaving this world and going to the other world desirous of birth in the Pure Land. In these lines we can clearly see T'an-luan's rootage in the soil of *sūnyata* philosophy. T'an-luan further states:

> Why is birth in the Pure Land expounded? When the Five-fold Path of Nembutsu is practiced by the so-called human beings of this world, a fore-thought becomes the cause of an after-thought. The so-called human beings of the defiled land and those of the Pure Land are neither decidedly identical with each other nor decidedly different from each other. The same holds true with the fore-thought and the after-thought. Why?
>
> Because if they were identical, there would be no law of cause and effect; if different, there would be no continuity between them [*Taishō*, vol. 40, p. 827b].

This two-fold question and answer is highly significant in that T'an-luan is suggesting that "birth" ultimately means "conversion." "The so-called human being of the defiled world" is an unenlightened man and "the so-called human being of the Pure Land" is an enlightened man. The relationship between these two types may be compared to that of Saul and Paul. Saul was a man bent on persecuting Jesus, Paul was a man who faithfully followed the footsteps of Jesus. Are these two men different or the same? The same relationship is seen in the life of Shinran. Yamabushi Bennen may correspond to Saul in that he was bent on persecuting Shinran. Myōhōbō, known as Bennen before he was converted by Shinran, would thus correspond to Paul. Is Bennen different from Myōhōbō or is he the same? In answering such a question, T'an-luan resorted to the typical dialectic of Mādhyamika logicians. In these particular passages, we must not overlook that T'an-luan has drawn out the innermost meaning of "birth" (*ōjō*) by suggesting the spiritual transformation that takes place in man's mind at the experience of conversion. The above shows clearly that T'an-luan interpreted the religious experience of "birth" not in terms of actually leaving this world and going to the other world, but in terms of the inner experience of man's mind. This might be said to be another example of T'an-luan's version of demythologization.

(2) Ideas of *Jiriki* and *Tariki*

We have seen in the above how T'an-luan made a great contribution to the Pure Land ontology and soteriology through his characteristic interpretations. Shinran understood the experience of enlightenment or salvation in terms of "birth in the Pure Land," mainly through T'an-luan's dialectical exegesis. Shinran thus had through T'an-luan's exegesis a great deal to learn from Vasubandhu's presentation of the full significance of "Pure Land." T'an-luan, while standing upon *śūnyata* philosophy, positively accepted the schematized representation of the Pure Land, in full recognition of the raison d'être of Pure Land Buddhism which arose in defense of the cause of universal salvation. Nevertheless, T'an-luan was well aware that the ultimate meaning of "birth in the Pure Land" consisted not in the matter of geography or physical movement but in spiritual birth or conversion, which he clearly expressed in Mādhyamika terms as "birth of non-birth." On the other hand, the final realization Shinran attained was that the essence of Nembutsu is none other than the whole connotation of "Pure Land," for the essence of Pure Land is *nirvāṇa* itself. Pure Land is not a static or physical place but a dynamic reality or a ceaseless functioning of *satori* itself. It is not only a place all men are expected to reach, it is something to be realized amidst the actual human existence beset with all forms of predicament and suffering.

Shinran was perceptive enough to see the essence of Nembutsu practice in Vasubandhu's "single-mindedness," which was expressed in his confession in praise of Amida. He reached the conclusion that Vasubandhu's "single-mindedness" was the key to unlock the mystery of Nembutsu practice. With his keen insight, he perceived that it did not in fact belong to Vasubandhu as a man, but that it was Amida's Original Vow materialized as Vasubandhu's aspiring heart. Shinran also perceived in the "single-mindedness" a unity of the so-called three minds—sincerity, faith, aspiration for birth—contained in Amida's Eighteenth Vow. In other words, he discerned the essence of the Eighteenth Vow realized in Vasubandhu's "single-mindedness" led by his insight that Vasubandhu achieved the unity in order to enable unenlightened sentient beings to acquire understanding, since although Amida put forth the three minds as a prerequisite insuring the efficacy of Nembutsu, there is no other authentic cause for attaining *nirvāṇa* than "Faith." Shinran's contention was that Nembutsu can be a right cause for all people to attain *nirvāṇa* because the Faith in Nembutsu is essentially not man's but Amida's. He used the term "*tariki*" (Other Power) in order to express this. Defining "*tariki*" in the *Kyō-gyō-shin-shō* chapter on Practice, he states:

"The 'Other Power' is none other than the Power of Amida's Original Vow."
Hōnen was also, of course, fully convinced that the practice of reciting Nembutsu was effective for all people of the latter day as the sole cause of attaining *nirvāṇa*; that it was not because Nembutsu is sincerely recited by men, but
because Nembutsu was in accordance with the spirit of Amida's Original Vow.
This is the very reason why he could be so emphatic in expounding the teaching
of Nembutsu as the founder of the Jōdo Sect. However, he did not distinguish
precisely enough the two aspects of Nembutsu: *jiriki* and *tariki*. For Hōnen
all Nembutsu was, so to speak, *tariki*, because Nembutsu itself, as the sacred
practice selected by Amida's Compassionate Vow, was superior to all other
practices. On the other hand, Shinran's historical mission was to scrutinize the
inner motive of Nembutsu practice. He made a minute examination of the sacred
practices leading one to birth in the Pure Land, which he recorded in the "Faith"
chapter of the *Kyō-gyō-shin-shō*. In the course of this process, the ideas of *jiriki*
and *tariki* played a vital role. The examination of "Faith" cannot help but lead
to the examination of the vows and sūtras from which it derives and the modes
of birth which it gives rise to. For vows are the basic principle or the prime,
spiritual force of which the sūtras are the expressions, and the ensuing modes of
birth are an indication of the quality of faith which produced them.

The terms *jiriki* and *tariki* Shinran adopted from T'an-luan can of course be
traced to their popular usage. Ordinarily *jiriki* stands for "self-power" or "self-
effort," and *tariki* for "Other Power" or "external help." It was T'an-luan, however, who gave a religious significance to these popular terms. For T'an-luan,
tariki was not simply an antonym to *jiriki*, but moreover it covered the transcendental extension of the term. It is not that he totally discarded the popular, relative meaning of *tariki*, but that he added to it a transcendental meaning to make
it a religious term. T'an-luan transformed a popular term into a religious one. So
the term *tariki* itself was not created by T'an-luan. It had existed far prior to him,
and it can even be found in Vasubandhu's *Treatise on the Pure Land*.

In the following let us look into the significance of the task T'an-luan performed in clarifying the dual meaning of *tariki*. When *tariki* means simply a
dependence upon something else, and as long as the "faith" is characterized as
such, such a "faith" is not instrumental in leading to one's enlightenment, to his
true independence from all external things. By *tariki* "Faith" T'an-luan meant
the establishment of the True Self, while by *jiriki* "faith" he meant our enslavement to our self-power, our limited, relative human power. *Tariki* "Faith" must
be something that enables man to establish his True Subjectivity. The establishment of True Subjectivity is none other than salvation, *nirvāṇa*, *mokṣa*, or "birth
in the Pure Land." Only the *tariki* "Faith" in its religious sense makes man truly
autonomous or sets him free.

It is generally believed that when we embrace the faith of *tariki*, we lose our
subjectivity. In such a case, *tariki* means not Vow Power but simply dependency
upon something else. Such a faith enslaves man rather than sets him free. When

we accept Vow Power through Nembutsu, Vow Power is realized in us. Then it is Vow Power that is our real Subjectivity. As long as faith remains *jiriki*, our subjectivity also remains relative, enslaved, limited, and dependent. It is at this moment a transformation takes place. Furthermore, T'an-luan went so far as to see *tariki* Faith as the effect rather than the beginning of the Vow. In other words, he considered that the fact of man's embracing *tariki* Faith is the realization of the Original Vow of Amida, and not the beginning of man's religious life. He saw the effect (realization or accomplishment) in the cause where an ordinary man would see merely the beginning. To the eyes of an unenlightened man, our act of believing is the start of religious life. For T'an-luan, however, our belief was none other than the realization of Amida's Original Vow. This interaction between Amida and man (though, essentially, they are not necessarily distinct from each other as between God and man) was called by T'an-luan "*ekō*." This Shinran inherited from him.

(3) The Idea of *Ekō*

We have seen in the above that the term *ekō* has an important bearing on the event of "transformation" or the moment of birth in the Pure Land. As with *tariki*, *ekō* was a common term in India. It meant either "transformation" or "transferring of merit accumulated by someone for the benefit of others." In this case, too, everyday language came to be given a religious meaning: *pariṇāma* which in Sanskrit originally meant a "change" or a "transformation," came to be used by Buddhists as "merit-transference." At least up until the time of Hōnen, *ekō* invariably meant man's act of transferring merit to others. But for the first time in Buddhism, the term *ekō* was given to mean Amida's transference of merit towards men. For Hōnen Nembutsu was always man's *ekō*, while for Shinran it was always Amida's. It was Vasubandhu who used the term *ekō* for the first time, presenting its two directions: going and returning. He meant by "going *ekō*" a Pure Land aspirant's direction from the defiled world to the Pure Land, while by "returning *ekō*" he meant an enlightened bodhisattva's direction from Pure Land to the defiled world. That is to say, for Vasubandhu there were two directions of *ekō*: one from the realm of *mayoi* (illusion) to the realm of *satori* (enlightenment), the other from the realm of *satori* to the realm of *mayoi*. T'an-luan accepted Vasubandhu's conceptions of the two directions of *ekō* and developed them further. T'an-luan, while accepting the ideas of the two directions of *ekō* shown by Vasubandhu, finally concluded that they were in fact reducible to one, the "returning *ekō*" alone, the direction of *ekō* from *satori* to *mayoi*. He showed it to be Amida's and not man's, and he qualified it as *tariki ekō*, the *ekō* motivated by the Power of Amida's Original Vow.

It was accordingly thought to be Amida's working itself that man acquires Faith, for essentially there is only one *ekō*. It is now apparent that Shinran's well-known teaching of "Faith in the Other Power" is thus indebted to this insight of T'an-luan into the nature of *ekō*. In the *Jōdo Ronchū* T'an-luan declares:

> If we clearly look into the source of this idea, Tathāgata Amida is the promotive agent [*Taishō*, vol. 40, p. 843c].

This declaration was quoted by Shinran in the Chapter on Practice of the *Kyō-gyō-shin-shō* [*Shinshū Shogyō Zensho* (hereafter SSZ), vol. 2, p. 36]. T'an-luan pointed out that ultimately our aspiration for the Pure Land itself originates from Amida. He then continues:

> Of all things our birth in the Pure Land and the works of the bodhisattvas of other lands, arise from the power of the vows of Tathāgata Amida. Why is it so? Should things not arise from the power of the forty-eight vows of the Buddha, they would have been taken in vain [*Taishō*, vol. 40, p. 843c].

Shinran expressed the meaning of *tariki ekō* in his own words as "*fu-ekō*" ("non-*ekō*"). *Fu-ekō* means "not man's *ekō*," hence Amida's. He states in the *Kyō-gyō-shin-shō*:

> Therefore it is clearly known that this Nembutsu practice is not the practice of self-power by common men and sages. Therefore it is called the practice of *fu-ekō* [Chapter on Practice, SSZ, vol. 2, p. 33].

Again, Shinran reversed the meaning of the expression "*Hotsugan ekō*" (to aspire for birth and transfer the merit) that had invariably been taken as man's action toward Amida, and says:

> *Hotsugan ekō* refers to the Tathāgata's (Amida's) aspiration, in which he, having already taken the Vow, endows sentient beings with their Practice [Chapter on Practice, SSZ, vol. 2, p. 22].

In this way Shinran's *Kyō-gyō-shin-shō* might be said to be permeated throughout by the insight of *tariki ekō*. In this respect T'an-luan's influence upon Shinran's teaching is indeed considerable. In conclusion, it may be said that in the light of T'an-luan's insight, Shinran executed the task of examining the quality of Nembutsu Faith mainly from the viewpoints of *tariki* and *ekō*, and clarified that the Original Vow of Amida, that is usually regarded as the Other Power by man, realized itself in man's Faith, thus truly establishing his Subjectivity. That Amida's Vow realizes itself as man's Faith and at the same time Faith proves the presence of the Vow, and that the evidence of the realization of the Vow is none other than man's Faith—all this was the central theme of the *Kyō-gyō-shin-shō*. Without T'an-luan's genius Shinran could not have succeeded to the extent he did in making this clear.

CHAPTER 19

PURE LAND BUDDHIST HERMENEUTICS: HŌNEN'S INTERPRETATION OF *NEMBUTSU*[1]

—ALLAN A. ANDREWS

I Introduction

How do Buddhists understand and interpret the *dharma*? Several recent studies have explored this question. Robert A. F. Thurman, in his article "Buddhist Hermeneutics,"[2] correctly notes,

> One can hardly set out to win liberation and enlightenment, or even to live properly in an ethical sense, until one has decided which of these teachings [of the Buddha] is right, and what ways lead to their realization. Thus, it is clear that the hermeneutical enterprise in the [Buddhist] tradition is an essential part of praxis on whatever level, an essential vehicle on the way of enlightenment. We should note that since the various scriptural passages are contradictory on the surface, scriptural authority alone will not fully settle the hermeneutical questions, since the scriptures are in a sense the basis of discussion (Thurman 1978, 23).[3]

Thurman then claims, and attempts to substantiate on the basis of the Mādhyamika philosophical views of the Tibetan master Tsong Kha pa (1357-1419), that,

> In the final analysis, rationality (*yukti*), inference (*anumāna*), or philosophic logic (*nyāya*) becomes the highest authority (*pramāṇa*) for deciding which scriptural passage is ultimately valid (Thurman 1978, 23).

In a response entitled, "Chinese Buddhist Hermeneutics: The Case of Hua-yen," Peter N. Gregory points out that Chinese Buddhists relied less on logic for their hermeneutics, especially the Mādhyamika logic of negation, and more on the construction of hierarchical classifications of scriptures (*p'an-chiao, hangyō*), which served their need to interpret in affirmative terms which teachings were more valid than others (Gregory 1983, 231-34).

In this paper I propose to look at an instance of interpretation in the Japanese Buddhist tradition. The instance is Hōnen's interpretation of the value of the Pure Land scriptures and especially his view of the *nembutsu* teachings of the *Sūtra on the Buddha of Limitless Life*.[4] I hope to demonstrate that although

Hōnen's hermeneutics embrace a wide range of principles, ultimately they were based on neither reason nor on a doctrinal classification, but upon the authority of a revered teacher, and in the final analysis on Hōnen's own experience of certainty of salvation achieved through the guidance of that teacher.

II Hōnen's Use of Doctrinal Analysis

Hōnen's interpretation of the Pure Land scriptures is to be found in his *Senchaku hongan nembutsu shū* (*Senchaku shū* or *Senjyaku shū*),[5] "Treatise on the *Nembutsu* Selected by the Original Vow," composed in 1198. Hōnen opens this work with a sweeping doctrinal analysis segregating all scriptures and doctrines into two categories, the *dharma*-gate of the sages and the Pure Land *dharma*-gate[6] (Ōhashi 1971, 88-93). Unlike schemata based on stages in the teaching career of Śākyamuni Buddha which had dominated Chinese Buddhist hermeneutics (Thurman 1978, 29-31; Gregory 1983, 232-33),[7] this analysis is founded on an historical view of the flowering and decline of the Buddhist faith; that is, on the widely accepted doctrine of the three periods of the *dharma*—the ages of perfect *dharma*, superficial *dharma*, and degenerate *dharma*.[8] Hōnen maintains that the world has entered the age of degenerate *dharma*, when the true teachings have largely been lost and the spiritual capacities of sentient beings have deteriorated as well, and therefore that the scriptures and doctrines on gaining enlightenment through learning and discipline—that is, the *dharma*-gate of the sages—are no longer applicable and only the teachings on Pure Land rebirth—i.e., those of the Pure Land *dharma*-gate, which were intended by Śākyamuni for the age of degenerate *dharma*—remain valid.[9]

Thus Hōnen's hermeneutical principle for designating the Pure Land teachings and scriptures as more effective (though not truer) than all others was a doctrinal classification which, similar to those that had dominated Chinese Buddhist hermeneutics (and indeed Japanese hermeneutics until Hōnen's time), asserted on the basis of a Buddhist view of history that some scriptures were more appropriate to the age and efficacious than others.

III Hōnen's Interpretation of the *Nembutsu* of the Eighteenth Vow

As is well known, Hōnen interpreted the *nembutsu* of the *Sūtra on the Buddha of Limitless Life*'s eighteenth vow, the "original vow," as invocational *nembutsu*, that is, as calling upon the name of Amida Buddha with the utterance, "*namu Amida Butsu.*" Moreover, Hōnen interpreted this *nembutsu* as sufficient by itself for achieving salvation through rebirth into Amida Buddha's pure buddha-land. This interpretation and its logic are revealed most clearly in the third chapter of the *Senchaku shū*, entitled "Passages Showing that Amida Tathāgata Made *Nembutsu*, and No Other Works, the Practice of the Rebirth Original

Vow." Hōnen opens this chapter with the citation of three proof texts, the first of which is the "rebirth original vow," the eighteenth vow of the *Sūtra on the Buddha of Limitless Life*:

> When I become a Buddha, if there should be sentient beings anywhere in the ten regions of the universe having sincere and deep faith and aspiration to be reborn into my buddha-land and who, by making even ten reflections [on me], are not reborn there, then I will not accept perfect enlightenment (Ōhashi 1971, 101).[10]

This scriptural passage has been considered by Pure Land Buddhists since Hōnen as the most important Buddha-*dharma* of all. They see it as the supreme expression of Buddha wisdom and compassion and as a virtual guarantee of the eventual salvation of all sentient beings. Of course what was at issue for Hōnen in this passage was the meaning of "reflections" (i.e., Buddha-reflections), because he saw this term as defining the practice by means of which beings could gain rebirth in the Pure Land. The original term, *nen* (Chinese, *nien*) is rather ambiguous.[11] It can mean "to recollect," "keep in mind," "think about," and even "one instant." My English rendering is intended to convey this ambiguity. Although Hōnen's understanding of the meaning of this term is implied in the two other proof texts with which he opens this chapter (citations of the Chinese Pure Land master Shan-tao), before considering these passages let us first examine Hōnen's explicit, unequivocal interpretation of the eighteenth vow as invocational *nembutsu*.

In order to clarify the meaning of the *nembutsu* of the eighteenth vow as invocational *nembutsu*, Hōnen examines several of the *sūtra*'s forty-eight vows to show that with each vow Dharmākara Bodhisattva (i.e., Amida Buddha during his *bodhisattva* career) selected from among the qualities of countless buddha-lands only the pure qualities or characteristics which he wanted his buddha-land to possess. Hōnen maintains:

> As for the eighteenth, the *Nembutsu* Rebirth Vow, we find that among all those buddha-lands there were some for which the rebirth-practice was generosity, some for which it was moral conduct, some for which it was patience and humility, some for which it was tireless effort, some for which it was meditation and some for which it was wisdom (such as faith in the highest truth) ... Or there were various lands for each of which there were several practices, such as erecting reliquaries and dedicating images, supporting monks, or even being filial to parents and revering teachers and elders ... Yet all the above practices from generosity and moral conduct to filial piety were rejected and only the exclusive utterance of the Buddha's name was chosen ... (Ōhashi 1971, 104).

With the phrase "exclusive utterance of the Buddha's name"[12] Hōnen leaves no doubt that in his view the meaning of *nen* in the eighteenth vow, and therefore the practice Amida Buddha (Dharmākara) selected for earning Pure Land rebirth, is invocational *nembutsu* alone, and not some kind of meditation upon the Buddha.

IV   Contemporary Views of *Nembutsu*

This interpretation of *nembutsu* as solely sufficient invocation of the Buddha's name was widely at variance with the generally accepted view of *nembutsu* in Hōnen's time. The prevailing view was based on the tenth century Tendai treatise on *nembutsu*, the *Essentials of Pure Land Rebirth*.[13] This work attempted to integrate the Tendai meditative form of *nembutsu* based upon the *Mo-ho chih-kuan*[14] of Tendai (T'ien-t'ai) founder Chih-i (538-597), with the devotional forms of *nembutsu* found in the popular Pure Land scripture, *Sūtra of Contemplation on the Buddha of Limitless Life*[15] (Andrews 1973, 107-20). The *Essentials* maintained that authentic *nembutsu* is contemplative *nembutsu*, a rigorous exercise consisting of visualizing the magnificent form of Amida Buddha in order to achieve *nembutsu samādhi*, a deep enlightenment experience. Invocational *nembutsu*, calling upon the name of Amida Buddha, was considered a practice which should accompany contemplative *nembutsu* in order to bring about a more intense meditative state. As an independent practice, the *Essentials* considered invocational *nembutsu* as suitable for only the least spiritually capable of persons, and especially as a sort of last resort for such people as a way to gain rebirth into the Pure Land of Amida when they are about to die and fall into hell or some other painful transmigratory state.[16] Moreover, while the *Essentials* acknowledged *nembutsu* as the best of all practices for achieving Pure Land rebirth, it taught that *nembutsu* was most effective when accompanied by other practices such as performance of good deeds and observance of monastic precepts (Andrews 1973, 72-75, 90-91).

This view of the true meaning and proper use of *nembutsu* is reflected in an interesting document contemporary with Hōnen, the *Kōfukuji sōjō*, or *Kōfukuji Temple Petition for the Suppression of Sole Nembutsu Practice*, submitted to the throne in protest of Hōnen's movement in 1205. It includes a criticism of Hōnen's interpretation of *nembutsu* typical of the view of establishment Buddhism in that age. In Article Seven of the *Petition*, "The Error of Misunderstanding Nembutsu," we find the following charge:

> First, the Buddha reflected upon has a name and a person. With regard to the person there is the phenomenal and the noumenal aspects. With regard to the *nembutsu* itself, there is vocal *nembutsu* and mental *nembutsu*. The mental *nembutsu* includes both reflection upon and contemplation of the Buddha. Contemplation can be either non-meditative or meditative, performed with either deluded or enlightened mind. The degrees of shallowness and depth are manifold; the shallow is inferior, the deep superior. Thus to invoke the name orally is neither contemplative nor meditative *nembutsu*; it is inferior and superficial *nembutsu* … Concerning the passage, "even ten reflections," of that [eighteenth] vow, this is provided for the most inferior beings. With contemplative *nembutsu* as the foundation, yet extending all the way down to invocational *nembutsu*, with many Buddha-reflections as the primary teaching, yet

not discarding even ten reflections, this shows the great compassion and power of the Buddha. The way of easy guidance and sure rebirth is by contemplative *nembutsu* and many Buddha-reflections (Kamata and Tanaka 1971, 38-39).[17]

For the author of the *Kōfukuji Petition*,[18] as for most contemporary clerics, nembutsu was primarily a meditative practice. Invocational *nembutsu*—calling upon the name of a Buddha—was considered merely an aid to meditation on the Buddha's form ("phenomenal aspect") or essence ("noumenal aspect"). By itself, invocation was considered a practice suitable only for those most burdened with bad *karma*, and then only marginally effective for their Pure Land rebirth in certain circumstances. To totally reject the efficacy of other practices as Hōnen did in the *Senchaku shū* was considered by establishment Buddhism of the time as absolutely blasphemous and heretical. Hōnen's position was therefore audacious and even foolhardy.[19]

V Hōnen's Hermeneutics: The Appeal to Reason

What was the basis of Hōnen's bold reinterpretation of *nembutsu* as solely invocation and sufficient for Pure Land rebirth?[20] In other words, what were his hermeneutical principles? As we indicated above, in the final analysis Hōnen had recourse to the authority of a revered teacher for his different and challenging interpretation of *nembutsu*. Yet he does not dispense with reason entirely as a means of discovering the Buddha's meaning. The initial justification we find in the *Senchaku shū* for his interpretation is based on reason. Following his assertion, which we have examined above, that Amida choose only *nembutsu* as the practice of the original vow, Hōnen poses this question from a hypothetical interlocutor:

It seems correct to survey the various vows, applying the principle of [Amida's] rejecting the gross and evil and choosing the good and refined. But why in the case of the eighteenth vow did Dharmākara [i.e., Amida Buddha] reject all the other practices and exclusively choose only the single practice of *nembutsu* as that of the rebirth original vow?

Hōnen responds:

The holy one's[21] intentions are difficult to fathom and not easy to set out, but I will attempt to explain them by means of two principles—(1) that of superiority versus inferiority and (2) that of ease versus difficulty.

First, with respect to superiority versus inferiority, *nembutsu* is superior while the other practices are inferior because the Buddha's name is the bearer of infinite karmic merits. All of Amida Buddha's inner meritorious qualities, such as his four kinds of wisdom, three Buddha-bodies, ten powers of comprehension, and four certainties, and all of his outer meritorious functions, such as his Buddha-marks, his brilliance, his *dharma*-preaching and his saving of sentient beings, each and every one of these resides in Amida's name. Thus the karmic merit of his name is superior. The other practices are not like this. Each practice has only its own merit. Thus the other practices are inferior ...

Thus, is it not because the karmic merit of the Buddha's name is superior to the merits of the other practices that the inferior practices were rejected and the superior adopted as the practice of the original vow? (Ōhashi 1971, 104-105)

Although Hōnen is literally telling us why he thinks Amida Buddha chose the invocation of his name as the original vow's *practice* for Pure Land rebirth, he is also revealing some of the reasoning he pursued in coming to the conclusion that *nen* of the eighteenth vow meant only calling upon Amida's name. He reasoned that to call upon Amida's name gains for the cultivator all the karmic merit of Amida himself—all the merit implied in his Buddha-wisdom and compassion and all the merit achieved in Amida's use of these as well. Other practices, reasoned Hōnen, merely earn for the cultivator a limited amount of merit from the cultivator's performance of that particular meritorious deed or act itself.

To return to Hōnen's reasoning:

Regarding the principle of ease versus difficulty, *nembutsu* is easy to cultivate while all other practices are difficult to cultivate ... Because *nembutsu* is easy it can be used by all sentient beings, but because all other practices are difficult, they cannot be used by all those with various spiritual abilities. And thus was it not for the purpose of bringing about the universal rebirth of all sentient beings that the difficult practices were rejected and the easy adopted as the practice of the original vow?

Let us suppose that donating images and founding temples had been made the practices of the original vow. Then those in poverty would have no hope of rebirth. But the poor and lowly are much more numerous than the rich and high-born. If wisdom and intelligence had been made the condition of the original vow, then the dull and foolish would have no hope of rebirth. Yet the dull and foolish are much more numerous than the intelligent. If wide learning and experience had been made the condition of the original vow, then those with little learning and experience would have no hope of rebirth. Yet the unlearned are much more numerous than the learned. If moral conduct and observance of the precepts had been made the practices of the original vow, then those who violate or who have not adopted the precepts would have no hope of rebirth. Yet those who violate the precepts are much more numerous than those who observe them. We should see that it is the same with the various other practices. It is important to understand that if any of those practices had been made the condition of the original vow, then those gaining rebirth would be few and those not reborn would probably be many.

Thus it was that Amida Tathāgata, conceiving in the distant past when he was the monk Dharmākara a great and universal compassion, in order to embrace all sentient beings selected not the donation of images, the founding of temples or any other of the sundry practices for his rebirth original vow, but only the single practice of the *nembutsu* of calling upon his name (Ōhashi 1971, 105-106).

We find here once again that although Hōnen is ostensibly explaining why Amida decided to select invocational *nembutsu* as the practice for rebirth, he is revealing as well the reasoning that went into his own decision to interpret the *nembutsu* of the vow as easy invocation of the name. In short, Hōnen reasoned that the compassion of Amida would not exclude even the least spiritually capable of sentient beings, those capable of no other good deed than to call upon Amida Buddha in total reliance. This passage is justly famous for affirming the universality of Pure Land salvation. It is also a remarkable expression of Hōnen's insight in discerning this breadth and of his courage in teaching it.

VI Hōnen's Hermeneutics: The Appeal to Scripture

Recourse to reason was not the only way in which Hōnen arrived at and justified his interpretation of the eighteenth vow. In fact, reason was for him and his contemporaries a rather unreliable tool. As Hōnen says, "the holy one's intentions are difficult to fathom and not easy to set out ... " A more reliable criterion for interpreting scripture was recourse to alternative scripture. Toward the end of the third chapter of the *Senchaku shū* Hōnen poses this hypothetical question:

> The *Sūtra* [*on the Buddha of Limitless Life*] says "ten reflections," while the interpretations [of the *Sūtra*][22] have "ten utterances." What is the difference between reflections and utterances? (Ōhashi 1971, 108)

He responds:

> The terms reflection and utterance[23] are one and the same. How do we know this? In the section of the *Contemplation Sūtra*[24] on the lower rebirth of the lower grade of beings it says, "Urged to call unceasingly, he completes ten reflections; when he calls '*namu* Amida Butsu,' by calling on the Buddha's name he sets aside with each reflection the evil deeds generated during eight billion eons of transmigration." According to this passage it is clear that utterance is the same as reflection and reflection the same as utterance.

What is happening here is that Hōnen is interpreting one passage of scripture on the basis of another. Both constituted for him Buddha-preachments,[25] and therefore true Buddha-*dharma*. The passage in question is the eighteenth vow of the *Sūtra on the Buddha of Limitless Life*; the passage being used as a guide to its meaning is that on the rebirth of the worst of sentient beings[26] as described in the *Contemplation Sūtra*. The *Contemplation Sūtra* describes how such a person, even though he is destined for hell because of extremely bad *karma*, gains salvation on his death bed by calling upon the Buddha ten times. In this passage the term "reflection" (*nen*) is clearly used in such a way as to mean invocational *nembutsu*, in for example, "urged to call unceasingly he completes ten reflections," and "by calling on the Buddha's name he sets aside with each reflection ... " By justifying his interpretation in this way, Hōnen reveals one of the bases for this interpretation—the authority of an alternative scripture.

VII   Hōnen's Hermeneutics: The Appeal to the Teachings of a Revered Master

What were Hōnen's hermeneutical criteria? On what basis did he interpret the all important *nembutsu* of the eighteenth vow as invocation? We have already seen that he had recourse to several criteria—the use of his own limited human reason and the authority of an alternative Pure Land scripture. As his most important hermeneutical criterion, however, Hōnen used a quite different standard—the judgment of an authoritative teacher. In the final analysis Hōnen based his interpretation of the eighteenth vow upon the teachings of the T'ang Chinese Pure Land master, Shan-tao (Jap. Zendō, 613-681).

As we have mentioned, Chapter Three of the *Senchaku shū* opens with three scriptural citations, the eighteenth vow of the *Sūtra on the Buddha of Limitless Life* (which we have already examined), and two quotations, actually paraphrases, of this vow by Shan-tao. Here is the way Hōnen presents these:

> In the first volume of the *Sūtra on the Buddha of Limitless Life* it is written: "When I become a Buddha, if there should be sentient beings anywhere in the ten regions of the universe having sincere and deep faith and aspiration to be reborn into my buddha-land and who, by making even ten reflections [on me], are not reborn there, then I will not accept perfect enlightenment.
>
> Quoting this passage, the *Amida Buddha Contemplation Method* [27] has: "When I become a Buddha, if there should be sentient beings anywhere in the ten regions of the universe aspiring to be reborn into my buddha-land who call upon my name with at least ten utterances, in dependence on the power of my vow, and are not reborn into my land, then I will not accept perfect enlightenment."
>
> Quoting the same passage, the *Hymns to Rebirth* [28] has: "When I become a Buddha, if there should be sentient beings anywhere in the ten regions of the universe who call on my name with at least ten utterances and are not reborn [into my land], then I will not accept perfect enlightenment." That Buddha, having perfected buddhahood, now resides in his land. Thus we should know that the vows he originally made were not in vain, and that sentient beings who call upon him will assuredly be reborn into his land." (Ōhashi 1971, 101).

Having presented these three proof texts, Hōnen does not comment upon the relationship of the second and third of these (the two passages by Shan-tao) to the first (the eighteenth vow) until the end of Chapter Three, where he poses the question and answer we examined above about the discrepancy between "reflection" and "utterance." We have seen that he considered the former to mean the latter, that is, Buddha-reflection to mean utterance of the name of the Buddha. However, there at the beginning of Chapter Three we see that it is strongly implied in this juxtaposition of the text of the eighteenth vow with these paraphrases of it by Shan-tao that *based upon Shan-tao's rendering* Hōnen had already interpreted the *nembutsu* of the eighteenth vow as invocation.

Who was this Shan-tao whose understanding of the eighteenth vow Hōnen seemed to value so highly? Shan-tao was a prominent Pure Land master of the early T'ang period (618-907) who taught and evangelized in the vicinity of the capital, Changan. Although he was a specialist in Buddha contemplation, having composed the important treatise *Amida Buddha Contemplation Method* (cited above) on the subject of this demanding discipline, he was also concerned with the salvation of the average, karmically burdened lay person. Especially important for Hōnen's thought and for us, he was the first Pure Land Buddhist thinker to explicitly relate the eighteenth vow to the *Contemplation Sūtra's* passage on the rebirth of the worst of beings, and thus the first not only to interpret explicitly and unequivocally the *nembutsu* of the vow as invocation, but also to assert that every instance of this invocation, every utterance of the name of Amida Buddha, is therefore endowed with the compassionate, saving power of Amida's vow.

We have already seen two important passages in which this position was set out. The first of the two passages by Shan-tao which Hōnen cites at the beginning of Chapter Three has,

> ... if there are sentient beings ... who call on my name with at least ten utterances *in dependence on the power of my vow* ...

The emphasized phrase (my emphasis of course) is not literally stated in the vow, but is Shan-tao's contribution. The second of the two passages concludes, as we have seen, in this fashion:

> That Buddha, having perfected buddhahood, now resides in his land. Thus we should know that the vows he originally made were not in vain, and that sentient beings who call upon him will assuredly be reborn into his land.

The assertion here is that because Amida's vow has been fulfilled in his acceptance of perfect enlightenment, the condition of that acceptance—rebirth for all those who call upon Amida—has also been fulfilled.[29]

Hōnen first encountered Shan-tao's writings in Genshin's *Essentials of Pure Land Rebirth*. Later he found Shan-tao's detailed commentary on the *Contemplation Sūtra*[30] and there discovered his teachings on the unfailing efficacy of the invocational *nembutsu* of the original vow (Tamura, 1972, 90-92). This discovery, in 1175, was crucial to Hōnen's teachings and career, for it brought about his conversion to the Pure Land path. In the conclusion to the *Senchaku shū* Hōnen reveals:

> A long time ago in my own humble searchings when I first opened this scripture [of Shan-tao's *Commentary on the Contemplation Sūtra*] and came generally to

comprehend its fundamental truths, I immediately ceased cultivation of other practices and took refuge in *nembutsu*. From that day to this, whether for my own practice or for teaching others, I have made *nembutsu* my sole concern (Ōhashi 1971, 162).

Here we have Hōnen's own confession that it was in Shan-tao's teachings that he found the true meaning of the original vow, and moreover a powerful influence upon his subsequent career. Hōnen openly admits that his reliance upon Shan-tao was total. In answer to the following hypothetical question:

The various masters of the Kegon, Tendai, Shingon, Zen, Sanron and Hossō schools have written many works on the Pure Land *dharma*. Why do you rely exclusively on the one master Shan-tao and not on these other masters?

Hōnen responds:

Even though these other masters have composed Pure Land works, they do not base themselves upon the Pure Land way, but rather only upon the way of the sages.[31] Thus I do not rely on them. Master Shan-tao bases himself exclusively on the Pure Land way and not upon the way of the Sages. Thus I rely solely upon Shan-tao (Ōhashi 1971, 158).[32]

Finally, so profound for Hōnen were the teachings on *nembutsu* of Shan-tao, so impressive the impact of these upon him, that he was convinced that Shan-tao had been a very manifestation, an *avatāra*, of Amida Buddha himself.[33] In the conclusion of the *Senchaku shū* we find this eulogy:

When we reverently seek the fundamental reality we realize that it is the Dharma Prince of the forty-eight vows [Amida Buddha]. The teaching arising from his ten eons-long path to perfect enlightenment is reliance on the *nembutsu*. When we humbly search for the derived manifestation we find that it is the Path Master of sole *nembutsu* practice [Shan-tao]. The message of his perfectly realized *samādhi* is complete faith in Pure Land rebirth. Though the fundamental reality and the derived manifestation[34] are not identical, their guidance to emancipation is one (Ōhashi 1971, 162).

In the final analysis, the "ten reflections" of the eighteenth vow meant to Hōnen ten utterances of that prayer of homage to Amida Buddha because, many years before he had composed the *Senchaku shū*, Hōnen realized in utterance of that prayer of homage the fulfillment of his own personal search for an assured means of rebirth into the Pure Land.[35]

VIII Conclusions

To summarize, we have seen several hermeneutical principles at work in Hōnen's reinterpretation of the nature and power of *nembutsu*: 1) A doctrinal analysis based upon a Buddhist view of history; 2) recourse to imperfect but helpful human reason; 3) the use of scriptural authority; 4) reliance upon the authority of an enlightened teacher; and 5) the weight of personal religious experience—an experience of certain salvation. One may question whether Hōnen's personal experience was a hermeneutical principle or merely a compelling influence upon his views. I would suggest that in so far as Hōnen advances this experience as evidence of the correctness of his interpretation, as we have seen him do above, it becomes for him a criterion of interpretation, that is, a hermeneutical principle.

In conclusion, although Hōnen does use reason to justify his interpretations, reason is much less important and reliable in his eyes than scriptural authority or the teachings of an enlightened master. In general, there seems to be little concern here for the rational inference and philosophical logic which Robert Thurman sees as the highest authority for deciding scriptural validity. Doctrinal analysis of the kind Peter Gregory finds typical of Chinese Buddhist hermeneutics is important for Hōnen, but only to establish the priority of Pure Land teachings and scriptures in general. It is clear that Hōnen relies most heavily upon the authority of an enlightened master, a master whose teachings were instrumental in his own conversion to the Pure Land path and to his own assurance of salvation. And though we have examined only one instance of interpretation by Hōnen, this interpretation was his major contribution to his age and to Japanese religious history.

We cannot generalize any farther from this single instance with any confidence, yet the important place of patriarchal authority and personal experience in Hōnen's thinking raises a number of questions. Is a preference for these hermeneutical principles peculiar to Hōnen, to the new Buddhism of which Hōnen was precursor, to Japanese Buddhism in general, to the Pure Land tradition as a whole? Would close examination of important interpretations of other Buddhist thinkers reveal a similar hermeneutics? We would like to suggest that the case of Hōnen is not exceptional. The more we know about the career of a Buddhist thinker, especially the nature of his or her crucial religious experiences, the more clearly would we see that such experiences were central to that figure's thinking, and in particular to his or her interpretation of scripture.

In the religious life we find again and again that human reason must give way before sacred power, or that at best, reason is but a means to try and make understandable what is ultimately beyond reason.

REFERENCES

Akamatsu Toshihide, 1966.
Zoku Kamakura Bukkyō no Kenkyū (Further Studies on Kamakura Period Buddhism). Kyoto.

Andrews, Allan A., 1973.
The Teachings Essential for Rebirth: A Study of Genshin's Ōjōyōshū. Tokyo.
Coates, Harper Havalock and Ryugaku Ishiruka, 1925.
Hōnen the Buddhist Saint: His Life and Teachings. Kyoto.
Gregory, Peter N., 1983.
"Chinese Buddhist Hermeneutics: The Case of Hua-yen," *Journal of the American Academy of Religion*, 51/2, 231-50.
Ikawa Jōkei, ed., 1967.
Hōnen Shōnin den zenshū (The Complete Biographies of Hōnen Shōnin). Revised ed. Takaishi, Osaka Pref.
Inagaki, Hisao, trans., 1966.
Zendō's Exposition on the Merit of the Samādhi of Meditation on the Ocean-like Figure of Amida Buddha. Kyoto.
———, trans., 1984.
"Shan-tao's Method of Meditation on Amida Buddha," *Ryūkoku Daigaku ronshū*, no. 425, 20-41.
Ishii Kyōdō, ed., 1955.
Shōwa shinshō Hōnen Shōnin zenshū (Shōwa Period Revision of the Complete Works of Hōnen Shōnin). Tokyo.
Kamata Shigeo and Tanaka Hisao, eds., 1971.
Kamakura kyū-Bukkyō [Nihon shisō taikei 15] (Traditional Kamakura Period Buddhism [A Collection of Japanese Thought, Vol. 15]). Tokyo.
Mochizuki Shinko, 1942.
Chūkoku Jōdo Kyōrishi (History of Pure Land Doctrines in China). Kyoto.
Morrell, Robert E., 1983.
"Jōkei and the Kōfukuji Petition," *Japanese Journal of Religious Studies* 10/1, 6-38.
Nakamura Hajime, Hayashima Kyōshō and Kino Kazuyoshi, trans., 1963.
Jōdo sambukyō (The Three Part Pure Land Scripture), 2 vols. Tokyo.
Ōhashi Toshio (Shunnō), ed., 1971.
Hōnen-lppen [Nihon shisō taikei 10] (Hōnen and Ippen [A Collection of Japanese Thought, Vol 10]). Tokyo.
Shigematsu Akishisa, 1964.
Nihon Jōdokyō seiritsu katei no kenkyū (Studies on the Process of Establishment of Japanese Pure Land Buddhism). Kyoto.
T., 1924-32.
Taishō shinshū daizōkyō (Taishō Period revised edition of the Chinese Buddhist Canon). Ed. by Takakusu Junjirō, 100 vols. Tokyo.
Tamura Enchō, 1956.
Hōnen Shōnin den no kenkyū (Studies on the Biographies of Hōnen Shōnin). Kyoto. *Teihon Shinran*, 1976.

Teihon Shinran Shōnin zenshū, 5; Shūroku hen, I (The Authentic Complete Works of Shinran Shōnin, V; Compilation section, 1). Ed. by the Shinran Shōnin zenshū kankōkai. Kyoto.

Thurman, Robert A.F., 1978.

"Buddhist Hermeneutics," *Journal of the American Academy of Religion*, 46/1 19-40.

NOTES

[1] An earlier version of this paper was delivered to the Japan-American Buddhist Studies Conference commemorating one hundred years of Buddhism in Hawaii held in Honolulu, July, 1985.

[2] Hermeneutics is the science of interpretation, especially of the meaning of scripture. The term ultimately derives from the name of the Greek deity, Hermes, messenger of the gods.

[3] Bracketed additions are mine.

[4] *T. 360* (*Taishō shinshū daizōkyō* text no.), *Fo-shuo Wu-liang-shou ching* (Jap., *Bussetsu Muryōju kyō*), the most influential Chinese version of the larger *Sukhāvatī-vyūha-sūtra*.

[5] T. 2608. We will use the version annotated by Ōhashi Toshio (Ōhashi 1971).

[6] *Shōdō mon* and *Jōdo mon*, respectively.

[7] This method of evaluation assumed that the *sūtras* which Śākyamuni had presumably delivered later in his teaching career (such as, for example, the *Lotus Sūtra*) contained more advanced doctrines for more advanced disciples. Each school tended, naturally, to place its texts at the end of this progression, that is at the end of the Buddha's life or teaching career, and claim that its doctrines were therefore truer than those of other schools. One of the most influential of Chinese schemata, that of the T'ien-t'ai master Chih-i (538-597), was accepted by much of Japanese Buddhism in Hōnen's day.

[8] *Shōbō, zōhō* and *mappō*, respectively.

[9] As Hōnen acknowledges, this analysis was actually developed by the Chinese Pure Land master Tao-ch'o (Jap., Dōshaku, 562-645).

[10] It is interesting and significant that Hōnen omits from his citation of this vow its last phrase, "excepting those who have committed the five irredeemable evils and slandered the true *Dharma*" (T. 360, XII, 268a).

[11] Extant Sanskrit versions of the *Sūtra on the Buddha of Limitless Life* indicate that *nien* is a translation of *citta*, "mind," "thought," "consciousness," (Nakamura et al. 1963, 1, 283, n. 136). Of course Hōnen had no access to Sanskrit originals.

[12] *Moppara shō Butsugō*.

[13] T. 2682, *Ōjō yōshū*.

[14] T. 1911, Jap., *Maka shikan*, "Great Quiescence and Insight."

[15] T. 365, *Fo-shuo kuan Wu-liang-.shou-fo ching* (Jap., *Bussetsu kan Muryōju Butsu kyō*).

[16] This view of the function of invocational *nembutsu* was based upon a passage of the *Sūtra of Contemplation on the Buddha of Limitless Life* describing the rebirth of an extremely evil person by calling upon the name of Amida Buddha. One tendency of the *Essentials of Pure Land Rebirth*, however, was to consider almost everybody then living to be such a person because Śākyamuni's buddha-world had by then entered the age of degenerate *dharma* (Andrews 1973, 44-45).

[17] For an alternative rendering see Morrell 1983, 30-31.

[18] The Hossō priest Jōkei, 1155-1213 (Morrell 1983, 7-15).

[19] He was of course exiled for this stand in 1207. As Morrell noted, the one intolerable religious attitude in this eclectic age was intolerance (1983, 13).

[20] Hōnen's interpretation was undoubtedly influenced by the growing popularity of invocational *nembutsu*. However, here we will be concerned with how Hōnen himself justified his interpretation of scripture, rather than with the historical influences at work upon him.

[21] Amida Buddha's.

[22] Interpretations of the eighteenth vow of the *sūtra* by Chinese master Shan-tao. See below.

[23] *Nen* and *shō*, respectively.

[24] *Sūtra of Contemplation on the Buddha of Limitless Life*. See notes 15 and 16.

[25] Both the *Sūtra on the Buddha of Limitless Life* (which presents Amida's eighteenth vow) and the *Contemplation Sūtra* are considered sermons of Śākyamuni Buddha.

[26] This passage, called *gebon geshō*, "lowest rebirth of the lowest class," in Pure Land doctrinal discussions, is possibly the most important passage for the history of Pure Land Buddhism next to the eighteenth vow itself. For the text see T. 365, XII, 346.

[27] T. 1959, *Kuan-nien A-mi-t'o fo hsiang-hai san-mei kung-te fa-men* (Jap., *Kannen Amida Butsu sōkai sammai kudoku hōmon*). See the translation of Inagaki (1966 and 1984).

[28] T. 1980, *Wang-sheng li-tsan chieh* (Jap., *Ōjō raisan ge*).

[29] See also Shan-tao's *Commentary on the Sūtra of Contemplation on the Buddha of Limitless Life*, T. 1753, section four on non-meditative practices, XXXVII, 272a-b and 277 a-c.

[30] T. 1753, *Kuan Wu-liang-shou fo-ching shu* (Jap. *Kan Muryōjubutsu kyō sho*).

[31] The reference here is to the *dharma*-gate of the sages and the Pure Land *dharma*-gate discussed above.

[32] We should note that in the first chapter of the *Senchaku shū* Hōnen specified Shan-tao as one of the patriarchs of his Pure Land School (Ōhashi 1971, 93).

[33] This view of Shan-tao did not originate with Hōnen, but had apparently been current in China (Mochizuki 1942, 182-83).

[34] *Honji* and *suijaku*, respectively.

[35] There is evidence of an even closer nexus between Hōnen and Shan-tao. Hōnen's biographies, including those compiled shortly after his death, relate that after his conversion experience in 1175 Shan-tao appeared to him in a dream and commended him for propagating the exclusive cultivation of *nembutsu*. Such an event would have meant to Hōnen a personal transmission of the *dharma* from master to disciple and a clear mandate to interpret the

nembutsu of the original vow as he did. This episode is related in, for example, the *Genkū shōnin Shinikki* (Teihon Shinran 1976, V, 177) and the *Ichigo monogatari* (Ikawa 1967, 774a), both composed before 1227, and of course in the forty-eight chapter biography (Coates and Ishizuka 1925, 205-206). Another early text, the *Mukan shōsō ki*, records that the dream occurred in 1198 (Ishii 1955, 862). The *Shinikki* ("The Private Life of Saint Genkū) has:

> After considering carefully for awhile this [discovery of Shan-tao's teachings], while sleeping he had a dream … He climbed a high mountain and immediately saw the living Shan-tao. From the hips down he was golden, from the hips up [he appeared] as usual. The eminent priest said, "Even though you are of humble status, the *nembutsu* has arisen everywhere under the heavens. Because you will spread the sole invocation of the name to all sentient beings, I have come. I am Shan-tao." Because of this, he propagated this *dharma* and year by year it came to flourish more and more until there was nowhere to which it had not spread (Teihon Shinran, V, 177).

Tamura (1956, 248-256) argues against the actual occurrence of this event, proposing that it was invented to generate a patriarchal line of transmission between Hōnen and Shan-tao for the developing Pure Land School, but Shigematsu (1964, 447-487) and Akamatsu (1966, 204-205) consider the account credible.

JAPANESE AND CHINESE TERMS

Chih-i 智顗
Fo-shuo kuan Wu-liang-shou-fo ching (Bussetsu Kan Muryōju Butsu kyō) 佛説観無量寿佛経
Fo-shuo Wu-liang-shou ching (Bussetsu Muryōju kyō) 佛説無量寿経
Gebon geshō 下品下生
Genkū Shōnin shinikki 源空聖人私日記
Genshin 源信
Hōnen 法然
Honji suijaku 本地垂迹
Ichigo monogatari 一期物語
Jōkei 貞慶
Kōfukuji sōjō 興福寺奏上
Kuan-nien-A-mi-t'o-fo hsiang-hai san-mei kung-te fa-men (Kanen Amida Butsu sōkai sammai kudoku hōmon) 観念阿弥陀佛相海三昧功徳法門
Kuan Wu-liang-shou-fo-ching shu (Kan Muryōjubutsukyō sho) 観無量寿佛経
Mo-ho chih-kuan (Maka shikan) 摩訶止観
Moppara shō Butsugō 専称佛号
Mukan shōsō ki 夢感聖相記
Namu Amida Butsu 南無阿弥陀佛
Nembutsu 念仏
Nen (nien) 念

Nen (shō) 念（声）
Ōjō yōshū 往生要集
P'an-chiao (hangyō) 判教
Senchaku hongan nembutsu shū 選択本願念仏集
Shan-tao (Zendō) 善導
Shōbō, zōhō, mappō 正法, 像法, 末法
Shōdō mon, Jōdo mon 聖道門, 聖道門
Taishō shinshū daizōkyō 大正新脩大蔵経
Tao-ch'o (Dōshaku) 道綽
Tendai (T'ien-t'ai) 天台
Wang-sheng li-tsan chieh (Ōjō raisan ge) 往生礼讃偈

CHAPTER 20

DAVID, SHANKARA, HŌNEN

—FRITHJOF SCHUON

David, Shankaracharya and Hōnen are spiritual personalities who are in many respects quite different, but who have in common the fact that they each represent an altogether fundamental mode of spirituality, and that they do so in a perfect, unsurpassable and incisive manner.

David is the great personification of prayer; of discourse addressed, from the depths of the heart, to the Divine Person. He thus incarnates all the genius of Israel, all the great Semitic message, which is that of faith; hence all the mystery of man standing before his God, and having nothing to offer but his soul; but offering it entirely, without reticence or reservation. *De profundis clamavi ad Te Domine*; the creature who stands thus before his Creator knows what it is to be a human being, and what it is to live here below. David represents the man of virtue contending with the powers of evil, yet invincible because he is a man of God.

It is thus that David, in his Psalms, spreads out before us all the treasures of the dialogue between the creature and the Creator. Everything is manifested therein: distress, trust, resignation, certitude, gratitude; and all is combined and becomes a song of glory to the Sovereign Good. It is easy to understand why Jesus is "son of David"; and why—by way of consequence—Mary could be called "daughter" of the Prophet-King,[1] independently of the fact that she is his descendant according to the flesh.

To be a Prophet is to open a way; David through his Psalms opened the way of prayer, even though he was not, to be sure, the first to know how to pray. Metaphysically speaking, he manifested in concrete and human mode—not in abstract and doctrinal mode—the reciprocity between *Māyā* and *Ātmā*; he incarnated so to speak—and this was the purpose of his coming—all the varied and paradoxical play between contingency and the Absolute, and in this respect he even opened indirectly a way towards gnosis. But he always remains man and, consequently, does not seek to draw away from the human point of view, as is especially attested by Psalm 139: "O Lord, thou hast searched me, and known me. Thou knowest my downsitting and mine uprising, thou understandest my thought afar off ... " And later: "For there is not a word in my tongue, but lo, O Lord, thou knowest it altogether. Thou hast beset me behind and before, and laid thine hand upon me. Such knowledge is too wonderful for me; it is high, I cannot attain unto it."

Independently of the fact that the Psalms, being inspired by the Divine Spirit, must contain implicitly all wisdom,[2] these Texts are not lacking in passages capable of directly vehicling esoteric meanings. It is thus that the first of the Psalms speaks of him whose "delight is in the law of the Lord; and in his law doth he meditate day and night." The law of the Lord is, on the one hand Revelation, and on the other, the Will of God; as for meditation, it signifies a contemplation and not a cry of the soul. Moreover, this meditative contemplation comprises two modes or two degrees: the "day" and the "night"; the first concerning the literal and immediate truth, and the second, esoteric truth. "The Lord knoweth the way of the righteous: but the way of the ungodly shall perish," for only on the side of the Immutable is there stability, peace and life. And the fourth Psalm speaks to us thus: "But know that the Lord hath set apart him that is godly for himself: the Lord will hear when I call unto him." This invocation, in fact, is the very essence of the soul of the righteous, at whatever level we envisage the prayer of the heart.

*

* *

Aside from the esoteric allusions necessarily contained in the Psalms, it could also be said, from another point of view, that it is Solomon who represents esoterism most directly; thus David and Solomon appear as two inseparable poles, or as the two sides of one and the same Revelation.

David is the builder of Jerusalem; he represents, for Israel, the passage from nomadism to sedentarism. As for Solomon, he is the builder of the Temple; from David comes the body, from Solomon the heart.[3] Solomon also had sanctuaries built for foreign divinities; through this universalism, he entered into conflict, not with the formless Truth, but with the Sinaitic, Mosaic, Israelite form of this Truth. Moreover, we may consider the three Books of Solomon to be a spiritual mountain, the Song of Songs being—in the opinion even of the Kabbalists—the summit or the heart; or the wine, in the initiatory sense of the word.

As regards the problem of doctrinal formulation, one should not lose sight of the fact that for the Semites, prior to their contacts with the Greeks, metaphysics pertained in large measure to the inexpressible; now, not to know how to express something—not to know that one can express it or possibly not to wish to express—it is in no wise not to conceive it. And all the more so is this the case in a perspective of transcendence where the accent is on the fear of God, whence the prohibition of pronouncing the supreme Name; whence too the reticence to articulate the divine mysteries.

*

* *

In Shri Shankaracharya, the distinction between *Ātmā* and *Māyā* does not appear as a mystery which is brought out "in the final analysis"; it is expressed from the outset without a veil, which is to say that it constitutes the message itself. As for the veil, which is exoterism, or legalism, Shankara abandons it to others.

Like the inspired Kings of the Biblical world, Shankara is a Prophet, but not the Founder of a religion; his message presupposed a preexisting framework. This is not to say that his message is merely partial; if it can have this appearance in relation to the Hindu system viewed in its totality, it is because, geometrically speaking, it is like the point which does not encompass the periphery; but it cannot be said that this is because something is lacking in the point, which is perfect and can suffice unto itself. Moreover, Providence foresaw for Shankara a quasi-exoteric complement, namely Ramanuja, the great spokesman of Vaishnavite monotheism: the convinced adversary of the Shankarite and Shaivite metatheism, yet tolerated by the Shankarite school as an elementary stage. Even within *Advaita-Vedānta*, the necessity for worship is taken into account: the disciples of Shankara do not deprive themselves of adoring and invoking divinities, for they know that they are human beings and that it is proper to put everything in its place. One cannot transcend *Māyā* without the grace of a divinity which is included within *Māyā* who is *Ātmā* of course, but within *Māyā*, as we ourselves are. The contact between man and God presupposes a common ground.

One could speak of the "Shankarite miracle," for this intellectual phenomenon is almost unique in its character at once direct, rigorous, explicit, and complete; just as the Semites, through their Prophets, have brought the world the great message of Faith, so the Aryans, through Shankara—and in a certain manner also through the Greeks—have brought it the great message of Intellection. This is not to say, obviously, that Shankara was the first in India to speak of this mystery, for one finds it formulated first in the Upanishads, and later by the great commentator Badarayana; but Shankara offers a particularly precise and complete crystallization of it, unique in its perfection and fecundity.

The entire message of the Upanishads, of the *Brahma-Sūtras* of Badarayana, and finally of Shankara, may be condensed into the following words: "*Brahma* alone is real; the world is illusion, *Māyā*; the soul is not other than *Brahma*."

*

* *

Some scholars have quite improperly concluded that the Shankarite advaitism—"non-dualism"—stems in the final analysis from Nagarjuna, hence from mahayanic Buddhism which Shankara condemns implacably; the reason for this false assimilation is that there is a certain parallelism between advaitism and the Nagarjunan perspective in the sense that both represent a metatheistic immanentism; but the starting points are totally different. No doubt, the Buddhist *Nirvāṇa* is nothing other than the Self, *Ātmā*; but whereas for the Hindus the starting point is that reflection of the Self which is the "I," for the Buddhists on the contrary the starting point is entirely negative and moreover purely empirical: it is the *Saṃsāra* as the world of suffering, and this world is merely a "void," *shūnya*, which it is not worth the trouble to try to explain. The Buddhists deny the concrete existence of the soul and consequently also that of the Self—they conceive in negative mode that which the Hindus conceive in positive mode— and the Hindus, for their part reject no less categorically this negativism of the Buddhists, which appears to them like the negation of the Real itself.

Here one may nonetheless wonder—and we cannot avoid this doctrinally important parenthetical insertion—why a mind like Shankara indulged in casting invective even on the very person of the Buddha; now it is excluded that a Shankara could have "indulged" himself; in fact, he exercised in this case a function which we will term a "self-defensive symbolist interpretation"; we meet with such examples in the sacred Scriptures themselves. Shankara's mission was not only to formulate the *Advaita-Vedānta*, but also to protect the vital milieu of this doctrine against the Buddhist invasion; but he could not have the mission of explaining the intrinsic validity of Buddhism, which did not concern the Hindu world. If Shankara's mission had been to explain traditional universality and thereby the validity of all the forms of revelation and spirituality, it could then be said that he erred in judging Buddhism and the Buddha Shakyamuni; but, again, Shankara's mission was altogether intrinsic—not extrinsic as the study of the diverse traditional forms would have been—consequently he could overlook, and wanted to overlook, the possible value of foreign traditions; he did not practice the "science of religions" (*Religionswissenschaft*).

On the plane of metaphysics as such—and it is this which alone counts in the final analysis—Shankara was one of the most eminent authorities who has ever lived; his scope was of a "prophetic" order, as we have said, which means that he was as infallible as the Upanishads. The doctrinal and institutional work of Shankara marked the inauguration of a millennium of intellectual and spiritual flowering;[4] to say Hindu wisdom, is to say Shankara.

*

* *

Like Shankara, Hōnen Shōnin was not the founder of the perspective that he personified, but he was its most explicit and incisive representative, and this is precisely what allows us to say that he was the personification of his message. Doubtless—from the point of view of "avataric" phenomenology—he is not situated at the same level as David and Solomon, or as Shankara; the Buddhist equivalent of these rather would be Nagarjuna, the great spokesman of original *Mahāyāna*. But Nagarjuna—while he eminently represented the invocatory branch of *Mahāyāna* and is considered to be the first patriarch of this school[5]— was hardly explicit concerning the perspective here in question; thus it became necessary later on to expound in detail this particular doctrine, and this was done by the other patriarchs of the so-called "devotional" Buddhism, Hōnen being the seventh and last of them; his predecessors—after the Indian Vasubandhu—were Chinese, followed by one Japanese.[6]

If David incarnates the meeting with God and Prayer, and Shankara metaphysical Truth, Intellection and Meditation, Hōnen for his part will be like the incarnation of Faith and Invocation; his perspective and his method coincide, as regards the essential, with the way of the "Russian Pilgrim" and the Hindu *japa-yoga*, as well as with the *prapatti*—saving trust—of the Vaishnavites. This is to say that it is the way of easiness, of Grace; the word "easiness" is not to be taken here in a pejorative sense, it rather means that the technique of this way is easy. Grace is conditionally acquired; but concrete perseverance is difficult *de facto*, for in the final analysis, it demands all that we are; man cannot bear the "divine climate" for long, except on condition of gently dying to the world and to himself. In fact, no way, if it is really spiritual, could be "easy" in the vulgar sense of the word.

*

* *

The fundamental idea of the way of *Amitābha* (*Amida* in Japanese) coincides in substance with this saying of Christ: "With men it is impossible, but not with God: for with God all things are possible" (Mark 10:27). This is the Buddhist perspective of the "power of the other" (*tariki*, in Japanese), not of "self-power" (*jiriki*); it means that man adopts an attitude of faith "which moves mountains," combined with a divine and sacramental support which, for its part, is what in reality brings about salvation; there is something analogous in the case of Christian communion, which in fact communicates an incommensurable grace without man having any part in it, except as regards receptivity, which clearly has its requirements.

But the sharp alternative between a "way of merit" and a "way of grace"—for that is what the distinction between the principles *jiriki* and *tariki* means in Japanese Buddhism—this alternative is, we think, more theoretical than practical; in concrete reality, there is rather an equilibrium between the two procedures, so that the distinction evokes the Far Eastern symbol of the *Yin-Yang*, composed, as is known, by a white half containing a black dot, and a black half containing a white dot, this being the very image of harmonious complementarity.[7] Shinran, the disciple of Hōnen, wished to place the accent on the "power of the other," which from a certain mystical point of view is defensible, on condition of not reproaching Hōnen for stopping halfway and of having mistakenly maintained an element of "self-power"; for, as initiative and activity are natural to man, we do not see what advantage there would be in depriving him of them. Faith, it seems to us, is much more easy to realize if one allows man the joy of collaborating with it; in our personal activity there is in fact a criterion of concrete reality and a guarantee of efficacy, whereas faith alone—as a condition of salvation—has no support which is ours and which we could control. Hōnen knew as well as Shinran that the cause of salvation is not in our work but in the grace of Amida; but we must in fact open ourselves in some fashion to this grace, otherwise it would suffice to exist in order to be saved.

The great Semitic message, as we have said in speaking of David, is that of faith; now the fact that devotional Buddhism is founded upon saving faith could cause one to think that in both cases it is a question of the same attitude and the same mystery, and consequently that the two traditional positions coincide. Now, aside from the fact that the element of faith exists necessarily in every religion, there is here this distinction to be made: the Semitic or Abrahamic faith is the fervent acceptance of the omnipotent Invisible and consequently submission to Its Law; whereas the Amidist faith is trust in the saving Will of a particular Buddha, a trust linked to a particular and well-defined practice: namely the invocation *Namomitābhaya Buddhaya*: or *Namu Amida Butsu*.[8]

Way of altogether human Prayer; way of metaphysical Discernment; way of saving Trust: The three ways can be combined because man has many chords in his soul, or in other words, because human subjectivity comprises different sectors. It is true that Prayer and Trust pertain to the same sector; but such is not the case with metaphysical Discernment, whose subject is not the sensible soul, but pure intelligence; which—far from creating an antagonism—permits the simultaneity of parallel approaches. The proof of this is the altogether lyrical piety of a Shankara, his hymns and invocations to the feminine as well as masculine aspects of the transcendent and immanent Divinity: to the Self who a priori is infinitely "other," but who in reality is infinitely "ourselves."

NOTES

[1] As is attested by the *Magnificat*, which is altogether in the line of the Psalms.

[2] We do not, however, believe that one can draw "any meaning from any word," for hermeneutics has its laws as does every science; but it is a fact that these rules have often been lost sight of.

[3] David, however, chose Mount Zion—as a kind of replacement for Mount Sinai—the seat of the Ark of the Covenant; Solomon placed it in the Holy-of-Holies.

[4] For he did not limit himself to writing treatises, he also founded spiritual centers whose influence was immense and which still exist in our time.

[5] Founded on the worship of *Amitābha* Buddha, the great manifestation of saving Mercy.

[6] Namely, T'an-luan, Tao-ch'o, Shan-tao and Genshin. Eminent Japanese precursors who are not counted as Patriarchs were Kūya and Ryōnin.

[7] For example, man bears in his soul a feminine element, and woman, a masculine element, and it is necessarily thus, not only because every person has two parents, but also because each sex belongs to one and the same human species.

[8] "Salutation to the Buddha *Amitābha*." The second of the two formulas cited is the Japanese adaptation of the Sanskrit formula.

CHAPTER 21

MUTUAL TRANSFORMATION OF PURE LAND BUDDHISM AND CHRISTIANITY: METHODOLOGY AND POSSIBILITIES IN THE LIGHT OF SHINRAN'S DOCTRINE[1]

—TAKEDA RYŪSEI

(TRANSLATED BY JAN VAN BRAGT)

"What can, or must, Buddhism learn from Christianity?" From my experience of encounters with Christian theologians, seminarians, and ordinary faithful, I have come to the conviction that, rather than learning from some element of Christianity (doctrine, or view of life, or worldview, or others), we Buddhists must lend an ear to all that Christianity is teaching and arguing. Buddhism must first of all learn from the attitude Christianity is showing nowadays, of trying to learn from Buddhism, and from the earnestness and humility this implies. What is, after all, the theological or doctrinal basis that lies at the bottom of that effort to learn from other religions? I have the impression of discerning in that attitude the very religious core of Christianity.

In this essay I want to take up the writings of, successively, Nishitani Keiji, John Cobb, Takizawa Katsumi, and Gordon Kaufman, and to reflect on the relationship of Christianity and Pure Land Buddhism from the perspective of some of the problematics that these authors have introduced. In my last section I shall broach the subject of "religious pluralism." This is a position that wants to uproot the traditional concepts by means of which the religious phenomenon has been conceived, for example, the very ideas of "Christianity," "Buddhism," and so on. Its problem is, then, no longer simply the mutual relationship of the two religions, Christianity and Buddhism. It tries to rethink from the bottom up the very phenomenon of two religions endeavoring to learn from each other.

But, before I enter into my investigations, permit me to stress my strong conviction that, in the praxis of the interreligious dialogue, the existential relationship with the dialogue partner is of central importance. In my own case, the encounter with the four people mentioned above was such an existential thing, something beyond all doctrines and academic theories. It was rather the case that the meaning of the doctrines and theories emerged for me from the existential encounter. For me, these four persons are truly "bodhisattvas of returning transference," and especially the Christians among them I cannot but call "Christian bodhisattvas." It is in my *nembutsu* world that these people appear to me in this way.

I Nishitani Keiji's Ideas on the Buddhist-Christian Dialogue

Nishitani discovers the path to mutual understanding in a doctrine that affords liberation at the same time that it implies exclusivity.[2] He insists that we must descend deep into the realm of faith and doctrine, and quotes as the reason that this is precisely "the deepest and innermost realm that humankind has reached in its long history." He therefore stresses that also the encounter of East and West cannot be called a true and radical encounter "as long as the two do not come to a real understanding by descending into that innermost level or realm." However, this realm is "at the same time precisely the place where the most vexing aporias originate that obstruct all mutual understanding."[3]

Nishitani then concludes that there is no other way but to break through the very level of faith and doctrine, after having reached it—into a "totally new level wherein even the innermost core of the human heart is transcended."[4] The place that makes possible a "true encounter," in other words, "a mutual understanding that goes beyond even the innermost core of the human heart," is "a level wherein humans are simply human, purely 'sons of man'." It is to this place that we must return. What is required is that "we resolutely and radically divest ourselves of all the fixed forms and categories that shut up all our thoughts, feelings and acts of will within an established and immutable-looking framework." This is a level wherein "the human being becomes a totally 'unveiled body,' barefoot and barehanded, without a thread either on the head or on the back, and is able, at the same time, to open and unveil also his/her innermost heart for everybody to see."[5]

Nishitani looks for the elements that could make possible the realization of such a "true encounter" in the following four "basic historical conditions of the present": (1) "the fact that at present the whole world is rapidly becoming 'one world'"; (2) the fact that, in art, morals, and philosophy, it is this one world that has become the stage; (3) the fact that science-technology has become "the main actor of the drama of the emergence of this 'one world,' first of all by making communication all over the globe easy and rapid"; but more basically (4) by the fact that this science-technology, on account of having "objectivity" as its basic character, is in the process of bringing the hearts of all humans and peoples to the same common level of thoughts and intentions.

The universal pattern of our times, that which characterizes our contemporary lives, is brought about precisely by "secularization." Secularization designates "the piecemeal liberation of human endeavors from the shackles of religious doctrine and theology that have long dominated them."[6] However, the root-cause that led to our present "one world," accompanied as it is by a radical and universal secularization, is as yet a "hidden ground." I would like to suggest that, given the fact that the root-cause of the emergence of the "one world" remains unrevealed, we must conclude that this "one world" is not truly realized as yet.

What kind of reality is that "one world"? This "one" is a problem. The fact that its root-cause is not visible to us is another. The root-cause of the contemporary "one world" must be understood as that which in our times made one world out of the dispersed localized or "parochial" worlds that existed in modern times. As long as this root-cause is hidden, the "one world" we are presently thinking of is, in fact, still a chimera. Only when this root-cause is unveiled will it appear whether the world brought about by it is "one world" or not.

What is the concrete methodology of the encounter of religions? Nishitani maintains that the only possible path to mutual understanding "can only be found by exposing oneself directly and with all one's might to the factual, profound, and complicated situation of the present world, and to grasp in its midst some new point of departure." How would this complexity be related to the "oneness" of the "one world"? It has to be a relationship of the "many" to the "one." Basing itself on the theory of emptiness, Buddhism has traditionally presented this relationship by the formula "many-*sive*-one" (多即一). This *soku* philosophy, however, is no longer adapted to reality. Buddhists may seriously argue about *soku* and emptiness, but would this mean that they are earnestly tackling the problems of reality in the direction indicated by Nishitani, of "exposing oneself to the real situation of the present world"? Does not their real attitude show the exact opposite? While with their bodies they are firmly immersed in the luxuries and pleasures of the secular world, their hearts keep aloof from the secular world by judging it to be illusory. In the world they are called "monks" but they are living in comfortable houses on great lots of land.[7]

Could this possibly be called a way of life of total exposure to the factual situation of the present world? These priests are nothing but entrepreneurs who make their living from the management of funerals, cemeteries, and parking places; people who have turned the dead into commercial objects. On seeing them, I cannot but think of the "clerics" against whom Nietzsche directed his fiery invectives in *The Antichrist*.[8]

Nishitani also says that the "level where the self is a naked body" has the same meaning as the "Pure Land" of which Pure Land Buddhism speaks. He points out that the Pure Land is the "fatherland whereto living beings must return, and that in Shinran's *Notes on 'Essentials of Faith Alone'* it is called the 'City of Dharma-nature,' the hometown to which one is meant to return."[9] According to Nishitani, the Pure Land is "the Fatherland, essentially the Buddha's Enlightenment, the Awakening we have to reach."[10] Indeed, if one thinks only of the Pure Land as such, Nishitani's understanding is correct. However, would it be possible to say that the place of the Pure Land in Pure Land thought and its salvific significance reveals the identical meaning as what Nishitani intends when he says that "the level on which the self is a bare body" is the place of "living in the world as an enlightened one"? Did it or did it not have such a meaning in Shinran's own self-understanding? Shinran uses the expressions "City of Dharma-nature" and "returning to one's hometown" in connection with his idiosyncratic interpretation of the traditional idea of *raikō* (来迎 the coming of Amida with a suite of bodhisattvas to one's deathbed), while commenting on a text by Fa-chao wherein the latter speaks of "Avalokiteśvara and Mahāsthāmaprāpta come of themselves to welcome them." There, Shinran clearly tries to read elements of his idiosyncratic soteriology, such as "rejecting this defiled world" and "coming to the *saha* world," into the expression "returning to the city of Dharma-nature." Without reference to these soteriological elements, the "life" of the religious existence by which the individual *nembutsu* practitioner is moved would be lost in these expressions. "To reject this defiled world" is certainly not something that has to do only with awakening of self-awareness.

Moreover, in Shinran's particular way of thinking, the opposite idea of "rejecting the Pure Land to return to the world of life-death," the so-called "returning transference,"[11] is involved. This corresponds to the idea of the bodhisattva path in Mahāyāna: wandering endlessly in *saṃsāra* with an ultimate aim of profiting all living beings by teaching them and setting them on the path to buddhahood. In Nishitani's understanding, "returning to the city of Dharma-nature" is an event within self-awareness or awakening; would this also be the case with Shinran's "returning from the city of Dharma-nature to the saha world"? It is clear that the expressions "rejecting" and "coming" contain in their meaning what Nishitani understands by them, but besides this, there is strongly present in Pure Land thought a dynamic pragmatism, that points over and beyond that meaning to an infinite openness to positive involvement in all the phenomena of "this world." It is precisely by way of that limitless openness to the practice of the bodhisattva path that we can conform to the demand which Nishitani directs at all present-day religionists: that they expose themselves directly and with all their might to the profound and complicated conditions of present reality.

Nishitani writes that, in the present interreligious situation, it is more important and urgent to pay attention to the vast commonalities among the religions than to focus on the particularity of the religion one believes in. Still, in his famous essay "God and Absolute Nothingness," he writes:

> Absolute Nothingness is a term that has its genealogy in Buddhism. It is true that Meister Eckhart speaks of a "Godhead" beyond the personal God and calls this also an Absolute Nothing. Still, there is a basic difference between that Nothing and the Nothingness in Buddhism, a difference on the level of the general difference between Christianity and Buddhism, or between Oriental spirit and Western spirit.[12]

Thus, Nishitani clearly points to a basic difference between the Absolute Nothingness of Buddhism and the Nothing of Eckhart. This even becomes a central theme in the essay. The two notions belong to worlds that are already different. Nishitani recognizes that, from the viewpoint of difference, the two are totally different and no single point of sameness can be detected between them. Nevertheless, Nishitani endeavors to compare them.

The question then becomes: what kind of relationship or world does there lie between those wholly different realities and, on the other hand, the philosophy (or comparative thought) of Nishitani himself, who compares the two? What is the point of contact between these heterogeneous concepts and comparative thought? What kind of situation does comparative thought reveal Buddhism's nothingness and Eckhart's Nothing to be in? Does it reveal that each is sufficient unto itself? If so, comparative thought becomes unnecessary. Or does it reveal that the two are complementary? Or does comparative thought endeavor to create something new, something that could not be detected in the compared realities before the comparison, something that is neither Eckhart's Nothing nor Buddhism's Nothingness? Would comparative thought lay claim to the revelation of a new reality that had not been paid attention to nor had been realized in any of the two?

Nishitani maintains that Eckhart's Christian experience in itself contains a correspondence with Buddhist experience. This is a matter of rather great importance for Nishitani, "because I believe that, not only for different sects but also for different religions, the awareness of a greater sameness is more important at present than the awareness of difference."[13] He also says: "A mental attitude of burying oneself exclusively in the particularity of one's religion naturally makes one's eyes turn towards the past and necessarily lands one in conservatism," while it is necessary in our present situation to evoke "the spirit of trying to open new possibilities of religion in view of the future." What Nishitani looks for is that "the religious life in each of the religions would, from within that very life, become aware of a position of universality greater than that which it had traditionally been conscious of."[14]

What, after all, is the meaning of "a universality greater than one had hitherto been conscious of"? "The awareness one had hitherto" (awareness N) is different from that "greater awareness" (awareness X). Still, insofar as the claim is that they arise from "inside that life itself," they must both be contained in the religious life itself. Indeed, religious life implies awareness of some kind (awareness $N + X$); religious life does not obtain apart from the self-awareness of the religionist. Religious life exists essentially as religious self-awareness. However, seen from Nishitani's standpoint, in this religious self-awareness the self-awareness of a "greater universality" (awareness X) has not yet been reached. It must then be a self-awareness that comes to itself only by an encounter with other thought, philosophy, religion, and science. The self-awareness of a more universal position is also presented as "a path that opens new possibilities into the future for the present religions." To which concrete circumstances would these "new possibilities" point with regard to each religion? In the same vein as Nishida Kitarō, Nishitani also strongly states that these new possibilities do not intimate the creation of a new religion, different from both Buddhism and Christianity.

Nishitani circumscribes this "greater universality" also by writing: "the various religions should not stop at their established forms, but [reach] a standpoint of greater universality." The first requirement is thus that the religions break down the "existing forms" that they have built up in history. Those are the historically contingent religious forms that the various religions have created over a long time, by building a unique tradition with definite doctrines, "theologies," rituals, and various cultural elements, and by a course of repeated developments, struggles, backslidings, and reformations. These are the determinations that Nishitani himself calls "historically restricted on all sides." Nishitani considers that, by a "comparative thinking" about the relationships of the various religions, it becomes possible to bring to light "a religious life that takes the ground of man's eternal essence as its foundation, or at the least as the foundation of the vanguard of that religious life." This would precisely be "awareness X," which is then no longer "comparative thought" but goes beyond comparison and reveals itself as creative thinking.

Nishitani then clearly declares that "seen from the viewpoint of the history of world spirituality, religious life has come at present to a point where it must return to a standpoint of greater universality, based on the essence of the human, with regard to spiritual content and with regard to the factual historical relationships as well."[15] This "great universality" is no longer the universality that has been claimed and sought for by each of the religions, and that could be discovered within the various religious truths. From the standpoint of that "great universality," all universality to be detected within each religion and sect is relativized. Nishitani, however, discovers that "great universality" in mysticism. "From the viewpoint of universality in the religious life, there is nothing as universal as mysticism." Mysticism contains something very universal that pervades all the main religions. In a word, mysticism can be defined as precisely "the religious life that takes the essence of the human as its foundation."

The reason why I am deeply interested especially in Nishitani's "Eckhart theory" and want to attach great importance to the theory of interreligious dialogue propounded therein is that Nishitani offers an Eckhart interpretation according to which, in Eckhart, the two moments that in Japanese Buddhism came to be separated from each other, namely, Zen Buddhism and Pure Land Buddhism, cross and interpenetrate one another. In other words, the reason is that I have been made painfully aware, by my dialogue with Christians, of an urgent task to be performed, namely, the realization of a truly religious encounter of *nembutsu* and Zen within the same Buddhism. An important element herein is the question of what Pure Land Buddhism can/must learn from Zen. No matter how much the Buddhist-Christian dialogue flourishes and deepens, how could we be speaking of a dialogue of world religions, if a religious dialogue among the various schools belonging to the same Buddhism would prove to be impossible? Within Buddhism, Pure Land and Zen are two major schools that are summoned in an especially urgent way to enter into dialogue. It goes without saying that the Pure Land school (which includes Shin, Jishū, and so on) must also engage in religious dialogue with the other schools, such as Tendai, Shingon, and Nichiren, but the dialogue with Zen is one of our most important tasks, especially in view of the future of the propagation of Shin Buddhism in North America.[16]

Nishitani himself, rather euphemistically, gives us a first hint when he writes: "It is impossible to deny that there is something akin to Zen in Shinran's religious experience of dwelling, as a foolish being, in the state of non-retrogression and naturalness (*jinen hōni*)."[17] Also, people like Nishida Kitarō and Suzuki Daisetz, while having their basis in Zen religious experience, have shown interest in the thought of the Pure Land school and written about Shinran and the Myōkōnin. They thus appeared to recognize a "little universality" (over against Nishitani's "great universality") or, we might say, a common religious truth between Zen and *nembutsu*. Of course, at the same time, within the *nembutsu* school, the three major sects that derived from Hōnen, namely, Chinzei, Seizan, and Shinshū, will have to overcome their sectarian closedness and engage in mutual religious dialogue.

Unfortunately, in all this we run into a steep wall: how far will each religion and sect be capable of "the effort to divest itself from all the established doctrines and theological tenets," in order for this "great universality" to come into its own? In fact, to divest oneself in this way is of extreme difficulty for the concrete individual believer, and is it not also rather unrealistic when one actually engages in interreligious dialogue? What does this "divesting oneself" really mean, after all? It might be possible to do this on a somewhat theoretical-conceptual level. Would there really be no way for that "great universality" to come to the fore without this divesting? Would it not be that actual religious dialogue comes to be, not by divesting but rather by each religion positively putting forth and laying bare "all its established doctrines and theological theories" and confronting them squarely with the particular doctrines and theories that the other religion has built up in its history? Thereby the religious diversity would come to the fore as the factual problem it is. I wish to state that, especially in this "postmodern" present, creative interreligious dialogue must be undertaken from a standpoint of religious pluralism. It must go in the direction of what I like to call a "pluralistic religious dialogue."

II John Cobb's Theory of the Dialogue
between Pure Land Buddhism and Christianity

In chapter six of his well-known book *Beyond Dialogue*,[18] Cobb tackles the question, "What Buddhists Can Learn from Christians?"[19] The basis of the thesis he defends in that chapter is the idea that Pure Land Buddhists can learn from Christianity by recognizing that Amida is Christ. He then argues that the potential fruitfulness of this recognition appears most clearly if one gives attention to the following two points: (1) the meaning of Amida Buddha being personal; (2) the meaning of Amida being ethical.

The first refers to the problem of how universality and personality can be conceived of together. In Pure Land Buddhism and Christianity both are considered in much the same way. Still, Cobb argues that in Christianity there can be found in the relationship of God and us humans a personal character that has no equivalent in the mainstream of Pure Land thought. As a process theologian, who bases his thought on Whitehead's philosophy, Cobb's understanding of the personal character of the God-man relationship is very different from that of the traditional theology, which considered God to be immovable (divine immutability) and one-sidedly active in the relationship. On his part, he understands the personality of the God-man relationship as a "personal interaction between God and human beings."[20] In the relationship God is active but at the same time passive.

Here, Cobb points out an element that is lacking in the Pure Land Doctrine: Amida does not "listen to" the "prayers" of sentient beings. Or, to put it in terms of Whiteheadian theology, in Pure Land Buddhism there is, indeed, something that corresponds to God's "Primordial Nature," namely, Amida Buddha's Primal Vow, but the "Consequent Nature" of God is not represented. I do not want to enter here into Whitehead's philosophy, but I find this remark by John Cobb to be very important. We must carefully analyze the structure and content of the term "listening to," when it is said that Amida does not listen to our prayers.

In this connection, we might refer to the "Meditative Good" chapter of Shan-tao's Commentary on the *Meditation Sūtra*.[21] There, Shan-tao characterizes the relationship between Amida and sentient beings as a threefold relationship: "intimate karmic relation," "close karmic relation," and "superior karmic relation." In that analysis, however, the relationship is not seen from the viewpoint of activity and passivity, put into question by Cobb. Shan-tao elsewhere clearly says that, when sentient beings recite the *nembutsu*, the Buddha reacts favorably to that *nembutsu* recitation, precisely because it is the *nembutsu* that is the content of the Primal Vow of the Buddha. The religious act of the sentient being is thus perfectly predetermined by the Buddha, and in that sense sentient beings are passive. Shan-tao wrote the above text as an answer to the question: "Why is it said that the Buddha's Light, that is all-pervading, embraces only the people who recite the *nembutsu*?" From that point it could be said that the Buddha's Light is limited by the reciters of the *nembutsu*. It can also be said, however, that the implication is that the Buddha's Light turns non-reciters into reciters of the *nembutsu*. Thus, one can interpret this doctrine in the sense that the universality of the Buddha is here located in his active power to convert all sentient beings into *nembutsu* reciters. Anyway, even if it is said that Amida "listens" to sentient beings, the sense of this listening is fundamentally different from God's listening to people's prayers.

This may suffice to indicate that we should, indeed, pay heed to what Cobb proposes to us Pure Land people a proposal that he finally formulates as follows:

> At least in Christian experience and teaching it has seemed appropriate to believe that the One that gives gracious character to ultimate reality also responds perfectly to all that happens in the world. It is hard to see that anything of worth would be lost to Buddhists if they assimilated from the Christian knowledge of Christ the conviction that our lives are in this way of importance to Amida.[22]

We come now to the second point, the ethical character of the figure of Amida, especially in relation to the stress put on social ethics in Christianity. Also on this point Cobb's considerations are extremely well-taken. He is most certainly not suggesting that Buddhism or Pure Land Buddhism would be an unethical religion. He fully recognizes the moral character of Buddhism, stressing that Buddhist cultures are beautifully structured also ethically, meet the needs of society, and uphold socially desirable behavioral patterns by means of Buddhist ideas. He goes so far as to say that "on the whole, Buddhist societies probably function better than Christian ones, and could well be said to be more moral."[23] Cobb further points out the pacific and humanistic character of Buddhism. He refers to the negation of the caste system in Śākyamuni's sangha and to the fact that, contrary to the Christians who have taken up arms in the name of Christ, Buddhists have not waged wars for the sake of the Buddha. In a word, Buddhists have a more tolerant spirit in questions of religion than Christians. Finally, he remarks on the presence in Buddhist societies of moral ideals, a sense of responsibility, loyalty, and diligence, a spirit of not pushing oneself, of fortitude and discipline. In all these senses the morality of Buddhist societies must be said to be of a high quality.

What is lacking in Buddhism, at least when seen from a Christian viewpoint, is, according to Cobb, not moral virtue or goodness, but "a trans-social norm by virtue of which society is judged." Also with regard to this point, Cobb argues with much circumspection. He does not want to suggest that Buddhist humanism does not function as a normative check, but he indicates that, in the case of Buddhism, this check works only with regard to social roles or moral relationships that militate against the individual other. Consequently, Buddhism shows a tendency to attach supreme importance to human relationships as such, and the welfare of the individual is considered to be the norm to check the system and structure of actual society. He describes this characteristic of Buddhist societies as follows:

> But this potential principle of leverage is rarely thematically developed. On the whole, Buddhism does not encourage attention by its adherents to critical evaluation

of social and political programs or exhort them to be in the forefront of movements of social protest. This seems to be because the mode of the relation of individuals to trans-social reality, namely, to Emptiness or to Amida, does not direct them to a judgment of social structures and their historical roles.[24]

This remark faithfully describes at the least the actual situation of Japan's traditional Buddhist world, and cannot be said to show any intention of criticizing Buddhism in a negative way. Cobb himself says that his remarks are merely "descriptive comments." And he recognizes that even in Christianity itself the clarification of the relationship between religion and social justice is still very much a task of the future. On this point, too, Cobb is self-critical. In Cobb's theology, God is certainly not seen as an absolute Lord who likes to give heteronomous and despotic commands. In Christianity the image of God is not first of all that of one who commands; there is a more numinous idea of God's existence: the God who offers and calls. This image is in greater continuity with that of Amida. From there Cobb proposes that, by learning from Christianity, Pure Land doctrine can further extend the original image of Amida.

The core of what Cobb tries to say with regard to Buddhism, and especially Pure Land Buddhism, can be found in the difference he indicates between Buddhism and Christianity as to their attitudes to the actual world of *pratītya-samutpāda*, especially when confronting the problems of socio-ethical reality. The world of *pratītya-samutpāda* includes both what is actual and what is possible. According to Cobb, Buddhism has concentrated on the attainment of a nondiscriminating wisdom beyond the dualism of subject and object, by way of awakening to the fact that the world of reality has the *pratītya-samutpāda* nature. The focus, namely, is on the aspect of actuality. Christianity, on the other hand, focuses on the aspect of possibility. This indication has great doctrinal meaning for Buddhism and especially for Pure Land Buddhism, which has developed in close unity with the historical world.

If, then, in the perspective of "Amida Buddha is Christ, and Christ is Amida Buddha," the calling voice of Amida could be experienced not merely in the absolutely present individual ("for me, Shinran, only"), but beyond that as a summons with a social and world-historical meaning, Pure Land Buddhists would have to cease being concerned only with the liberation from the illusory and perverted ignorance found in the individual, and would naturally hear in Amida's summons also the demand for a right attitude with regard to social and historical reality.

The liberation from individual ignorance must also be the liberation from social and historical ignorance. But Cobb maintains that we must use the idea of liberation or freedom to evoke better concepts and theories. If we want to live according to the call of Amida that summons us to individual liberation and at the same time to the liberation of society, we have to consider carefully how our social activity and decisions can truly contribute to social liberation. Cobb concludes: "Pure spontaneity works well in immediate human relations, but is a poor basis for public policy."[25] This theological criticism is worthy of our attention.

III Takizawa Katsumi's Ideas on the Dialogue of Pure Land Buddhism and Christianity

The centerpiece of Takizawa's theology is certainly his theory of a "primary contact between God and man," antedating that of the "secondary contact" in Christ. But, since I have earlier discussed this theory from the standpoint of Pure Land doctrine,[26] I shall not develop it here. Only, when Takizawa equates the "primary contact" with "Amida's Primal Vow" and understands the "secondary contact" as the moment of the "attainment of faith," I cannot but find this problematic. The problem lies in the relationship between the "practice" spoken of in "the realization and fulfillment of the bodhisattva practice by Dharmākara Bodhisattva" and the "*nembutsu* practice of ordinary sentient beings." It is the problem of the "karma" that embraces both the pure karmic activity of the Buddha (Donran calls Amida's Vow-practice "the karmic power of the Great Vow") and the sinful karma of sentient beings—both are described as "the threefold karma of body, speech, and mind." I fear that this problem is not taken into consideration in Takizawa's theology.

But, as I said already, I cannot enter into this discussion here. Now I want to give a moment's thought, from a Pure Land perspective, to what Takizawa calls "absolute negation."[27] For Takizawa, the "negation" in absolute negation is not a judgment or decision by us humans, nor is it an arbitrary human activity. He qualifies it as follows: "A negation that simply arises without any negating agent; a negation that is unconditionally there right from the beginning of human existence and will always be there and be valid ever anew till the very end."[28] In human existence, therefore, this negation is there, previous to any human initiative, from the very moment that humans exist, without the need of any preconditions, and will be there till the very end, whether this end is seen as the point that humans become inexistent or as the time that the whole universe passes into nonexistence (the eschatological end).

Commenting on the Buddhist expressions "Buddha and sentient beings are one," "the pure and the impure are not two," Takizawa interprets these as referring to the unique point that is the point of contact while being the dividing line between the everyday finite self and the true infinite self that is absolutely creative; an uncrossable borderline but, at the same time, a point of contact that does not allow any separation. Precisely in the fact that the absolutely formless subject is unconditionally present, Takizawa saw the eternally unchanging but forever new "basic situation (*Grundsituation*)" of human existence.[29]

According to Takizawa, all human beings, without exception, whether consciously or unconsciously, willingly or unwillingly, are placed in a unique and nonpareil universal situation, "the basic situation of the unity of true Buddha and ordinary human." Each human being, although being nothing more than a contingent objective manifestation of the true formless subject, is placed in that basic situation as one free subject.

A foundation that simply exists, totally independent from all human reason and will; without it or outside of it, no particular situation of any kind can actually exist. It is the real and universal ground of human life and history. Consequently, there can be nothing whatsoever in any place or time on earth that could do away with the irreversible relationship between one's unique basic situation and one's particular situation, or that could keep away from the human being the knowledge of that original state of affairs.[30]

The structure of Christianity, which Takizawa calls "the schema that is universal to all Christianity up to now," can also be considered to be the general schema of Jōdo Shinshū. God and man are seen in a dualistic relationship of total mutual separation; Jesus of Nazareth is the only mediator between the two, and this mediatorship is symbolized in the visible cross of Golgotha; there exists a community of people who believe in that particular form as in their only and absolute refuge; this church is the only sacred haven in the real human world; the world outside it is an abyss of endless darkness; all people of other faiths are beings drowning in that abyss: it is their ineluctable destiny.

Takizawa, while maintaining that this is the schema or way of thinking of all Christianity, declares it to be in reality a chimera or false image. The logic behind this declaration is as follows. Takizawa puts the reason for this mistake of Christianity in the fact that Christians, in the bind of that schema, have not known about the inseparable, nonidentical, and irreversible relationship that exists between God and human beings.

Judging from the way he speaks about that "one particular form within the world," we can discern in Takizawa a pluralistic standpoint. He defines the schema that he sees as universal in Christianity as "one particular form" and criticizes traditional Christianity for the error of absolutizing that particular form. He then adds that, for that reason, Christianity cannot free itself from the medieval heteronomy. On the other hand, he also writes that, to the extent that it presupposes that image of human existence as something evident, Christianity stays within the general framework of the modern autonomy. In other words, Takizawa states that both the lapse into medieval heteronomy and the fall into modern autonomy derive from the same "one single mistake": the blindness to the inseparable, nonidentical, and irreversible unity of God and human being. Therefore, the mistake can only be corrected from "the one point, the insight that true Buddha and sentient beings, while being one, remain forever two."

A grave problem may be lurking here, however: the danger that precisely "the one point" of which Takizawa speaks implies, in turn, the tendency of falling into the "absolutization of one particular form." In other words, even when it is said to always contain a moment of negativity (as absolute negation), as long as it is thought of as having the nature of "a unity," "one point," or "a single point," this "one" is, in the final analysis, a unity of the same nature as the "one absolute" found in making Jesus the "sole mediator," "the only refuge," or "the only sacred haven"—which Takizawa makes the object of his critique of the general Christian schema. What difference would there be between the two, when it comes to religious experience? The Buddhist *soku* certainly does not designate a unity in whatever sense; if one describes it by means of the expression "one," one commits a great mistake. Is it not because one grasps it as "one" that one is obliged to bring in a distinction such as Takizawa's distinction of "primary contact" and "secondary contact"?

In intention, Takizawa's Christology wants to be inclusivistic, but I cannot help feeling that, in its inner nature, it is an expression of Christian absolutism. How would his view of Jesus differ from that of the idea of Jesus as mediator in the traditional Christian schema, criticized by him? When he presents Jesus as the point of contact between God and humans, we can ask why such a contact point is needed. For a contact point to be decisively needed, one must presuppose a decisive opposition between God and the human. Without a decisive breach, the need for a contact point that links the two becomes thin. The nature of a contact point is determined by the poles to be linked (God and the human), and by the respective nature of the poles. It can be said that Hisamatsu's criticism was directed at these basic elements that are more constitutive of Christianity as such, and not, as Takizawa's interpretation of this critique understands it, at a generally held schema of Christianity that can be called a false image. Hisamatsu levels a radical critique at the idea of God, in whatever meaning it may be believed in by Christians. And the same goes for his critique of Shinran.

Further, which role would the historical reality of Jesus in Christianity play in Hisamatsu's critique of Christianity? Which meaning is to be given to the historical existence and life of Jesus as the one who realizes the love of God in the figure of the Son of God? The meaning that the cross of Jesus has for the Christians, that of the historical reality of salvation by God, will not crumble, whatever critique Hisamatsu may level against it. But Hisamatsu's critique is not directed against such historical realities. Does he not rather want to put into question the very God who was the object of Jesus' self-awareness? It is precisely because his critique of Christianity is directed at that point that it is so basic (*gründlich*). For this is the very foundation on which Christianity exists as Christianity.

Let me finally touch on Takizawa's theory of the "Original Immanuel" and "derivative Immanuel." I shall present it only schematically and then add a few observations on it.

Immanuel in the primary, original sense = actual reality; to awaken to the primary Immanuel = discovery of actual reality = faith in Jesus Christ by the working of the Holy Spirit (as Karl Barth sees it).

Immanuel in the secondary, derivative sense = the fact of somebody believing in the primary Immanuel = the fact of God being with us to the extent that we believe in Him.

Seen from a Buddhist perspective, this is a theory of Buddha-nature or *tathāgatagarbha* (Buddha-womb). The problematic point is the relationship between original and derivative Immanuel. My difficulties with this theory can be summarized in the following four points:

1. If the original Immanuel can be directly discovered provided one awakens to it, is not the derivative Immanuel then unnecessary? Or again, if the original Immanuel is seen as the object of awakening, discovery, or faith, does it then not cease to be in the strict sense (or according to the definition) original Immanuel?

2. If the original Immanuel can become object of awakening, the derivative Immanuel becomes indeed unnecessary. If one then would hold that the awakening itself is the derivative Immanuel, is not the derivative Immanuel then by itself sufficient, since one can discover the way of being of the original Immanuel within the derivative one?

3. Whereby is someone's awakening to the original Immanuel brought about? If one holds that the original Immanuel is present in the ground of the self, the awakening becomes an awakening to the way of being of the original self. In that case, Jesus Christ becomes unnecessary. If one would equate this with "faith in Jesus Christ by the working of the Holy Spirit," it would cease to be the discovery of the original Immanuel. This is precisely what Hisamatsu criticizes. It is precisely in the idea that one cannot actually exist without reliance on Christ that Hisamatsu discovers a remnant of medieval heteronomy. One might come somewhat nearer to Hisamatsu's standpoint if one talked of a self-realization of the original Immanuel. However, the basic problem lies in the idea itself of an original Immanuel. In the way Takizawa here speaks of "with the inclusion even of non-Christians" or of "a gracious visitation of God," we can detect again traces of a feeling of Christian superiority. If one sets one false step in that direction, one falls into absolutism or religious pride. Does not Takizawa, totally against his intentions, fall into a dangerous all-one theory or a hidden inclusivism?

4. Takizawa defines the existence of "the actual human being" as "the actual human being wherein Christ is present totally independently from the person's consciousness, in other words, wherein God and man are mutually inseparable."[31]

Here again we can detect the same tendency. Takizawa himself considers that the structure of this "actual human being" is the same structure as the one the Zen man Hisamatsu discovered in the ground of his being. But, what would be, for Hisamatsu, the meaning of that God of which it is said that "God and man are mutually inseparable"? Could Hisamatsu, after all, admit a God in that sense? No, he must absolutely negate even such a God.

IV Four Questions Directed at Pure Land Buddhism by Gordon Kaufman

In this section I want to comment on the keynote speech, entitled "Religious Diversity and Religious Truth," delivered by Gordon Kaufman at the "Shinran and the Contemporary World" Symposium, which was organized to commemorate the 350th anniversary of Ryūkoku University in Kyoto. On that occasion, after having argued the necessity of a pluralistic conception of religious truth, Kaufman applied this view to Shinran's Pure Land doctrine and formulated four critical questions concerning it.[32]

These questions were not meant as a mere criticism of another religion's doctrine, but grew out of the belief that "the various Buddhist ways of understanding human life and the world have significant contributions to make in the pluralistic conversation about religious truth in which we all are becoming increasingly engaged." Kaufman added, however, that "if this conversation is to go forward, we must speak clearly and forthrightly with each other about what we understand and what we do not understand." With the intention of reflecting on the idea of a "pluralistic truth" as proposed by Kaufman, and as a like-minded partner, I want to present here these four questions and, afterwards, offer a short response.

(1) The Question of the Pure Land

How are we to understand this "Pure Land" at present? Does there really exist in the afterlife a very different place from this present world, a Pure Land of peace and joy? Many religious mythologies speak of a similar place, but, "in the light of modern scientific cosmology and our modern knowledge of the grounding of human existence in the evolution of life and the earth's ecology, it is difficult to make much sense of this kind of thinking." Kaufman says that he did not find much discussion about this problem in the doctrinal writings of the Jōdo Shinshū he had access to, and asks himself how ordinary Shin faithful are thinking about the Pure Land. Could it be that this question is not so terribly important for them? Do Buddhist teachers not discuss these issues when instructing their students? "Do common folk, for the most part, believe that their faithful repetition of the *nembutsu* will assure their entry into some sort of Pure Land—wherever that might be—after they die?

(2) Questions Concerning Amida Buddha

Who—or what—is Amida Buddha? Is Amida some sort of "cosmic person," a kind of god? If so, how are we to conceive this sort of being today? If Amida is not a person of some sort, how should we think of the "vows" he is supposed to have made? Vows are made by personal beings, beings who can carry out purposes they have set for themselves: were Amida's vows made at some particular time and place (like ordinary vows), and then carried out later through his personal activity? How are we to understand the claim that Amida's vows bring about effects in this world, such as transferring women and men into the Pure Land?

We are told that the making and carrying out of Amida's vows took many "kalpas" of time—apparently billions of years—but how should this be understood? It is difficult to see just what this highly mythical sort of thinking could mean if taken in anything like its literal sense; but if we do not take it in this way, what does it really signify?

Amida is said to be "the primordial Buddha who embodies the essence of all Buddhas"; and this ultimate reality is taken to be utterly "formless," characterizable by such various terms as "emptiness, suchness, dharma-body, thusness, oneness." If such characterizations are really appropriate, is it not quite misleading to put such emphasis on the importance of a particular personal name ("Amida") and to suggest that this reality makes "vows" and then acts in certain specific ways to carry them out?

Kaufman then goes on to insist:

These questions are not mere quibbles: they go to the heart of the claims of Shin Buddhism. For all salvation from the evils of this world, all movement into the Pure Land of fulfillment and bliss, is said to depend on the activity of Amida Buddha, the great Other-Power apart from which we wicked human beings could have no hope at all. I am most interested in learning more about how modern Shin Buddhists understand these central symbols about Amida Buddha.

(3) A Radical Dualism

Kaufman's third and most basic question concerns "the radical dualism suggested by the symbols of the Pure Land and Amida's Vow, a dualism that runs through all Shin Buddhist thinking":

The entire understanding of human existence and its problems appears to rest on sharp contrasts like that between the Pure Land and this world, Other-Power and self-power: everything right and good and true is concentrated in the one side of this contrast; everything evil and false and wrong is to be found on the other.

This clear dualism is inherent in the symbolic basis of all things Jōdo Shinshū is speaking of. However, further exploration reveals that Shin Buddhists are not in fact speaking (as I just have) about a simplistic or straightforward dualism between this world and some other reality: on the contrary, this very dualism, it is claimed, is itself a delusion and confusion; entry into the Pure Land is nothing else than the discovery that this powerful dualism—experienced to deep levels by the self which lives in this world of *saṃsāra*—is really false, an illusion. *Saṃsāra* is really *nirvāṇa*, and *nirvāṇa* pervades all of *saṃsāra*. Shinran has expressed this as follows: "the person of true *shinjin* can be called equal to Tathāgatas ... even though he himself is always impure and creating karmic evil ... the heart of the person of *shinjin* already and always resides in the Buddha Land."[33]

We must take note of what this seems to imply about our humanness and the meaning of our human activities. For Shinran every thread of the human sense of a capability or power to do something on our own, to act in some meaningful or significant way, appears to be part of the illusion of *saṃsāra*: even the believing in Amida's Primal Vow and the reciting of his Name are said to be given through and as the activity of the Buddha. The person of *shinjin* realizes that Amida's Primal Vow to liberate him has been fulfilled in the infinite past, and has always been working to grasp him. Thus, everything of any importance that we might do or not do appears to have been caused by Amida Buddha long before our appearance on earth.

Kaufman maintains that this scheme does not carry conviction for us. Since we are told that "human judgments of good and evil hold no meaning from the deeper standpoint of the Primal Vow, even our apparent power to do evil is undercut here." Kaufman then considers:

This position seems to undermine all human sense of responsibility, on the one hand, and, on the other, to declare all apparent evil in this life—torture or murder, injustice of all sorts, poverty, disease, the suffering in war, polluting the environment, even the perpetration of a nuclear holocaust—to be our deluded interpretation of what is actually the beneficent outworking of Amida's Primal Vow.

As Other-Power becomes almighty, self-power disappears into nothingness, and the Buddha's mind and the mind of the practicer become one, the distinctions necessary to maintain some sort of humanness and decency in life all seem to dissolve away completely. The sharp dualism running through the mythology and symbolism of Amida's Vow and the Pure Land has now become so decisively dissolved that all distinctions essential to on-going human life—good and evil, right and wrong, truth and falsehood, reality and illusion—evaporate into nothingness; and with them goes all human meaning, all discrimination of evils and problems in human existence, all human address of these problems and evils.

Or would it be so that the undercutting of the radical initial dualism does not have these implications?

(4) Three Criteria of Truth

Next, Kaufman broaches the question of "in what respect, and why, we should regard any or all of these Shin Buddhist claims as true." He says:

As nearly as I can see, for Shin Buddhists themselves this judgment is made on the basis of three criteria of truth: First and foremost, virtually unquestioned authority is given to certain scriptural texts (particularly those dealing with Amida's Vow), and to a specific line of interpreters of those texts—the Pure Land line culminating in Shinran. Second, cogency of argumentation on specific points or positions in these texts is valued highly. Third, there appears to be a claim that the positions taken and points made make sense of our everyday experience of life and its problems, in a way that is ultimately totally convincing.

He then goes on to comment:

It is not difficult to understand why these three criteria might well appear adequate to persons living and thinking within the circle of Shin Buddhism, [where the authority—that is, the ultimate truth—of these scriptural texts and this line of Pure Land interpretation is taken for granted; and where, therefore, human life and the problems of life are experienced, defined, and interpreted largely in Shin Buddhist terms.] At the same time, however, it is clear that arguments which invoke only these three criteria are completely internalist in character: they give us a self-confirming circle of interpretation and proof, in which nothing external to the perspective of Shin Buddhism—no ideas, evidence or arguments—is drawn upon. It should not be surprising, then, if outsiders find it difficult to understand many of the specific pieces of this picture or the picture as a whole; and if they regard it as but one more religious point of view, the expression of but one voice among the many engaged in the ongoing conversation of humankind about ultimate questions—with no more claim to genuine truth than any of the others.

Kaufman concludes as follows:

Such truth will emerge, I have been arguing today, only in the full conversation of all those many voices; and the real truth of the claims of Shin Buddhism, thus, will be discovered only through that wider conversation, not in the largely internalist dialogue that Shin writers—like the representatives of most other religious communities and traditions (including Christian theologians)—ordinarily conduct.

Which attitude should we Shin people take towards questions such as these posed here by a Christian theologian? We should first of all receive them with humility, and absolutely refrain from considering them a priori as the superficial and puerile questions one can expect from an outsider. The frank questions directed at Shin doctrine by Gordon Kaufman touch the very core of Shinran's thought, and we must respond to them in a "theological" fashion. Since all four questions are intimately interrelated, I shall try, in the remainder of my paper, to react to them as a whole, while leaving a detailed treatment for a later occasion.

The basic view underlying Kaufman's four questions has to do with the problem of religion and science, and thus points to the question of how Pure Land Buddhism is responding to the decisive change of worldview that science has brought about and is confronting religion with. This problem is not simply restricted to the sole realm of doctrine; we must take it up as a most personal challenge on the level of our religious existence, which is prior to doctrinal systematization. The question is here asked of Pure Land Buddhism's response to the change in worldview and the mechanization of the human being worked by science.

According to Nishitani Keiji, the continuity between the temporal-sensual world (the standpoint of *scientia*) and the eternal-suprasensual world (the standpoint of *sapientia*) has been severed by science in its modern guise. As one kind of knowledge, science stays within the field of *scientia* in the traditional sense; as to its basic spirit, however, it has become something of a totally different quality. The reason is that the two-level world view that lay in the background of traditional *scientia* has been lost. Moreover, from the standpoint of modern science, the traditional view of seeing all sensual things, within that two-level world, as transient-unreal-illusory has disappeared. Instead, modern science came to see, within the impermanent and ever changing phenomena, a mathematically measurable movement, and it interpreted this as a change in the combination of unchanging elements. It was the discovery that the sensual world is ruled by unchanging laws.

What does this mean for religion? Instead of seeing unchanging reality beyond and outside of changing things, one now came to grasp unchanging reality within the changing things themselves, and to see the changing phenomena as expressions of unchanging realities (laws). While formerly the changing things were experienced, in the perspective of a negative impermanence and in the consciousness of their contingency, as bringers of dissatisfaction or *Angst*, modern science has brought a sense of stability and order that precisely overcomes such feelings of *Angst*. That sense of stability had traditionally been supplied by metaphysics, but since modern times science has taken the place of metaphysics. It has inserted the infinite, as it were, right into the middle of the finite. This standpoint of the infinite is precisely the standpoint of pure intellect, of scientific cognition.

When we try to adapt to this scientific worldview, the traditional worldview of Pure Land Buddhism, as expressed in the motto "Reject this world and aspire for the next world," appears to lose all meaning. The traditional Pure Land view of salvation, based as it was on the two-level world of defiled land and Pure Land, according to which salvation consists precisely in rejecting the defiled land to be born into the Pure Land, has gradually lost its religious efficacy and power. Moreover, the dichotomy of defiled land and Pure Land became an especially clear-cut one, at least when seen from our actual situation, by the fact that death was seen as lying between the two. Therein lies the reason why our present Pure Land establishment has degenerated into mere "funeral Buddhism." Or, if this be an overstatement, we can at least say that the financial base of the Shin establishment relies for the greater part on funerals and services for the dead.

As Tanabe Hajime has argued, Pure Land Buddhism, as a religion living in our present times, must base itself on the historico-critical awareness of the philosophy of science. It must not wait any longer to reject the two-level worldview, wherein one passes from the defiled land to the Pure Land through death.

The old metaphysical tenets hitherto contained in Pure Land doctrine have now lost the religious power to save the suffering masses, which it possessed in the past. We must subject the basic doctrines of our Pure Land Buddhism—on the Pure Land, Birth, *nembutsu*, and Buddha bodies—to a radical reinterpretation.

At several historical turning points, Pure Land Buddhism has, in fact, experienced and overcome critical situations that shook the very bases of its existence. Basing himself on the value judgment that the path must fit the times and the capabilities of people, Tao-ch'o chose the Pure Land Gate as the only Buddhist path, with rejection of the Gate of the Sages; and, continuing in the same line, Shinran came to a clear awareness that, in these Latter Days or Extinction of the Dharma, all the doctrines left by Śākyamuni Buddha had lost their relevance. From there his Copernican turn from Śākyamunism to Amidism.

Would not now (after the birth of science) be the time to reject a Pure Land Gate that sees the Pure Land only in the afterlife; or at least a Pure Land Gate that, now as before, bases itself on a two-level worldview? Supposing, then, that Pure Land Buddhism is still viable as a path of salvation, which direction would still be open to it? I personally see no other direction than that of the practice of the bodhisattva path of Mahāyāna Buddhism, which can be discovered within Pure Land Buddhism. The "Other-Power," which Tanabe Hajime conceived of as a philosophy of metanoetics, also had its origin in such a bodhisattva path. The bodhisattva path found in Pure Land Buddhism is none other than the path of Dharmākara Bodhisattva. And this is not simply a myth, but has its historical basis in Śākyamuni Buddha. Precisely in a life that lives consciously the vow-mind of Dharmākara Bodhisattva (the compassionate mind born from the Dharma-nature of suchness) as the subjective basis of the existence of the self as ordinary human, we can bring forth the religious particularity of Pure Land Buddhism in the present situation, wherein we must make our own the historico-critical self-awareness of the philosophy of science. In his *Philosophy of Elemental Subjectivity*, Nishitani wrote the following sentences, wherein I find hints of a standpoint very similar to the one I just outlined:

> We must see both [divinity and humanity] in a relationship such as that found to exist between the transferences of going and returning. Therein we find the fundamental spirit that differentiates all high religions from mere superstition … In the Pure Land Gate of Buddhism there is the saying "directly attaining Birth, leading a life of gratitude." It expresses the idea of speedily attaining *nirvāṇa* by entrusting oneself to the vow-power of Amida's Great Vow, and thus obtaining the fruit of benefiting others in one's returning transference. Therein the "mind of true other-benefiting" is stressed. We can recognize the same basic spirit in Shinran's words: "The desire to attain buddhahood is the will to bring all living beings to the other shore, and this in turn is the true *shinjin* to benefit others." Here "*shinjin*" means being saved by going to one's Birth borne by Amida's vow-power and, carried by that same vow-power, returning to save all others; continuing Amida's vow of Great Compassion in one's own practice; living the life of Amida Buddha.[34]

Nishitani points out that this experience and practice of living the life of Amida Buddha evokes similar experiences and emulations (*Nachvollziehung*), and that a religious organization is precisely the crystallization as historical reality of this process. With regard to the relationship between the religious organization and experience-practice, Nishitani then rings a warning bell, which we, as a traditional religious organization, would do well to listen to: All religious organizations have as their basis and vital axis some powerful experience and praxis (for example, that of the founder), which unifies the network of experiences and practices of the organization. That network is given life precisely by the original "aspiration" that continues to work within it. Experience is a truly living *Erlebnis* only as long as it continues to originate and live as a response to the aspiration; as soon as the aspiration vanishes, it ossifies into dogma. When the aspiration weakens and dogmatism sets in, praxis becomes formalistic and the organization becomes rigid; and an ossified organization further plugs up the well from which living aspiration springs, so that it withers by the loss of a source of inner life. It then maintains itself only by extrareligious forces. It has then turned into a "religion"-less shell of religion. Indeed, it must be said that what brings forth and bestows life on religious formations as historical products —their source of life—is religious aspiration.[35]

Religion, thus, must find a place within itself for modern science as the element that at present offers the chance to return once more to the place of that most basic aspiration and to discover anew the "inner source of life" that is gradually disappearing from the traditional religious organizations. That basic aspiration is, further, the existential element that makes us consciously engage in the religious pluralism and concomitant interreligious dialogue, which constitute one more important task for present-day religions.

When we next pay attention to the "opening up of nihility," which came about together with the mechanization of the human, the above may apply again. From a Pure Land perspective it can be said that an awareness of radical nihility cannot arise from within "ordinary people" (*bonbu*). Rather, we must locate the essence of "ordinary people" in the fact that nihility cannot consciously present itself in them. On the other hand, it is also true that nihility reveals itself in a deeper way precisely where nihility cannot be self-consciously grasped. This is, in fact, the place where Tanabe's "metanoia" comes to awareness. However, also in this case, it remains true that "metanoia" in Tanabe's sense cannot be realized from within ordinary man and that this impossibility precisely defines "ordinary man."

The absolute Other-Power propounded by Pure Land Buddhism is absolutely affirmed as Other-Power precisely at the ground of ordinary man's existence, wherein neither nihility nor metanoia can be self-consciously realized. About the manner wherein the "opening up of nihility" is realized, Nishitani says that "it naturally comes to self-awareness when the human being faces its own existence without self-deceit." But does there not lie a still deeper nihility in the incapability of facing oneself without self-deceit? Is it not precisely there that the abyss of the human's basic ignorance (*avidyā*) is to be found? The extreme form of nihility occurs when nihility cannot be opened to self-awareness. Nishitani says that "nihility cannot free itself from itself." How, then, could a human being suspended over such an abyss of nihility ever face itself without self-deceit? The possibility of facing itself in this way would already mean the liberation from nihility.

Nishitani, moreover, time and again cites Eckhart's thought as a perspective that does not resort to the opposition of theism and atheism. He characterizes Eckhart's idea of God as a tendency to elevate the personal relationship of God and the human to a "suprapersonal" level, and sees in it an overcoming of nihility. According to him, Eckhart grasps the personal relationship of God and a human being as a living relationship within the soul between the "image of God" and its *Urbild*. As a result, God's "essence" is a completely "image-less" (*bildlos*) godhead, which he then calls a "nothing" beyond all forms. When the soul becomes perfectly one with the godhead that is the essence of the God that is nothing, it returns to the true self and obtains perfect freedom. This "nothing" in Eckhart's thought, while being the ground of the personal God and the other-side aspect of God, is at the same time "my ground" and is realized as my most this-side front. Nishitani considers that in this Eckhartian view is contained the turn to the "absolute this-side" that he discovered in "emptiness." Indeed, Nishitani interprets the idea of emptiness in Buddhism in this way: while it is spoken of as a transcendence toward the other-side, it is realized as something beyond the opposition of other-side and this-side and, in that sense, as the "emergence of the horizon of the absolute this-side."

What, then, should be our central concern when we pursue this kind of reasoning? When it is said that the self becomes perfectly one with the "nothing" that is the essence of God, the basic question is, of course, how this perfect unity can be reached, whereby this turnabout can occur. From the perspective of Mahāyāna Buddhism, the answer is that, for that purpose, the "practice" of the bodhisattva path is required. When we understand Eckhart from a Pure Land perspective, the "nothing" of the godhead corresponds to the formless "suchness" or "Dharma-nature": in the light of the doctrine of the Buddha-bodies one would speak of the "Dharma-nature Dharma Body," and in light of the "adornments of the Pure Land," the "uncreated Dharma body of true wisdom" comes to mind. As an "ordinary being," fully aware that I cannot perfectly fulfill the practice of the bodhisattva path, I cannot reach the place in which the "Dharma-nature Dharma body" is realized directly "in my own ground" as the this-side aspect of the self, without relying on some mediation. We have Shinran's confession: "I am one for whom any practice is difficult to accomplish, so hell is to be my home whatever I do."[36] This is an expression of Shinran's self-awareness of absolute limitation as to the path of practice, arrived at through the very "practice" of this bodhisattva path. This is a state of mind that opens up for the first time within the confrontation of the own "practice" with the "practice" of Dharmākara Bodhisattva. When this practice of the bodhisattva path is lost sight of, all the doctrines of the Pure Land Gate will lose their validity and vitality, just as the various paths of Śākyamunism have lost theirs.

V Religious Pluralism and Shinran's Pure Land Doctrine

Let me refer here for a moment to John Hick's thought. He bases himself on a new understanding of the religions, one that has mainly been promoted by Wilfred Cantwell Smith. One speaks here of a "dynamics of traditions": the different traditions, which have hitherto been called by the names of Buddhism, Christianity, Islam, Hinduism, Judaism, Confucianism, and so on, are certainly not homogeneous and static substances but rather "living movements" that have undergone great inner changes over time. What is here called a "tradition" is no longer seen as an unchanging fixed substance but as a "complex reality with a rich content," in which, by a cumulative process, all kinds of diverse elements have met, come to grips, and been amalgamated.

In the present meeting of these different traditions, Hick pleads for "a transformation of human experience from self-centeredness to Reality-centeredness." In the midst of that problematic, he discerns three possible intellectual options: exclusivism, inclusivism, and pluralism. I shall not speak here of the different standpoints taken by Christian theologians, since these are well known; instead, I shall try to indicate how these options shape up in the perspective of Pure Land thought.

(1) Exclusivism

As so many others, Shinran's Pure Land doctrine also easily falls into exclusivism. The reason is that its basic standpoint is one of "rejection and option": between all Buddhas and the sole Amida Buddha, between miscellaneous practices and the sole practice of the *nembutsu* of the Primal Vow, between all sūtras and the Greater Sūtra of Immeasurable Life.[37] Shinran, for instance, holds the tenet: "Only those who say the Name all attain birth";[38] and again: "You should know that only those who obtained true *shinjin* will dwell in the true Land of Recompense";[39] "Only those who dwell among the truly settled will be born in that Buddha Land";[40] "Only the saying of the *nembutsu* is the heart of great compassion that is thoroughgoing";[41] "With a foolish being full of blind passions, in this world that is a flaming house of impermanence, all matters without exception are lies and vanities, totally without truth and sincerity; the *nembutsu* alone is true and real."[42] The soteriological reason for this is then formulated as follows: "The Name of this Buddha surpasses the names of all the other Tathāgatas, for it is based on the Vow to save all beings."[43] It is the tenet that the Name of Amida is the "treasury of all merit," the supreme Name beyond all other merits.

However, when one considers the true meaning of the "choice" made by Dharmākara Bodhisattva, which serves as the basis for the "rejection and option" of Pure Land Buddhism, it appears that this "rejection and option" does not intend any exclusivism but, on the contrary, an extreme inclusivism. This appears clearly from the following text by Hōnen:

> Since the *nembutsu* is easy, it is open to everyone while the various other practices are not open to all types of people because they are difficult. Was it not in order to bring all sentient beings without exception to Rebirth that [Dharmākara] in his Original Vow cast aside the difficult practices and chose the easy one?[44]

(2) Inclusivism

An inclusivist understanding can easily be drawn from Pure Land doctrine as well. The object at which the Original Vow is directed is said to be the "sentient beings throughout the ten quarters." In other words, the ocean of all living beings in all possible worlds. The Light that "envelops and does not reject" is thought to embrace all sentient beings without discrimination of nationality, race, social class, gender, or culture. No single human being should be excluded from Amida Buddha's salvation on account of any of these differences. Interpreting the restrictive clause of the 18th Vow, "Excluded are those who commit the five grave offenses and those who slander the right dharma," Shinran simply states that "all the sentient beings throughout the ten quarters, without a single exception, will be born in the Pure Land."[45] The "form of the Buddha of Unhindered Light [Amida]" is said to be a "form that gathers up the wisdom of all Buddhas." From the fact that Amida Buddha's being is seen as embracing all other buddhas, it can be inferred that the basic standpoint of the doctrine of salvation by Amida Buddha is an inclusivist one.

On the other hand, however, it is believed that people who rely on miscellaneous practices "are not bathed in the light, are not taken up and protected, and do not share in the benefit of 'being embraced without rejection'." [46] Thus, people outside the pale of practicers in accordance with the Original Vow have been excluded from Amida's salvation. While it is said that "This Tathāgata pervades the countless worlds; it fills the hearts and minds of the ocean of all beings. Thus plants, trees, and all attain buddhahood,"[47] when it comes to the soteriological point of contact between Amida and sentient beings, the religious efficacy of Amida's "taking up and not rejecting" is made dependent on whether one practices the *nembutsu* as the practice of the Original Vow.

Therefore, if one considers the sole practice of the *nembutsu* of the Original Vow to be the only causal practice that saves all sentient beings, the religion of salvation by Amida is made to represent an exclusivistic standpoint. In that case, people that do not practice the *nembutsu*—Christians, Muslims, Jews, Hindus, and so on—are not saved by Amida Buddha. And the expression, "sentient beings throughout the ten quarters," of the Original Vow is then finally made to mean the sole practicers of the single practice of the *nembutsu*. It follows that, if we do not succeed in converting all human beings of the world into *nembutsu* practicers, Amida's Primal Vow will not be fulfilled.

Even when believing that Amida "fills all minds in the ocean of living beings," if we stick to the *nembutsu* prescribed by the Original Vow, we are open to the same criticism that Hick has leveled against the so-called inclusivism or universality of Christianity. No matter how universal the object of the Original Vow ("the sentient beings throughout the ten quarters") is deemed to be, the underlying logic will be an exclusivistic one: the reality of salvation will touch only the nembutsu practicers, and all people that engage in other religious practices will be excluded.

If so, how could we arrive at a way of thinking whereby salvation by Amida's Original Vow becomes truly universal? The answer must lie in the direction of a pluralistic standpoint.

(3) Pluralism

Hick's pluralism is built on the presupposition that "ultimate divine reality" is "One." From the perspective of that presupposition, it can be considered to be a kind of inclusivism. It differs fundamentally, however, from the inclusivistic standpoint we have been considering above. That inclusivism is a standpoint whereby one considers the ultimate truth of a particular religious tradition to include the truth of all other religions.

In Hick's theory, the "ultimate divine reality" is not seen within one particular religious tradition, but is viewed, within the basic field wherein all great religions originate, as the ontologically "preexistent One." He speaks of a development from that basic "One" to the particular concrete "Many" of the different religions. Hick further tries to find the proof of that development from the One to the Many in the fact that the same kind of evolution occurs in each of the traditions of all great religions. Therein lies the characteristic trait of Hick's pluralism.

Personally, I cannot agree with Hick's pluralistic standpoint. My basic difference with Hick is that I do not posit such an ultimate "One" as a presupposition of all religions. One claims such a "One" within each particular religion, but this forever refers to an ultimacy within the particular tradition, and cannot become an ultimate One among the different religions. At the present juncture it is impossible to know whether or not one can presuppose such a "One" among the various religions. More still, if such an underlying One could be known, there would be no meaning to the interreligious dialogue.

(4) The Point of Contact Between Pluralism and Shinran's Pure Land Doctrine

In the doctrinal system of Shinran's Pure Land Buddhism one finds classifications of doctrine proper to Shinran. They are called respectively *nisōshijūhan* (二双四重判 four-pronged classification in two steps) and *shinkegihan* (真仮偽判 classification in true, provisional, false). They have the doctrinal classifications of general Buddhism as their intellectual background, and take the Original Vow of Amida Buddha as their soteriological norm. The *nisōshijūhan* classifies and judges the various doctrines Śākyamuni preached during his lifetime; it is a classification of inner-Buddhist doctrines. The *shinkegihan*, which can be called Shinran's absolute doctrinal classification, has the discernment of true and provisional as its core and serves to judge between the doctrines of the Path of Sages and the Pure Land Gate. When we consider Shinran's Pure Land doctrine from the viewpoint of religious pluralism, both doctrinal classifications appear to be irrelevant, at least as doctrinal classifications. It is the various non-Buddhist doctrines, which in the doctrinal classification scheme belong to the category of the "false," that come into question here.

From the standpoint of religious pluralism, I want to pay attention to the following two points: (1) the fact that the Path of Sages is classified as provisional; (2) the fact that all religions and thought systems outside of Buddhism are branded as "perverted and wrongly adhered to." We could say that this is a doctrinal element in Shinran's Pure Land Buddhism that radically distances it from any positive attitude toward the dialogue among world religions and religious pluralism.

To overcome this serious handicap, the following two pluralistic methods need to be pursued. First, the ground on which the *shinkegihan* itself is based must be reconsidered. And second, the ground on which the very Original Vow of Amida Buddha, hitherto considered as absolute truth, is based as a soteriological method must be rethought. I shall discuss the second point, in the context of the truth claim of religious pluralism.

With regard to the refutation of the Path of Sages, we must give attention to the fact that the question of whether the Buddhist doctrines remain valid or not over the three ages of True Law, Semblance Law, and Latter Days Law has been taken as the actual standard for understanding the Path of Sages and the Pure Land Path as, respectively, provisional and true. This means that this classification has certainly not been put forth as a mere dogma. It was the actuality of the historical situation that led to the division of the whole of Buddhism into the two gates. It is precisely in this historical actual basis for the discernment of true and provisional that we discover a point of contact between religious pluralism and Shinran's Pure Land doctrine.

To make a long story short, at the present historical situation, 734 years after Shinran's death, the classification of Path of Sages and Pure Land Gate as provisional and true has ceased to correspond to the historical situation. This, however, does not at all mean that the *shinkegihan* has lost its essential meaning. Rather, to rework a *shinkegihan* that has ceased to correspond to the historical situation so as to make it correspond to the present historical situation is in accord with the original spirit wherein it was first set up. Shinran originally constructed his unique *shinkegihan* in order to put forth the true meaning of Amida's universal and absolute salvation. The religious basis of the truth of Pure Land Buddhism has always been sought in its soteriological contact point with the historical situation.

The historical situation is not limited to the mere Buddhist view of a history in three stages. While staying basically rooted in that view, but taking in also the results of the contemporary historical sciences and of the philosophy of history, we must base ourselves on the present historical situation wherein a communication in real-time has become possible across the boundaries of regions, nations, peoples, and cultures. We must build anew a *shinkegihan* that is adapted to the context of the world situation, which moves in these synthetically organic connections.

In the present situation, and seen from the standpoint of religious pluralism, an inner-Buddhist interreligious dialogue must come into being between the people of the different sects of the Path of Sages (*Lotus*, Hua-yen, Esoteric Buddhism, Zen, and so on) and the faithful of Shinran's Pure Land Buddhism, by way of a new recognition of the historical situation as sketched above, and in such a way as to be able to respond to the global tasks discovered in that situation.

This brings us to the second point: that all religions and thought systems outside of Buddhism having been branded as "perverted and wrongly adhered to." (As is well known, it is especially in the second part of the sixth chapter of his *Kyōgyōshinshō* that Shinran confronts in detail the various alien doctrines and perverted views in order to distinguish the true from the false.)

It goes without saying that the various views that were rejected as "false" by Shinran (the "62 perverted views and 95 false paths") were only the thought systems outside of Buddhism that were known in his time. Seen from the present-day history of thought, they represent only a very limited selection. And, on the other hand, to claim universal truth for a doctrine on the pretext that it is "true" in contrast with a limited number of other doctrines is not permissible any longer in the field of contemporary study of thought. If one nevertheless persists in clinging to this way of thinking, the truth claim either becomes a dogmatism or falls into a self-satisfied bigotry.

In fact, it may have been in order to avoid that dangerous trend that Shinran himself looked all over the sūtras and commentaries for relevant texts. It appears that Shinran did not stick to the sole subject-matter he took up; by contrast with extraneous doctrines, he endeavored to bring to light the universality of the Original Vow's truth. It could be maintained that Shinran's method was that of comparative philosophy. In the present historical situation, the question of whether the doctrine of salvation by Amida is true or not can be investigated only through a dialogue and comparison with all the thought systems that we know of at present. It is only in such a process that a new *shinkegihan*, that has the present historical situation as its basis, can originate.

From the pluralistic hypothesis the following questions arise. What, after all, is that "divine reality" that all great religions are supposed to intend? Can we, ultimately, consider as identical those elements of religion in East and West that are provisionally thought of as parallels: Yahweh and Brahman, the god Shiva and the Tao, the Trinity and the Trikāya (Three Buddha bodies), and so on? Did not East and West, each building up its own tradition in a particular and unique history, wrestle with different problems that cannot be brought under one common denominator?

With such questions in mind, John Hick strongly insists on the elaboration of the basic structure of a pluralistic theory that can positively recognize the plurality of religious "forms," and correctly value each of them while seeing them in an organic mutual relationship. Let me introduce here the basic structure of Hick's pluralistic theory by itemizing its essential characteristics:

(i) Ultimate Reality

1. There exists an infinite, majestic, and lofty reality.

2. It resides in the natural and social reality of our daily experience, or again in our own inner depths, while transcending us.

3. It is in our turning to it that our highest good consists.

4. What ultimately exists and is of ultimate value is the One.

5. To offer oneself totally to it is ultimate salvation, liberation, enlightenment, perfection.

6. It infinitely transcends all our language and thought; it cannot be caught in our human concepts, since it is infinite, eternal, and superabundant.

7. In order to express it in a way that does not depend on any particular tradition and is common to all, the term "ultimate reality" or "the real" is suitable.

It is precisely in the understanding of that ultimate reality that the fundamental problem of Hick's pluralist standpoint lies. On which level would a standpoint from which one can posit the proposition in point 4 originate? Is not the time when such a standpoint can originate the same as the moment when all dialogue among the great religions of the world has come to perfect fulfillment? At present, however, we only just entered the path of dialogue among the world religions. Is not it all too unrealistic, then, to posit such a proposition as a presupposition? Hick calls it a "hypothesis," but would not this hypothesis limit and distort the dialogue itself? Moreover, if this hypothesis proved to be true, it would follow that the dialogue itself is meaningless. It would therefore be irrational to make the determination of the truth or falsehood of this proposition into the goal of the dialogue. The "ultimate reality" contained in Hick's hypothesis has, after all, the same content as the "reality" intended by the "transformation of existence" that occurs in each religious tradition, the reality that is sufficiently present in the own religious tradition. It is, then, totally unnecessary to learn new things from other religious traditions.

(ii) The Real Itself

We come here to the distinction between the Real itself and the real as experienced and conceptualized by us humans (experiential reality). On this point Hick offers us the second proposition in the fundamental structure of his pluralistic theory. In a different formulation this becomes: "The Real itself is the One, but this One can nevertheless be experienced in various ways by us humans."

For Hick, precisely this proposition expresses the central reason why he had to come to his pluralistic hypothesis. Indeed, the logical basis of a pluralistic standpoint, propounds that all great religions reveal in themselves ultimate reality to the same degree, is located in the theory on the relationship between "Reality itself" and "experiential reality" that is taught in each of the great religions. This teaches us that, in Hick's view, the theoretical structure of pluralism is based on the fact that all religions themselves base themselves on a pluralistic view of reality. In other words, to negate the pluralistic understanding of religion amounts to negating the view of reality that is the ultimate ground of the salvation or enlightenment that one's own religion aims at.

(iii) The Reality of the Many "Forms"

With regard to the criterion whereby the grasp of "reality" of the various religious forms can be judged, pluralism proposes that: (1) within each of the particular forms a salvific power is at work; (2) particular traditions are fields wherein a transformation from self-centeredness to Reality-centeredness can be realized; (3) particular traditions each reveal "reality" in a different light. On the pluralistic standpoint, the criterion of truth is not simply looked for within the traditions themselves. By the same norm whereby the truth of the own tradition is established the truth of the other traditions must also be recognized at the same time. Precisely therein can be found the answer to the question which structure the new paradigm of religious truth in pluralism must have. And so we are faced anew with the problem of religious truth.

Personally I accept the truth theory of pluralism, according to which recognizing the criterion of one's own truth must mean at the same time recognizing the criterion of truth of the other. The reason for this is that as long as we do not base ourselves on that theory of truth, there can be no dialogue among the world religions. I am critical, however, of Hick's putting up the "One" of ultimate reality as a presupposition, and this for the following two reasons. One, because with this as a presupposition dialogue among the world religions becomes meaningless. Two, in the end because one arrives at an inclusivism, if one envisages the "One" of ultimate reality, be it only as a hypothesis.

It appears that an even more radical pluralistic standpoint is called for. Postponing a detailed argument to a later date, I would only like to suggest here by way of conclusion that, in order to come to a radical pluralism, at the least the following preconditions have to be considered:

1. We must not base our idea of an ultimate reality that latently pervades all great religions on a preconceived vision.

2. We must work with a postmodern worldview according to which, in true reality, all things in past, present, and future exist within the meshes of a net of organic nonsubstantial relationships.

3. All religions, no matter how limited they are by a particular tradition from the past, must be seen as forever open to infinite future possibilities. Each religion is a carrier of new creativity.

4. The religions must not resist the self-transformation demanded by the dialogue of world religions.

5. The religions must, therefore, see participation in interreligious dialogue and the transformation brought about by it, not as something imposed by other religions but rather as something that necessarily results from the ground on which their own religion is standing.

NOTES

[1] The following essay is a translation of one of the contributions to the 1997 Nanzan Symposium on the theme, "What Does Christianity Have to Learn from Buddhism?" The author is a Pure Land priest and professor of Religious Studies at Ryūkoku University in Kyoto, who looks back over his many years of interreligious dialogue to reflect on major issues.—*Ed.*

[2] For Nishitani's theory on the dialogue I base myself mainly on his essay "On the Encounter of Buddhism and Christianity: With Reference to Two Discourses by Martin Heidegger," in 西谷啓治著作集 [*Collected Writings of Nishitani Keiji*, hereafter NKCW], Volume 14 (Tokyo: Sōbunsha, 1990), 53-69.

[3] NKCW 14:55.

[4] NKCW 14:56.

[5] NKCW 14:56.

[6] NKCW 14:56.

[7] In his Letters (*Gobunshō*), Rennyo often criticizes the *bōzu* (monks or priests) in the following vein:

> Recently, however, even priests of high position, ignorant of what our school teaches about the settled mind, severely rebuke those among their disciples who happen to go to places where faith is discussed and listen to the dharma; thus, at times, discord arises. Consequently, since the priests themselves do not clearly hear the reality of faith, and since they deal with their disciples in such a manner, faith is not decisively settled either for them or for the disciples, and their lives then pass in vain. It is truly difficult for them to escape blame for harming themselves and others. This is deplorable, deplorable. (I, 1)

> These days, however, the priests in this region who are practicers of *nembutsu* are seriously at variance with the Buddha-dharma. That is, they call followers from whom they receive donations "good disciples" and speak of them as "people of faith." This is a serious error. Also, the disciples think that if they just bring an abundance of things to the priests, they will be saved by the priests' power, even if their own power is insufficient. This, too, is an error. And so between the priests and their followers, there is not a modicum of understanding of our tradition's faith. (I, 11)

Quoted from Minor and Ann Rogers, *Rennyo: The Second Founder of Shin Buddhism* (Berkeley: Asian Humanities Press, 1991), 143, 162.

[8] See my 親鸞浄土と西田哲学 [*Shinran's Pure Land Doctrine and Nishida's Philosophy*] (Kyoto: Nagata Bunshōdō, 1991), part II, ch. 6, "God, Humans, and Monks," 502-508.

[9] See *Notes on "Essentials of Faith Alone"* (Kyoto: Hongwanji International Center, 1979), 33.

[10] *Notes on "Essentials of Faith Alone,"* 62.

[11] The idea of "returning transference" (還相回向 *gensō ekō*), proper to Shinran's Pure Land doctrine, may not be understood apart from the "going transference" (往相回向 *ōsō ekō*). Both are only two aspects of the same soteriological reality, namely, Amida's Transference of Merit. One does not catch their essential meaning as long as one represents them as two points on a straight line. An interesting question is whether there is any idea in Christianity that corresponds to this "returning transference." Yagi Seiichi thinks it is not to be found in Christianity. Cf. Yagi Seiichi, パウロ・親鸞, イエス・禅 [*Paul and Shinran, Jesus and Zen*] (Kyoto: Hōzōkan, 1983), 57. On the other hand, Hisamatsu Shin'ichi criticizes this idea of Shinran as non-Buddhist.

[12] NKCW 7:3.

[13] NKCW 7:5.

[14] NKCW 7:6.

[15] NKCW 7:7.

[16] See my 親鸞とアメリカ: 北米開教の伝道の課題と将来 [*Shinran and America: The Task of the Propagation of Shinshū in North America and its Future*] (Kyoto: Nagata Bunshōdō, 1996).

[17] *Shinran and America*, 7.

[18] I rely here mainly on this work of John Cobb, Jr.: *Beyond Dialogue: Toward a Mutual Transformation of Christianity and Buddhism* (Philadelphia: Fortress Press, 1982).

[19] *Beyond Dialogue*, 128-36.

[20] *Beyond Dialogue*, 130.

[21] See 真宗聖教全書 (Kyoto: Kōbundō, 1992), vol. 1, 521-2. This text is extensively quoted in Hōnen's *Senchakushū* (956). The English translation of this text can be found in *The Pure Land*, N.S. 1 (1984), 20-21.

[22] *Beyond Dialogue*, 131-2.

[23] *Beyond Dialogue*, 132.

[24] *Beyond Dialogue*, 133.

[25] *Beyond Dialogue*, 136.

[26] I had occasion to discuss this theory directly with the author himself at a meeting of the Japan Society for Buddhist Christian Studies. For the theory itself see 滝川克己 Takizawa Katsumi, 現代に於ける人間の問題 [*The Problem of the Human Today*] (Tokyo: San'ichi Shobō, 1984), 164-70.

[27] I rely here on Takizawa Katsumi, 宗教を問う [*Questioning Religion*] (Tokyo: San'ichi Shobo, 1977), ch. 3: "Buddhism and Christianity: The Atheism of Hisamatsu Shin'ichi." I take as my main source the section "On the Basic Nature of What I Call Here 'Absolute Negation'." Takizawa's theology on "Buddhism and Christianity" is also discussed in a 120-page essay, taken up in Volume 7 of his collected writings 滝川克己著作集種 under the title 仏教とキリスト教:久松真一の 「無神論」 にちなんで. In this latter text, in the passage that summarizes Hisamatsu's theory, the term "absolute negation" is mentioned, but the idea is not especially discussed or criticized, whereas in the former it is. The reader should remember that Takizawa elaborates his ideas here in a running discussion with the "atheistic" Zen philosopher, Hisamatsu Shin'ichi.

[28] Takizawa Katsumi, *Questioning Religion*, 57.

[29] *Questioning Religion*, 58.

[30] *Questioning Religion*, 60.

[31] *Questioning Religion*, 66.

[32] In the following I shall use, as much as possible, Kaufman's own words without, however, indicating pages, since the official publication is still outstanding.

[33] *Letters of Shinran* (Kyoto: Hongwanji International Center, 1978), 26ff.

[34] (根源的主体性の哲学) [*The Philosophy of Elemental Subjectivity*], NKCW, vol. 1, 177-8.

[35] *Philosophy of Elemental Subjectivity*, 204-205.

[36] *Tannishō*, sec. 2.

[37] Cf. Hōnen's *Senchakushū*, ch. 4 [*The Pure Land*, N.S. 1, 3-11].

[38] Shinran, *Notes on "Essentials of Faith Alone,"* 30.

[39] Shinran, *Notes on the Inscriptions on Sacred Scrolls* (Kyoto: Hongwanji International Center, 1981), 54-5.

[40] Shinran, *Notes on Once-Calling and Many-Calling* (Kyoto: Hongwanji International Center, 1980), 34.

[41] *Tannishō*, sec. 4.

[42] *Tannishō*, sec. 15.

[43] *Notes on "Essentials of Faith Alone,"* 30.

[44] Hōnen, *Senchakushū*, ch. 3. Cited in *The Pure Land*, 5/2 (1983), 23.

[45] *Notes on the Inscriptions on Sacred Scrolls*, 35.

[46] *Notes on the Inscriptions on Sacred Scrolls*, 55.

[47] *Notes on "Essentials of Faith Alone,"* 42.

ACKNOWLEDGMENTS

We would like to thank the following authors, editors, and publishers for their consent to publish the articles in this anthology.

1. Bando Shojun, "'The Great Path of Absolute Other Power' and 'My Faith' by Kiyozawa Manshi." Translated with an Introduction by Bando Shojun. *The Eastern Buddhist*, vol. 5-2 (October, 1972), pp. 141-152.

2. Soga Ryojin, "The Significance of Dharmakara Bodhisattva as Earthly Savior." Unpublished translation by Wayne S. Yokoyama and Rev. Hiroshi Suzuki. This essay was originally published in *Seishinkai* (*World of Soul*) journal, Taisho 2.7 (July, 1913); found in *Collected Works* 2:408-421.

3. Kaneko Daiei, "The Meaning of Salvation in the Doctrine of Pure Land Buddhism." Translated and adapted by Sakamoto Hiroshi. *The Eastern Buddhist*, vol. 1-1 (September, 1965), pp. 48-63.

4. Daisetz T. Suzuki, "Shin Buddhism." *The Eastern Buddhist*, vol. 18-1 (Spring, 1985), pp.1-7; vol. 18-2 (Autumn, 1985), pp.1-8; vol. 23-1 (Spring, 1990), pp. 1-9. This series of articles is used with permission of the Matsugaoka Bunko (D. T. Suzuki Library).

5. Takeuchi Yoshinori, "Centering and the World Beyond." *The Heart of Buddhism*. Edited and translated by James W. Heisig. New York: The Crossroad Publishing Co, 1983, pp. 48-60.

6. Taitetsu Unno, "The Practice of Jodo-shinshu." *Buddhadharma* (Fall, 2002), pp. 24-29.

7. Omine Akira, "*Shinjin* is the Eternal Now." Translated by David Matsumoto. Institute of Buddhist Studies, Center for Contemporary Shin Buddhist Studies, (August, 1998), URL: http://www.shin-ibs.edu/ccsbsomn3.htm#anchor865218.

8. Alfred Bloom, "Shinran's Vision of Absolute Compassion." *The Eastern Buddhist*, vol. 10-1 (May, 1977), pp. 111-123.

9. Dennis Hirota, "Religious Transformation and Language in Shinran." Unpublished edited lecture.

10. Ueda Yoshifumi, "Freedom and Necessity in Shinran's Concept of Karma." Translated by Dennis Hirota. *The Eastern Buddhist*, vol. 19-1 (Spring, 1986), pp. 76-100.

11. Murakami Sokusui, "Joy of Shinran: Rethinking the Traditional Shinshu Views on the Concept of the Stage of Truly Settled." Translated by Eisho Nasu. *Pacific World: Journal of the Institute of Buddhist Studies*, Third Series, No. 3 (Fall, 2001), pp. 5-26.

12. Galen Amstutz, "Shinran and Authority in Buddhism." *The Eastern Buddhist*, vol. 30-1 (Spring, 1997), pp. 133-146.

13. Gerhard Schepers, "Shinran and Modern Individualism." *The Pure Land*, New Series, vol. 10-11 (December, 1994), pp. 241-250.

14. Futaba Kenko, "Shinran and Human Dignity: Opening an Historic Horizon." Translated by Kenryu T. Tsuji. *Pacific World: Journal of the Institute of Buddhist Studies*, New Series, No. 4 (Fall, 1988), pp. 51-59.

15. Ama Toshimaro, "Towards a Shin Buddhist Social Ethics." Translated by Robert F. Rhodes. *The Eastern Buddhist*, vol. 33-2 (Autumn, 2001), pp. 35-51.

16. Takagi Kenmyo, "My Socialism." Translated by Robert F. Rhodes. *The Eastern Buddhist*, vol. 33-2 (Autumn, 2001), pp. 54-61.

17. Kenneth K. Tanaka, "Ethics in American Jodo Shinshu: Trans-ethical Responsibility." *The Pure Land*, New Series, vol. 6 (December, 1989), pp. 91-116.

18. Bando Shojun, "Shinran's Indebtedness to T'an-luan." *The Eastern Buddhist*, vol. 4-1 (May, 1971), pp. 72-87.

19. Allan A. Andrews, "Pure Land Buddhist Hermeneutics: Hōnen's Interpretation of *Nembutsu*." Journal of the International Association of Buddhist Studies, 1987, pp. 7-25.

20. Frithjof Schuon, "David, Shankara, Hōnen." *The Eastern Buddhist*, vol. 20-1 (Spring, 1987), pp. 1-8.

21. Takeda Ryusei, "Mutual Transformation of Pure Land Buddhism and Christianity." Translated by Jan Van Bragt. *Bulletin of the Nanzan Institute for Religion and Culture*, Number 22, (Spring, 1998), pp. 6-40.

GLOSSARY

Akunin shoki—A term stressed in Jodo Shinshu referring to the evil person as the object of Amida Buddha's salvation.

Amida Buddha—The Buddha of Eternal Life and Infinite Light; according to the Pure Land teaching the Buddha who has established the way to Enlightenment for ordinary people; based on his forty-eight Vows and the recitation of his name *Namu-Amida-Butsu* one expresses devotion and gratitude.

Birth in the Pure Land—"Symbolic expression for the transcendence of delusion. While such a birth was thought to come after death in traditional Pure Land thought, Shinran spoke of its realization here and now; for example he states, 'although my defiled body remains in *saṃsara*, my mind and heart play in the Pure Land.'" (Unno)[1]

Bombu—Japanese term for foolish being, common mortal, passion-ridden being; the object of Amida's compassion.

Contemplation Sutra—Short title of the *Sutra on the Contemplation of Immeasurable Life*.

Dharmakara—Sanskrit name for the Bodhisattva who through five aeons of practice perfected his Vows to establish an ideal land where all beings can easily attain Enlightenment. On completion of his Vows he became Amida Buddha and established the western Pure Land.

Eko—Japanese term for transfer of merit, which in traditional thought was directed from the devotee to the Buddha so as to apply one's merit toward attaining Enlightenment. In Shin Buddhism, the direction is changed and Dharmakara-Amida's merit is turned toward beings to enable them to achieve Enlightenment.

Hinayana—Sanskrit term used by the Mahayanists to criticize early Buddhists for their limited or narrow perspective on the meaning of Buddha's teaching. It means literally "Small Vehicle." As a pejorative term it is not used in modern discussion to refer to Buddhists of South Asian background. The present term used is Theravada, the "Way of the Elders."

---

[1] Taitetsu Unno, taken from his Key Terms of Shin Buddhism, in the essay (contained in this volume) entitled, "The Practice of Jodo-shinshu."

291

Hiso-hizoku—A term used by Shinran when he was sent into exile; it indicated that he was neither a monk nor a layperson, and that his faith transcended these institutional and social definitions.

Honen (1133-1212)—Founder of the independent school of Pure Land (*Jodo*) Buddhism in Japan. He maintained that the traditional monastic practices were not effective in the Last Age (*mappo*) nor universal for all people, as intended by Amida's Vow. He incurred opposition from the establishment Buddhism and went into exile with several disciples, including Shinran. His major treatise, which was a manifesto of his teaching, was *Senchaku hongan nembutsu shu* (*Treatise on the Nembutsu of the Select Primal Vow*, abbreviated to *Senchakushu*).

Hozo—Japanese reading for the name "Dharmakara."

Jiriki—Self power; the consciousness that one achieves Enlightenment through one's own effort. In Pure Land Buddhism it is considered a delusory understanding of the true nature of practice and faith, which are supported and enabled through Amida's compassion.

Jodo—Japanese term for "Pure Land." Though all Buddhas have their Pure Lands, the Land of Amida Buddha became the most well-known and desired in China and Japan because of its comprehensive nature, its popular propagation, and its ease of entry through recitation of his Name.

Jodo Shinshu—Literally "The True Teaching (sect) of the Pure Land"; generally accepted as founded by Shinran, who was a disciple of Honen. In contrast to Honen's other disciples, Shinran stressed the centrality of true entrusting, or faith, as the fundamental basis of birth in the Pure Land and Enlightenment, and not the merit of practices directed to that end.

Jodo shu—Literally "The Pure Land Teaching (sect)." The tradition maintained by the successors of Honen.

Ki-ho-ittai—A term used in Shin Buddhism signifying the oneness of the Buddha or dharma and all beings, or foolish beings.

Larger Sutra of Eternal Life—The *Sukhavati-vyuha Sutra* which gives an account of Dharmakara (Jap. Hozo) Bodhisattva's Vows and his eventual fulfillment of them. The central Sutra for Shinran and part of a threefold complex of Sutras which include the *Sutra of Contemplation* and the *Smaller Pure Land Sutra*, which describes the Pure Land in detail. The title of the Sutra appears in various forms: *Sutra of Adornment of the Realm of Bliss*, *Sutra of Immeasurable Life*, or *Sutra of Limitless Life*.

Mahayana—The Larger Vehicle in contrast to the Hinayana, or Smaller Vehicle. It claimed to be more universal in opening Enlightenment to all beings, and inspired the emergence of the Pure Land teaching directed to ordinary beings—denoted as all beings in the ten directions. This tradition is characterized by a more complex philosophical development, an elaborate mythic and symbolic expression which emphasizes the cosmic character of the Buddha nature, and its inclusion of the key virtues of compassion and wisdom.

Mappo—A theory of the progressive degeneration of Buddhism after the passing of the Buddha. In the Pure Land tradition it was believed that Amida gave his teaching primarily for beings of the last age, who were spiritually decadent.

Meditation Sutra—A major Sutra of the complex of three Sutras of the Pure Land tradition initiated by Honen. This sutra was very influential in traditional Pure Land thought because of the system of meditations it describes, as well as the offer of salvation it provides to defiled people incapable of such practice. It gave the basis for the recitation of the Buddha's Name as a means of birth into the Pure Land.

Myokonin—"Literally, 'wonderful, good person.' Devout, sincere followers of Shin Buddhism who came from the lower classes in pre-modern times. They had little formal education, but their sayings are imbued with deep spirituality." (Unno)

Nembutsu—"The practice of reciting *Namu-Amida-Butsu* (the Name of Amida) is known as recitative *nembutsu*. There is also meditative *nembutsu*, which is a method of contemplation. *Nembutsu* is used synonymously with *myogo*, or the Name." (Unno)

Original Vow—A term referring to the Vows of Amida, which indicate that he worked for aeons and aeons in the past. "Original" is also translated as "Primal," or "Primordial" to suggest an event in the timeless past of eternity.

Pure Land—"Translation from the Chinese *ching-t'u* (*jodo* in Japanese). The term as such is not found in Sanskrit, the closest being the phrase 'purification of the Buddha Land.' Shinran describes it as the 'Land of Immeasurable Light,' referring not to a place that emanates light, but a realization whenever one is illumined by the light of compassion." (Unno)

Ranks of the Truly Settled (or Stage of the Truly Settled)—In Japanese *shojoju*; a stage in the process of the Bodhisattva becoming Buddha whereby he cannot backslide; the stage of non-retrogression where Enlightenment is guaranteed. In Pure Land thought it is to be attained in the future with our birth in the Pure Land. For Shinran it becomes a reality at the moment that we experience true entrusting in Amida Buddha's Vow.

Shan-tao (613-681)—An important scholar of Chinese Pure Land Buddhism whose teaching greatly affected Hōnen and Shinran through his commentary on the *Sutra of Contemplation* and systematization of Pure Land doctrine. He is credited with stressing the recitation of the *nembutsu* as the central act of Amida's Vow and Pure Land devotion.

Shingyo—Joyous trusting; the term from the Primal Vow denoting the mind of *shinjin*.

Shinjin—The term for "true entrusting," which according to Shinran is the primary cause for birth in the Pure Land. The western term "faith," commonly used to translate this term, does not completely express the special meaning given to this Japanese word. In Shinran's view it is the transference or infusion of Amida's true mind of compassion and wisdom into the person, yielding complete reliance on Amida's Vow for one's certainty of birth in the Pure Land. With this assurance of deliverance, recitation of *nembutsu* or religious practice becomes an expression of gratitude.

Shinran (1173-1262)—attributed founder of the Jodo Shin school of Buddhism.

Shinzoku-nitai—Term for the double theory of truth, mundane and supermundane. Initially a philosophical, epistemic distinction developed by the pivotal Buddhist teacher Nagarjuna (150-250 C.E.). In later Japanese Buddhism it was given a social interpretation in which the supermundane teaching denoted the path of salvation, while the mundane teaching referred to the morality and ethics prescribed by society.

Shojoju—*see* Ranks of the Truly Settled.

Sutra on the Contemplation of Immeasurable Life—*see* Meditation Sutra.

T'an-luan (476-542)—A major Chinese Pure Land teacher whose thought greatly influenced Shinran. See the essay in this volume by Shojun Bando entitled "Shinran's Indebtedness to T'an-luan."

Tariki—Other Power; "The working of the boundless compassion of Amida Buddha, which nullifies all dualistic notions, including constructs of self and other. According to Shinran, 'Other Power means to be free of any form of calculations (*hakarai*).'" (Unno)

Tathagata—Sanskrit term (Jap. *Nyorai*) used to refer to a Buddha. It means the one who comes and the one who goes—the thus come, thus gone one. *Tathata* means "truth" or "suchness"; consequently, one who comes from truth and goes to truth. The Buddhas as enlightened beings are manifested from the realm of truth.

SELECT BIBLIOGRAPHY FOR FURTHER READING

BLOOM, ALFRED, *Shinran's Gospel of Pure Grace*. Ann Arbor MI: Association for Asian Studies, 1965, 1991.

—*The Promise of Boundless Compassion: Shin Buddhism for Today*. Honolulu: Buddhist Study Center Press, 2002.

DOBBINS, JAMES, *Jodo Shinshu: Shin Buddhism in Medieval Japan*. Blooming-ton, IN: Indiana University Press, 1989.

HISAO INAGAKI, *The Three Pure Land Sūtras*. Kyoto: Nagata Bunshodo, 1994.

JODO SHINSHU HONGWANJI-HA, *The Collected Writings of Shinran*. 2 vols. Kyoto, 1997.

MATSUNAGA, DAIGAN AND ALICIA, *The Foundations of Japanese Buddhism*. 2 vols. Los Angeles: Buddhist Books International, 1974, 1976.

TABRAH, RUTH, *The Monk Who Dared*. Honolulu: Press Pacifica, 1995.

—*The Monk's Wife*. Honolulu: Buddhist Study Center Press, 2001.

TAITETSU UNNO, *River of Fire, River of Water*. New York: Doubleday Dell Publishing Group, 1998.

—*Tannisho: A Shin Buddhist Classic*. Honolulu: Buddhist Study Center Press, 1996.

—*Shin Buddhism: Bits of Rubble Turn into Gold*. New York: Doubleday, 2002.

TAMURA YOSHIRO, *Japanese Buddhism: A Cultural History*. Tokyo: Kosei Publishing Co., 2000.

TANAKA, KENNETH K., *Ocean: An Introduction to Jodo Shinshu Buddhism in America*. Berkeley: Ocean-Wisdom Publications, 1997.

UEDA YOSHIFUMI AND DENNIS HIROTA, *Shinran: An Introduction to His Thought*. Kyoto: Hongwanji International Center, 1989.

BIOGRAPHICAL NOTES

ALFRED BLOOM: Professor Emeritus, University of Hawaii, was the first Proctor of the Center for the Study of World Religions at Harvard University. He received his Ph.D. from Harvard University, and taught World Religions and Buddhism at the University of Oregon and the University of Hawaii. He was Dean at the Institute of Buddhist Studies, Berkeley, sponsored by the Buddhist Churches of America, and is an ordained Shin Buddhist priest. His publications include: *Shinran's Gospel of Pure Grace*; *Shoshinge: The Heart of Shin Buddhism*; *Strategies for Modern Living: A Commentary with Text of the Tannisho*; *The Life of Shinran Shonin: The Journey to Self Acceptance*; and *The Promise of Boundless Compassion: Shin Buddhism for Today*.

TAITETSU UNNO: Professor Emeritus of Religion, Smith College, is an ordained teacher in the Shin Buddhist tradition and serves on the Board of Directors of the American Buddhist Study Center in New York. He is the author of *River of Fire, River of Water*; *Tannisho: A Shin Buddhist Classic*; and *Shin Buddhism: Bits of Rubble Turn into Gold*.

CONTRIBUTORS AND TRANSLATORS

AMA TOSHIMARO: Professor of History of Japanese Thought at Meiji Gakuin University, Tokyo.

AMSTUTZ, GALEN: Coordinator, Reischauer Institute of Japanese Studies, Harvard University, Cambridge, Massachusetts.

ANDREWS, ALLAN A.: Late Professor of Religion, University of Vermont, Burlington, Vermont.

BANDO SHOJUN: Former Professor at Otani University; Resident Priest, Hoonji, Tokyo.

EISHO NASU: Tamai Professor, Institute of Buddhist Studies, Berkeley.

FUTABA KENKO: Late President of Kyoto Women's University; Former President, Ryukoku University; Professor, Ryukoku University.

HEISIG, JAMES W.: Research Fellow of the Nanzan Institute for Religion and Culture in Nagoya, Japan.

HIROTA, DENNIS: Professor of Asian Studies, Chikushi Jogakuen University, Fukuoka; Chief translator of the Collected Works of Shinran.

KANEKO DAIEI: Late Professor at Otani University. A major Shin thinker of the twentieth century.

KENRYU T. TSUJI: Former Bishop, Buddhist Churches of America; Former Resident Minister, Ekoji Temple, Springfield, Virginia.

MATSUMOTO, DAVID: Professor of Buddhism, Institute of Buddhist Studies; Director of the Center for Contemporary Shin Buddhist Studies.

MURAKAMI SOKUSUI: Late Professor Emeritus, Ryukoku University, Kyoto.

OMINE AKIRA: Professor, Ryukoku University; Emeritus Professor of Osaka University; member of the faculty of the Doctrinal Research Center of the Jodo Shinshu Hongwanji-ha.

RHODES, ROBERT. F.: Professor, Otani University, Kyoto.

SAKAMOTO HIROSHI: Former Professor, Otani University.

SCHEPERS, GERHARD: Professor of German Literature and Culture and Dean of the College of Liberal Arts, International Christian University, Tokyo.

SCHUON, FRITHJOF: Well-known, widely published proponent of the Perennial Philosophy, writing on metaphysical and religious themes.

SOGA RYOJIN: Late Professor at Otani University. A major Shin thinker of the twentieth century.

SUZUKI DAISETZ T.: Founder of the Eastern Buddhist Society; Professor, Otani University; Mahayana and Zen scholar-writer. In later years he concentrated on the study of Shin Buddhism.

SUZUKI HIROSHI: Rimban (Chief Minister) Higashi Hongwanji Hawaii Betsuin, Honolulu Hi.

TAKAGI KENMYO: Shin Buddhist priest during the Meiji Period (1868-1912); imprisoned on the charge of lese majeste; died at his own hand in prison.

TAKEDA RYUSEI: Doctor and Professor of Ryukoku University; Director, Center for Humanities, Science, and Religion; Director, Ryukoku Translation Center.

TAKEUCHI YOSHINORI: Late Professor Emeritus, Kyoto University, Kyoto.

TANAKA, KENNETH K.: Professor, Musashino Women's University, Tokyo.

UEDA YOSHIFUMI: Late Professor, Chikushi Gakuen, Fukuoka; Professor Emeritus, Nagoya University, Nagoya; Editor, Shin Buddhism Translation series, Hongwanji International Center, Kyoto.

VAN BRAGT, JAN: Honorary Research Fellow of Nanzan Institute for Religion and Culture; Professor Emeritus, Faculty of Arts and Letters, Nanzan University; and Professor, Hanazono University.

YOKOYAMA, WAYNE S.: Translator, Researcher, and Lecturer, Hanazono University, Kyoto.

INDEX

Index

Primal Vow, 67, 69, 166-167, 170, 200

Pure Land Buddhist, *xxiv*, 87, 94, 98, 199, 221, 231, 239, 290

Pure Land Buddhist Hermeneutics, *xxiv*, 231, 290

Pure Land Buddhists, 23, 27, 233, 262, 264

Pure Land Doctrine, 22-23, 27, 31-32, 262, 264-265, 269, 274, 277-278, 280-281, 285, 294

Pure Land Gate, 274, 277, 280-281

Pure Land Gate of Buddhism, 274

Pure Land Masters, 24, 71, 101, 135, 138, 218

Pure Land of Amida, 64, 234

Pure Land of Bliss, 134

Pure Land of Peace, 127, 162-163, 269

Pure Land of Ultimate Bliss, 74-76

Pure Land Path, 69-70, 87, 153, 209, 239, 241, 280

Pure Land Sūtra, *xiv-xvi*, 81, 84, 144, 222-223, 295

Pure Land School, *xvi*, 32, 34, 41, 64-65, 217, 219, 244-245, 261

Pure Land Sect, *xvi*, *xxiv*, 60, 62, 221

Pure Land Shin Sect, 3

Pure Land Teaching, *xiii-xviii*, *xxii*, *xxiv-xxv*, 33-34, 37, 74, 80, 133, 201, 218-219, 291-293

Pure Land Tradition, *xxi*, 68-69, 80-81, 83, 148, 217, 241, 293

Pure Land Way, 74, 76, 87, 100-101, 121, 125-126, 139, 143, 150, 154, 240

Pure Lands, 64, 292

raikō, 108, 258

rebirth, 24-26, 41, 44, 86, 144, 148, 151-152, 161-166, 232-240, 242, 244, 278

Rebirth into the Pure Land, 161, 163-164, 234, 240

Record in Lament of Divergences, A, see *Tannishō* (Shinran)

Rennyo, *xxiii*, 112-113, 136-137, 140, 158, 161-163, 176, 186-187, 190, 202-205, 212, 285

repentance, 28, 79, 113, 120

Rhodes, Robert F., 173, 189, 290, 297

Rōsenki, 4

Ryūju (Nāgārjuna), 60, 121, 144, 153, 217, 220, 222-223

saha world, 75-76, 258

Sakamoto Hiroshi, 19, 289, 297

Śākyamuni, Shakyamuni, 10, 56, 63-64, 69, 75, 77, 80-82, 104, 125, 134, 138, 169, 190-191, 232, 243-244, 250, 263, 274, 280

salvation, *xv-xviii*, *xxi-xxiii*, *xxv*, 15-19, 22-27, 32, 41-42, 53-54, 62, 66, 79-81, 83-85, 108, 111, 115, 117, 120, 123-124, 128, 132-136, 156, 159, 161-162, 166-167, 170, 190, 192, 205, 218, 220-222, 226-227, 232-233, 237, 239, 241, 251-252, 267, 270, 273-274, 278-279, 281-283, 289, 291, 293-294

salvation of women, 80

samboghakāya, 86, 152

saṃsāra, 55, 66, 103, 111, 120, 144, 151, 201, 250, 258, 271

Sangowakuran, *xxi*, 118

satori, 15, 68, 118, 146, 226, 228

Schepers, Gerhard, *xxii*, 155, 160, 290, 297

Schuon, Frithjof, *xxiv*, 247, 290, 297

Seishin shugi ("Spiritualism"), *xvii*, 4, 182, 186

Seishinkai ("Spiritual World"), 4, 184, 186, 289

Self Power, self-power, *xviii*, *xxiv*, 130-132, 292

Senchaku Hongan Nembutsu Shū (Hōnen), 218-219, 232, 246

Seven Pure Land Patriarchs, the, 219

Titles in The Perennial Philosophy Series by World Wisdom

A Buddhist Spectrum by Marco Pallis, 2003

The Essential Ananda K. Coomaraswamy, edited by
Rama P. Coomaraswamy, 2004

*The Essential Titus Burckhardt: Reflections on Sacred Art, Faiths, and
Civilizations*, edited by William Stoddart, 2003

Every Branch in Me: Essays on the Meaning of Man, edited by
Barry McDonald, 2002

*Islam, Fundamentalism, and the Betrayal of Tradition: Essays by Western
Muslim Scholars*, edited by Joseph E. B. Lumbard, 2004

*Journeys East: 20th Century Western Encounters with Eastern Religious
Traditions* by Harry Oldmeadow, 2004

Living in Amida's Universal Vow: Essays in Shin Buddhism, edited by
Alfred Bloom, 2004

Paths to the Heart: Sufism and the Christian East, edited by
James S. Cutsinger, 2002

Returning to the Essential: Selected Writings of Jean Biès, translated by
Deborah Weiss-Dutilh, 2004

Science and the Myth of Progress, edited by Mehrdad M. Zarandi, 2003

Seeing God Everywhere: Essays on Nature and the Sacred, edited by
Barry McDonald, 2003